essential
JMF
JAVA™ MEDIA FRAMEWORK

D0308487

ISBN 0-13-080104-6

90000

9 780130 801043

Titles in the PH/PTR *essential* series:

Essential JNI: Java Native Interface

Essential JMF: Java Media Framework
  Designing Media Players

  Essential JTAPI: Java Telephony API Designing
  Telephony Projects with Java

Series Editor Alan McClellan is coauthor of the best-selling Java by Example, Graphic Java: Mastering the AWT, and Automatic Solaris Installations: A JumpStart Guide (SunSoft/Prentice Hall). He is an award-winning software technical writer with over ten years of experience in the computer industry.

essential
JMF
JAVA™ MEDIA FRAMEWORK

ROB GORDON

STEPHEN TALLEY

Prentice Hall PTR
Upper Saddle River, NJ 07458
http://www.phptr.com

Editorial/Production Supervision: *Vincent J. Janoski*
Acquisitions Editor: *Gregory G. Doench*
Editorial Assistant: *Mary Treacy*
Manufacturing Manager: *Alexis R. Heydt*
Marketing Manager: *Kaylie Smith*
Cover Design: *Scott Weiss*
Cover Design Direction: *Jerry Votta*

© 1999 Prentice Hall PTR
Prentice-Hall, Inc.
A Simon & Schuster Company
Upper Saddle River, NJ 07458

Prentice Hall books are widely used by corporations and government agencies for training, marketing, and resale. The publisher offers discounts on this book when ordered in bulk quantities. For more information, contact: Corporate Sales Department, Phone: 800-382-3419; FAX: 201-236-7141; E-mail: corpsales@prenhall.com; or write: Prentice Hall PTR, Corp. Sales Dept., One Lake Street, Upper Saddle River, NJ 07458.

Printed in the United States of America
10 9 8 7 6 5 4 3 2 1

ISBN 0-13-080104-6

Prentice-Hall International (UK) Limited, London
Prentice-Hall of Australia Pty. Limited, Sydney
Prentice-Hall Canada Inc., Toronto
Prentice-Hall Hispanoamericana, S.A., Mexico
Prentice-Hall of India Private Limited, New Delhi
Prentice-Hall of Japan, Inc., Tokyo
Simon & Schuster Asia Pte. Ltd., Singapore
Editora Prentice-Hall do Brasil, Ltda., Rio de Janeiro

Still Kathy, Matthew, Kilian and Kieran
Rob

To Mom
Steve

CONTENTS

Chapter 6 **The Controller** 71

Chapter 16

Implementing the Player Interface   261

Chapter 19

Creating Custom Controls 339

Chapter 20

Creating Control Panel Controls 357

Chapter 21   **Creating a Custom Control Panel** 397

Part IV

Appendices

PREFACE

What This Book Is About

This book describes the *Java Media Framework* (JMF) API and how to use it to integrate audio and video playback into Java applications and applets.

The JMF API consists of three pieces: playback, capture and video conferencing. This book covers only the first piece, specifically, the *Java Media Player* API.

This book does not stop at the API, however. It also discusses the different implementations of that API, how they differ, and even their failure to conform to the API. Where the API is open to interpretation, a discussion of various interpretations is undertaken.

This discussion appears in the context of developing a framework for building your own custom Player implementation. The framework code appearing in this book provides all the API-compliance code necessary for building an API-compliant Java Media Player, leaving you to focus on the media-specific coding issues.

Finally, this book has sprinkled throughout examples from the *Essential* JMF Toolkit, a collection of reusable Java classes for many multimedia occasions.[1]

Who Should Read This Book?

This book is written for the Java engineer or aspiring Java engineer who needs to integrate audio and video into his applications or applets. It assumes some familiarity with the Java language but you need not be an expert. Webmasters with JavaScript and perl experience could easily adopt some of the examples in this book for rudimentary multimedia applications. In other words, if you are interested in Java and multimedia, this book becomes you.

Who Should Buy This Book?

Everyone.

Structure of This Book

This book contains four distinct parts. We have even named the parts and inserted a decorative page between them so there is no doubt as to which is which.

Part I, "Using the Java Media Framework," comprises the first ten chapters. Part I was written for the reader who wants to learn to *use* the JMF Player. After finishing Part I, you will know all there is to know about using a Player for playback of currently supported media types.

If that is not enough to satisfy you, Part II, "Extending the Java Media Framework," will show you how to build a complete Player to support a new media type. Not only will Part II show you how to do this, but when you are finished, you will have a good deal of code available to use with still newer and more exciting media types.

In addition, Part II covers the building of a custom GUI for a Player, again providing lots of reusable code. And, if that were not enough, Part II covers the creation of a new DataSource for support of an actual protocol, the NNTP protocol for downloading articles from news groups. Put together the custom Player and DataSource developed in Part II and you have a Java Media Player for reading articles from your favorite news group. Strange, but elegant!

In Part III, "Building JMF Applets and Applications," a simple media mixer application is presented. Using this application you can generate HTML for inclusion in your web pages that need to playback multiple media sources. The MultiPlayer class, also presented in Part III, can then be dropped right into your applet to play the media described by the HTML.

The books finishes up with a collection of appendices in Part IV. Herein you will find complete reference material for the JMF API and the *Essential*

---

1. Cocktail parties, bar mitzvahs, baptisms, etc.

JMF Toolkit. There is also a discussion of the use of the JMF with various browsers, some potentially useful URL resources and a virtual glossary, to boot.

Using This Book

The first three parts of this book can, more or less, stand alone. If you do not have an immediate need to create your own Player, reading Part I and referencing the appendices as needed will meet your needs.

If you need to create your own custom Player to support a new media format, Part II is for you. If you are in a real hurry, you may be able to get by with just reading Chapter 18, "Creating a Custom Player." You can at least start there and refer back to earlier chapters in Part II as necessary. In any case, understanding Part II really depends upon having the knowledge and wisdom contained in Part I. If you did not get such knowledge from somewhere else, you may as well get it from there.

If you need an easy way to play multiple media files from an applet, go directly to Part III.

Part IV is the work horse section of the book: It is there when you need it, ready and willing.

We recommend you do not read this book backwards. We cannot guarantee that there are no hidden, satanic messages.

Gathering the Pieces

To derive the fullest benefit and pleasure from reading this book, you will need to have the following pieces of software installed on your computing device.

- A version of the JDK
- The Swing component set from the Java Foundation Classes
- An implementation of the JMF
- The *Essential JMF* example source and Toolkit

A section is dedicated to the acquisition and installation of each of these pieces. In addition to this software, there is the presumption that some fundamental software already exists on your computer, specifically, the necessary audio and video device drivers. For Solaris and Windows machines that have not been butchered by an overzealous system administrator, this a safe assumption.

Downloading JDK

To use Sun's implementation of the JMF, you will first need to have installed some flavor of JDK 1.1.*x*. The latest version is available at http:// java.sun.com/products/jdk/1.1/.

Intel's implementation does not require JDK 1.1. If you still have a version of JDK 1.02 sitting around and will only be using Intel's JMF, you are set. However, to use the examples included with this book, you will need JDK 1.1.

As part of installing your JDK, you will want to set the JDK_HOME environment variable to reference the directory in which the JDK was installed. This environment variable is referred to in later discussions.

Downloading Swing

Since all the GUI code written for this book uses Swing components, you will need to have the Swing jar files installed on your system.

The Swing component set is available from The Swing Connection. To download the Swing classes, go to http://java.sun.com/products/ jfc/index.html#download-swing. The downloaded file is a ZIP file containing jar files for different platforms. After unzipping the downloaded file, say in /jfc (d:\jfc for Windows), you will want to change your CLASSPATH as shown below, depending on which platform you are running.

Swing on Solaris

On Solaris, you will want to include swing.jar in your CLASSPATH. For example, using ksh, type:

```
% export CLASSPATH="/jfc/swing.jar:$CLASSPATH"
```

Swing on Windows

If you are running on a Windows machine and want the Windows Look & Feel, you will also need to add windows.jar to your path.

```
% set CLASSPATH=\
        c:\jfc\swing.jar;c:\jfc\windows.jar;%CLASSPATH%
```

Including only swing.jar file in your CLASSPATH will give you the Java (or Metal) Look & Feel.

If you are new to Swing, there is more information on the above topics in the README file that comes with the Swing distribution and resides in the install directory.

Downloading JMF

You can obtain a copy of a JMF implementation from either Sun or Intel. If you will be using JMF on Solaris, you are limited to Sun's implementation. If you will be running on Windows 9*x* or Windows NT, you can choose between Sun and Intel.

Downloading Sun Implementation

Sun's implementation of the JMF can be downloaded from `http://java.sun.com/products/java-media/jmf/1.0/`.

Installing Sun Implementation On Solaris

Solaris installation is accomplished with a shell script. For example, if you have downloaded the JMF distribution file into `/home/me/tmp` and you want to install JMF in `/home/me/jmf`, you would perform the following steps:

```
% cd /home/me
% sh /home/me/tmp/jmf101-solaris2-sparc.bin
% export JMFHOME=/home/me/jmf
```

The JMF will now be installed in `/home/me/jmf` and the `JMFHOME` environment variable will have the value `/home/me/jmf`.

The following table describes the recommended configuration for using Sun's JMF on a Solaris platform.

Recommended Configuration for Solaris	
Processor	SPARCstation 10, SPARCstation 20, or UltraSPARC-based workstation
O/S	Solaris 2.5.*x* or Solaris 2.6
JDK Software	JDK 1.1.*x*
Add'l Hardware	24-bit frame buffer (8-bit is acceptable)

Up-to-date installation instructions and system requirements can be found in `$JMFHOME/html/setup.html` after you have downloaded and installed the JMF. This file also contains instructions for running the sample code that comes with the JMF distribution.

Before using Sun's JMF on Solaris, you need to augment two environment variables. First, you must add the JMF classes to your `CLASSPATH`.

```
% export CLASSPATH="$JMFHOME/lib/jmf.jar:$CLASSPATH"
```

You must also modify your `LD_LIBRARY_PATH` variable so that the *Java Virtual Machine* (JVM) can find the native libraries required by the JMF.

```
% export LD_LIBRARY_PATH="$JMFHOME/lib:$LD_LIBRARY_PATH"
```

Installing Sun Implementation on Windows

Sun's JMF for Windows 9*x* and Windows NT is installed using InstallShield. Simply double-click on the downloaded file and the installation begins. Note the name of the directory in which you install the JMF and set the JMFHOME environment variable to this value. This environment variable is referred to throughout this Preface.

The following table describes the recommended configuration for using Sun's JMF on a Windows machine.

Recommended Configuration for Wintel	
Processor	486 or Pentium 100Mhz or better
O/S	Windows 9*x* or Windows NT 4.0
Memory	Windows 9*x*: 12MB; Windows NT: 24MB
JDK Software	JDK 1.1.3 or greater
Additional Software	Microsoft DirectShow (for MPEG)

Up to date installation instructions and system requirements can be found in $JMFHOME/html/setup.html after you have downloaded and installed the JMF. This file also has instructions for running the sample code that comes with the JMF distribution.

Before using Sun's JMF on a Windows machine, you need to augment two environment variables. First, you must add the JMF classes to your CLASS-PATH.

```
c:> set CLASSPATH="%JMFHOME%\lib\jmf.jar;%CLASSPATH%"
```

You must also modify your PATH variable so that the JVM can find the native libraries required by the JMF.

```
c:> set PATH="%JMFHOME%\lib;%PATH%"
```

Downloading Intel Implementation

Intel's JMF implementation can be downloaded from:

http://developer.intel.com/ial/jmedia/JMDownload.htm.

Installing Intel Implementation

The Intel JMF is also installed with InstallShield. The installation is a piece of cake. You simply double-click on the downloaded file and the installation begins. The only thing you need to note is the name of the directory in which you install. As a convenience, set the environment variable JMFHOME to this value. We refer to JMFHOME throughout this Preface.

The following tables describe the minimum and recommended configurations for using Intel's JMF.

Minimum Configuration	
Processor	Pentium
O/S	Windows 9*x* or Windows NT 4.0
Memory	Windows 9*x*: 12MB; Windows NT: 24MB

Recommended Configuration	
Processor	Pentium or Pentium II w/MMX technology
O/S	Windows 9*x* or Windows NT 4.0
Memory	Windows 9*x*: 16MB; Windows NT: 32MB

In addition to these requirements, you will want to have the latest Direct-Draw drivers for your graphics card.

The EJMF FTP Site: Support Code, Examples

Source code and class files for all the examples presented in the book, as well as the *Essential JMF* Toolkit, are available from the Prentice Hall `ftp` site, `ftp.prenhall.com`. This site is accessible via anonymous `ftp`.

A single ZIP file contains all the necessary files. In the following discussion, this file is referred to as the "EJMF support code." It is named `ejmf_support.zip`.

Downloading the EJMF Support File

The following sequence of steps illustrates how to download the EJMF support code. You type the **bold**. The computer types the rest.

```
% ftp ftp.prenhall.com
Connected to iq-ss3.prenhall.com.
220 iq-ss3 FTP server(UNIX(r) System V Release 4.0) ready.
User (iq-ss3.prenhall.com:(none)): anonymous
331 Guest login ok, send ident as password.
Password: <type your user name, e.g. username@someisp.net>
230 Guest login ok, access restrictions apply.
ftp> cd /pub/ptr/professional computer_science.w-022/
gordon/essential_jmf
250 CWD command successful.
ftp> bin
200 Type set to I.
```
(1)

```
ftp> get ejmf_support.zip
200 PORT command successful.
150 ASCII data connection for ejmf_support.zip
   (38.11.232.6,1099) (19818 bytes).
226 ASCII Transfer complete.
20184 bytes received in 5.93 seconds (3.40 Kbytes/sec)[2]
ftp> bye
Goodbye.
```

Installing the EJMF Support Classes

Before unzipping the downloaded EJMF support file, choose a directory in which you will the install *Essential JMF* support code. This is called the installation directory. When you unzip, be sure you are in this directory.

Once you have unzipped the examples file, set the EJMF_HOME environment variable to point to the installation directory. For example, if you unzip ejmf_support.zip in /home/me/ejmf, you would set EJMF_HOME as follows.

```
% export EJMF_HOME=/home/me/ejmf
```

Or, on a Windows machine:

```
c:> set EMF_HOME=c:\home\me\ejmf
```

Within this directory, you will find three major subdirectories. Additionally, the source directory contains a directory for example source and one for Toolkit source.

Directory Name	Description
$EJMF_HOME/src	Contains the source files for all the examples and the *Essential JMF* Toolkit.
Within $EJMF_HOME/src/ejmf are two more directories which separate out examples and Toolkit source	
$EJMF_HOME/src/ejmf/examples	Contains example source.
$EJMF_HOME/src/ejmf/toolkit	Contains Toolkit source.
$EJMF_HOME/classes	Contains the class files for all the examples and the *Essential JMF* Toolkit.
$EJMF_HOME/docs	Contains the javadoc output for the *Essential JMF* Toolkit.

---

2. Do not take these file sizes and transfer times at face value. A test run generated these values.

CLASSPATH Considerations

The following entries should be added to your CLASSPATH in order to run the examples and use the *Essential JMF* Toolkit.

```
$EJMF_HOME/classes
$EJMF_HOME/src
```

The latter is not strictly necessary for running the examples, but is required if you want to rebuild either the examples or Toolkit class files.

The ejmf.properties File

Some of the examples and much of the Toolkit code use the java.util.Properties class to reference property data stored in $EJMF_HOME/classes/lib/ejmf.properties.

The mixer example from Chapter 24 uses an entry in this file to name the directory in which to load and store its session information. If a MIXER_HOME value is defined, it is used as the "current directory" for mixer data files. If it is not defined, the Java property user.dir is used.

To easily access the media files available with the EJMF support code, place the following entry in the ejmf.properties file:

MEDIA_HOME=*ejmf_home*

where *ejmf_home* is full path name of the EJMF installation directory.

Building the EJMF Support Classes

Class files for both the examples and the Toolkit are included with the EJMF support code so, once installed, you are ready to roll. However, if you need to rebuild the class files, you have two options.

Brute Force

The brute force method dictates that you visit every directory you want built and type:

```
% javac -d $EJMF_HOME/classes *.java
```

This will get the job done, albeit with a little extra typing.

Using GNU make

Alternatively, GNU make files are provided along with the EJMF support code. If you want to use these make files, you must either have GNU make or be willing to get it. You can find information on the GNU Project at http://www.cfcl.com/free/orgs/DP/P/GNU.html. GNU make can be downloaded from `ftp://prep.ai.mit.edu/pub/gnu/`. We used Version 3.76-1 of GNU `make` in our work.

The following `make` variable must be set for the `make` files to properly work. These are set in the file `$EJMF_HOME/src/ejmf/Makefile.master`.

`BIN` – The value of this variable should name the directory in which "remove file" and "remove directory" equivalents reside. The `BIN make` variable is used in the file `$EJMF_HOME/src/ejmf/Makefile.cmd` to point to the directory in which these commands reside.

Making the EJMF Class Files

To build the EJMF class files for the examples and the Toolkit, perform the following steps:

```
% cd $EJMF_HOME/src/ejmf
% make TARGET=all all
```

The above `make` command can be executed from within any directory within the directory tree rooted at `$EJMF_HOME/src/ejmf` to build a subtree.

Cleaning the EJMF Class Files

To clean the EJMF class files, perform the following steps.

```
% cd $EJMF_HOME/src/ejmf
% make TARGET=clean clean
```

The above `make` command can be executed from within any directory within the directory tree rooted at `$EJMF_HOME/src/ejmf` to clean a subtree of its corresponding class files.

The README File

The `ftp` site also contains a README file that resides in the same directory as the EJMF support file. This file will contain an update history of the example source accompanying *Essential JMF*. Please refer to it to track changes to the *Essential JMF* Toolkit.

Reporting Problems

Comments, suggestions, compliments and abuse intended for the authors can be sent to `feedback@phptr.com`.

Help From Fellow Travellers

Appendix D, "Resources," contains instructions for subscribing to three Java Media-related mailing lists. We encourage you to join the fray.

Some Conventions

A Word About Listings and Code Segments

Code that appears in this book in a numbered listing can also be found among the example source code available from the *Essential JMF* `ftp` site. Generally a Listing corresponds to either a complete Java source file or a complete Java method. In cases where a class or method is excerpted, ellipses will appear at the beginning and end of the Listing to identify this fact.

In some instances, code snippets will appear in `courier` but otherwise not offset from the normal flow of the prose. This is done in short examples to illustrate a very general usage or technique. These code snippets do not appear, as such, as part of any example.

Secret Meaning Behind Typeface Selections

All code listings and output, all method and function names, commands, directories, and all URLs appear in `courier`.

User input appears in **`bold courier`**.

Special terms, upon their introduction, variables, and parameters to be substituted for appear in *italics*.

Text within figures appears in helvetica.

Weak attempts at humor appear in footnotes.

A Thousand Words About Pictures

The class diagrams that appear in this book were all constructed using Rational Software's Rational Rose visual modeling tool. They are all constructed from the Unified Modeling Language (UML). See Appendix E, "Unified Modeling Language Notation," to learn enough about UML to understand the diagrams that appear in this book.

A big thanks to Rational Software Corporation for their complementary use of Rational Rose. What's in a name? No other modeling tool would have been as sweet.

A Word About Sexist Language

We have been very impressed with the sensitivity displayed by some authors of technical books in their efforts to avoid sexist language in their writing. After all, the computer, that quintessential human expression of masculine rationality and logic, could use a little softening around the edges.

One particularly tortured public display of post-modern sensibilities appears in Dan Heller's book *The Motif Programming Manual*. Mr. Heller spends nearly 500 words to inform the concerned reader that he (he is a "he") is going to use "he" when in need of a singular pronoun. Like a good cybernaut, Heller then softens the blow with a : (but one is still left with a taste of political correctness in his mouth.

We, too, struggled with this decision. Many late nights were spent listening to Lou Reed's "Walk On The Wild Side" ("shaved her legs and then he was a she/She said, hey babe, take a walk on the wild side") without resolution. We just could not "take a walk on the wild side." Our obstinacy, however, had nothing to do with a secret desire to perpetuate oppressive patriarchal power structures or even a failure to adequately deconstruct gender roles.

You see, we went to the source. We did what any two living, white males would do: we consulted two dead, white males, Mr. Strunk & Mr. White. We agree with them when they say: "The furor recently raised about *he* would be more impressive if there were a handy substitute for the word" and that the use of "he" for embracing both genders "has no pejorative connotation."

Throughout this book, you will find "he" where you have come to expect it, accompanied by neither apology nor emoticon.

A Footnote

We are going on the optimistic assumption that our readers will complete this book as experts in the JMF in spite of stupid footnote humor.

ACKNOWLEDGMENTS

The *wisdom* that "you can't judge a book by its cover" must have originated with the *fact* that you can't judge the number of people who contributed to a book by the number of authors listed on its cover. To wit, there is a long list of people whose involvement with this book improved it and made it possible.

We had a crack team of reviewers who shared our pain down to the very end, turning around chapters in a day's time. Neither their thoroughness nor thoughtfulness suffered under such deadlines. They worked well together without even knowing each other. Shawn "G. Love" Bertini of QuickStream Software, Jan Martin Borgersen of IBM, Peter Rivera of LSI Logic, and Andrew Wason of SoftCom all provided valuable comments after reading a draft of this book. Our work was much improved by theirs.

In two cases, our talents were not up to the task of providing the necessary artistic flair required in the book. For that, we relied on the talented Max Eisele, erstwhile college professor now branching into web design work. Check out her work at http://dialup.pcisys.net/~meisele/. Max did the spaceship animation that appears in Chapter 18 and the colorful icons that appear in Chapter 21.

Our Prentice Hall editor Greg Doench displayed an abiding and faithful patience. No book can have too much of that. He also brought others into the picture as needed, including Lisa Iarkowski, Gail Cocker and Mary Treacy.

Lisa and Gail made us look like better desktop publishing types than we really are. Mary is simply a presence. She makes things happen, not the least of which is, shall we say, the dispersal of funds.

There is one professional support type who deserves an entire, typo-free paragraph of her own. Julie Bettis's performance as our copy editor was above and beyond the call. The most and best that can be said of her is that she cares about her work and she treated our work as if it were hers. Perfection is a tough standard but she pushed us toward it. Besides all that, she, for the most part, liked our jokes.

Rob adds: Gratitude, like charity, begins at home, so it is with my wife and boys that I must start when thanking the many people who have helped me with this book. Their patience is as much a part of this book as any reviewer's comment, artist's graphic or editor's guidance. Kathy, Kieran, Kilian and Matthew deserve billing as honorary co-authors.

In no way does this diminish my gratitude and indebtedness to my co-author, whose name does appear on the cover, Steve Talley. Working with Steve was a treat. I have rarely seen such talent in a single person in my fifteen years in the computer industry. Talent aside, he laughs at my jokes. That alone qualifies him as perfect co-author material.

There are also a few people whose contribution to my effort on this book cannot be described by a title nor linked to a particular chapter. It can only be said that their involvement was timely and necessary: Bob Senese, Pat McBride, Pete Cullinan, Bart Henderson, Mark Pattridge, Phil Russo, Bill Pollack, Tim Joyce, Dennis Bartlett, and Jim Blaha.

Finally, my dad deserves acknowledgment for teaching me the value and satisfaction that comes from finishing what you start; my mom, for teaching me the power of faith.

Steve adds: In these times of Dilbert-esque scenarios being played out all over the computer industry, it is rare that someone would choose to thank his manager above all others. However, I'll buck the trend and thank Andy Rudoff for allowing me the latitude to complete this book. Without his support (and occasional chess game) this undertaking would not have been possible.

Next to thank are the family members who, without knowing the specifics of this endeavor, have given me the support and confidence to write a book. Now you know. Free copies to anyone who can define JMF after skimming through this book.

Like a second family, Jenn, Jeff, Sandee and Jon Rudnick have also provided invaluable support throughout this project. They were good enough to remind me of the life that can be enjoyed if I don't spend twenty hours a day at the office.

Finally, a special thanks to my co-author. Risking a Hallmark sentiment, Rob is an inspiration in both wit and lore. I have learned much from him about Java, careers, and life – most notably that the three are not necessarily related.

Rob is a true friend with whom I hope to continue to work, in some capacity, in the future.

Rob: Anyone we missed?
Steve: Yes. I think we should thank [!][Gg]od[s|dess[es]] we are finished!
Rob: Phew, good call there, Steve. Wouldn't want to offend anyone.
Steve: Nope. Furthest thing from my mind. How about you, Rob, any last words?
Rob: Yes. After working so iduously on this book, it is time to get some sleep.
Steve: "Iduously"?
Rob: We worked our ass off.
Steve: Well put. With that in mind, don't code like my co-author.
Rob: Don't code like my co-author.

essential

JMF

JAVA™ MEDIA FRAMEWORK

Part I

USING THE JAVA MEDIA FRAMEWORK

Chapter 1   *INTRODUCTION*

Part I of this book is written for the user of the *Java Media Framework*. The material contained in this section is written with the goal of in mind of getting a Player working in an applet or an application.

What follows is a brief overview of Part I.

Why JMF?

In Chapter 2, "Why JMF?," we take a brief look at the JMF in the context of both the other *Java Media* APIs and related or competing products. This chapter will give you a sense of the larger picture of multimedia programming in Java.

The Basics of JMF Programming

In Chapter 3, "The Basics of JMF Programming," we hit the ground running with programming examples. By the end of this chapter you will be able to write a simple applet or application that incorporates a JMF Player.

JMF Architecture

In Chapter 4, "JMF Architecture," we step back and take a look at The Big Picture. This chapter provides an architectural overview of the JMF Player, laying the groundwork for an in-depth look at each of the pieces in subsequent chapters.

The Clock

The piece of the JMF API that describes timing services supplied by a Player is covered in Chapter 5, "The Clock."

The Controller

The Controller is discussed in Chapter 6, "The Controller." The Controller interface defines a state machine implemented by a Player. The different Controller states define different levels of Player readiness. These states, the transitions from state to state and the accompanying events are covered in detail in this chapter.

The Player

In Chapter 7, "The Player," we see how the major pieces of the JMF come together in a Player. In addition, we introduce the GUI components associated with a Player.

Player Controls

A Control associated with a Player provides a standard way to present non-standard Player features to a user. Chapter 8, "Player Controls," describes the Control interface and discusses how it relates to the operation of a Player.

Synchronizing Multiple Players

In Chapter 9, "Synchronizing Multiple Players," an important feature of the Player API, the ability to synchronize multiple Players, is discussed.

Locating the Player

Chapter 10, "Locating the Player," discusses the little known facts surrounding the algorithm used by the JMF Manager class when locating a Player to playback media of a certain type.

Chapter 2   *WHY JMF?*

Introduction

In the early days of Java, what must have been a hundred Internet years ago, the promise of content-rich, multimedia-laden, dynamic web pages featuring animation, audio and video, was the talk of everyone, everywhere, from lackey webmasters to cyber-samurai CEOs, from Peoria to Wall Street. The web, no, the world was on the verge of yet another of those mini-revolutions spun off by the big revolution of our times, the Information Revolution.

Yet, the early features of Java only hinted at the possibilities: the audio capabilities of applets were limited to a single format;[1] there was no support for video; animation was limited to a series of GIF images.

It was not until the introduction of the Java Media APIs that Java began to meet the increasing demand for multimedia. The Java Media APIs, of which the *Java Media Framework* (JMF) is one, support the integration of a wide range of audio and video formats, advanced imaging, animation, two- and three-dimensional graphics and modeling, as well as speech and telephony support, into Java applications and applets.

---

1. The Java Development Kit 1.2 will support additional formats.

3

The Java Media Framework

The JMF consists of a suite of three APIs designed for the capture and play-back of audio and video. The first of these APIs, and the subject of this book, is the JMF Player API. The other two APIs that make up the JMF describe video and audio capture capabilities and video conferencing capabilities.

The JMF Player API is the most mature of these three APIs, having been implemented by three vendors. Sun has released implementations for both Solaris and Wintel platforms. Intel has released an implementation for Wintel platforms. Finally, RealNetworks has released a Player implementation that supports their RealAudio and RealVideo media data types.

The Java Media Player

Before you dirty your hands with the details of coding to the JMF Player API, it would be helpful to survey some of the features of a Player.

Ease of Use

Applications and applets can create and control media playback for any standard media type using only a few method calls.

Cross Platform Multimedia

A Java application or applet written to the JMF Player API is capable of operating on any Java platform that supports a conforming implementation of the Player API.

However, since the JMF Player API is not part of the core Java packages, the classes and libraries that constitute an implementation of it must be installed separately from the *Java Development Kit* (JDK) or *Java Runtime Environment* (JRE).

Support For Many Popular Formats

The JMF Player API is independent of any particular media data type. Instead, each implementation of a Player is written to support a particular type of media data. The Player is then easily integrated with the installed JMF. The API does not at all constrain the Player in the type of the media data it presents.

Current implementations of the JMF support audio formats such as AIFF, AU, MIDI, MPEG-1 Layer 1/2, PCM, RMF, and WAV. Video codecs supported include Apple Graphics (SMC), Apple Animation (RLE) Cinepak, H.261, H.263, Indeo 3.2, Motion-JPEG, and MPEG-1.

For a complete list of the media types supported by various implementations, visit the URL mentioned in Appendix D, "Resources."

Support For Common Protocols

A JMF Player can obtain media data using the FILE, FTP, HTTP and RTP protocols. This allows access to local and non-local media data sources, either streamed or non-streamed.

Extensibility

The design of the JMF makes it easy to incorporate support for new media data types and data source protocols. To support a new data type, a new Player is developed and registered with the JMF configuration service. To support a new data source protocol, a similar approach is taken. In this way, the JMF scales across different types of media data types and different delivery mechanisms.

The registration of either of these elements is trivial. The work of developing them is not so. However, complete examples of building both a new Player and support for a new protocol are presented later.

In Part II, "Extending the Java Media Framework," we will develop a framework that provides an abstract Player implementation compliant with the JMF API. All that is left to implement a new Player is to supply the media- and device-dependent code.

Additionally, an example of how to extend the JMF to support a new protocol for obtaining media data is presented in Part II. Support for an actual protocol, the NNTP protocol for news group transmission, will be developed to work with the JMF. Think of the efficiencies as you use a Player to scroll news group postings across your screen all day!

Synchronization of Multiple Media Sources

The JMF Player API describes a simple mechanism to synchronize the play back of multiple media sources.

Push and Pull Data Sources

The JMF supports both *push* and *pull* modes for acquiring media data. When acquiring media in pull mode, the client initiates data transfer and controls the flow of data from the source.

In push mode, data transfer is initiated by the source serving the media data. The server, then, is also responsible for controlling the flow of data. The JMF Player supports the Real-time Transport Protocol (RTP) for the delivery of various types of streaming media data.

Along with these features, the JMF Player offers the benefit of being part of a larger multimedia effort within the Java "community." Sun and its partners are involved in the development of other APIs for multimedia programming that place the JMF within a related set of programming tools that enhance and complement its capabilities.

The Java Media APIs

The Java "community" has undertaken a large effort to augment the core of the Java language by specifying and implementing APIs that, among other things, allow easy integration of multimedia functionality into Java applications and applets. Sun is promoting the subset of these APIs that relate to multimedia under the general banner of the Java Media APIs. The JMF is one of these APIs. Let's take a quick look at the functionality specified by the other APIs.

Java 2D API

The *Java 2D* API provides a framework for device- and resolution-independent, two-dimensional graphics.

The Java 2D API is currently specified as a collection of classes that will appear in the `java.awt` package. The Java 2D classes contained in JDK 1.2 conform to the Java 2D API 1.0 specification.

Java 3D API

The *Java 3D* API is a set of classes for writing three-dimensional graphics applications and applets. It gives developers high-level constructs for creating, manipulating and rendering three-dimensional geometry.

The Java 3D API is a standard extension to Java residing in the `javax.media.j3d` package. Supporting math classes are in the `javax.vecmath` package.

Java Advanced Imaging API

The *Java Advanced Imaging* API allows sophisticated, high-performance image processing to be incorporated into Java applets and applications. It is a set of classes providing imaging functionality compatible with the Java 2D and the *Java Foundation Classes* (JFC).

The Java Advanced Imaging API is a standard extension to Java and is currently specified in the `javax.jai` package.

Java Speech API

The *Java Speech* API allows Java applications and applets to incorporate speech technology into their user interfaces. The API defines a cross-platform API to support command and control recognizers, dictation systems and speech synthesizers.

The Java Speech API is a standard extension to Java and is specified in the `javax.speech` package.

Java Sound API

Java Sound API is a high-quality, 32-channel audio rendering and MIDI-controlled sound synthesis engine featuring a new Java audio API. Java Sound uses the Headspace Audio Engine from Headspace, Inc. It will be integrated into the Java Virtual Machine in JDK 1.2.

The same sound engine is currently being used in Sun's JMF 1.0.1 for rendering the audio of a JMF Player.

Java Telephony API

The *Java Telephony* API is an object-oriented application programming interface for Java-based computer-telephony applications ranging from call center applications to web page integration of phone services.

The Java Telephony API is a set of interfaces and abstract classes defined in the `javax.telephony` package.

There are currently two implementations of the Java Telephony API; IBM's CallPath and Lucent Technologies Passageway Telephony Services.

For more information on the Java Telephony API, see *Essential JTAPI* by Spencer Roberts (Prentice Hall, 1998).

All of these APIs are in various stages of specification, the progress of which can be followed at `http://java.sun.com/products/java-media`.

As you can see, some of these APIs are explicitly related to the JMF. The audio rendering portion of the JMF is also used by the Java Sound API and the Java Telephony API. The Java 3D API is useful for developing animations that can be played with a JMF Player. A custom Player implementation may take advantage of the Java Advanced Imaging API to integrate special effects into the playback of its media.

The above discussion places the JMF in the context of a larger Java multimedia effort. Now let's look at some products from other vendors to understand the place of the JMF within a broader set of available tools for audio and video presentation.

Related Products

There is also a variety of other "player" products on the market that compete in varying degrees with the JMF Player. A few words on the more popular products follow.

Beatnik Plug-in

The Beatnik Plug-in from Headspace, Inc. plays a variety of music and audio file formats including RMF, MIDI, MOD, AIFF, WAV, and AU files. It is supported on Macintosh PowerPCs, Windows 95 and NT machines. Since it uses the Headspace Audio Engine, it does not require a high-end sound card. It does its processing entirely in software, and requires only a DAC (digital-to-analog converter) to play audio to your speakers via stereo output.

Microsoft DirectShow

Microsoft DirectShow (formerly ActiveMovie) is a media-streaming architecture for the Windows platform. It supports both capture and playback of multimedia streams in a variety of formats. MPEG, Apple QuickTime, AVI, and WAV files are all supported for playback. Capture can be based on either Video for Windows (VFW) or Windows Driver Model (WDM).

Microsoft com.ms.DirectX Package

The Microsoft DirectX package provides the classes and interfaces needed by Java programs and applets to access the services and features of the DirectX Component Object Model (COM) interface for Microsoft Windows.

This is a fairly low-level interface, providing nothing more than a Java wrapper for accessing the DirectX libraries.

QuickTime for Java

QuickTime for Java presents the QuickTime 3 API as a set of Java classes. These classes offer equivalent APIs for using QuickTime functionality on both MacOS and Windows. QuickTime for Java supports the MacOS Runtime for Java (MRJ) on MacOS and the Sun JDK 1.1 on Windows NT and Windows 95/98.

RealMedia and RealSystem G2

RealMedia from RealNetworks, Inc. is tailored for on-demand streaming media at relatively low bandwidths. It uses proprietary compression technology together with the Real Time Streaming Protocol (RTSP) to obtain "near broadcast" quality sound and video and fast download performance.

RealMedia defines a client-server architecture wherein the popular Real-Player is served by servers capable of streaming using RTSP. The wide appeal of RealPlayer is the content it provides in conjunction with major commercial broadcast outlets.

The technology upon which RealPlayer is built is called RealSystem G2. RealSystem G2 supports both local and streaming media in RealVideo and RealAudio formats, as well industry standard media data types such as AVI, WAV, ASF, VIVO, MPEG, JPEG, AU, AIFF. RealSystem G2 includes a development kit for the integration of playback of these formats from within an application.

An implementation of the JMF Player using RealMedia technology is available from RealNetworks, Inc. See Appendix D, "Resources," for details.

Macromedia ShockWave

Shockwave from Macromedia, Inc. plays streaming multimedia content over the Internet. It is limited to playing content produced by Macromedia's Flash, Director and AuthorWare products but that has not impeded its wide acceptance. It operates as a plug-in and is shipped as a standard piece of both Netscape's Communicator and Microsoft's Internet Explorer.

Well, Why?

Many of these products are quite popular and have gained widespread acceptance. It is hard to go anywhere on the Internet without running into content that requires one or another of them. To the Java programmer, however, most suffer from the same disadvantage: they are not easily-accessible from Java. The exception to this, QuickTime for Java, is not available for UNIX platforms. If you need a cross-platform audio and video playback solution for application and applet development, then the JMF is just the ticket.

Additionally, by using the JMF Player, you situate your development within a rich milieu of related and compatible APIs. As the other pieces of JMF mature, you will be able to take advantage of capture and conferencing features. Likewise, as the other Java Media APIs mature, you will be able to integrate them with your JMF applications for a cross-platform, multimedia solution.

Summary

We have seen an overview of the features of the JMF Player. We have seen how it fits into the larger of picture of Java multimedia development. We have seen some related media playback solutions for Internet development. Finally, we have observed that if you are doing Java multimedia development, the JMF, with its current functionality and the promise of future integration with complementary APIs, is a good choice.

But enough of that. It sounds too much like marketing hype. Let's write some code.

Chapter 3

THE BASICS OF JMF PROGRAMMING

Introduction

The best place to start with JMF programming is where the `java.applet.AudioClip` interface leaves off. Before the days of the JMF, the closest Java came to providing multimedia functionality was animated GIFs and looping audio files in Sun's AU format. The shortcomings associated with these two approaches to multimedia programming are obvious. Not only are they limited in their richness of presentation but they do not comprehend the wide array of available media formats. If a sound file were not in AU format, it could not be used in an applet. Likewise, if your animation could not be encoded in a multi-image GIF file, it could not appear in your applet or application. Complex AWT programming can produce some animation, but a lot of work was and is required to match the sophistication of the output generated by commercial animation programs.

The JMF enhances the previous capacities for Java multimedia programming. This chapter starts with a JMF port of an old applet using the `java.applet.AudioClip` interface. From there, incremental complexity will be added to our example applet until it incorporates the minimally useful set of JMF API calls. These examples will eventually end up replacing animated GIFs with video files.

An AudioClip Example

To set the context for our evolving JMF example, let's look at a simple applet that loops through a sound file using the `java.applet.AudioClip` interface. If you are currently using this functionality in your web page, it may look something like Listing 3.1 below.

Listing 3.1 *Applet Using AudioClip Interface*

```
package ejmf.examples.basics;

import java.applet.Applet;
import java.applet.AudioClip;
import java.net.URL;
import java.net.MalformedURLException;
import java.io.*;

public class OldAudio extends Applet {
    private AudioClip      clip;
    public void start() {
        clip.loop();
        // Or, to play just once, use play()
        // clip.play()
    }

    public void stop() {
        clip.stop();
    }

    public void init() {
        String media;
        if ((media = getParameter("MEDIA")) == null) {
            System.err.println(
                    "Invalid MEDIA file parameter");
            return;
        }
        clip = getAudioClip(getCodeBase(), media);
    }
}
```

(1) `clip.loop();`

(2) `clip = getAudioClip(getCodeBase(), media);`

The use of the `AudioClip` interface is straightforward. The clip is started in [1] after being retrieved using `getAudioClip` in [2]. The audio clip can either be played continuously using the `loop` method, as above, or once using the `play` method. To run the above example, the following HTML file is available with the *Essential JMF* source.

Listing 3.2 *HTML File for OldAudio Example: OldAudio.html*

```
<applet code=ejmf.examples.basics.OldAudio.class
        width=100 height=100>
<param name=MEDIA
        value=../../../../classes/media/issues.au>
</applet>
```

This HTML file can be loaded into `appletviewer` to give you the impression you are sitting in on a marketing meeting. This example can be run from the `$EJMF_HOME/src/ejmf/examples/basics` directory by typing the following command.

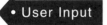 **Running OldAudio Example**

% appletviewer OldAudio.html

We will now look at how both the looping and single play strategies can be implemented using the JMF API.

Playing Audio Using JMF

Playing an audio file in an applet using the JMF API is no more complex than the simple interface provided by `java.applet.AudioClip`. However, as our example evolves, more JMF-induced complexity will enter the picture. Do not let this scare you. What this complexity buys you is a whole lot of flexibility. As we build larger examples using the JMF API, you will see not only the value of this complexity but you will also see a method to the apparent madness.

The next two examples model the one-shot playing of an audio clip and the looping of an audio clip.

One-Shot Play of Audio Using JMF

The one time playing of an audio file represents the minimal JMF example. Such a bare bones approach only makes sense with audio files as there is no video to display. As we will see, displaying video properly requires just a little more JMF expertise.

The minimal interaction with JMF requires two steps:

1. Create a `Player`.
2. Start the `Player`.

There is much more but, for now, let's look at a synopsis of the JMF API calls used in the audio example. First, we will look at how a `Player` is created in JMF API Synopsis 3.1.

JMF API Synopsis 3.1 *Creating a Player*

Class	`javax.media.Manager`
Method	`createPlayer`
Arguments	`java.net.URL`
Return	`javax.media.Player`
Description	Creates a `Player` from a URL.
Method	`createPlayer`
Arguments	`java.media.MediaLocator`
Return	`javax.media.Player`
Description	Creates a Player from a `MediaLocator`.

These two methods are the most common ways of creating a `Player`. The `javax.media.MediaLocator` is much like a URL but there need not be a `URLStreamHandler` installed on the system to use one. We will see more about the `MediaLocator` in Chapter 10, "Locating the Player." The JMF API also provides the `createPlayer` method with other signatures which will be introduced later.

JMF API Synopsis 3.2 describes the method used to start a `Player`.

JMF API Synopsis 3.2 *Starting a Player*

Interface	`javax.media.Player`
Method	`start`
Arguments	`void`
Return	`void`
Description	Starts the `Player`.

Aside from creating and starting the `Player`, the following example code represents a typical applet.

Listing 3.3 *Playing JMF Audio in a Typical Applet*

```
      import java.applet.Applet;
      import java.net.URL;
      import java.net.MalformedURLException;

(3)   import javax.media.Player;
(4)   import javax.media.Manager;
(5)   import javax.media.NoPlayerException;

      public class JMFAudioOnly extends Applet {
          private Player      player;
          public String       media;

          public void init() {

              if ((media = getParameter("MEDIA")) == null) {
                  System.err.println(
                      "Invalid MEDIA file parameter");
                  return;
              }
              try {
                  URL url = new URL(getCodeBase(), media);
(6)               player = Manager.createPlayer(url);
              } catch (NoPlayerException e) {
                  System.out.println("Could not create player");
              } catch (MalformedURLException mfe) {
                  System.out.println("Bad URL");
              } catch (IOException ioe) {
                  System.out.println("IO error creating player");
              }
          }

          public void start() {
(7)           player.start();
          }

(8)       public void destroy() {
              player.stop();
              player.close();
          }
      }
```

The Player is created at [6] using the createPlayer method provided by the javax.media.Manager class. It is then started at [7]. These steps correspond nicely to the steps necessary to play an AudioClip. To make the calls in lines [6] and [7] possible, the proper classes must be imported by the Java compiler. Lines [3] through [5] take care of this.

The role of the destroy method when using a Player within an applet is very important. destroy is called by the browser when leaving a page. The destroy method above [8] stops the Player and then closes it. If this is not done there are possibly two negative side-effects. First, if, say, your Player is playing audio, that audio will continue to play while the user is visiting the next page. Second, as long as the Player object is referenced by the browser, it will own all the resources allocated to it. This may prevent another Player from operating properly in subsequent page visits.

Note that the package name for the JMF classes begins with javax and not the usual java. This is because the JMF API represents an extension to the core Java packages.

To run the example Listing 3.3 using appletviewer type:

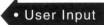 **• User Input**   **Running JMFAudioOnly Example**

```
% appletviewer JMFAudioOnly.html
```

If you run the example HTML file unchanged, you will feel like you are still in a meeting with the marketing folks. The HTML file shipped with the *Essential JMF* examples appears below.

Listing 3.4 *HTML File for JMFAudioOnly Example: JMFAudioOnly.html*

```
<applet code=ejmf.examples.basics.JMFAudioOnly.class
        width=100 height=100>
<param name=MEDIA
        value=../../../../classes/media/issues.au>
</applet>
```

As you see, the HTML files appearing in Listing 3.2 and Listing 3.4 are very similar. They differ only in value of the code argument value. To play another sound clip, edit the JMFAudioOnly.html file and change the MEDIA tag to supply another audio file.

Since the HTML files for the remaining examples in this chapter all derive from the previous two files, they will no longer be displayed in text. They all are available with the *Essential JMF* source.

Looping Play of Audio Using JMF

Playing an audio clip through once was easy enough. Looping an audio clip continuously adds just a little twist. There is not a single call as with Audio-Clip. To loop through a clip using JMF, we have to learn a bit about two more features of a JMF Player:

- Player events
- Media time

For now these two topics will be covered only briefly, enough to make progress on your looping audio applet or application. Later, they will get in-depth coverage.

In order to cause a `Player` to loop through some media source, your applet must be able to recognize when the media is finished playing. This is done easily enough with a listener that listens for events.

The JMF event-handling mechanism is similar to the Java 1.1 delegation event model.[1] The architecture is simple: some object fires *events* which can be listened for and acted upon by *listeners*.

In our case, the `Controller` is the object which fires `Controller-Events`. When discussing JMF events, a distinction needs to be made that has heretofore been ignored. A JMF `Player` implements the `javax.media.Controller` interface. The `Controller` piece of a `Player`, among other things, maintains state information and fires events in response to state changes. One such event is the `EndOfMediaEvent` which signals that the end of the media associated with the `Player` has been reached. Your applet must recognize this event, "rewind" the media, and start it again.

In the next example, a listener especially tailored to receiving `EndOf-MediaEvents` will be built and discussed. Two new JMF methods are introduced. The first `getSourceController` reports from which `Controller` an event was fired.

JMF API Synopsis 3.3 *The getSourceController Method*

Class	`javax.media.ControllerEvent`
Method	`getSourceController`
Arguments	`void`
Return	`javax.media.Controller`
Description	Retrieves from a `ControllerEvent`, the `Controller` that fired the event.

1. The idea is the same but the JMF's event mechanism cannot be said to follow exactly the AWT 1.1 event model. `ControllerListener` does not implement `java.util.EventLis-tener`, and `ControllerEvent` does not extend `java.util.EventObject`. This disparity can only be described as an historical nuance.

The return value of getSourceController will be used to invoke set-MediaTime to rewind the Player. setMediaTime is a method that is available from a Player by virtue of it implementing the javax.media.Clock interface.

JMF API Synopsis 3.4 *The setMediaTime Method*

Interface	javax.media.Clock
Method	setMediaTime
Arguments	javax.media.Time
Returns	void
Description	Positions the media at the time designated by the Time argument.

What does a listener that is interested in Controller events look like? Listing 3.5 presents the listener we will use for our looping example. Notice that our LoopListener class implements ControllerListener [14]. Before jumping into the body of the code, it is also worth noting the import statements that are required in lines [9]-[13]. Lines [9] and [10] are required for every ControllerListener.

Listing 3.5 *A Simple ControllerListener*

```
(9)   import javax.media.ControllerListener;
(10)  import javax.media.ControllerEvent;
(11)  import javax.media.Controller;
(12)  import javax.media.Time;
(13)  import javax.media.EndOfMediaEvent;
(14)  class LoopListener implements ControllerListener {
(15)      public void controllerUpdate(ControllerEvent event) {
(16)          Player p = (Player) event.getSourceController();
(17)          if (event instanceof EndOfMediaEvent) {
(18)              p.setMediaTime(new Time(0));
(19)              p.start();
          }
      }
}
```

For readers familiar with the AWT, this listener holds no surprises:[2] There is a single method implementation, controllerUpdate [15], that takes some kind of event as an argument. In our case, that event is a Controller-Event. Of course, a listener may implement other methods but it must provide

2. For a good discussion of the AWT 1.1 event model, see *Graphic Java 1.1 Mastering the JFC Volume I: AWT,"* David Geary (Sunsoft Press, 1998).

controllerUpdate in order to satisfy the ControllerListener interface and field ControllerEvents. JMF API Synopsis 3.5 summarizes the controllerUpdate method.

JMF API Synopsis 3.5 *controllerUpdate Method*

Interface	javax.media.ControllerListener
Method	controllerUpdate
Arguments	javax.media.ControllerEvent
Return	void
Description	Invoked by the Controller when an event is posted.

Returning to Listing 3.5 you can see that the work of the listener for our looping example is done in lines [16] through [19]. First, the Controller which generated the event is extracted from the ControllerEvent object at [16]. It is cast to a Player so that we can later use the start method.

After detecting that the incoming event is, in fact, an EndOfMediaEvent in line [17], the listener calls setMediaTime [18] with a Time object whose value is initialized to zero, effectively rewinding the media. The start in line [19] kicks off the Player again. The use of the Time class and the EndOfMediaEvent require the import lines at [12] and [13]. Again, we will see more about the Time class and all the ControllerEvents in later chapters.

Lines [12] and [18] expose yet another dimension of a JMF Player that will be explored in detail later. For now suffice it to say that each media has a time value associated with it. By manipulating this time value, a programmer can change the point in the media at which the Player is to play. One way to think of it is as a programmatic seek function.

The complete listing of the looping JMF audio clip answers the final question: how does the listener get registered with the Player?

Listing 3.6 *Looping JMF Audio Applet*

```java
// Only novel import statements reproduced here.
import javax.media.Controller;
import javax.media.ControllerEvent;
import javax.media.ControllerListener;
import javax.media.Time;
import javax.media.EndOfMediaEvent;

public class JMFAudioLoop extends Applet {
    private Player      player;
    private String      media;

    public void init() {
        if ((media = getParameter("MEDIA")) == null) {
            System.err.println(
                "Invalid MEDIA file parameter");
            return;
        }
        try {
            URL url = new URL(getCodeBase(), media);
            player = Manager.createPlayer(url);
            player.addControllerListener(
                                new LoopListener());
        } catch (Exception e) {
            e.printStackTrace();
        }

    }

    public void start() {
        player.start();
    }

    public void destroy() {
        player.stop();
        player.close();
    }
}

class LoopListener implements ControllerListener {
    public void controllerUpdate(ControllerEvent event) {
        Player p = (Player)event.getSourceController();
        if (event instanceof EndOfMediaEvent) {
            p.setMediaTime(new Time(0));
            p.start();
        }
    }
}
```

(20)

(21)

(22)

The `start` method of `JMFAudioLoop` differs from the previous applet, `JMFAudioOnly`, appearing in Listing 3.3 only at line [20]. This line creates a new `LoopListener` object and registers it with the `Player` as being interested in `Player` events. The listener is registered using `addController-Listener`.

JMF API Synopsis 3.6 *Adding a Listener to a Controller*

Interface	`javax.media.Controller`
Method	`addControllerListener`
Arguments	`javax.media.ControllerListener`
Returns	`void`
Description	Registers `ControllerListener` object as interested in `ControllerEvents` for a given `Controller`.

Notice that at line [21] the `Controller` needs to be cast to a `Player` so that in [22] the `start` method may be used.

As is the case in general with the event delegation model, a `Player` may have an arbitrary number of listeners. Later examples will illustrate applets or applications with multiple listeners registered on a single `Player`.

The above example may be run using `appletviewer` by typing the following command in the `$EJMF_HOME/src/ejmf/examples/basics` directory.

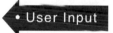 **Running JMFAudioLoop Example**

```
% appletviewer JMFAudioLoop.html
```

If the last example did not sound like a marketing meeting, this one certainly will.

Before moving on, let's review how the above applet works. There are six JMF-related steps constituting the looping audio example:

1. Definition of a `ControllerListener` class.
2. Creation of a `Player`.
3. Registration of a listener with `Player`.
4. Starting the `Player`.
5. Detection of `EndOfMediaEvent`.
6. Resetting the media time to zero and restarting the `Player`.

In the next example, step (5) will be expanded to handle an additional JMF event. We will also see one of the features of the JMF that separates it from the simple `AudioClip` interface: the provision of a GUI component for interactive control of a `Player`.

The Control Panel Component

In the previous example, the applet was designed to programmatically "rewind" the audio and replay it without any interaction with the user. This may be adequate for some applications, but the JMF provides GUI components to allow the user to interact with a `Player` when interaction is desirable.

The JMF API specifies a method to query a `Player` for its default user interface `Component`. Such a `Component` might contain buttons to stop, start or rewind the `Player`. Figure 3.1 shows the default control panel for the Intel implementation of the JMF.

Figure 3.1 *Default Control Panel Component for Intel JMF*

Figure 3.2 shows the default control panel for Sun's implementation.

Figure 3.2 *Default Control Panel Component for Sun JMF*

Each control panel layout contains a play/pause button, two volume control arrows and a speaker which acts like a mute button. Additionally, a slider bar shows the progress of the media. The use of these components is straightforward. There is one trick, however. Holding down the right mouse button over the start button on the Sun control panel component will display a GUI component for adjusting the rate of the `Player`.

The `Player` method that retrieves this `Component` is `getControlPan-elComponent` and is described below.

JMF API Synopsis 3.7 *Obtaining GUI Control Component*

Interface	`javax.media.Player`
Method	`getControlPanelComponent`
Arguments	`void`
Returns	`java.awt.Component`
Description	Returns a `java.awt.Component` which can be used to control a `Player` from the GUI.

There is a restriction on the use of the `getControlPanelComponent` method. It may only be called when the `Player` is at least in the *realized* state. As was mentioned, a `Player` by virtue of its implementing the `Controller` interface, has a state associated with it. Further, these states are ordered. A `Player` can be in one of the six states listed below. One state is "greater than" another if it appears later in the list.

Table 3.1 *Ordered Player States*

State	Description
unrealized	Initial state. `Player` object instantiated.
realizing	Determining required resources and information about media. Acquiring non-exclusive use resources.
realized	All non-exclusive use resources have been acquired.
prefetching	Acquiring necessary exclusive use resources.
prefetched	All resources have been acquired.
started	`Player` is running, `Clock` has started.

It is possible for a `Player` to step through each step until it is *started*. In all the examples so far, a `Player` has simply been started using the start method. The `ControllerListener` that was registered with the `Player` was only interested in the `EndOfMediaEvent` in order to rewind the `Player`. All intermediate state transitions were ignored.

We have now come to an example that requires a bit more sophistication on the part of the `ControllerListener`. As mentioned above, a `Player` must be *realized* in order for a call to `getControlPanelComponent` to be legal. This means the `ControllerListener` is going to have to pay attention to state changes and act when the `Controller` reports that the *realized* state has been reached. It does this by looking for the `RealizeCompleteEvent`. Since the main-line of the applet remains unchanged from the previous example, we will only look at the `ControllerListener` code. In this case, the `ControllerListener` interface is implemented by `AudioControlListener`.

The `init` method from the applet that creates an `AudioControlListener` object and passes it a `JPanel` component is shown in Listing 3.7.

Listing 3.7 *JMFManualControl: Creating A ControllerListener*

```
public class JMFManualControl extends JApplet {
    private Player       player;
    private PlayerPanel playerpanel;
    private String       media;

    public void init() {
        playerPanel = new JPanel();
        playerPanel.setLayout(new BorderLayout());
        add(playerPanel);
            if ((media = getParameter("MEDIA")) == null) {
                System.err.println(
                    "Invalid MEDIA file parameter");
                return;
            }
    }

    public void start() {
        try {
            URL url = new URL(getCodeBase(), media);
            player = Manager.createPlayer(url);
            player.addControllerListener(
                new AudioControlListener(playerPanel));
            player.start();
        } catch (Exception e) {
            e.printStackTrace();
        }
    }

    public void destroy() {
        player.stop();
        player.close();
    }
}
```

(23)

(24)

The `JPanel` is created at [23] and passed to the `AudioControlListener` at [24]. The `AudioControlListener` source appears in Listing 3.8. The `JPanel` argument to the constructor is used to display the control panel.

Listing 3.8 *Displaying the Control Panel Component*

```
(25)    import javax.media.RealizeCompleteEvent;

        public class AudioControlListener
                            implements ControllerListener {
            private JPanel      panel;
            private Component    cpc;

            public AudioControlListener(JPanel panel) {
(26)            this.panel = panel;
            }

            public void controllerUpdate(ControllerEvent ev) {
                Player p = (Player)ev.getSourceController();
                if (ev instanceof EndOfMediaEvent) {
                    p.setMediaTime(new Time(0));
                }
(27)            else if (ev instanceof RealizeCompleteEvent) {
(28)                Component cpc = p.getControlPanelComponent();
                    if (cpc != null) {
(29)                    SwingUtilities.invokeLater(
                            new AddComponentsThread(cpc));
                    }
                }
            }

(30)        class AddComponentsThread implements Runnable {
                private Component c;
                public AddComponentsThread(Component c) {
                    this.c = c;
                }

                public void run() {
(31)                panel.add(c, BorderLayout.CENTER);
(32)                panel.validate();
                }
            }
        }
```

What separates this example from the previous ones is the added complexity within the ControllerListener code.

At line [27], an additional if clause is added to the controllerUpdate method to respond to a RealizeCompleteEvent (imported at [25]). Now that the Player has reached the *realized* state, the control panel Component can be retrieved [28]. What happens next can only be described as a distraction from our main task. In short, a Runnable object is created and scheduled for deferred execution by the event dispatching thread. That Runnable, defined at [30], is responsible for adding the control component to the JPanel object, panel, at [31], and then calling validate [32] to force a layout of panel.

All of this happens as a result of the call to SwingUtilities.invoke-Later [29]. A long story is going to be made short here: Swing components can be accessed by only one thread at a time. Generally, this is the event-dispatching thread. If you need access to the GUI from outside event-handling or drawing code, then you can use either invokeLater or invokeAndWait method from the SwingUtilities class. "Outside event-handling or drawing code" means somewhere other than within methods like the Component.paint method or an event listener method (e.g. actionPerformed). The bottom line is that controllerUpdate is not one of these. Hence, the call to SwingUtilities.invokeLater. For the long version of this story see either http://java.sun.com/products/jfc/tsc/swingdoc-archive/threads.html or *Graphic Java 1.1 Mastering the JFC Volume II: Swing* by David Geary.

We now return to our regularly scheduled discussion of the JMF.

There is one thing absent from this example that appeared in the JMFAudi-oLoop example. In the EndOfMediaEvent branch within controller-Update, there is no call to the start method. This is because the control panel provides a button which is tied to the start method of the Controller. When the media is finished playing, the controllerUpdate method will rewind it. The user can then restart it using the control panel.

To run this example from the $EJMF_HOME/src/examples/basics directory type the following:

▸ • User Input   **Running JMFManualControl Example**

% **appletviewer JMFManualControl.html**

This is the first example whose GUI is of any interest. The whole point of obtaining the control panel from the Player is to display it so the user can manipulate it. When this applet is run, you should see one of the control panels shown in Figure 3.1 or Figure 3.2.

You are encouraged to run this example because watching the applet come up and run exhibits a shortcoming with the above code's interaction with the Controller. You may notice that the sound starts to play before the control panel is rendered.[3] This happens because the forward movement of the Player through its different states is asynchronous with respect to the user code. When the applet code receives the RealizeCompleteEvent, the Player continues to make progress through its ordered states as described in

---

3. This behavior may not manifest itself at all times on all machines. The point is that the current example does not solve the general problem of media being played before the control panel is displayed.

Table 3.1 on page 23. If it happens to take the user code longer to render the control panel than it does the `Player` to arrive at the started state, you will hear the audio play before the control panel is displayed. In Chapter 6, "The Controller," we will take a detailed look at how the `Controller` transitions from one state to the next. With that new knowledge, we will create an example that eliminates the problem of the media playing before the control panel is rendered. Although not necessarily a big problem with an audio-only media format, it is more serious with a video format.

There is a related point that needs to be made about the above example and its interaction with the `Controller`. The `JMFManualControl` applet comes up with the sound already started because the `start` method was called to kick off the `Player`. Calling the `start` method should be understood as a request to "move through the `Controller` states until the *started* state is reached." We will see later how a `Player` can be created and left in a state such that the media does not play until the user presses the start button on the control panel or explicitly moves the Player into the started state. Solving this problem will also solve the premature rendering problem.

Discussion of these problems will be deferred. After we look at `Controller` state transitions, we will return to them. For now, one more basic element of a `Player` will be introduced. It is time to introduce video to the mix.

The Visual Component

What fun would a web page be with only sound and not video? Obtaining the `java.awt.Component` into which a `Player` renders it video parallels obtaining the control panel component. There is a single method that returns the Component and it must not be called before the `Player` is in the *realized* state.

JMF API Synopsis 3.8 *Obtaining a Player's Visual Component*

Interface	`javax.media.Player`
Method	`getVisualComponent`
Arguments	`void`
Returns	`java.awt.Component`
Description	Returns the Component into which a Player's video will be rendered.

A minor change to the `ControllerListener` from the `JMFManualControl` example nets a `Player` that displays its video. The new `ControllerListener`, `VideoTooListener` appears in Listing 3.9.

Listing 3.9 *Displaying Player Visual Component*

```
public class VideoTooListener
                    implements ControllerListener {
    private JPanel panel;
    private Component cpc, vc;

    public VideoTooListener(JPanel panel) {
        this.panel = panel;
    }
    public void controllerUpdate(ControllerEvent event) {
        Player p= (Player) event.getSourceController();
        if (event instanceof EndOfMediaEvent) {
            p.setMediaTime(new Time(0));
        }
        else if (event instanceof RealizeCompleteEvent) {
            SwingUtilities.invokeLater(
                    new AddComponentsThread(p));
        }
    }

    class AddComponentsThread implements Runnable {
        private Player player;
        public AddComponentsThread(Player player) {
            this.player = player;
        }
        public void run() {
            cpc = player.getControlPanelComponent();
            if (cpc != null)
                panel.add(cpc, BorderLayout.SOUTH);
            vc = player.getVisualComponent();
            if (vc != null)
                panel.add(vc, BorderLayout.NORTH);
            panel.validate();
        }
    }
}
```

(33) **(34)** **(35)**

Two new lines of code are all that are needed to display the video associated with a `Player`'s media. In line [33] the visual component is obtained from the `Player` and then at [34] added to the parent container for display. The call to `validate` at [35] forces the `JPanel` to be laid out to accommodate its new members. Again, as good Swingers, we do the GUI work on the event thread.

The problems discussed for sound are also present with the display of video. The `Player` may actually start the media before the video is rendered. Again, the solution to this problem will be deferred until Chapter 6.

These current shortcomings notwithstanding, let's look at the input to this example and its output. Notice the input HTML refers to a media format that supports video.

Listing 3.10 *HTML for Video Player: JMFVideoToo.html*

```
<applet code=ejmf.examples.basics.JMFVideoToo.class
    width=340 height=260>
<param name=MEDIA
    value=../../../../classes/media/safexmas.mov>
</applet>
```

The mov suffix represents a QuickTime movie. This example can be run from the $EJMF_HOME/src/ejmf/examples/basics directory by typing:

◄ • User Input   **Running JMFVideoToo Example**

```
% appletviewer JMFVideoToo.html
```

Running appletviewer as above presents the following output frame when using Sun's JMF classes.

Figure 3.3 *Displaying Visual and Control Components*

Now that we have seen a few examples using the JMF, let's take a look at some classes that will reoccur throughout this book. These classes are part of the *Essential JMF* (EJMF) Toolkit and facilitate the integration of the JMF into applications and applets.

Introducing the EJMF Toolkit

The structure of the preceding examples is quite similar. There is the main-line applet code that creates and starts the `Player`, and the `ControllerListener` code that responds to `Controller` events. Within the `ControllerListener` code there is also some AWT and *Java Foundation Classes* (JFC) code necessary for displaying the various components associated with a `Player`.

In order to simplify the presentation of examples as well as provide some easy-to-use code for loyal readers, this section will introduce the `PlayerPanel` and `PlayerDriver` classes, both from the `ejmf.toolkit.util` package. These classes take care of some of the details of creating a `Player`, as well as abstracting some of the differences between the use of a `Player` within an applet and application.

As the last example highlights, a JMF `Player` displays its visual and control panel components within a `java.awt.Container`. The particular `Container` used by the `JMFManualControl` is a `JPanel` from the JFC. The examples throughout this book will be displaying a `Player`'s visual and control components within a `PlayerPanel`, an extension of `JPanel`.

The `PlayerPanel` class provides the following functionality:

- A `JPanel` into which the GUI components of a player can be placed

- A simple interface for adding the GUI components associated with a `Player`

- Standard borders and layout manager

- Display of a status message while `Player` is being created

Along with the `PlayerDriver` class, the `PlayerPanel` class provides a consistent structure for the book's examples. `PlayerDriver` is the base class from which all the examples extend. It is also an `abstract` class, relying on its subclasses to implement the `abstract` method `begin`.

The `PlayerDriver` class provides the following functionality:

- Creation of a `Player`
- A `JFrame` in which the `PlayerPanel` is displayed
- The ability to run as either an applet or an application
- A hook, the `abstract` method `begin`, for user-supplied action once the `Player` is created

The relationship between `PlayerDriver` and `PlayerPanel` is depicted in Figure 3.4.

Figure 3.4 *Class Diagram for PlayerDriver and PlayerPanel*

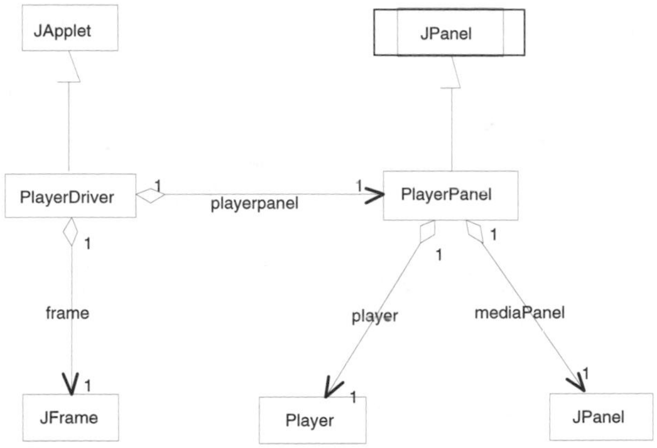

As you can see, `PlayerDriver` extends `JApplet` and has a reference to a `PlayerPanel`. When constructed, the `PlayerDriver` takes as input a `MediaLocator` and passes it off to the `PlayerPanel` for creation of the `Player`. The `JPanel` reference maintained by `PlayerPanel` is the Container in which a `Player`'s GUI `Components` are displayed.

The display of the GUI `Components` is left entirely to the user. It is intended that the `begin` method defined by a subclass of `PlayerDriver` perform this work. `PlayerPanel` displays a message informing the user that the media is being loaded until one of either the visual or control panel components is displayed.

With an overview of the operation of `PlayerDriver` and `PlayerPanel` behind us, let's look at each of them more closely

EJMF Toolkit PlayerDriver

We won't spend too much time on `PlayerDriver` since it does not add much to our discussion of the JMF API. It does, however, provide a simple harness for driving a `Player` applet or application. With that in mind, we will focus on how it is used.

Listing 3.11 is a skeletal example class extending `PlayerDriver`.

Listing 3.11 *Using PlayerDriver*

```
(36)    import ejmf.toolkit.util.PlayerDriver;
(37)    import ejmf.toolkit.util.PlayerPanel;

(38)    public class APlayerClass extends PlayerDriver
            implements ControllerListener
        {
            private PlayerPanel playerpanel;
            private Player player;

            public static void main(String args[]) {
(39)            main(new APlayerClass(), args);
            }

(40)        public void init() {
(41)            super.init();
                // Do your own init thing.
            }
(42)        public void begin() {
(43)            playerpanel = getPlayerPanel();
(44)            player = playerpanel.getPlayer();
                ...
(45)            player.addControllerListener(this);
                ...
(46)            player.start();
            }

            public void controllerUpdate(ControllerEvent event) {
                ...
            }
        }
```

Starting at the top you see that both `ejmf.toolkit.util.Player-Driver` [36] and `ejmf.toolkit.util.PlayerPanel` [37] are imported. `PlayerDriver` is required since `APlayerClass` extends from it [38] but generally, `PlayerPanel` is necessary too.

The full advantage of `PlayerDriver` is derived from a call to its `main` method at [39]. The `main` method takes an object reference to the example class plus the command line arguments, in the case of an application, as its arguments. If `PlayerDriver` is used as an applet and the subclass defines an `init` method [40], this `init` method must call `super.init` [41].

The sole syntactical requirement placed on a subclass of `PlayerDriver` is that it implement `begin` [42]. The `begin` method is where the action is, and it is where typical operations like getting the `PlayerPanel` [43] and the `Player` [44] are performed.

Once the `Player` is obtained, it registers itself as a `ControllerListener` [45]. Finally, the `Player` is started at [46].

This skeletal example highlights the `getPlayerPanel` [43] method, one of the useful `public` methods defined by `PlayerDriver`. It and two other handy methods provided by `PlayerDriver` are described in EJMF Toolkit Synopsis 3.1.

EJMF Toolkit Synopsis 3.1 *Useful PlayerDriver Methods*

Class	`ejmf.toolkit.util.PlayerDriver`
Method	`getPlayerPanel`
Visibility	`public`
Arguments	`void`
Return	`ejmf.toolkit.util.PlayerPanel`
Description	Returns the `PlayerPanel` associated with this `PlayerDriver`.
Method	`redraw`
Visibility	`public`
Arguments	`void`
Return	`void`
Description	Lays out and resizes `JFrame` associated with `PlayerDriver`.
Method	`getFrame`
Visibility	`public`
Arguments	`void`
Return	`com.sun.java.swing.JFrame`
Description	Returns the `JFrame` associated with this `PlayerDriver`.

All the above methods will be sprinkled throughout examples presented in subsequent sections of this book. Don't be shy about using them yourself.

EJMF Toolkit PlayerPanel

If `PlayerDriver` is the harness, then `PlayerPanel` is the horse. It creates the `Player` and provides a `JPanel` in which to display the `Player`'s visual and control panel `Components`. In addition, it provides a simple interface for adding those `Components`.

`PlayerPanel` defines a single constructor which takes a `MediaLocator` as its argument. A `Player` is created from that `MediaLocator`. The constructor for `PlayerPanel` is excerpted in Listing 3.12.

Listing 3.12 *PlayerPanel Constructor*

```
(47)   private Player player;

       public PlayerPanel(MediaLocator locator)
           throws IOException, NoPlayerException {
(48)       player = Manager.createPlayer(locator);
(49)       mediaPanel = new JPanel();
           . . .
       }
```

PlayerPanel's constructor first creates the Player [48] using the javax.media.Manager method createPlayer and stores it in the player member data field at [47]. It then creates a JPanel [49] for display of the Player's GUI Components. Whether or not the mediaPanel is ever used is up to the client of PlayerPanel.

PlayerPanel does, however, prescribe how mediaPanel is used. Specifically, it determines the layout of whatever Player Components are added. It does this by defining an interface by which Components can be added. This interface is comprised of the four methods described in EJMF Toolkit Synopsis 3.2.

EJMF Toolkit Synopsis 3.2 *Adding Player Components to PlayerPanel*

Class	ejmf.toolkit.util.PlayerPanel
Method	addControlComponent
Visibility	public
Arguments	void
Return	java.awt.Component
Description	Adds the default control panel component to the BorderLayout.SOUTH position of PlayerPanel's mediaPanel. The Component that is added is returned, null if the Player has no control panel component.
Method	addControlComponent
Visibility	public
Arguments	java.awt.Component
Return	java.awt.Component
Description	Adds the Component passed as an argument to the BorderLayout.SOUTH position of PlayerPanel's mediaPanel. Returns the same Component.

EJMF Toolkit Synopsis 3.2 *Adding Player Components to PlayerPanel*

Class	`ejmf.toolkit.util.PlayerPanel`
Method	`addVisualComponent`
Visibility	`public`
Arguments	`void`
Return	`java.awt.Component`
Description	Adds the default visual component to the `BorderLay-out.CENTER` position of `PlayerPanel`'s `mediaPa-nel`. The `Component` that is added is returned, `null` if the `Player` has no visual component.
Method	`addVisualComponent`
Visibility	`public`
Arguments	`java.awt.Component`
Return	`java.awt.Component`
Description	Adds the `Component` passed as an argument to the `Border-Layout.CENTER` position of `PlayerPanel`'s `mediaPa-nel`. Returns the same `Component`.

All four of these methods require that the `Player` be realized. A quick look at the source of a representative pair of these methods shows why.

Listing 3.13 *addVisualComponent and addControlComponent*

```
public Component addVisualComponent() {
    return addVisualComponent(
        player.getVisualComponent());
}

public Component addControlComponent() {
    return addControlComponent(
        player.getControlPanelComponent());
}
```
(50)

(51)

Both of these methods invoke calls ([50] and [51]) on a `Player` that require it to be realized.

Once the `Player` components are placed into some AWT `Container`, the `Container` needs to be redrawn so the components can be laid out and the `Container` resized if necessary. The `PlayerDriver` redraw method is useful for accomplishing this task.

Before we look at a full-blown example using `PlayerPanel`, there is one more method worth looking at. We have already seen `getPlayer` at [44] in

Listing 3.11 on page 32 but since it is so central to the use of `PlayerPanel`, it is worth an EJMF Synopsis.

EJMF Toolkit Synopsis 3.3 *PlayerPanel getPlayer*

Class	`ejmf.toolkit.util.PlayerPanel`
Method	`getPlayer`
Visibility	`public`
Arguments	`void`
Return	`javax.media.Player`
Description	Returns the `Player` associated with the `PlayerPanel`.

Now we have all the pieces required to see our first official *Essential JMF* example using the *Essential JMF* Toolkit. Does it get any better?

The GenericPlayer

The first example fitted to the *Essential JMF* Toolkit takes the JMF functionality we have seen so far and integrates it with what we know about `Player-Panel`. There is no new functionality of the `Player` exposed with this new example. It is simply an illustration of the use of `PlayerDriver` and `PlayerPanel`. Specifically, a new class `GenericPlayer` is built which extends `PlayerDriver`. Listing 3.14 presents the complete source for the `GenericPlayer` example.

Listing 3.14 GenericPlayer Example

```
package ejmf.examples.genericplayer;

public class GenericPlayer extends PlayerDriver
    implements ControllerListener
{
    private PlayerPanel playerpanel;
    private Player player;

    public static void main(String args[]) {
        main(new GenericPlayer(), args);
    }

    public void begin() {
        playerpanel = getPlayerPanel();
        player = playerpanel.getPlayer();

        player.addControllerListener(this);
        player.start();
    }

    public synchronized void controllerUpdate(
                    ControllerEvent event) {

        if( event instanceof RealizeCompleteEvent ) {
            Runnable r = new Runnable() {
                public void run() {
                    playerpanel.addControlComponent();
                    playerpanel.addVisualComponent();
                    redraw();
                }
            };
            SwingUtilities.invokeLater(r);
        } else if (event instanceof EndOfMediaEvent) {
            player.setMediaTime(new Time(0));
        }
    }
}
```

(52)

(53)
(54)

(55)
(56)
(57)

Although not exposing any new Player functionality, the Generic-Player example does illustrate the use of three PlayerPanel methods that we will see over and over and over again. First, the Player associated with the PlayerPanel is retrieved at [52]. The Player value returned is used both to add the GenericPlayer object as a ControllerListener [53] and to start the media playback [54].

The other two relevant `PlayerPanel` methods are called within the `Runnable` used for GUI update. The default control panel `Component` is added to the media `JPanel` at [55] while the visual component is added at [56].

Finally, at [57], `redraw` is called to layout the newly added `Components`.

We will see use of the `PlayerPanel` class throughout the remainder of this book. Its use simplifies those pieces of code that need to interact with the JMF. Further, it provides a convenient wrapper for a `Player` that can be used within either an applet or application.

Summary

This chapter has presented the basic elements of creating a JMF `Player` within either an applet or application. We have seen how to create and start a `Player` and field events fired by the `Controller` as it moves from one state to another. Using the `ControllerListener` interface, we saw examples of listeners which field `ControllerEvents` within their `controllerUpdate` method.

We saw how the `RealizeCompleteEvent` signals that a `Player` is ready to provide its control and visual components. We also fielded the `EndOfMediaEvent` in order to rewind the media. There was only brief discussion of the entire set of `Controller` states. That subject will be covered in depth in Chapter 6.

Finally, we introduced the `PlayerDriver` and `PlayerPanel` classes from the *Essential JMF* Toolkit. Both will be used throughout this book for presenting examples. They also provide a convenient vehicle for dropping `Players` into your own applets or applications. As we progress, more functionality will be added to the *Essential JMF* Toolkit. In the next chapter, we will learn about methods for fine tuning a `Controller`'s state transitions.

Chapter 4　　　*JMF Architecture*

Introduction

In the last chapter we got our feet wet with JMF programming. Using very nearly the minimum possible number of pieces of the JMF API, we built a few small applets that play media. In this chapter, we are going to step back and take a look at the Big Picture. Whereas methods from the API were thrown out without much discussion in Chapter 3, this chapter will be all discussion with nary a method name.

The JMF is really two things. It is a specification for implementing a `Player` and its constituent parts, and it is an API against which you can write code to use a `Player`. The distinction is useful because there is but one API and multiple implementations.

This chapter provides an overview of the JMF API specification. It does not discuss any specific implementation, nor does it discuss how to implement the API. Where the implementations covered by this book fail to conform to the API, mention is made of that fact where relevant throughout the book. In Part II, "Extending the Java Media Framework," we will look in detail at how to implement the JMF API. Here, the overall architecture is covered only in such depth as necessary to understand how to use existing implementations of JMF `Players` to play supported media formats. If you need support for

39

unsupported formats, you will need to reference Part II. For now, we will direct our attention to understanding the JMF Player API.

Overview of a JMF Player

We will start with a picture. Figure 4.1 is a class diagram depicting the major components of the JMF Player API. A close look will reveal that a Player is the successive extension of a set of Java interfaces.

Figure 4.1 *The JMF Player Class Diagram*

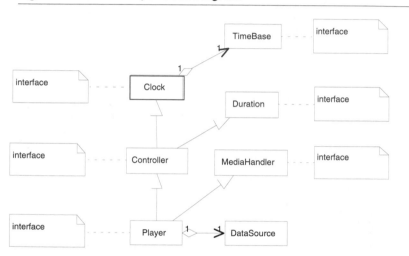

If all you want to do is write applications and applets that *use* a Player, knowing the interface definition and reading this book is sufficient. All you need to know to write code using a Player is specified by these interfaces and clearly explained by this book. The details that make it all work for a particular Player on a particular platform have already been solved by Sun, Intel, and others who have *implemented* the JMF Player API.

We will proceed in this chapter to describe a Player and its constituent parts so that you can become an expert *user*. Later, again in Part II, we will describe a Player and its constituent parts in such excruciating detail that you can become an expert at implementing the JMF API and demand a high salary from the kind of web start-up companies you read about in *Wired* magazine all the time.

The User's View: A Synopsis

As a user, the first piece of the JMF API that concerns you is a Player. The Player is the piece of the API that an application or applet will reference most frequently. You may recall from the previous chapter that the discussion focused primarily on the `Player`. In fact, you could, for example, incorporate a `Player` into a web page without referencing any of its constituent parts. Although that, being the simplest case, is quite useful, more needs to be said about a `Player` so that it can be used in more complex situations. This section gives a brief overview of the pieces of a `Player`. Subsequent sections go into more detail, enough to understand specific pieces of the API as they are introduced incrementally throughout the book.

As Figure 4.1 shows, a `Player` implements the functionality of a `Controller` and a `MediaHandler`.

As a `Controller`, a `Player` performs three responsibilities:

1. Managing acquisition and release of the system resources needed for rendering media.

2. Implementing a state machine that tracks the acquisition and release of system resources. Movement from state to state can be thought of as changes in the degree of "readiness" of a `Controller`.

3. Notifying interested parties about state changes. Any object that supports the `ControllerListener` interface can register with a `Controller` as a listener for `ControllerEvents`. After such registration, the `Controller` informs the listener when something of note happens by sending it an event.

A `Controller` extends the `Clock` and `Duration` interfaces. The `Duration` interface is very simple and merely defines the manner in which the length of media is reported.

The `Clock` interface specifies the functionality required to support the basic timing and synchronization needs of `Player`. A `Clock` has a reference to an object that implements the `TimeBase` interface. A `TimeBase` object provides a constant source of time, typically representing real time.

This structure allows a single `Clock` implementation to be extended by any number of `Controller` implementations. Likewise, any number of `Player` implementations may extend the same implementation of the `Controller` interface. This is useful since a `Player` is always limited to supporting only a single media type. However, the action of the `Controller` is not at all bound to the content of the media or its location. This loose coupling between a `Controller` and media allows a single `Controller` implementation to provide its services to many `Players`.

A `Player` has a `DataSource` object that provides media data to the `MediaHandler`. Because the `MediaHandler` is responsible for reading media data, it is the part of the `Player` that understands media format or *content type*. The `MediaHandler` interface is not that important from the user perspective since a `Player`'s `DataSource` is typically set at `Player` creation time by the `Manager` class which functions as a `Player` *factory*.[1]

A `Player` is limited to supporting only a single medium by virtue of its having only a single `DataSource` as shown in Figure 4.1. A `DataSource` describes the location of media data and the protocol with which the data is retrieved.

With this quick look at the structure of a `Player` out of the way, let's look a bit more closely at all the pieces. We'll start with the `Player` since that is where a user will start. From there, we will work our way up the inheritance tree as shown in Figure 4.1.

The Player Interface

A JMF `Player` is an object that processes a stream of data over time. Typically, the data comes from an audio or video file in one of the popular media formats, for example MPEG or QuickTime. However, it is not limited to a file. Media may also be read from an FTP or HTTP connection. As a `Player` reads data, it renders the data in whatever fashion is appropriate. Video is typically rendered to your display, audio to your speakers.

The `Player` API is the interface that pulls the rest of the API together to provide the above functionality. As you can see from Figure 4.1, the `Player` extends either directly or indirectly the major interfaces provided by the API. The `Player` extends two of these interfaces, `Controller` and `MediaHandler`, directly.

In addition to implementing these interfaces, the `Player` performs the following tasks.

- Reading media data from a `DataSource`, by virtue of being a `MediaHandler`.

- Rendering media.

- Providing user methods for obtaining the AWT `Components` used to render media and control the `Player`'s operation.

- Optionally, managing multiple `Controllers`.

Let's look at each of these roles briefly. They will be expanded upon in later chapters.

Rendering Data

The `Player` is the object that eventually draws on the screen for video media and generates audio for audio media. A `Player` reads data from a `DataSource` and massages that data as needed to render it in the appropriate way. Typically it does this using platform-specific native libraries that know how to send data to video and audio cards, or take advantage of a native CODEC.

---

1. A *factory* as defined by Gamma, et al. in *Design Patterns* provides "an interface for creating families of related of dependent objects without specifying their concrete classes."

A `Player`, however, need not necessarily rely on native libraries when rendering data. You will see in Part II of this book a `Player` implementation that renders its "video" using only `Components` from the *Java Foundation Classes* (JFC).

Access to AWT Components

Even if a `Player` relies on special video and sound cards to render media, it still must supply the user application some access to the video and audio streams so that they can be integrated into the application. For example, the application needs to be able to determine the placement of rendered video on the display. Similarly, an application may want to display a control panel to allow the user to interact with the `Player` from a GUI.

The `Player` meets both of these needs by providing a getter for each of the `Player`'s visual component and control panel component. The visual component is the AWT `Component` into which video is rendered. The control panel component is similar to, though much simpler than, the control panel of your CD player or VCR. `Player`'s differ in what they present, and an application can further customize the control panel, but basically the default control panel allows you to start, stop, rewind, change volume and position the media to any location.

Managing Multiple Controllers

A `Player` is designed to allow you to bring multiple `Controllers` under a single point of control. A master `Player` may have multiple slave `Controllers`. Any operation on the master `Player` is distributed to all the slave controllers. Likewise, multiple similar events generated by slave `Controllers` are collapsed into a single event by the master `Player` and passed to its `ControllerListener`.

This functionality is used to synchronize multiple `Players`. If you have a sound track and a video as separate media, you can create a `Player` for each and overlay the sound on the video by synchronizing the two `Players`. The `Player` interface provides methods that make this quite simple. Synchronizing multiple `Controllers` is the subject of Chapter 9, "Synchronizing Multiple Players."

The MediaHandler Interface

In addition to the responsibilities discussed above, the `Player` also implements the `MediaHandler` interface. An instance of a `MediaHandler` is defined by the type of media (or *content type*) it supports. As a result, an implementation of a `Player` is associated with a single content type. Conversely, each different media format will require a different `MediaHandler` object.

The functional role of a MediaHandler is to establish the association between a DataSource and a Player.

The DataSource Interface

Whereas a Player is defined by the media format it supports, a DataSource is defined by the protocol it supports. Together the two define the what and the how of retrieving media: an instance of a Player defines what kind of data is to be rendered, the DataSource defines how to get that data from wherever it resides to the Player. An implementation of a Player is capable of playing media of a single format.

Since it reads media data, a DataSource is also responsible for managing a connection to a Player's media data. That connection may be as simple as an open file descriptor or as complex as a socket over the Internet.

A DataSource also provides a set of controls for manipulating its data. These controls are specific to a particular implementation of DataSource and are not specified by the JMF API. Using a specialized control, an application can directly manipulate attributes of a DataSource. For example, the URL-DataSource class could be extended to provide a control that allows the user to set its HTTP proxy host and port values. Because the controls associated with a particular DataSource are not specified by the API, an application must determine the controls supported by a DataSource at run-time.

There are two flavors of data source. A pull data source involves data transfer initiated by the client or Player. Examples of this kind of source are DataSource implementations for the HTTP and FILE protocols.

A push data source involves data transfer initiated by some server. Examples of push data sources include video-on-demand (VOD) and broadcast data. Real-time Transport Protocol (RTP) can also be used as a transport mechanism for streaming push data sources.

The Controller Interface

The Controller interface extends both the Clock and Duration interfaces. Both of these interfaces will be discussed later in the chapter. What we are interested in here is the operation of the Controller as a state machine. Although a Controller can certainly be implemented independently of a Player, we will limit this discussion of a Controller in its role as a state machine that drives the operation of a Player.

The Controller state machine divides the work of preparing a Player into five resource allocation phases. Each state represents a different level of preparedness toward playing the media on the part of the Controller.

Controller States

The `Controller` states are ordered so that the further along in the state progression a `Controller` is, the closer a `Player` is to being able to play. This arrangement allows the user to exercise fine control over potentially time consuming operations and the allocation of system resources.

The way this control is exercised is by "listening" to the `Controller` as it reports state changes. Any instance of a class that implements the `ControllerListener` interface may register itself with a `Controller`, declaring its interest in events generated by the `Controller`. When some significant event occurs, the listener object gets notified. By monitoring these events as a `ControllerListener`, your application can determine exactly what state a `Controller` is in at any given time.

State Transitions

The `Controller` provides methods for changing its state. Whenever one of these state changing methods is invoked, a `ControllerEvent` is posted. As a `Controller` moves closer to being ready to play, it is said to be moving in the forward direction. In the process, a `Controller` generally acquires more of the resources it needs for playing. Forward transition methods are asynchronous and cause a `ControllerEvent` to be generated after the completion of the transition.

Backward transition methods are executed synchronously. Backward transition methods render a `Player` less ready to play. Generally, backward transition methods relinquish resources a `Player` has acquired.

Some transition operations affect a transition across multiple states. For this reason the `Controller` is able to report its *target* state as well as its *current* state. The target state is the final state at which the `Controller` will come to rest based on some transition method invocation. The current state is the state in which the `Controller` resides when the query is made.

The Duration Interface

The `Duration` interface provides a means to obtain a `Time` object from the `Controller`. The `Time` class encapsulates time for the JMF. The `Time` object provided by the `Duration` interface represents the total playing time of the `Controller`.

The Clock Interface

We all learned in kindergarten that a clock keeps time. That may be enough for the "all I needed to know I learned in kindergarten" crowd but it will not do in a world of "Internet time." The times are a changin' and now we have *media time* and *time-base time* to consider.

Media Time

The `Clock` associated with a `Player` keeps track of media time for a particular medium. Media time is that little counter at the bottom of the viewfinder on your video camera. It is what is reported by the LED read-out on your compact disc player.

Media time does not answer the question "What time is it?" Rather, it answers the question "What point in the media stream am I viewing (or hearing)?" or, the more colloquial, "Like, wow, man, where does that wicked Eddie Van Halen lick start in 'Runnin' With the Devil'?"

Media time can be manipulated. Just as you can rewind your VCR or play your *Abbey Road* album backwards, you can change the media time kept by an object that implements the `Clock` interface. The `Clock` interface defines methods for manipulating media time.

Time-Base Time

Time-base time is not so pliable. It just keeps on ticking. Time-base time is the flow of time against which media time is measured. The system time-base time is based on the time-of-day clock maintained by the native operating system.

A `Clock` may use a `TimeBase` other than the system `TimeBase`. It is not uncommon for video or audio boards to have an on-board hardware clock. A `Player` designed to render to such a device may opt to use this hardware clock as its `TimeBase`. The only requirement on the time-base time source is that its value be monotonically increasing.

The JMF API does not explicitly require it, but it is also useful that a `Clock`'s time-base time reflect real time. If it does not, your media may not play at the same speed at which it was recorded. This is clear from the relationship between media time and time-base time.

Mapping Time-Base Time to Media Time

When a `Clock` is started, it is responsible for maintaining a mapping between media time and time-base time. The point in time at which this mapping is applied is called the *time-base time start time*. From this point in time until the `Clock` is stopped, media time is synchronized with time-base time. The point in media time that maps to time-base start time is known as *media start time*. The progression of media time is a function of time-base time. As long as the `Clock`'s rate is unity, each tick of media time reflects a tick in time-base time. For `Clock` rates other than unity, for example, when fast forwarding media, the appropriate scaling is applied to derive media time from time-base time.

Building a Player

Manager: The Player Factory

The JMF provides a factory class for creating Players. The Manager class is a singleton and provides for, among other things, creating a Player.

Besides creating Players, the Manager class also provides access to system-dependent resources such as DataSources and the system TimeBase.

One of the most important roles of the Manager class is to algorithmically determine the available content and protocol support. This is transparent to an application and occurs when a new DataSource or Player object is requested from the Manager class. This algorithm will be discussed in detail in Chapter 10, "Locating the Player".

Keep in mind that the JMF API defines a Player interface. Recall from Java 101 that you cannot create an instance of an interface. To create a Player object, you must go through the Manager class.

Identifying Media

In order to create a Player object, the Manager needs a DataSource object. The Manager can also take an instance of a URL or MediaLocator and create a Player, but it must first construct a DataSource from these. What type of media object is passed to the Manager will determine the algorithm used to create a Player. The Manager uses the javax.media.PackageManager class provided by a JMF implementation to locate the supported Players for a given installation. The details of these algorithms are also covered in Chapter 10, "Locating the Player." For now, the brief descriptions offered below will suffice.

Each type of media object, and an outline of the algorithm Manager uses to create a Player from that media object, is described below.

DataSource

A DataSource is the most complete form of a media object. From it, you can retrieve information about both media content and the protocol used to retrieve the media. Given a DataSource, the Manager compares its content type with a list of supported Players for that content type. The Manager tries to create a Player from each element in this list in turn. When it succeeds, it returns a Player object. An exception is thrown if the Manager cannot find an appropriate Player.

MediaLocator

A MediaLocator is like a URL except that you can create a MediaLocator without having an instance of java.net.URLStreamHandler loaded in the JVM. What this amounts to is that support for such streaming protocols such as FTP, GOPHER and HTTP need not be available.

Presented with a `MediaLocator`, the `Manager` extracts the associated protocol and uses it to search a list of supported `DataSources` that is provided by the `PackageManager`. For those `DataSources` that support the `Media-Locator`'s protocol, a further search is done looking for a `Player` that supports the content type provided by the `DataSource`. If a `Player` can be instantiated, it is returned by the `Manager`.

URL

When the `Manager` is asked to create a `Player` from a URL, the `Manager` simply wraps the URL in a `MediaLocator` and applies the algorithm for building a `Player` from a `MediaLocator` as described above.

The Player as Implemented

The design of the JMF segments the job of getting media from a source to an output device fairly nicely. Three major functional components are identified and described by the API. Because of the delineation in their presentation, it is easy to take the next step and imagine some implementation that provides as clean a delineation in your thinking of them.

Unfortunately, it is not that simple. Keep in mind that the API defines only Java interfaces; the `Player`, `Controller` and `Clock` are all interfaces. The single most important implication of this fact is that there is no way to create, say, a `Clock` object, within your application, since a Java interface cannot be instantiated. The same holds for creating a `Controller` or `Player`. In the case of a `Player`, references to `Player` objects can only be obtained via the `Manager` class which acts as a `Player` factory. However, there is no analogous way to create a `Controller` or a `Clock`. The API dictates that the `Player` provides the `Controller` and `Clock` functionality.

What this means is that applications written to an implementation of the JMF API will almost always be dealing with a `Player` object. This `Player` will also be a `Controller` and a `Clock` since it will implement those interfaces as well. This has implications for determining when certain methods may and may not be called. There are some `Clock` methods, for example, that may not be called when the `Clock` is running. As we will see, the `Player` API relaxes this constraint. Specifically, some methods which are not allowed on a started `Clock` may be called on a `Player` when the `Clock` is started. In this case, it is the `Player`'s responsibility to stop the `Clock`. This is just one of several examples where the `Player` provides more flexibility than the `Clock`. When discussing the `Clock` and `Controller` APIs in Chapter 5, "The Clock" and Chapter 6, "The Controller," these loosened constraints are discussed. The important thing to keep in mind is that when your code references a `Player` object, many of these constraints are relaxed.

Summary

This chapter has presented the nickel tour of the JMF Player architecture. We have seen that a Player derives its functionality by extending various interfaces defined by the JMF API. Namely, the API defines the Clock, TimeBase, Controller, Duration and MediaHandler interfaces, all of which contribute to the Player interface.

The Clock interface provides timing functionality, and the Controller interface provides a resource allocation state machine. These interfaces define the major functionality of a Player.

The Duration interface allows a Controller to report the length of its media and the TimeBase interface provides something akin to wall clock time. Finally, a MediaHandler reads data from a DataSource and presents it to the Player.

Since interfaces don't get you very far in Java, there must be a way to actually create Player objects. The Manager factory class provides this capability. We saw that the Manager returns a Player object given a media object. A media object may either be a DataSource, a URL, or a MediaLocator.

At this point, all we have is a vocabulary to take with us as we look at different aspects of the JMF API in greater detail. Many topics introduced here will be revisited and elaborated upon in later chapters. We will start with an in-depth look at the Clock API.

Chapter 5   THE CLOCK

Introduction

The progression of time is central to the operation of a JMF `Player`. The questions of *when* a `Player` is to begin, for *how long* it is to play and at *what rate* all depend on some mechanism for measuring the progression of time.

That mechanism within the JMF is an instance of an object that implements the `Clock` interface.

This chapter looks at the `Clock`'s role in the playing of media. In addition to the `Clock` API, we will discuss two closely related APIs defined by the JMF. One of these, the `TimeBase` interface, must, in fact, be referenced by an implementation of the `Clock` interface. The other, `Time`, provides an abstraction—as if time were not already abstract enough—for handling the notion of time across the various classes defined by the JMF API.

Throughout this chapter, much of the discussion of the `Clock` interface takes place within the context of a `Player`. This is because the `Player`, as the most common implementation of a `Clock`, is the focal point of the JMF. As we progress through Part I, we will build on our current discussion by looking at other important parts of the `Player`, such as the `Controller`, `Duration`, and `MediaHandler` interfaces. By the end of Chapter 7, "The Player," we will

51

have a complete understanding of every aspect of the `Player` interface. For now, let's concentrate on the `Clock` interface.

What's Time?

The `javax.media.Time` class provides a uniform and abstract means for representing time across different pieces of the JMF. All methods defined by the API that refer to time use a `Time` object to do so.

A `Time` object can be constructed in one of two ways as shown in JMF API Synopsis 5.1.

JMF API Synopsis 5.1 *javax.media.Time Constructors*

Class	`javax.media.Time`
Constructor	`Time`
Arguments	`long`
Description	Creates a `Time` object representing `long` nanoseconds.
Constructor	`Time`
Arguments	`double`
Description	Creates a `Time` object representing `double` seconds.

A `Time` object can report its value either in seconds or nanoseconds.

JMF API Synopsis 5.2 *Accessor methods for Time*

Class	`javax.media.Time`
Method	`getSeconds`
Arguments	`void`
Return	`double`
Description	Returns the number of seconds represented by the `Time` object.
Method	`getNanoseconds`
Arguments	`void`
Return	`long`
Description	Returns the number of nanoseconds represented by the `Time` object.

The `Time` object is used by the JMF API to either represent a point in time, as in `getMediaTime`, or an amount of time, as in `getDuration`. The use of the `Time` object is straightforward enough but it leaves open the question of who or what maintains a more concrete idea of time. Is it a clock ticking away somewhere? Let's explore this question.

Time Base Time

The class diagram of a `Player` from Figure 4.1 on page 40 shows that a `Clock` must contain a reference to an object that implements the `TimeBase` interface. As part of that implementation, `TimeBase` provides a source of time that represents real time. This source of time is called the *time-base time*. Time-base time has the following characteristics.

- It is read-only.

- It is monotonically increasing.

Time-base time can be derived from any of a variety of sources as long as that source meets these requirements. The system hardware clock would certainly suffice, as would the JVM's `System.currentTimeMillis`. Time-base time may also come from a hardware clock on a video or audio rendering device. The origin of time-base time is not important from a user's perspective. We simply need to understand `TimeBase` as an ever increasing source of time that a program can read.

The `TimeBase` class defines only two methods. These methods allow a program to query a `TimeBase` object for the current time. We will see here the first use of the `Time` object described above.

JMF API Synopsis 5.3 *Accessor Methods for TimeBase*

Interface	`javax.media.TimeBase`
Method	`getTime`
Arguments	`void`
Return	`javax.media.Time`
Description	Returns a `Time` object representing the current time-base time.
Method	`getNanoseconds`
Arguments	`void`
Return	`long`
Description	Returns the current time-base time in nanoseconds.

A Clock provides access to its TimeBase with the getTimeBase method.

JMF API Synopsis 5.4 *Clock TimeBase Accessor*

Interface	javax.media.Clock
Method	getTimeBase
Arguments	void
Return	javax.media.TimeBase
Description	Returns the TimeBase object associated with Clock object.

Once retrieved the Clock's TimeBase object can be used to get the current time-base time.

```
long now = player.getTimeBase().getNanoseconds();
```

This concept of "now" is relative to when time-base time began. For example, the TimeBase returned by the getSystemTimeBase method of the javax.media.Manager class considers the beginning of time-base time as the time when the class first gets loaded by the JVM. This detail should not be relied upon when coding, rather it is pointed out to indicate the range of possible sources for the time basis.

The Clock API provides methods for setting and getting a Clock's TimeBase. JMF API Synopsis 5.5 describes setTimeBase.

JMF API Synopsis 5.5 *Setting TimeBase for a Clock*

Interface	javax.media.Clock
Method	setTimeBase
Arguments	javax.media.TimeBase
Return	void
Description	Set the time-base for Clock.

It is important to emphasize that setTimeBase does not set time-base time. It simply associates a time-base with a Clock. Time-base time cannot be manipulated but a Clock's time-base can change. One way to set a Clock's TimeBase is simply to pass a null object as the TimeBase argument. This resets the TimeBase to its default value.[1]

1.This does not work on Sun's JMF 1.0.1 release.

```
// reset Player time-base to default value
try {
    player.setTimeBase(null);
} catch (IncompatibleTimeBaseException e) {
    // exception handling here
}
```

The above code illustrates the fact that setTimeBase throws an IncompatiableTimeBaseException. We will learn more about this exception when we cover synchronizing Players in Chapter 9, "Synchronizing Multiple Players."

The JMF provides a time-base time tied to the system clock. This TimeBase is available from the Manager class.

JMF API Synopsis 5.6 *Accessor for Default System TimeBase*

Class	javax.media.Manager
Method	getSystemTimeBase
Arguments	void
Return	javax.media.TimeBase
Description	Returns the default system TimeBase object.

A Clock's default time-base is not necessarily the same as the system time-base. Do not assume

```
player.setTimeBase(null)
```

and

```
player.setTimeBase(Manager.getSystemTimeBase())
```

are the same. It is certainly possible that they could be, but the JMF does not specify that this must be the case. The above two lines are equivalent only if a Clock uses the system time-base as its default time-base.

Nowhere in our discussion of time, Time and TimeBase has there been any mention of playing media. We have yet to address the questions posed in the first paragraph of this chapter, the questions of when, for how long and at what rate does a Player play. To fully answer these questions, we will need the concept of media time.

Media Time

We have digressed just a bit from our discussion of Clock to explain some of the related parts of the JMF. We have seen two classes, Time and TimeBase, which provide a way for applications to deal with time. Now we will see how the Clock ties these classes together with the idea of *media time*.

An implementation of the Clock interface keeps media time. It does not maintain real-time, nor time-base time. The Clock object ticks only when media is playing. When the Clock is ticking, media is playing and the Player is in the started state. When the Clock is not ticking, the media is stopped and the Player is in the stopped state.

Recall from page 46 in Chapter 4 that media time tracks time within a media stream. Just like you can manipulate the point in a song you are playing on your CD player, you can manipulate media time using the Clock API.

A clear understanding of the relationship between media time and time-base time is essential to proper use of the Clock API. Furthermore, the description of some of the Clock methods refer to both media time and time-base time so before we look at the Clock API in detail, an explanation of the mapping of media time to time-base time will be undertaken.

Mapping Time-Base Time to Media Time

The JMF specification defines very clearly the relationship between media time and time-base time. Consider the following definitions:

mediaTime The current time in media time coordinates.

mediaStartTime A value that represents the time at which the media starts in media time coordinates.

timeBaseTime The current time in time-base time coordinates.

timeBaseStartTime A value that represents the time-base time at which the media is started.

rate A scale factor that determines how "fast" media time is to progress relative to time-base time. *rate* need not be integral and may be negative, indicating that the media is playing in reverse.

These values can be used to calculate media time as a function of time-base time.

$$mediaTime = mediaStartTime + \\ (timeBaseTime - timeBaseStartTime) * rate \qquad \text{(EQ 1)}$$

This equation says that we can determine how far we have progressed into some media by looking at how much time-base time has transpired. To this fundamental understanding, two qualifications must be added. If the media is started somewhere "in the middle," we adjust by adding at what point it did start. This is the *mediaStartTime* value. Secondly, if we are, say, fast-forwarding the media, we need to multiply the elapsed time-base time by some value. This value is *rate* in the above equation. If we are fast-forwarding, *rate* will be greater than one. If we running the media "slowly," *rate* will be less than one.

mediaStartTime and *timeBaseStartTime* define a point in time at which the `Clock` is said to be *synchronized* to the time-base time. Specifically, it is the time at which a `Player` is started. Continuing the VCR analogy, it is the point in time at which you push the play button.

This discussion should make clear that there is some expectation that time-base time reflect real time. If a `Player`'s rate were set to a value of one (1.0), the `Player` would be expected to play its media at the normal or expected speed. Just as if you had recorded *Seinfeld* on your VCR, you would expect the tape to last thirty minutes when viewed at normal speed.[2]

Mapping Media Time to Time-Base Time

All of the above calculations are implicit in the `Clock`'s ongoing maintenance of media time. For example, a `Clock` would implement `getMediaTime` to recalculate the media time at each call. This would imply some implementation of (EQ 1) above to transform time-base time to media time. The reverse translation, media time to time-base time, is not something a `Clock` needs for its internal calculations but is provided as a convenience to you, the user.

JMF API Synopsis 5.7 *Mapping Media Time to Time-Base Time*

Interface	`javax.media.Clock`
Method	`mapToTimeBase`
Arguments	`javax.media.Time`
Return	`javax.media.Time`
Description	Takes a media time value as input and returns the corresponding time-base time.

`mapToTimeBase` cannot be called on a stopped `Clock`. If `mapToTimeBase` is called on a stopped `Clock`, a `ClockStoppedException` is thrown. When a `Clock` is stopped, there is no relation between media time and time-base time.

With the discussion of the relationship between media time and time-base time now behind us, let's take a close look at the methods defined by the `Clock` API. We will start with `syncStart` since that is how a `Clock` starts.

---

2. By the time you read this, *Seinfeld* will no longer be airing on prime time television, leaving a hole in our cultural tapestry second in size only to the cancellation of *Ellen*.

Starting a Clock

A Clock is started with the syncStart method. As its name implies, it does a little more than simply start the Clock. It also synchronizes media time and time-base time.

Recall that while time-base time keeps increasing, media time can start, speed up, slow down and stop arbitrarily. To synchronize media time and time-base is to lock the flow of media time to the flow of time-base time.

A real life example may be helpful here. Assume that every morning you need to get out of bed at 6:00AM in order to do all the things you need to do to be at that desk by 8:00AM. You have been having trouble getting out of bed. The alarm is just not enough to jolt you from your sweet dreams of an IPO. You decide to try a new tactic. You set your CD player to kick on at six bells and you load Black Sabbath's *Paranoid* and queue up track #4, "Iron Man,"[3] because that is what you are. Now every morning at 6:00 sharp, Ozzie Osbourne growls "I am Iron Man" into your sleepy little head and you fly out of bed, run to the mirror and sing along with him. There is no stopping you. You are now good for 1000 lines of bug-free code.

What does this little story have to do with the JMF? The wall clock time at which you leap from your bed is the time-base start time. Just before Ozzie starts screaming, the media time of the tape is zero. Using the vocabulary of the JMF, you would say the media time of zero is synchronized with the time-base time 6:00AM. When 6:00AM rolls around, the CD player turns on and plays "Iron Man." When the CD starts playing, media time starts ticking. So in setting the CD play time, you have established the time-base time at which the media time begins ticking; media time is synchronized with a time-base time.

Once you finally arrive at the office, the programmatic way to do this is with the syncStart method of the Clock API.

JMF API Synopsis 5.8 *Starting the Clock*

Interface	javax.media.Clock
Method	syncStart
Arguments	javax.media.Time
Return	void
Description	Synchronizes media time with time-base time and moves the Clock into the Started state.

---

3. If you are a woman reading this, please substitute Helen Reddy's "I Am Woman."

Immediate Time-Base Synchronization with syncStart

To start a `Clock` immediately, you can pass `syncStart`, a `Time` value that represents a time that is less than the current time-base time. The safest way to do this is to get the current time from the `Clock`'s `TimeBase` object and use it as an argument to `syncStart`. The following `syncStart` call will start the `Clock` immediately.

```
long now = clock.getTimeBase().getNanoseconds();
clock.syncStart(now);
```

Since there is non-zero overhead in fetching the current time and calling `syncStart`, by the time the `syncStart` is affected now will be in the past and the `Clock` will start immediately.

Deferred Time-Base Synchronization with syncStart

The argument to `syncStart` describes a time-base time. It is the time-base time at which the media is to be synchronized with the time-base. Typically, it is a relative value. For example, to start the `Clock` in ten seconds from the current time, your code would look something like:

```
double now = clock.getTimeBase().getTime().getSeconds();
double then = now + 10.0;
clock.syncStart(new Time(then));
```

More likely, since you will be manipulating a `Player` whose `Controller` implements the `Clock` interface:

```
double now = player.getTimoBase().getTime().getSeconds();
double then = now + 10.0;
player.syncStart(new Time(then));
```

Both of the above code samples start a Clock (or a Player) ten seconds in the future. Since the `Time` class defines two different constructors, care is taken here to use a `double` argument to the `Time` constructor to mean ten seconds. Using a `long` value as an argument to the `Time` constructor would create an object representing ten nanoseconds. That is not what is intended here.

Ten seconds after the time-base time of "now," the flow of media time begins as depicted by Figure 5.1

Figure 5.1 *Media Time and Time-Base Time*

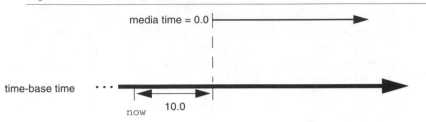

We will see applications of using a deferred time-base time synchronization in Chapter 9 where we discuss synchronizing multiple `Players`.

Tracking Time to Time-Base Synchronization

Between the time `syncStart` is called and the synchronization actually takes place, it may be helpful to track how much time remains before media time starts progressing in lock-step with time-base time. The `getSyncTime` method is useful for this purpose.

JMF API Synopsis 5.9 *Tracking Time Until Synchronization*

Interface	`javax.media.Clock`
Method	`getSyncTime`
Arguments	`void`
Return	`javax.media.Time`
Description	Reports transformed media time prior to synchronization with time-base time.

`getSyncTime` reports its value in *transformed* media time coordinates derived from applying (EQ 1) on page 56. According to the JMF API, `getSyncTime` "performs a countdown to the time-base start-time, returning the time remaining until the time-base start-time." Neither the Sun 1.0.1 nor the Intel 1.0 version of the JMF properly implements `getSyncTime`. The Sun JMF 1.0.1 implementation always returns a `Time` object representing zero. Intel mistakenly calculates "time to sync" using the media time calculation in (EQ 1) on page 56. If you want a countdown timer from the Intel implementation, you will need to subtract the return value of `getSyncTime` from media start time, that is, the value returned by `getMediaTime`. Let's work through an example.

Assume the `Clock`'s rate is 1.0, the media start time is 2.0 seconds, and a synchronization time of the current time plus 5.0 seconds is passed to `syncStart`. A call to Intel's `getSyncTime` immediately after the call to `syncStart` yields:

```
timeToSync = 2.0 + (-5.0) * 1.0
```

or -3.0. As time-base time approaches "sync time," the middle term approaches zero and the "time to sync" calculation approaches 2.0. So, the "time to sync" goes from -3.0 to 2.0. That is clearly not correct. However, subtracting the `getSyncTime` value from media time yields the expected value.

The following calculation of `timeToSync`, based on Intel's `getSyncTime` ranges from 5.0 to 2.0, which is what one would expect from a "countdown" timer.

```
timeToSync = clock.getMediaTime() - clock.getSyncTime();
```

Since the standard transformation mapping is used, once the synchronization point is reached, `getSyncTime` correctly reports media time.

Now let's look at a coding example that incorporates the salient points from the above discussion. Listing 5.1 shows the begin method from a standard `PlayerPanel` example, `GetSyncTime.java` in `$EJMF_HOME/src/ejmf/examples/clock/getsynctime`.

Listing 5.1 *getSyncTime and Media Time Synchronization*

```
public void begin() {
    double now;
(58)    player.setMediaTime(new Time(2.0));
    now = player.getTimeBase().getTime().getSeconds();
(59)    player.syncStart(new Time(now + 5.0));
    while (true) {
        double syncTime;
        syncTime = player.getSyncTime().getSeconds();
(60)        System.out.println("getSyncTime = " + syncTime);
(61)        System.out.println("timeToSync = " +
            (double)(player.getMediaTime().getSeconds()
                - syncTime));
        try {
            Thread.currentThread().sleep(1000);
        } catch (Exception e) {}
    }
}
```

Per our discussion, the media time is set to 2.0 seconds at [58]. At [59] `syncStart` is called to affect a synchronization of media time and time-base time at roughly five seconds in the future. The value of `getSyncTime` is then printed repeatedly at [60] while our `timeToSync` calculation is printed at [61]. From looking at the output below, you can see that the value of `getSyncTime` starts as a negative number and turns positive at roughly the time synchronization occurs. The value of the time to synchronization decreases as time-base time progresses.

• Program Output   **getSyncTime and Media Time Synchronization**

```
getSyncTime = -2.988
timeToSync = 4.9879999999999995
getSyncTime = -1.947
timeToSync = 3.947
getSyncTime = -0.9460000000000001
timeToSync = 2.946
getSyncTime = 0.056
timeToSync = 1.944
getSyncTime = 1.0570000000000002
timeToSync = 0.9429999999999998
getSyncTime = 2.06
```

(62)
```
timeToSync = -0.06000000000000005
getSyncTime = 2.9330000000000003
timeToSync = 9.999999999998899E-4
getSyncTime = 3.9389955000000003
timeToSync = 9.999999999998899E-4
getSyncTime = 4.9417257
. . .
```

At [62], the `timeToSync` value turns negative. This signals synchronization has occurred. Since `timeToSync` then starts reporting a positive number, you are going to have to be satisfied with testing against some threshold to determine if the synchronization time has been reached. If you are using `getTimeSync` to synchronize some other application event with the start of media, you are going to have to live with the imprecision of software-reported time.

Referring back at the output, you can see that after synchronization occurs, `getSyncTime` reports media time.

Figure 5.1 on page 60 shows synchronizing the beginning of media time with a time-base time. What if you wanted to start somewhere in the middle of the media? To see how this is done, we will look at `setMediaTime`.

Accessing Media Time

To set the media time, the `Clock` API provides the `setMediaTime` method.

Setting the media time is what you do when you position a video tape to start right at the beginning of the movie, after any previews. Once the media time has been set with `setMediaTime`, it is that media time that gets synchronized with time-base time. In the previous two code snippets illustrating the use of `syncStart`, the media time is assumed to be zero. A `Clock`'s media time defaults to zero if `setMediaTime` has not been called. On the other hand, to skip those previews, we may want to set the media time to twenty seconds. This means when the `Clock` starts ticking, as the result of a `syncStart` call, it will start at twenty. When the `Clock` is also a `Player`, the media will start playing twenty seconds into its media data.

The following code segment synchronizes the media time and time-base time immediately but positions the media time at twenty seconds. We will reference a `Player` object since that is the most common implementation of a `Clock`.

```
player.setMediaTime(new Time(20.0));
player.syncStart(player.getTimeBase().getTime());
```

The effect these two lines of code have on starting a `Clock` is illustrated in Figure 5.2. Compare Figure 5.1 and Figure 5.2.

Figure 5.2 *Media Time and Time-Base Time and setMediaTime Method*

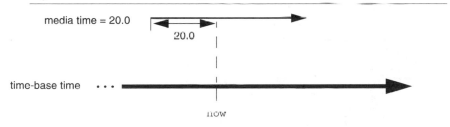

In Figure 5.1, the media is played from the beginning. In Figure 5.2, the `setMediaTime` call has the effect of skipping the first twenty seconds of the media.

Media time is reported by the Clock in two different ways. You can either get the media time as a Time object or in nanoseconds.

JMF API Synopsis 5.10 *Getting Media Time*

Interface	javax.media.Clock
Method	getMediaTime
Arguments	void
Return	javax.media.Time
Description	Returns a Time object representing the current media time.
Method	getMediaNanoseconds
Arguments	void
Return	long
Description	Returns the current media time in nanoseconds.

getMediaTime is fairly straightforward. It reports the current media time. However, there is a set of circumstances that needs elaboration. If a call to getMediaTime is made after a call to syncStart but before the time-base time start time has been reached, getMediaTime returns the Time value set by the last call to setMediaTime. In other words, if getMediaTime is called before synchronization, it will return the media start time as defined on page 56. A short example will illustrate this point.

Listing 5.2 contains just the begin method from a standard PlayerPanel example located in $EJMF_HOME/src/ejmf/examples/clock/getmediatime/GetMediaTime.java.

Listing 5.2 *getMediaTime Value Before Synchronization*

```
public void begin() {
    double now;
    player.setMediaTime(new Time(2.0));
    now = player.getTimeBase().getTime().getSeconds();
    player.syncStart(new Time(now + 5.0));
    while (true) {
        System.out.println(
            "getMediaTime = " +
                player.getMediaTime().getSeconds());
        try {
            Thread.currentThread().sleep(750);
        } catch (Exception e) {}
    }
}
```

(63)
(64)
(65)

At [63] `setMediaTime` is called with a value of two seconds. At [64] the `Clock` is started with a `Time` argument that calls for media time and time-base time to be synchronized roughly five seconds in the future. At this point, the code goes into a loop printing the return value of `getMediaTime`. The `sleep` call in the loop serves only to slow the output. If you run this example, you will see output very much like what is shown below.

• Program Output   **getMediaTime Value Before Synchronization**

```
getMediaTime = 2.0
getMediaTime = 2.0
getMediaTime = 2.0
getMediaTime = 2.0
getMediaTime = 2.0
getMediaTime = 2.0
getMediaTime = 2.0
getMediaTime = 2.1670000000000003
getMediaTime = 2.918
getMediaTime = 3.6681769
getMediaTime = 4.419453600000001
. . .
```

As you see, the first few times through the loop, before the synchronization takes place, `getMediaTime` reports the `Time` value set by `setMediaTime`. After approximately five seconds (7 * 750ms = 5250ms), the designated synchronization time, `getMediaTime` reports the true media time.

The JMF specification for the `Clock` API refers to the time reported by `getMediaTime` before synchronization as the *untransformed* media time. This means that the time-base time values from (EQ 1) on page 56 are treated as zero and the equation reduces to:

```
mediaTime = mediaStartTime
```

which is confirmed by the above output.

Clock Rate

Let's take a look at the *rate* factor in the second term of (EQ 1). The rate of the `Clock` determines how fast media time will transpire relative to time-base time. Common sense and the transformation equation tell us that the higher the rate, the faster media time will progress. A rate of 2.0, for example, means the media time will progress twice as fast as time-base time. This relationship is shown in Figure 5.3.

Figure 5.3 *Comparison of Media Time and Time-Base Time with Unity and Non-Unity Rate*

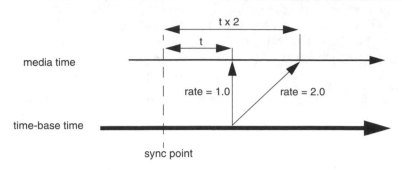

Basically, what this diagram says is that if you recorded the final hour-long episode of *Seinfeld* and then replayed it at a rate of 2.0, you could watch it in the usual thirty minutes.[4]

The Clock API provides getter and setter methods for reading and setting the rate value. Both of these reference the internal Clock value that corresponds to the rate factor in (EQ 1).

Setting Clock Rate

A Clock's rate is set with the setRate method. The JMF specification requires only that a Clock support a rate of 1.0 so the argument to setRate ends up being a suggestion. Different implementations may or may not support changing the Clock rate. The return value from setRate reports how closely Clock followed your suggestion. setRate may always return 1.0, in which case you can rest assured your requests are being ignored.

JMF API Synopsis 5.11 *Setting the Clock Rate*

Interface	javax.media.Clock
Method	setRate
Argument	float
Return	float
Description	Attempts to set the rate of the Clock and returns the rate value in effect after the call.

Even if a Clock supports changing the rate of the passage of media time, it is not required to follow your suggestion precisely. The Clock API states that

4. Thus saving time to watch *the* episode of *Ellen* at rate=2.0 and thereby viewing both in the time it would normally take to view either.

a `Clock` "should" set its rate as close to the requested value as possible. The only rate value a `Clock` is required to set exactly is 1.0.

`setRate` may also be used to request a negative rate. A negative rate turns the `Clock` into a countdown timer, running in the opposite direction of its `TimeBase`. All the limitations on `setRate` still apply; a negative rate value is still only a request that may be amended or ignored entirely. When a negative rate is set on a `Clock` that is also a `Player`, the media is played in reverse.

Whenever `setRate` is called and the rate is changed, to the requested value or otherwise, a `RateChangeEvent` event will be fired.

Getting Clock Rate

The `Clock` API provides a getter method for querying a `Clock`'s rate. A synopsis of `getRate` is shown below and it speaks for itself.

JMF API Synopsis 5.12 *Getting Clock Rate*

Interface	`javax.media.Clock`
Method	`getRate`
Arguments	`void`
Return	`float`
Description	Returns the rate at which the `Clock` is moving relative to its `TimeBase`.

Just as a negative value to `setRate` means the `Clock` should run in reverse, a negative return from `getRate` means the `Clock` is running in reverse.

Stopping a Clock

In the absence of any error or intervention on the part of the user, a started `Clock` will run until the end of media has been reached. As the examples from Chapter 3 illustrate, when this happens an `EndOfMediaEvent` is fired by the `Controller`. There are two direct and explicit ways a `Clock` can be stopped before media expires. First, a call to the `stop` method can be made. Second, the user can set a stop time at which the `Clock` will stop.

Stopping Immediately

The `stop` method stops the `Clock` immediately. It is a synchronous call and does not return until the `Clock` moves to the `Stopped` state. Moving to the stopped state means that media time is no longer synchronized with the

Clock's TimeBase; the time-base time keeps on slipping into the future while the media time stops.

JMF API Synopsis 5.13 *Stopping a Clock with stop Method*

Interface	javax.media.Clock
Method	stop
Arguments	void
Return	void
Description	Moves the Clock to the Stopped state.

If the Clock is a Controller, as is typically the case, a StopByRequestEvent is posted by the Controller in response to the invocation of the stop method.

Stopping at a Specified Time

If you would like to stop media at some specified time, the Clock API provides the setStopTime method.

JMF API Synopsis 5.14 *Setting Stop Time*

Interface	javax.media.Clock
Method	setStopTime
Arguments	javax.media.Time
Return	void
Description	Sets the media time at which the Clock is to stop.

When the media time reaches the time specified by the Time object argument, the Clock will stop. Of course, if that Clock object is a Player, the media will also stop playing. The media time represented by the Time object is called the *media stop time*. If the value passed to setStopTime represents a time the Clock has already passed, the Clock stops immediately.

The notion of having "passed" a particular time is a function of the Clock's rate. If the rate is negative, the Clock is stopped when media time becomes less than or equal to the media stop time. If the rate is positive, the Clock is stopped when the media time becomes equal to or greater than the media stop time. When the Clock does stop, its stop time is cleared.[5] Restart-

---

5. Intel's JMF implementation does not properly conform to the API on this point. It fails to clear the stop time.

ing the Clock at this point, assuming no subsequent actions to stop the Clock, will cause the Clock to run until the end of media time.

setStopTime can always be called on a stopped Clock. If a Clock is started, setStopTime can only be set once without having been reset. Media stop time is reset either upon the Clock's having reached the designated stop time or by an explicit action on the part of the user. The Clock API provides the static final member data value Clock.RESET that can be used with setStopTime to clear the media stop time. To explicitly clear the media stop time, use the following call.

```
player.setStopTime(Clock.RESET);
```

If you call setStopTime on a started Clock whose media stop time has been previously set and there has been no intervening resetting of the stop time, a StopTimeSetError will be thrown.

The media stop time can also be queried using the getStopTime method provided by the Clock interface.

JMF API Synopsis 5.15 *Setting Stop Time*

Interface	`javax.media.Clock`
Method	`getStopTime`
Arguments	`void`
Return	`javax.media.Time`
Description	Return the media time at which the Clock is to stop.

Restrictions on Clock Methods

Many of the methods defined by the Clock interface are state-dependent. These methods are their state requirements are summarized in Table 5.1.

Table 5.1 *Restrictions on Clock Methods*

Method	*stopped*	*started*
`mapToTimeBase`	ClockStoppedException	Legal
`setMediaTime`	Legal	ClockStartedError
`setRate`	Legal	ClockStartedError
`setTimeBase`	Legal	ClockStartedError
`setStopTime`	Legal	StopTimeSetError (if stop time is already set)
`syncStart`	Legal	ClockStartedError

Summary

That completes coverage of the Clock API. This chapter has discussed the different flavors of time comprehended by the JMF and, specifically, the Clock, TimeBase and Time APIs. The relationship between these interfaces was also discussed.

A Clock tracks media time but also has an associated TimeBase object. The TimeBase object is a read only, monotonically increasing source of time. On the other hand, media time can be stopped, started, and explicitly set. The rate at which a Clock runs can also be manipulated, including being set to a negative value for reversing media time. The Clock API defines a mapping of media time to time-base time. This mapping is applied only when a Clock is started, in which case media time is said to be synchronized with time-base time. When a Clock is stopped, the two time flows are no longer synchronized.

Most of the discussion of the Clock API has been outside of the context of any useful applications. The API has been laid out and explained in detail. In the next chapter, we will look at an application of some of the Clock methods as we take an in-depth look at the Controller API.

Chapter 6   *THE CONTROLLER*

Introduction

In Chapter 3, "The Basics of JMF Programming" we focused on getting a JMF applet up and running and only gave cursory consideration to the Player as either a state machine or a Controller. In Chapter 4, "JMF Architecture" an architectural overview of a Player and all its parts was presented. In the last chapter we took an in-depth look at a key element of a Player, the Clock interface. This chapter and the next take a closer look at two of the larger pieces of the Player architecture.

This chapter is dedicated entirely to a detailed look at the Controller interface. The Controller implements a state machine controlling the progression of a Player's resource allocation. As a state machine, the Controller moves from state to state in response to user requests in the form of method calls defined by the Controller API.

The Controller interface extends the Clock interface discussed in Chapter 5. As with the Clock interface, the Controller interface is most commonly implemented as a Player. For this reason, the discussion of the Controller in this chapter will often be in the context of a Player. Since the Player is the focal point of the JMF, some of the examples and discussion

71

within this chapter will refer to a `Player` implementation of the `Controller` interface.

This chapter will elaborate on `Controller` states, the state transition methods and `ControllerEvents`. We will start with a state transition diagram that lays out the `Controller` states. From there we will look at the methods that cause state transitions. After seeing how a `Controller` moves from state to state, we will look at the events generated to inform a listener of such changes. We will finish with an example of a tool that graphically depicts state changes.

Controller States

`Controller` states are defined by both the `Clock` interface and the `Controller` interface. The `Clock` interface defines two states: *stopped* and *started*. The `Controller` further divides the stopped state into five other states: *unrealized, realizing, realized, prefetching* and *prefetched*. These five `Controller` states are ordered. As a `Controller` moves from the unrealized state to the prefetched state, the amount of overhead required to actually play media data is reduced by some amount. As a `Controller` moves from the unrealized state toward the started state, it is said to be moving in a forward direction. Otherwise, it is moving in a backward direction.

There are two flavors of states, *static* and *transient*. When the `Controller` is in a static state, a method call is required to transition out of the state. A transient state is entered by the `Controller`, some work is done and then the `Controller` exits the state. No explicit user method invocation is required to trigger a transition from a transient state. The unrealized, realized and prefetched states are static states. The realizing and prefetching states are transient states.

The started state is a hybrid of these two types of states. Moving in the forward direction, an explicit user method call moves the `Controller` into the started state. However, when in the started state, there are a handful of reasons why a `Controller` may move to the stopped state without explicit user action, most notably the `EndOfMediaEvent` that reports that a `Controller` has reverted to the prefetched state after playing its entire media.

Since different implementations of the `Controller` interface may perform different initialization sequences, the following description of each state is rather general.

Unrealized

A `Controller` object has been instantiated. This is the state a `Player` is in when it is created using `Manager.createPlayer`. At this point, the `Player` does not know anything about its media source.

Realizing

In the realizing state a `Controller` is attempting to acquire the non-exclusive resources it needs. Any rendering resources that can be acquired non-exclusively are obtained by the `Controller` while it is realizing. A `Controller` may also download resources from the Internet while in this state.

Realized

In the realized state the `Controller` has completely acquired non-exclusive use resources, including information about its media. A realized `Controller` knows how to render its data. We will see that many of the `Controller` and `Clock` methods that were previously illegal are now legal operations.

Prefetching

While prefetching, a `Controller` attempts to acquire any exclusive use resources it needs. For example, in the prefetching state, the `Controller` may obtain exclusive access to a sound or video device. While prefetching the `Controller` may also buffer media data.

Prefetched

In the prefetched state, the `Controller` is all but started. Its start-up latency has been reduced as much as possible. The `Controller` has all the resources it needs.

Started

In the started state the `Clock` is started and the media is playing.

State Transitions

Though the state descriptions do not specify exactly what qualifies a `Controller` as being in a particular state, the transitions between states and the events generated as a result of a transition are precisely specified. Figure 6.1 depicts the states, the events which cause a transition, and the events fired as a result of each transition. A brief discussion of the syntax used in the diagram will clarify this.

State Transition Syntax

The Unified Modeling Language is used to depict the state machine for a JMF `Controller`. The general model is that the *event* that causes a transition from one state to another is a method call by the user. The *send event* that occurs as a result of the transition is a `ControllerEvent` and the target of the send event is a ControllerListener. The arrows denote the direction of each transition. The syntax of the UML is as follows:

event(args)[condition]/action^target.sendEvent(args)

For our purposes, we omit the *condition* and *action* and argument fields. The *target* is always a ControllerListener so it is also omitted. Substituting JMF language, the notation is simplified to the form in which it appears below and in Figure 6.1.

method^ControllerEvent

In this representation either the *method* field or ControllerEvent field may be empty.

The static states are depicted with rectangular boxes. The other states, with rounded corners, are transient. Recall that, although the started state is a hybrid state, it is marked as a static state because an explicit method call is required to move into this state when the Controller is progressing forward.

As you can see from Figure 6.1, moving to the realizing and prefetching states is a response to the realize and prefetch methods, respectively. As a result of this movement, a TransitionEvent is fired.

Figure 6.1 *Controller State-Transition Diagram*

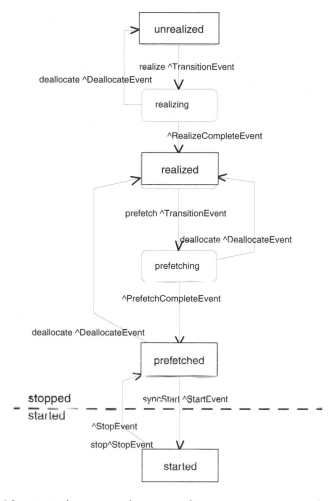

Movement into a transient state always appears as ^TransitionEvent. No explicit method call triggers this movement, however, upon entry to the transient state, a TransitionEvent is fired. An example of this type of transition is the movement from unrealized to realizing.

Transitions from transient states into static states are labelled with the subclass of TransitionEvent that is fired upon leaving the transient state. An example of this is the movement from realizing to realized when the RealizeCompleteEvent is fired.

The transition from started to prefetched is shown both as being affected by a trigger, the stop method, and also occurring without an explicit trigger. This is because many internal conditions can cause a Controller to stop and move back to the prefetched state. An error is one such condition. Reaching a predetermined media stop time (e.g. StopAtTimeEvent) or the end of the media (e.g. EndOfMediaEvent) are two others. The subclasses of StopEvent that signal these events are all discussed in "Controller Events" on page 78.

Now let's take a look at methods for changing the Controller's state.

State Transition Methods

A Player moves in the forward direction in response to any of three method calls. All the forward transition methods are asynchronous, meaning that calls to these methods return immediately. The completion of the state transition is signalled by a TransitionEvent, a subclass of ControllerEvent.

To track Controller changes, an object must implement the ControllerListener interface and register with the Controller. The Controller informs interested parties of its activity by firing ControllerEvents. Registered listeners can act in response to events to manage Controller start-up latency and defer certain operations until the Controller is in a state that supports those operations.

Backward-moving methods are synchronous but nonetheless cause a TransitionEvent to be generated. All TransitionEvents are covered in detail in "Controller Events" on page 78. First we will look at the methods for changing Controller states.

Controller State Transition Methods

JMF API Synopsis 6.1 describes two state transition methods specified by the Controller interface. These Controller methods are both asynchronous. Instead, they return immediately and a subsequent ControllerEvent signals that their work is complete.

JMF API Synopsis 6.1 *Forward Transition Methods*

Interface	javax.media.Controller
Method	realize
Arguments	void
Return	void
Description	Moves a Controller to the realizing state and return immediately. RealizeCompleteEvent signals that Controller has reached realized state.

JMF API Synopsis 6.1 *Forward Transition Methods (Continued)*

Interface	javax.media.Controller
Method	prefetch
Arguments	void
Return	void
Description	Move a Controller to the prefetching state and return immediately. PrefetchCompleteEvent signals that Controller has reached prefetched state.

That these methods, specifically realize, are asynchronous is what led to the problems seen in Chapter 3 when the media started playing before the Player control and visual components were rendered. Often, an application will want to ensure that these operations block the thread on which they are invoked until the transitions are complete. Later in this chapter we will look at a class from the *Essential JMF* Toolkit that provides this capability.

An additional Controller method forces reverse state transitions. The deallocate method is called to relinquish resources allocated to the Player. The deallocate method can be called from any state except the started state.

If deallocate is called when the Controller is prefetching or prefetched, the Controller is moved back to the realized state. If deallocate is called when the Controller is realizing, the Controller is moved back to the unrealized state.

JMF API Synopsis 6.2 *Controller State Transition Methods: deallocate*

Interface	javax.media.Controller
Method	deallocate
Arguments	void
Return	void
Description	The current operation is terminated and any resources held by the Player are released. This method generates an error if the Player is in started state. A DeallocateEvent is posted.

Clock State Transition Methods

There are also state transition methods defined by the Clock interface. JMF API Synopsis 6.3 describes the Clock methods syncStart and stop methods. A Controller implements these methods by virtue of extending the Clock interface.

The syncStart method moves the Controller from the prefetched state to the started state. Like all other forward transition methods, syncStart is asynchronous.

The syncStart method may only be called on a Controller if the Controller is in the prefetched state. Failure to meet this requirement will result in a NotPrefetchedError being thrown. If syncStart is called when the Clock is started, a ClockStartedError is thrown.

The stop method moves the Controller from the started state into the prefetched state and stops the Clock. Like deallocate, stop is synchronous.

These two methods are described in JMF API Synopsis 6.3

JMF API Synopsis 6.3 *Clock Transition Methods: syncStart and stop*

Interface	javax.media.Clock
Method	syncStart
Arguments	javax.media.Time
Return	void
Description	Synchronizes media time with a real or base time clock and moves the Player into the started state. A StartEvent is posted.
Method	stop
Arguments	void
Return	void
Description	Stops the Clock and moves the Controller into the prefetched state. A StopEvent is posted.

Controller Events

At this point, we have covered the Controller states in detail and the methods used to affect state changes. This section will now discuss how to monitor state changes, and will describe in detail the ControllerEvents that are fired in response to changes within a Controller.

Recall in Chapter 3 we were exposed to a few of the events that a Controller fires in response to changes to its state or resource appropriation. The RealizeCompleteEvent signalled to the user code that the Player was sufficiently initialized and that it could report its control panel and visual components. At the end of playing the example media, the EndOf-MediaEvent signalled that the entire media had been played. In both cases these events were fielded by an instance of a class that implemented the ControllerListener interface. Specifically, this class defined a controllerUpdate method. After registering with a Controller using the

`Controller`'s `addControllerListener` method, a listener would then have its `controllerUpdate` method called whenever a significant change occurred within the `Controller`.

When an object is no longer interested in hearing about `Controller-Events`, it can remove itself as a listener using the `removeControllerListener` method.

`addControllerListener` and `removeControllerListener` are described in JMF API Synopsis 6.4.

JMF API Synopsis 6.4 *Adding and Removing ControllerListeners*

Interface	`javax.media.Controller`
Method	`addControllerListener`
Arguments	`javax.media.ControllerListener`
Returns	`void`
Description	Registers `ControllerListener` object as interested in `ControllerEvents` for invoking `Controller`.
Method	`removeControllerListener`
Arguments	`javax.media.ControllerListener`
Return	`void`
Description	The object passed as an argument is removed from the list of `ControllerListeners` for invoking `Controller`.

There are over twenty changes that a `Controller` considers "significant" enough to reports to its `ControllerListeners`. All of these changes are reported as an instance of `ControllerEvent` or one of its subclasses.

A `ControllerEvent` is capable of reporting its source. The methods for obtaining the source of a `ControllerEvent` are summarized in JMF API Synopsis 6.5. All `ControllerEvent` objects can report their sources in two different ways. One way, the `getSource` method, is the conventional means for getting the object from which an event originates.

The second method, `getSourceController`, is a type-safe method that saves the application the need to cast the return of `getSource`. The `ControllerEvent` methods are described in JMF API Synopsis 6.5.

JMF API Synopsis 6.5 *Retrieving ControllerEvent Source*

Class	`javax.media.ControllerEvent`
Method	`getSource`
Arguments	`void`
Return	`java.lang.Object`
Description	Returns the `java.lang.Object` that generated the event. In this case, a `javax.media.Controller`.
Method	`getSourceController`
Arguments	`void`
Return	`javax.media.Controller`
Description	Returns an object representing the `Controller` that fired the event.

There are four types of events which are fired by a `Controller`: *transition* events, *change* events, *close* events, and *control*[1] events. These are described in the following sections.

Transition Events

Transition events mark state changes. Three transition events signify the `Player`'s movement into one of the static states: `RealizeCompleteEvent`, `PrefetchCompleteEvent` and `StartEvent`. Movement out of the started state is marked by a `StopEvent`.

In addition to reporting its source `Controller`, a transition event can report the `Controller`'s past, present and future states.

---

1. The JMF API does not use the term "control" events. We improve upon its omission here.

JMF API Synopsis 6.6 *TransitionEvent Methods*

Class	`javax.media.TransitionEvent`
Method	`getPreviousState`
Arguments	`void`
Returns	`int`
Description	Returns an `int` representing the state the `Controller` was in *before* reported transition occurred.
Method	`getCurrentState`
Arguments	`void`
Returns	int
Description	Returns an `int` representing the state the `Controller` is currently in.
Method	`getTargetState`
Arguments	`void`
Return	`int`
Description	Returns an `int` representing the state the `Controller` is destined for at the time of reported transition.

These methods give complete information about what transition the `Controller` is undertaking. The `getCurrentState` method reports what state the `Controller` is in. `getPreviousState` reports the last state the `Controller` was in. Comparing these two states allows you to determine whether a `Controller` is moving in the forward or backward direction. Finally, `getTargetState` tells you whether or not the `Controller` is finished with its transition. For example, if `prefetch` is called when the `Controller` is in the unrealized state, the `RealizeCompleteEvent` will report a target state of prefetched.

Each of these methods returns an `int` corresponding to the `static final` variables in the `Controller` interface.

These state methods each return an `int` value corresponding to one of the `static final` variables provided by the `Controller` interface. These values are summarized in Table 6.1.

Table 6.1 *Controller State Definitions*

State	Definition
unrealized	Controller.Unrealized
realizing	Controller.Realizing
realized	Controller.Realized
prefetching	Controller.Prefetching
prefetched	Controller.Prefetched
started	Controller.Started

Of the `Controller` states, `getState` may return any of the possible values. `getTargetState`, on the other hand, will never return either of the transient states, `Realizing` or `Prefetching`.

Subclasses of TransitionEvent

The following four events are direct subclasses of `TransitionEvent`.

`RealizeCompleteEvent` – Posted when the `Controller` has successfully reached the realized state. Additionally, a `RealizeCompleteEvent` is posted if `realize` is called and the `Controller` is already realized.

`PrefetchCompleteEvent` – Posted when the `Controller` has successfully reached the prefetched state. Additionally, a `PrefetchCompleteEvent` is posted if `prefetch` is called and the `Controller` is already prefetched.

The `RealizeCompleteEvent` and the `PrefetchCompleteEvent` are subclasses of `TransitionEvent` that signal movement into the realized and prefetched states, respectively. Vanilla `TransitionEvents` are posted when the `Controller` transitions to the realizing and prefetching states.

`StartEvent` – Posted when the `Controller` is started. This is equivalent to the `Player` moving into the started state. The `StartEvent` can report both the media time and the time-base time at which the `Controller` was started. JMF API Synopsis 6.7 describes the methods used for retrieving those values.

JMF API Synopsis 6.7 *StartEvent Methods*

Class	javax.media.StartEvent
Method	getMediaTime
Arguments	void
Return	javax.media.Time
Description	Returns the Time object passed to the constructor of the StartEvent. This value is intended to represent the media time at which the Controller was started.
Method	getTimeBaseTime
Arguments	void
Return	javax.media.Time
Description	Returns the Time object passed to the constructor of the StartEvent. This value is intended to represent the time-base time at which the Controller was started.

StopEvent – Posted when the Controller is stopped. A StopEvent reports the time at which it stops. JMF API Synopsis 6.8 describes the getMediaTime method for retrieving this value.

JMF API Synopsis 6.8 *StopEvent Methods*

Class	javax.media.StopEvent
Method	getMediaTime
Arguments	void
Return	javax.media.Time
Description	Reports the javax.media.Time object passed to the constructor of the StopEvent. This value is intended to represent the media time at which the Controller was stopped.

There are six special cases of StopEvent.

Special Cases of StopEvent

The API defines six subclasses of StopEvent. A ControllerListener can test for a specific type of StopEvent if it needs to determine the specific reason a Player has stopped.

StopByRequestEvent – Posted after a Player has been stopped in response to a stop method invocation.

`StopAtTimeEvent` – Posted when the `Controller` reaches the point in its media time where the user has requested it to stop via a call to `setStopTime`.

`EndOfMediaEvent` – Posted when the end of the media is reached.

`RestartingEvent` – Posted if a `Controller` has been started and must return to the prefetching state to satisfy some user request. For example, a `Controller` may be started but have not yet buffered all its media data. If `setMediaTime` is called with a media time beyond its buffered media data, the `Controller` would transition to the prefetching state and post a `RestartingEvent`.

`DataStarvedEvent` – Posted to indicate that a `Controller` has lost data or has stopped receiving data. This event may occur when a `Player` is reading a push data source and is rendering its media faster than the data source can supply data.

`DeallocateEvent` – Posted at the completion of a deallocation operation performed in response to a call to the `deallocate` method.

Change Events

Change events directly extend `ControllerEvent` and inform `Controller-Listeners` of interesting changes in a `Controller`'s status other than state transitions. These changes may occur in response to some method call. For example, the `setMediaTime` method call will cause a `MediaTimeSetEvent`. A `RateChangeEvent` may also be posted as a result of a `setRate` call.

A change event also may occur in response to some internal change to the `Controller`. An example of this is the `DurationUpdateEvent` which is fired when a `Controller` recalculates the playing time of its media.

`MediaTimeSetEvent` – Posted in response to a call to `setMediaTime`. The `MediaTimeSetEvent` reports the new media time set by the call as described in JMF API Synopsis 6.9.

JMF API Synopsis 6.9 *MediaTimeSetEvent Method*

Class	`javax.media.MediaTimeSetEvent`
Method	`getMediaTime`
Arguments	`void`
Return	`javax.media.Time`
Description	Reports the new media time set by a call to `setMediaTime`.

StopTimeChangeEvent – Posted in response to a setStopTime method call if the call *changes* the Clock's stop time.

JMF API Synopsis 6.10 *StopTimeChangeEvent Method*

Class	javax.media.StopTimeChangeEvent
Method	getStopTime
Argument	void
Return	javax.media.Time
Description	Returns the new stop time that caused this event to be generated.

RateChangeEvent – Posted in response to a setRate method call if the call *changes* the rate at which the Controller is playing its media. The RateChangeEvent is capable of reporting the new rate with the getRate method described in JMF API Synopsis 6.11.

JMF API Synopsis 6.11 *RateChangeEvent Method*

Class	javax.media.RateChangeEvent
Method	getRate
Arguments	void
Return	float
Description	Reports the new Clock rate.

DurationUpdateEvent – Posted by a Controller when it recalculates the duration of its media. For example, when a Player is managing multiple Controllers, DurationUpdateEvents may be fired as Controllers are added or removed from the managed set. The duration of each managed Controller is determined and if that duration is greater than the Player's current duration, a DurationUpdateEvent will be fired.

A DurationUpdateEvent reports the new duration for a Controller using the getDuration method described in JMF API Synopsis 6.12.

JMF API Synopsis 6.12 *DurationUpdateEvent Method*

Class	javax.media.DurationUpdateEvent
Method	getDuration
Arguments	void
Return	javax.media.Time
Description	Reports the new duration of the Controller.

Close Events

Close events are fired in response to a Controller shutting down. A Controller may shut down in response to a close method call or it may shut down as a result of some error condition. After a Controller has been closed, it is no longer usable. Calling methods on a closed Controller may result in errors, depending on the implementation. To "re-open" a Controller, it must be created anew using the javax.media.Manager class's createPlayer method.

ControllerClosedEvent is a direct extension of ControllerEvent. It adds a message-reporting method that elaborates on why a Controller was closed or, in the case of ControllerErrorEvent, information about the error.

JMF API Synopsis 6.13 *ControllerClosedEvent Method*

Class	javax.media.ControllerClosedEvent
Method	getMessage
Arguments	void
Return	java.lang.String
Description	Returns a string that provides some explanation of the close event.

ControllerClosedEvent – Posted in response to invocation of the close method on a Controller.

The API defines a subclass of ControllerClosedEvent that is intended for reporting catastrophic failures in the Controller. The firing of a ControllerErrorEvent signals that the Controller is closed as a result of an error. Three subclasses of ControllerErrorEvent provide notification of specific problems.

Special Cases of ControllerErrorEvent

The following error events which are posted in response to a Controller closing due to an error all extend ControllerErrorEvent. In general, an implementation of the JMF should only extend ControllerErrorEvent to report errors that require the Controller to close.

ConnectionErrorEvent – Posted as a result of a failed read on a connection to a streaming media source when obtaining data from the server of this media.

InternalErrorEvent – Posted when some error internal to the Controller occurs. This event would be posted, for example, if there were some error
in the native video rendering hardware.

ResourceUnavailableEvent – Posted when realize or prefetch fails.
It signals some failure in completing these steps in the Player state progression.

Control Events

The API leaves open the possibility that a Controller implementation may
support custom Controls. These Controls are specialized mechanisms for
manipulating some aspect of a Controller's operation.

Only one control event is specified by the JMF. It is specific to the Player
interface.

CachingControlEvent – Posted to notify listeners of a change to the
Player's media download progress.

Custom Control Events In Sun's Implementation

The Sun implementation of the JMF supports an additional control event not
specified in the API. It is mentioned here for completeness but will not work
when run on other implementations of the JMF. With that caveat out of the
way, here it is.

SizeChangeEvent – Posted in response to a change in the size of the screen
area in which a Player's video is rendered. To change the size of this area,
Sun's implementation of the JMF provides the setSize method on a Video-
SizingControl. The VideoSizingControl is not part of the JMF API.

Controller Events Class Hierarchy

If a picture is worth a thousand words, a class diagram is worth at least two
thousand. A class hierarchy rooted at ControllerEvent is shown in Figure
6.2.

Figure 6.2 *ControllerEvent Class Hierarchy*

Stopping a Player

There is a simplification to Figure 6.1 that needs to be clarified. The transition from the started state to the prefetched state collapses multiple StopEvent subclasses into a single transition. This is the arrow labelled with ^StopEvent. As Figure 6.2 illustrates, there are six subclasses of the StopEvent.

One subclass of StopEvent requires special discussion. Notice that the DeallocateEvent extends from StopEvent. This means that deallocating a Player in the prefetched state will post a StopEvent even though the Player is already in a stopped state. Attention must be paid to this subtlety in the design of your ControllerListener code. If you are listening for a

StopEvent, you must take care to distinguish a generic StopEvent from a DeallocateEvent. Confusing the two may cause your stop code to be executed under inappropriate circumstances. If you were to deallocate in the prefetched state, a DeallocateEvent would be posted. If not explicitly handled as an instance of a DeallocateEvent, it could be mistakenly treated as a StopEvent. To avoid this problem, you would want to write the StopEvent handling in your controllerUpdate method similar to one of the code snippets below.

The first snippet ignores the DeallocateEvent on the assumption it is unimportant to your application.

```
public void controllerUpdate(ControllerEvent e) {
    if (e instanceof StopEvent &&
        !e instanceof DeallocateEvent)
    {
        // do something.
    }
}
```

The second snippet is written to provide special handling of the DeallocateEvent.

```
public void controllerUpdate(ControllerEvent e) {
    if (e instanceof DeallocateEvent) {
        // do that wacky deallocate thing
    } else if (e instanceof StopEvent) {
        // do something.
    }
}
```

Controller State Machine In Action

The foregoing discussion of Controller states and events cries out for an example to assist in making sense of Player state transitions and ControllerEvents. The StateChanger example provides just the ticket.

The StateChanger Example

This example creates a Player and allows you to affect state changes from a GUI. As you select a state, the Player is moved to that state and the Controller events posted in response to the state transition are reported.

To run the StateChanger example, type the following command.

 **Running StateChanger Example**

```
% java ejmf.examples.statechanger.StateChanger \
    $EJMF_HOME/classes/media/safexmas.mov
```

The GUI for the StateChanger example appears in Figure 6.3.

Figure 6.3 *The StateChanger GUI*

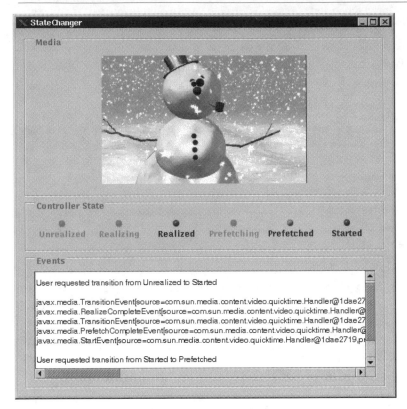

Each of the buttons in the Controller State panel represents one of the Controller states. Clicking on one of the buttons moves the Player to the selected state. The ControllerEvents that are fired as the Player moves to the desired state are displayed in the Events panel. When the Player reaches the realized state and the visual component becomes available, the Player is rendered in the Media panel. The current Player state is represented by a green ball.

You are encouraged to run this example and observe the events that result from various state changes. Exercising this example will help you understand the Controller piece of a JMF Player. In the next section, we will take a look inside StateChanger to improve our comprehension of Player state transitions and Controller events.

Identifying Controller State

Since most of the StateChanger example deals with JFC code, we will only look at pieces of it here. The complete source is included with the *Essential JMF* source at the Prentice Hall ftp site and resides in the $EJMF_HOME/ src/ejmf/examples/statechanger directory when installed.

Most of StateChanger's work is done within its actionPerformed method. StateChanger implements the actionListener interface and registers itself on each of the state buttons. The actionPerformed method determines the button that was selected, and based on the current state of the Player, calls the appropriate Player method to move the Player into the requested state. It also reports the requested action in the Events panel.

We will look at the source of the actionPerformed method, focusing on those parts that use pieces of the JMF API.

Listing 6.1 *actionPerfomed Method of StateChanger*

```
public void actionPerformed(ActionEvent event) {

    Object source = event.getSource();
    if (source instanceof JRadioButton) {
        String userEvent =
            "User requested transition from " +
            Util.stateToString(currentState) + " to ";
        if (source == realizing || source == realized) {
            if (currentState != Controller.Realized) {
                writeEvent("\n" + userEvent +
                Util.stateToString(
                    Controller.Realized) + "\n");
            }
            switch(currentState) {
                case Controller.Unrealized:
                    player.realize();
                    break;
                case Controller.Started:
                    player.stop();
                case Controller.Prefetching:
                case Controller.Prefetched:
                    player.deallocate();
                    break;
                default:
                    setState(Controller.Realized);
            }
```

(1)

(2)

(3)

(4)

(5)
```
        } else if(source == prefetching ||
                  source == prefetched) {
          if (currentState != Controller.Prefetched) {
          writeEvent("\n" + userEvent +
          Util.stateToString(
              Controller.Prefetched) + "\n");
        }
```
(6)
```
          switch(currentState) {
            case Controller.Unrealized:
            case Controller.Realizing:
            case Controller.Realized:
                player.prefetch();
                break;
            case Controller.Started:
                player.stop();
                break;
            default:
                setState(Controller.Prefetched);
        }
```
(7)
```
        } else if (source == started) {
          if (currentState != Controller.Started) {
          writeEvent("\n" + userEvent +
          Util.stateToString(
                  Controller.Started) + "\n");
          player.start();
        }
      }
    }
}
```

The `actionPerformed` method has three main parallel sections. Lines [1] and [2] test for and affect state changes in response to clicking the Realizing or Realized button. If the `Player` is started, `stop` is called [3] and execution falls through to call `deallocate` [4]. In other words, to go from the started state to the realized state, the `Player` must be stopped and then deallocated.

Line [5] tests for a click on either the Prefetching or Prefetched button. Line [6] affects state changes in response to clicking either of these buttons. Finally, line [7] marks the beginning of the code executed in response to a click on the Started button.

The operation of the code is summarized in Table 6.2. The state corresponding to the user selection appears in the left and the current state in the center column.

Table 6.2 *StateChanger State Progressions*

Selected State	Current State	Method Call(s)
`Realizing` or `Realized`	`Unrealized`	`realize`
	`Started`	`stop, deallocate`
	`Prefetching` or `Prefetched`	`deallocate`
`Prefetching` or `Prefetched`	`Unrealized` or `Realizing` or `Realized`	`prefetch`
	`Started`	`stop`
`Started`	all except `Started`	`start`

It should be noted that what is true in this example is true in general with JMF `Controllers`. A `Controller` will never pass through a transient state when its state machine is moving in the backward direction. This is highlighted by the `StateChanger` example by disabling the transient states after the `Controller` has passed them in the forward direction. You can view the complete source in the `$EJMF_HOME/src/ejmf/examples/state-changer` directory.

Getting Controller Status

The `StateChanger` example relies on the `Controller` method `getState` to determine `Player` state. It uses this value to update the GUI, disabling those illegal states and enabling possible future states.

JMF API Synopsis 6.14 *Getting Controller State with getState*

Interface	`javax.media.Controller`
Method	`getState`
Arguments	`void`
Return	`int`
Description	Returns the current state of the `Controller` as declared by the `static final` class variables in `Controller` (See Table 6.1).

Some state transition methods may cause a `Player` to traverse multiple states. The most obvious example is the `Player start`. Called from the unrealized state, `start` will cause the `Controller` to pass through all the intervening states on the way to the started state. In this case, the started state is said to be the *target* state for the `Controller`. The `Controller` method `getTargetState` returns the target state value.

JMF API Synopsis 6.15 *Getting the Target State of the Controller*

Interface	`javax.media.Controller`
Method	`getTargetState`
Arguments	`void`
Return	`int`
Description	Returns the intended final state of the `Controller`.

The legal values returned by `getTargetState` are described in Table 6.1 on page 82.

You may have noticed that these methods are similar to those summarized in JMF API Synopsis 6.6 on page 81. `Controller` state information is available directly from the `Controller` object itself or a `TransitionEvent` it generates.

Controller Duration

In addition to extending the `Clock` interface, the `Controller` also extends the `Duration` interface. This interface consists entirely of the lone method `getDuration`. It is intended to represent the duration of the `Controller`'s media as a `Time` object.

The `getDuration` method is described in JMF API Synopsis 6.16.

JMF API Synopsis 6.16 *Getting the Duration of Controller's Media*

Interface	`javax.media.Duration`
Method	`getDuration`
Arguments	`void`
Return	`java.media.Time`
Description	Gets the `Duration` of the `Controller`'s media, or `DURATION_UNKNOWN` if unknown.

The `Controller` implements this method to report the amount of time needed to play its media at the default rate of `1.0`. If this value cannot be determined, `DURATION_UNKNOWN` is returned.

Although the `Duration` interface is implemented by the `Controller`, only a `Player` knows enough about its media to report its duration. Applications can query a `Player` for its duration as soon as the `Player` has been created. However, this method may return DURATION_UNKNOWN if the Player has not been realized, or possibly prefetched. Generally, the closer that a Player is to being in the Started state, the more reliable its getDuration method is likely to be. For example, a Controller that reports DURATION_UNKNOWN while in the Realized state may report a known value in the Prefetched state.

Restrictions on Method Invocation

Not every Controller method is available in every state. Recalling that a Controller implements the Clock interface, the Clock methods we saw in Chapter 5 are also available from a Controller. However, because an unrealized Controller is not required to have complete information about a Clock, many Clock methods are unavailable until a Controller is realized.

Table 6.3 lists the Controller methods whose legal invocation is constrained to certain states.

Table 6.3 *Restrictions on Controller Methods*

Method	Unrealized Realizing	Realized/ Prefetching	Prefetched	Started
getTimeBase	NotRealizedError	Legal	Legal	Legal
setTimeBase	NotRealizedError	Legal	Legal	Clockstartederror
setMediaTime	NotRealizedError	Legal	Legal	Clockstartederror
setRate	NotRealizedError	Legal	Legal	Clockstartederror
setStopTime	NotRealizedError	Legal	Legal	SetStopTimeError
getStartLatency	NotRealizedError	Legal	Legal	Legal
mapToTimeBase	ClockStoppedException			Legal
syncStart	NotPrefetchedError		Legal	ClockStartedError
deallocate	Legal	Legal	Legal	ClockStartedError

Events, Errors, and Exceptions

The preceding discussion introduced some new terminology that needs elaboration. We saw that some methods generate *errors* when called under inappropriate conditions, while others may generate *exceptions*. This language is consistent with the normal Java language usage in that JMF errors extend from java.lang.Error and exceptions extend from java.lang.Exception. Additionally, all errors defined by the API are rooted at javax.media.MediaError and all exceptions are rooted at javax.media.MediaException.

It is important to keep in mind that both of these are distinct from `ControllerEvents`, which extend from `java.lang.Object` and are generated under normal `Controller` operating conditions.

Media Errors

Media errors are thrown when an application calls a method that is illegal in the invoking object's current state. Errors are thrown in situations where you should know better; you have control over the `Player` state and you mistakenly call an inappropriate method. Most of the inappropriate method invocations described in Table 6.3 result in a `javax.media.MediaError` being thrown.

Typically, errors should not be caught by an application. Instead, they are a result of a programming error and their cause should be determined and fixed.

The subclasses of `javax.media.MediaError` are summarized below.

`ClockStartedError` – Thrown when a method is invoked that is not legal on a `Clock` in the `Started` state.

`NotPrefetchedError` – Thrown when a `Controller` is not `Prefetched` and an operation requiring that it be so is attempted.

`NotRealizedError` – Thrown when a `Controller` is not `Realized` and an operation requiring that it be so is attempted.

`StopTimeSetError` – Thrown when the stop time has been set on a `Started Clock` and `setStopTime` is invoked again.

Media Exceptions

Media exceptions are thrown as a result of a call to a method that cannot complete successfully because of something beyond the application's control. As Table 6.3 shows, the `mapToTimeBase` method will generate a `ClockStoppedException` if the `Clock` is not started. Likewise, `addController`, a `Player` method we will meet in Chapter 9, "Synchronizing Multiple Players," will generate an `IncompatibleTimeBaseException` if you attempt to synchronize two `Controllers` with incompatible time bases.

The subclasses of `javax.media.MediaException` are described below.

`ClockStoppedException` – Thrown when a method that expects the `Clock` to be `Started` is called on a `Stopped Clock`.

`IncompatibleSourceException` – Thrown when `setSource` is invoked and the `MediaHandler` cannot support the `DataSource`.

`IncompatibleTimeBaseException` — Thrown when `setTimeBase` is invoked using a `TimeBase` that the `Clock` cannot support.

`NoDataSourceException` — Thrown when a `DataSource` cannot be found for a particular `URL` or `MediaLocator`.

`NoPlayerException` — Thrown when the `Manager` cannot find a `Player` for a particular `URL` or `MediaLocator`.

Like any Java exception, media exceptions should be tested for and handled within a `try-catch` block.

Having now learned all there is to know about JMF state transitions and events, errors and exceptions, we are going to look at an example that provides finer application control over state transitions. If you recall, all `Player` methods that cause forward moving transitions are asynchronous: a method is called, it returns, and at some later time a `ControllerEvent` shows up at a `ControllerListener` signalling the completion of the requested state transition.

In the section "The Control Panel Component" on page 22, we discussed the possibility that a `Player` may start before its control or visual components are rendered. The asynchronous nature of `Player` state transitions is at the root of this problem. The next section will show how, by wrapping some code around the `Controller` transition methods, we can make those methods appear synchronous to the main-line user code.

More from the EJMF Toolkit

We saw in "The GenericPlayer" on page 36 an example of creating a `Player`. The visual and control panel `Components` of the `Player` were created and displayed in response to a `RealizeCompleteEvent` fielded by the `controllerUpdate` method.

Since the `Player` was started using the asynchronous `start` method, progress toward prefetching and rendering media data was being made while our `controllerUpdate` thread retrieved the `Player`'s GUI `Components`. When we finally added these `Components` to a `Container` for display, a small amount of media time had already transpired. The first frame of video displayed was some number of frames from the beginning of the media source.

What is needed to solve this problem is the ability to call `Controller` methods and block the current thread until the `Controller` thread finishes. You have come to the right place. Another look into the *Essential JMF* Toolkit yields the `StateWaiter` class.

The StateWaiter Class

The StateWaiter class relies on the Java language wait and notify synchronization mechanism to provide synchronous versions of the asynchronous Player state transition methods. The StateWaiter class provides routines to allow the current thread to wait for a Player to reach a particular state. A StateWaiter object will first register itself as a ControllerListener on the given Player object. It will then set the desired target state, and block the current thread using wait. When the Player transitions to the desired state, notify is called from within controllerUpdate and the thread will continue.

Figure 6.4 contains a class diagram of the StateWaiter class.

Figure 6.4 *StateWaiter Class Diagram*

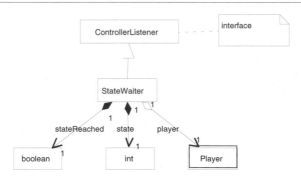

A StateWaiter object has a Player reference which it receives as an argument to its constructor.

EJMF Toolkit Synopsis 6.1 *StateWaiter Constructor*

Class	ejmf.toolkit.util.StateWaiter
Constructor	StateWaiter
Visibility	public
Arguments	javax.media.Player
Description	Creates a StateWaiter object that waits for state transitions on the Player passed as an argument upon construction.

It is this Player upon which a StateWaiter instance registers itself as a ControllerListener. That the StateWaiter class implements the ControllerListener interface makes this possible.

Two of StateWaiter's private instance data members, state and stateReached, maintain the desired target state and a boolean flagging whether that state has been reached, respectively. No public setter is available to set the target state. Rather, a `StateWaiter` object uses the `private` method `setState` to set the `state` data member in response to `Transi-tionEvents` signalled by the `Controller`.

EJMF Toolkit Synopsis 6.2 summarizes the `public` methods provided by the `StateWaiter` class.

EJMF Toolkit Synopsis 6.2 *StateWaiter public Methods*

Class	`ejmf.toolkit.util.StateWaiter`
Method	`blockingRealize`
Visibility	`public`
Arguments	`void`
Return	`boolean`
Description	Calls `realize` on the `StateWaiter`'s `Player` object and blocks the current thread until the player is `Realized`. Returns `true` if `Controller` reaches `Realized` state, otherwise `false` is returned.
Method	`blockingPrefetch`
Visibility	`public`
Arguments	`void`
Return	`boolean`
Description	Calls `prefetch` on the `StateWaiter`'s `Player` object and blocks the current thread until the player is `Prefetched`. Returns `true` if `Controller` reaches `Prefetched` state, otherwise `false` is returned.
Method	`blockingStart`
Visibility	`public`
Arguments	`void`
Return	`boolean`
Description	Calls `start` on the `StateWaiter`'s `Player` object and blocks the current thread until the player is `Started`. Returns `true` if `Controller` reaches `Started` state, otherwise `false` is returned.

EJMF Toolkit Synopsis 6.2 *StateWaiter public Methods*

Class	`ejmf.toolkit.util.StateWaiter`
Method	`blockingSyncStart`
Visibility	`public`
Arguments	`void`
Return	`boolean`
Description	Calls `syncStart` on the `StateWaiter`'s `Player` object and blocks the current thread until the player is `Started`. Returns `true` if `Controller` reaches `Started` state, otherwise `false` is returned.

If the `Controller` is stopped before the desired state is reached, or if it posts a `ControllerErrorEvent` indicating that the transition has failed, then the `StateWaiter`'s blocking methods will return `false`. Otherwise, if the desired state is reached, they will return `true`.

A Blocking Realize Implementation

Since the implementations of the `StateWaiter` methods are identical save the value of the target state, we will only look at one of the above methods, `blockingRealize`.

Listing 6.2 *Implementation of blockingRealize*

```
public boolean blockingRealize() {
(8)     setState(Controller.Realized);
        player.realize();
(9)     return waitForState();
}
```

Line [8] sets the desired target state and is the line at which the various blocking methods differ. Each passes a different value to `setState`. `setState` does one other important task. It registers the `StateWaiter` object as a listener on its `Player` object using the `private` method `addAsListener` [10] which, in turn, calls `addControllerListener` [11].

Listing 6.3 *Implementation of setState and addAsListener*

```
private void setState(int state) {
    this.state = state;
    stateReached = false;
    addAsListener();
}

private void addAsListener() {
    if (!listening) {
        player.addControllerListener(this);
        listening = true;
    }
}
```

(10)

(11)

The work of waiting is done at [9] by calling into waitForState. The blocking occurs at [12] from Listing 6.4 on page 101 when the java.lang.Object wait method is called.

Listing 6.4 *Implementation of waitForState*

```
private synchronized void waitForState() {
    while (listening) {
        try {
            wait();
        } catch(InterruptedException e) {}
    }
    return stateReached;
}
```

(12)

waitForState is not quite the final piece of code we need to look at to completely understand the StateWaiter class. All it does is wait [12]. As devilish detail, the wait is wrapped by a while loop testing listening to protect against the possibility of some thread other than StateWaiter's controllerUpdate calling notify. If this would happen, the blocking method may return prematurely.

We have yet to see the notify call that allows waitForState to return and, finally, blockingRealize to return with the guarantee that the Player is in the Realized state. The final piece of the puzzle appears in the controllerUpdate method. As we have seen, it is the controllerUpdate method that is responsible for fielding events from a Controller. Let's take a look at StateWaiter's controllerUpdate method appearing in Listing 6.5.

Listing 6.5 *controllerUpdate Method for StateWaiter Class*

```
public synchronized void
      controllerUpdate(ControllerEvent ev) {

   if(ev.getSourceController() != player) {
      return;
   }

   if (ev instanceof TransitionEvent) {
      int currState =
         ((TransitionEvent)ev).getCurrentState();
      stateReached = (currState >= state);
   }

   if( ev instanceof StopEvent ||
      ev instanceof ControllerClosedEvent ||
      stateReached)
   {
      removeAsListener();
      notifyAll();
   }
}
```

Line markers: (13), (14), (15), (16), (17), (18), (19)

controllerUpdate first does some preparatory work before determining
if it should notify any waiting threads. At [13] the current state is retrieved
from the ControllerEvent and used to determine if the desired state has
been reached. The boolean stateReached is set [14] to record whether the
Controller has reached the state expected by the outstanding blocking call
on StateWaiter. For example, if blockingRealize had been called, then
stateReached is set to true when a TransitionEvent signalling the
movement to any state greater than or equal to the Realized state is seen by
controllerUpdate.

There are three conditions under which one of StateWaiter's blocking
calls will return:

- If the Controller posts a StopEvent [15]
- If the Controller posts a ControllerClosedEvent [16]
- If the stateReached variable is set to true [17]

In any of these conditions is met, the waiting thread, the object calling the
blocking method, is removed from the StateWaiter's listener list [18] and
awakened from its wait [19]. This wait was executed at [12] by wait-
ForState which was originally called at [9] by blockingRealize.

A brief example of how to use StateWaiter is shown below in a short
code segment.

```
Player          player = Manager.createPlayer(...);
StateWaiter     sw = new StateWaiter(player);

sw.blockingRealize();
// Do Player gui stuff...
```

Let's now look at the use of `StateWaiter` in a complete example.

BlockingPlayer Example

Listing 6.6 presents an excerpt from the `BlockingPlayer` class. `Blocking-Player` is a refinement of the `GenericPlayer` that was used to introduce the *Essential JMF* Toolkit on page 36 in Chapter 3, "The Basics of JMF Programming." It uses `StateWaiter` to block on the `realize` and `prefetch` transition methods.

`BlockingPlayer` conforms to the *Essential JMF* example structure, extending `PlayerDriver` and implementing `begin`.

Listing 6.6 *BlockingPlayer Example*

```
public class BlockingPlayer extends PlayerDriver
    implements ControllerListener
{
    private PlayerPanel playerpanel;
    private Player player;
    ...
    public void begin() {
        playerpanel = getPlayerPanel();
        player = playerpanel.getPlayer();
        player.addControllerListener(this);

(20)    StateWaiter waiter = new StateWaiter(player);
(21)    if (!waiter.blockingRealize()) {
            return;
        }
        Runnable r = new Runnable() {
            public void run() {
(22)            playerpanel.addControlComponent();
(23)            playerpanel.addVisualComponent();
(24)            redraw();
            }
        };
        try {
(25)        SwingUtilities.invokeAndWait(r);
        } catch (InterruptedException e) {
        } catch (InvocationTargetException e) {
        }
(26)    if (!waiter.blockingPrefetch()) {
            return;
        }
(27)    player.start();
    }
    ...
}
```

Only the constructor and the `begin` method from the `BlockingPlayer` example appear in Listing 6.6. The creation of the `Player`'s GUI components has been moved out of the `controllerUpdate` method and into the `begin` method. Contrast this with the `GenericPlayer` example where the GUI `Components` are retrieved and displayed within the `ControllerUpdate` method.

To allow for retrieval of the GUI `Components` in-line, a `StateWaiter` object is created [20]. `StateWaiter`'s `blockingRealize` is then used to bring the `Player` to the `Realized` state [21] call. If this method returns `true`, the `Player` is realized. The `Player` must be realized before the call to `addControlComponent` since this method invokes getControlPanelComponent. addControlComponent is eventually called [22] (as well as the other GUI-manipulating methods at [23] and [24]) on the event queue thread run by the call to invokeAndWait [25].

The call to invokeAndWait represents a twist unseen in Generic-Player. If the goal is to ensure the GUI is completely built, laid out, and visible before the Player starts rendering media, then it does not make sense to schedule a thread on the event dispatching queue and proceed to start the Player. These is no assurance the thread will run before media is rendered. To avoid this indeterminate behavior invokeAndWait is used to run our GUI-building code instead of invokeLater. invokeAndWait does not return until the Runnable object passed as its argument completes execution.

Since the GUI components of the Player have been laid out before the media is prefetched [26] and the Player started [27], when the media is rendered, its first frame will be the first frame displayed.

Asynchronous Stop and Deallocate

Just as StateWaiter inverts the normal behavior of the forward moving state transition methods, making asynchronous methods synchronous, the Asynch-Stopper class makes the backward moving transitions asynchronous.

An AsynchStopper instance is created by associating it with a Controller. The description of the constructor appears in EJMF Toolkit Synopsis 6.3

EJMF Toolkit Synopsis 6.3 *AsynchStopper Constructor*

Class	ejmf.toolkit.util.AsynchStopper
Constructor	AsynchStopper
Visibility	public
Arguments	javax.media.Controller
Description	Creates a AsynchStopper object that can be used to perform asynchronous stop and deallocate operations on the Controller passed as an argument upon construction.

Normally, when stop is called on a Player, it does not return until the Player has been stopped. If this is not appropriate for your application or if the Player is known to take a "long" time to stop, then the stop method from AsynchStopper can be used. The same applies for the deallocate operation.

AsynchStopper's methods are described in EJMF Toolkit Synopsis 6.4.

EJMF Toolkit Synopsis 6.4 *AsynchStopper Methods*

Class	`ejmf.toolkit.util.AsynchStopper`
Method	`stop`
Visibility	`public`
Arguments	`void`
Return	`void`
Description	Stops the `Controller` on a separate thread.
Method	`deallocate`
Visibility	`public`
Arguments	`void`
Return	`void`
Description	Deallocates the `Controller` on a separate thread.

The implementation of these two methods is straightforward.

Listing 6.7 *AsynchStopper Methods*

```
public void deallocate() {
    new Thread() {
        public void run() {
            controller.deallocate();
        }
    }.start();
}

public void stop() {
    new Thread() {
        public void run() {
            controller.stop();
        }
    }.start();
}
```

As you see, both methods have the same signature as their `Controller` counterparts.

The use of `AsynchStopper` is also straightforward.

```
AsynchStopper as = new AsynchStopper(controller);
as.stop();
```

Together with `StateWaiter`, `AsynchStopper` gives you an added degree of flexibility when managing `Controller` state transitions. Of course, the use of these *Essential JMF* Toolkit methods does not alter the behavior of the `Controller` one iota. They simply allow your application to behave *as if* the `Controller` worked differently.

Summary

This chapter has focused on when and how a `Controller` moves from state to state as it acquires the resources it needs. As a `Controller` moves into different states, `ControllerEvents` are delivered to all `ControllerListeners` registered for that `Controller`. In this chapter we saw a state transition diagram that detailed the method calls that caused transitions as well as the events posted as a result of a state change.

State transitions are affected by `Controller` methods. All `Controller` methods that move the `Controller` in a forward direction are asynchronous. Methods such as `realize` and `prefetch` initiate a state transition and return immediately. Methods that move the `Controller` in a backward direction, such as `deallocate` and `stop`, are synchronous.

Some `Clock` and `Controller` methods are illegal in some states. If a method is called when the `Controller` is not in an appropriate state, a `javax.media.MediaError` is thrown. Typically, an application tracks state changes in the `updateController` method so it knows when it is okay to call various methods.

An alternative to explicitly tracking state changes when starting a `Player` is to use the `StateWaiter` class from the *Essential JMF* Toolkit. The `StateWaiter` class introduces synchronous versions of the asynchronous `Controller` state transition methods. The `BlockingPlayer` example illustrated the use of these blocking methods as provided by the `PlayerPanel` class. Conversely, the `AsynchStopper` class provided asynchronous versions of the synchronous `Controller` methods.

Now that the `Clock` and `Controller` interfaces have been fully explored, it is time to turn our attention towards bigger and better things. For the remainder of Part I, we will examine the most important piece of the JMF, the `Player` interface. We will begin this examination in the next chapter.

Chapter 7 THE PLAYER

Introduction

Having explored the `Clock` and `Controller` interfaces in the last two chapters, we are now ready to begin our discussion of the central element of the JMF, the `javax.media.Player` interface. Extending from the `Controller` interface, a `Player` offers several points of extended functionality not available with a simple `Controller`.

Throughout the remainder of Part I, we will be discussing different aspects of the `Player` in more detail. We will begin here by outlining some of the `Player`'s most important features.

Visual and Control Panel Components

Perhaps the most immediately useful part of the `Player` interface is the support for visual and control panel `java.awt.Components` used in rendering the media. Without a visual `Component`, a `Player` would not be able to render video media. Without a control panel `Component`, a user would not be able to easily control the playback of the media. And without an API specifying a programmatic way to obtain these `Components`, a JMF developer could not provide a robust, extendible media application.

The `getVisualComponent` and `getControlPanelComponent` methods are provided by the `Player` interface to programmatically retrieve these `Components`. These methods were discussed in detail in Chapter 3, "The Basics of JMF Programming."

GainControl

The `Player` interface provides a method for obtaining an object through which an application can manipulate the audio signal associated with a `Player`'s media. This object, an implementation of `javax.media.Gain-Control`, is returned by the `getGainControl` method. `getGainControl` is described in JMF API Synopsis 7.1.

JMF API Synopsis 7.1 *Obtaining Player GainControl*

Interface	`javax.media.Player`
Method	`getGainControl`
Arguments	`void`
Return	`javax.media.GainControl`
Description	Returns the `GainControl` associated with a `Player`.

The `GainControl` interface extends the `javax.media.Control` interface. A `Control` is a generic means for affecting the operation of a `Controller`. The `GainControl` is a more specific way of affecting the operation of a `Player`.

We will look at the topic of `Controls` and the `GainControl` in more depth in Chapter 8, "Player Controls."

The Start Method

As we learned in Chapter 6, "The Controller," the `syncStart` method is used to start a `Controller`. Unfortunately, however, the `syncStart` method is terribly picky about when and under what circumstances it is called. If it is called before the `Controller` is prefetched, then it will throw a `NotPrefetchedError`. If, however, it is called after the `Controller` has been started, it will throw a `ClockStartedError`. In short, it is the cranky old man of the JMF.

To avoid dealing with `syncStart`, the `Player` interface provides the `start` method. This method relaxes the tight restrictions set forth by `syncStart`. If the `Player` has not yet been prefetched when the `start` method is called, then the start method will prefetch it before beginning the media playback. If the start method is called while the Player is in the Started state, then it will simply post a StartEvent and return. In short, it is the relaxed, easy-going flower child of the JMF.

To illustrate the process that the start method undertakes, consider the following code snippet. Essentially, it is the syncStart equivalent to calling the start method.

```
public void poorMansStart(Time t) {
    int state = player.getState();

    if( state = Controller.Started ) {
        //... Post StartEvent
        return;
    }

    if( state != Controller.Prefetched ) {
        player.prefetch();
        //... Wait until done prefetching
    }

    player.syncStart(t);
}
```

(1)

(2)

(3)

(4)

If the Player has already started [1], a StartEvent is posted and the method returns. If the Player has not yet been prefetched [2], then the prefetch method must be called. Since the prefetch operation is asynchronous, some mechanism for waiting until the transition is complete must be implemented [3]. When using the start method, this functionality comes for free. Finally, after the Player has been transitioned to the Prefetched state, the syncStart method is called [4].

When You Gotta Play ASAP

The start method also has one other feature. Whereas the syncStart method takes a Time argument specifying the time-base start time, the start method simply starts the Player as soon as possible. It is roughly the equivalent of:

```
Time now = player.getTimeBase().getTime();
player.syncStart(now);
```

For the majority of media applications, such as the typical applet that plays a media clip when a web page is visited, the exact time-base start time does not need to be specified. In these cases, the sleeker, sportier, start method is preferred.

Relaxed Method Restrictions

In addition to the more flexible way of starting a `Player`, the `Player` interface relaxes some of the restrictions on two time-related methods. As you recall from Table 5.1, "Restrictions on Clock Methods," on page 69, the `setMediaTime` and `setRate` methods each require that the `Clock` on which they are invoked be stopped. If this is not the case, then they will throw a `ClockStartedError`.

As a `Clock`, a `Player` is duty-bound to uphold these restrictions. However, there is nothing preventing it from circumventing them. To wit, the `Player` interface allows its `setMediaTime` and `setRate` methods to be called while it is `started` by implementing a simple workaround: When one of these methods is called, the `Player` temporarily stops itself, executes the requisite operation, and restarts itself before returning.

In the process of stopping and restarting itself, the `Player` may post a `RestartingEvent`. Introduced in Chapter 6, this `StopEvent` indicates that the `Player` has temporarily stopped itself to set its media time or rate. In such a situation, the `Player` may need to prefetch more of its media data before continuing.

Restrictions on Method Invocation

Just when you thought you could relax, more methods, with more restrictions, appear. Table 7.1 summarizes the above discussion with respect to `setMediaTime` and `setRate` while describing state restrictions on all the methods introduced by the `Player` interface.

Table 7.1 *Restrictions on Player Methods*

Method	Unrealized Realizing	Realized/ Prefetching	Prefetched	Started
addController	NotRealizedError	Legal	Legal	ClockStartedError
getControlPanel Component	NotRealizedError	Legal	Legal	Legal
getGainControl	NotRealizedError	Legal	Legal	Legal
getVisual- Component	NotRealizedError	Legal	Legal	Legal
remove- Controller	NotRealizedError	Legal	Legal	ClockStartedError
start	Legal	Legal	Legal	Legal
setMediaTime	Legal	Legal	Legal	Legal
setRate	Legal	Legal	Legal	Legal
syncStart	NotPrefetchedError		Legal	ClockStartedError

With the exception of `syncStart`, those methods whose restrictions do not change from the `Controller` interface do not appear in 7.1. They are summarized in Table 6.3 on page 95. `syncStart` is reproduced here for emphasis. Contrary to what could be concluded from reading the `Player` API, `syncStart` may only be called with impunity from the `Prefetched` state.

DataSource Support

Briefly mentioned in Chapter 4, "JMF Architecture," was the `javax.media.MediaHandler` interface. This interface, extended by the `Player` interface, accounts for the part of the `Player` that connects to the media data.

The DataSource

Also briefly discussed in Chapter 4, the `javax.media.protocol.Data-Source` class establishes a protocol-specific data connection to the `Player`'s media. At this point a few more words must be said about the role that this class plays in the JMF.

A typical user of the JMF will never need to worry about the specifics of a `DataSource` implementation. It is sufficient to know that each `DataSource` class is specific to a particular transfer protocol. There are `DataSource` classes for the HTTP, FTP, and FILE protocols included in the standard JMF distribution. When a URL or `MediaLocator` is used by the `javax.media.Manager` class to create a `Player`, the `Manager` takes the responsibility of finding the appropriate `DataSource` for the given protocol.

Only if you need to provide support for an unsupported protocol should you concern yourself with the inner workings of the `DataSource`. If this is the case, then Chapter 22, "Creating a Custom DataSource," will answer all of your questions.

Connecting to the Media

The `MediaHandler` interface consists entirely of a single method. This method, `setSource`, is used by the `Player` to establish a connection to a `DataSource` object.

JMF API Synopsis 7.2 *Connecting a Player to a Media Source*

Interface	`javax.media.MediaHandler`
Method	`setSource`
Arguments	`javax.media.protocol.DataSource`
Return	`void`
Description	Sets the `DataSource` object for this `Player`. If the `Player` cannot use this `DataSource`, it throws an `Incompatible-SourceException`.

The `setSource` method is not meant to be called directly. Rather, it is intended that it be called by the `Manager` class as it searches for an appropriate `Player` for a given medium. After the `Manager` has created a `Data-Source` for a particular protocol, it attempts to set this `DataSource` on an appropriate `Player` object using the `setSource` method. If the `Player` for some reason cannot utilize the given `DataSource`, then the `setSource` method will throw an `IncompatibleSourceException`. This may occur when, for instance, a push medium is set on a pull-only `Player`.

Again, a typical user of the JMF need not be concerned about this implementation detail. It is presented here solely to illustrate the means by which a `Player` connects to its media. For a detailed discussion of the algorithm that is followed by the `Manager` class to connect a `Player` to a `DataSource`, see Chapter 18, "Creating a Custom Player."

Synchronized Managed Controllers

Last but not least of the major features of the `Player` interface is the ability to synchronize and manage other `Controllers`. `Controllers` placed under the control of a managing `Player` will be synchronized with each other and the master `Player`. Every state transition, property change, or closure invoked on the master `Player` will be propagated on to each of its managed `Controllers`. Similarly, every exception or error thrown by a managed `Controller` will be funneled through and reported by the master `Player`.

What this amounts to is the ability to play multiple media files simultaneously. Suppose, for instance, that you wanted to create an applet that displays an AVI video of John Elway leading the Denver Broncos to victory in Super Bowl XXXII. Rather than using the audio from the television broadcast of the game, you instead choose to overlay the WAV audio from the local Denver AM radio station's coverage of the game.[1] After creating a `Player` for the video, and another for the audio, you place one under the control of the other

---
1. A wise choice, since television football announcers couldn't call their way out of a phone booth.

and start the master player. At that point, you can watch John Elway repeatedly drive to the end zone while Dave Logan yells "Salute *That*, Denver!"

The specifics of how to play multiple media sources simultaneously is discussed in Chapter 9, "Synchronizing Multiple Players."

Summary

In this chapter we took a cursory look at some of the more important features of the `Player` interface. Extending the `Controller` interface, the `Player` offers support for visual and control panel `Components` for rendering its media. It also provides the `start` method, and relaxes state restrictions on the `Clock` methods `setMediaTime` and `setRate`. As a `MediaHandler`, a `Player` connects to its media through a `DataSource` object. This is done with the `setSource` method, called by the `Manager` class. Finally, the `Player` provides support for `Controller` management and synchronization. This allows multiple media to be played simultaneously.

Each of these features transforms the utilitarian `Controller` class into a refined and sophisticated mechanism for displaying media. Now that we have completed this brief look at some of the features of the `Player` interface, we will explore the `Player` in more depth. In the next chapter, we will look at how a `Player` can provide external control over some aspect of its operation. Then, concluding Part I, we will thoroughly examine the process of synchronizing multiple `Players`.

Chapter 8　　　　*PLAYER CONTROLS*

Introduction

In Chapter 7, "The Player," we caught a glimpse of the `getGainControl` method provided by the `Player` API. We saw that it returned a `GainControl` object. This object allows an application to control the volume of the audio track played by a `Player`.

The `GainControl` is a specific example of a general capability of the JMF API. A close look at `GainControl` reveals that it implements the `Control` interface. The `Control` interface is a generic mechanism by which an application can affect control over a JMF `Player`.

The JMF designers could not anticipate all the different flavors of `Player` implementations and all the possible operations on those `Players`, so instead they provided a simple means for a `Player` to present its operations to the user.

In this chapter we will first cover the general features of the `Control` interface and look at a couple of specific `Controls` defined in the JMF API.

Controls: An Overview

The JMF API specifies a fairly narrow range of operations that can be applied to a Controller or Player. Basically, the API describes a state machine and ways to move the Controller from one state to another. Beyond that, the API specifies a means to affect the gain level of a Player's audio signal and monitor the loading of media. We will look at these latter two possibilities in just a bit. First, we will consider the question: Wouldn't it be nice if there were a way to affect arbitrary control over media playback? Well, now there is a way!

The Control Component

The Control interface provides a uniform way for integrating arbitrary programmatic control over an object; it is an API-compliant way to provide possibly non-compliant functionality.

This leads to a problem: If the functionality provided by a Control is not specified, how is this functionality accessed?

The answer to this lies in the sole method defined by the Control interface. The getControlComponent method returns a java.awt.Component, the purpose of which is to provide the user with a GUI appropriate for manipulating its Control object. Since the API cannot specify the details of all conceivable Controls in such a way that would allow programmatic interaction with that Control, an application can present the Control's Component to the user. The user can then indirectly control the Player via the Control component.

JMF API Synopsis 8.1 provides the details on getControlComponent.

JMF API Synopsis 8.1 *Accessor Method for Control Component*

Interface	javax.media.Control
Method	getControlComponent
Arguments	void
Return	java.awt.Component
Description	Returns a java.awt.Component associated with a Control.

getControlComponent may return null but this means that the only way to use that Control would be programmatically, if at all. This implies that the class implementing the Control interface introduces additional public methods beyond getControlComponent. An application that used those methods would not be generally portable across different JMF Player implementations. It is rather pointless, then, to implement the Control interface and return a null Component.

What this discussion amounts to is that `Controls` are a mechanism predominantly for adding *custom* operations to a Controller. Since these operations are custom, that is, not specified by the API, the means of applying them are entirely the responsibility of the `Control` through the provision of a GUI component.

The reason for this qualified description of the purpose of `Controls` is that there are two `Controls` specified by the API, the `GainControl` and `CachingControl`. These are such common and useful `Controls` that they merited attention in the JMF API. Other than these two special cases, `Controls` are a very general idea supporting a wide range of possible ways for affecting operation of a `Controller` or a `Player`.

Whence Controls?

Just how generally the `Control` interface applies is indicated by the API itself. `Controls` can be found in three places.

1. A `Controller` may return `Control` objects, either individually or in an array.

2. The API defines a `CachingControl` interface that may be optionally supported by a `Controller` and returned by `getControls`.

3. The `Player` returns a `GainControl` object using `getGainControl`.

The `GainControl` is unusual in that it is a `Control` explicitly returned by a method invocation on a `Player` object. In that sense, it must clearly be considered a `Player` control. Doing so, however, represents a liberal interpretation of the JMF specification which states:

A Control is an object that provides a way to affect some aspect of a Controller's operation in a specific way.

Given that every `Controller` you see will almost always be a `Player`, it is useful to consider them as affecting the operation of a `Player` as well as a `Controller`. This interpretation violates neither the letter nor the spirit of the API.

`GainControl` is an unusual `Control` in another way. In neither Sun's nor Intel's implementation is it contained in the `Controls` array returned by the `Controller` `getControls` method. There is, however, nothing in the API that precludes a `GainControl` object from being returned by `getControls`. In fact, the `Player` framework introduced in Part II, "Extending the Java Media Framework," *does* include any `GainControl` associated with a `Player` in the return value from `getControls`.

Controller Controls

An implementation of `Controller` should provide the `Controls` it needs to make available all of its functionality to the user. The `Controller` API defines two methods by which a `Controller` can report its `Controls`. A single `Control` is returned in response to a `getControl` call, while all of a `Controller`'s `Controls` are reported in response to a `getControls` method call. These two methods are described in JMF API Synopsis 8.2.

JMF API Synopsis 8.2 *Accessor Methods for a Controller's Controls*

Interface	`javax.media.Controller`
Method	`getControl`
Arguments	`java.lang.String`
Return	`javax.media.Control`
Description	Returns an object that implements the `Control` interface identified by the `String` passed as an argument. The argument should identify a fully-qualified class or interface name.
Method	`getControls`
Arguments	`void`
Return	`javax.media.Control[]`
Description	Returns an array of `Control` objects.

The argument to the `getControl` should be a fully-qualified class or interface name. Imagine a `RateControl` from the *Essential JMF* Toolkit.[1] You would retrieve that `Control` as follows:

```
Controller controller;
...
Control rateControl = controller.getControl(
                    "ejmf.toolkit.controls.RateControl");
```

If all the `Controls` supported by a `Controller` are needed, `getControls` can be used. In this case, individual `Control` objects can be identified by testing whether they are an instance of a supported `Control`.

As part of the *Essential JMF* example source, there is a simple application for reporting the `Controls` available from a specific `Controller`. You will find this application in the `$EJMF_HOME/src/ejmf/examples/showcontrols` directory. This application can be run using the following command.

---

1. Come Chapter 19, you will no longer have to imagine such a thing.

 **Running ShowControls Example**

```
% java ejmf.examples.showcontrols.ShowControls \
        $EJMF_HOME/classes/media/hello.txt
```

Figure 8.1 shows the Control components from the custom text Player that will be implemented in Chapter 18, "Creating a Custom Player." Here we get a preview of its Control components.

Figure 8.1 *Custom Controls for Text Player*

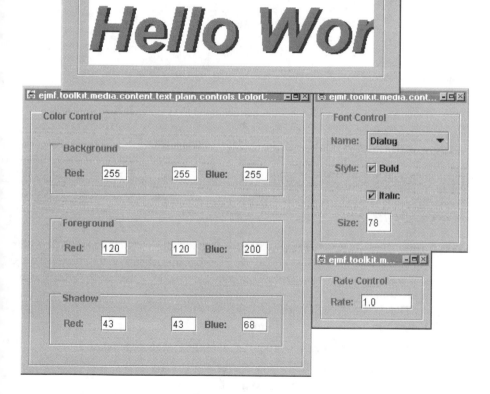

Although not the "killer app" the web has been waiting for, ShowControls is useful for a couple of reasons. First, it illustrates how to retrieve Controls from a Controller. Second, it is useful as a general mechanism for displaying the Controls available from a Controller. Listing 8.1 shows the meat of the ShowControls application, a method from the ejmf.toolkit.util.Utility class. The showControls method iterates over all the Controls, printing the class name and displaying the GUI component of each.

Listing 8.1 *Displaying a Player's Controls*

```
public static void showControls(Controller controller) {
        Control[] controls = controller.getControls();
        System.out.println("Control Names:");

        for(int i = 0; i < controls.length; i++) {
            String name = controls[i].getClass().getName();
            System.out.println(name);

            Component c = controls[i].getControlComponent();
            if( c != null && !c.isShowing() ) {
                JFrame frame = new JFrame(name);
                frame.getContentPane().add(c);
                frame.pack();
                frame.setVisible(true);
            }
        }
}
```

(1)
(2)
(3)
(4)

showControls first accesses the Controls array [1] from the Controller passed as an argument. The class name [2] and the GUI component [3] of each Control is then retrieved. The class name is printed and if the Control has a GUI component [4], it is displayed in a separate JFrame.

Gain Control

The JMF defines one standard Control available from the Player. The gain level of a Player's audio signal can be programmatically manipulated via the GainControl. As we saw in Chapter 7, a Player's GainControl is available from the getGainControl method.

The GainControl interface defines three major groupings of functionality to be supplied by objects that implement it.

- Methods for manipulating the amplitude of an audio signal.

- Methods for registering an object that is to be informed of changes in the gain value of an audio signal.

- Methods for manipulating the muted state of an audio signal.

It is tempting to think of gain and volume as interchangeable. This is workable, but not entirely correct. Gain is actually a measurable quantity whereas "volume" or "loudness" is rather subjective. What your typical teenage considers just right, his typical parents may think is unbearably loud.

Technically speaking, gain is a multiplier applied to an audio signal that modifies the amplitude of the signal. The larger the gain value, the greater the amplitude and the louder the music and the angrier the parent.

The `GainControl` interface allows you to specify the gain multiplier in either of two ways.

Gain Level Scale

The `GainControl` interface supports a *level scale* representing a linear understanding of audio signal strength. Values on the level scale range from 0.0 to 1.0. Values outside this range may often result in an uncomfortable level of distortion. A value of 1.0 represents the greatest possible gain value while still producing useful results. A value of 0.0 represents the lowest value and is indistinguishable from silence. As values range from 0.0 to 1.0 there is a corresponding linear increase in gain.

Since gain is a multiplier, it should be clear from the above discussion that an implementation must provide a mapping from a level value to a gain value. How this mapping is performed is implementation-dependent. As a user, however, all you have to know is that 0.0 is quiet and 1.0 is loud.

Gain Decibel Scale

The *decibel scale* comprises all possible `float` values. A gain of 0.0 dB means that the audio signal is neither amplified nor attenuated. Positive decibel values amplify the audio signals, while negative values attenuate, or decrease the amplitude, of the audio signal.

The following equation determines the relationship between a gain multiplier and a decibel value.

$$multiplier = 10.0^{(gainDB)/20.0}$$

(EQ 2)

It is often useful to think of this relationship using the alternative shown in (EQ 3).

$$gainDB = 20\log multiplier$$

(EQ 3)

To double the amplitude, then, you apply a multiplier of two. From (EQ 3) it follows that a ±6dB change in the decibel scale represents a doubling (or halving) of the signal strength.

$$gainDB = 20\log 2 \approx 6$$

(EQ 4)

Applying a multiplier of 0.5 to halve the signal strength results in a -6dB value.

$$gainDB = 20\log 0.5 \approx -6 \qquad \textbf{(EQ 5)}$$

The moral of the story for teenagers is that to double your fun and make your parents at least twice as angry, add 6 to the current decibel value. To halve your fun, subtract 6 from the current decibel value.

Manipulating Gain Value

The methods for manipulating the level scale are shown in JMF API Synopsis 8.3.

JMF API Synopsis 8.3 *GainControl Gain Level Methods*

Interface	`javax.media.GainControl`
Method	`setLevel`
Arguments	`float`
Return	`float`
Description	Sets the gain level of a `GainControl` object. Return the new level value. The return value will be different than the request value if the requested value could not be set.
Method	`getLevel`
Argument	`void`
Return	`float`
Description	Gets the current gain level of a `GainControl` object.

If `setLevel` is passed a value outside the range of 0.0 to 1.0, its return value will be different than its input value. Specifically, input values less than 0.0 will cause a return of 0.0. Input values greater than 1.0 will cause `set-Level` to return 1.0.

The methods for manipulating the decibel scale are shown in JMF API Synopsis 8.4.

JMF API Synopsis 8.4 *GainControl Gain Decibel Methods*

Interface	`javax.media.GainControl`
Method	`setDB`
Arguments	`float`
Return	`float`
Description	Sets the decibel scale value of a `GainControl` object. Return the new decibel value.

JMF API Synopsis 8.4 *GainControl Gain Decibel Methods (Continued)*

Interface	javax.media.GainControl
Method	getDB
Argument	void
Return	float
Description	Gets the current decibel scale value of a GainControl object.

Calling setDB(0.0) means the audio signal is neither amplified nor attenuated.

Keep in mind that if you use the level methods and decibel methods interchangeably, you are ultimately manipulating the same value, that is, the gain multiplier.

Relationship Between Decibel and Level Scales

The decibel and level scales are different representations of the same gain value. setLevel and setDB methods affect the gain multiplier in different ways. If you mix the use of setLevel and setDB, be aware of the following interactions between the two and the gain value.

- After setLevel(0.0) is used to make the audio output inaudible, getDB returns a value for which smaller values are equivalent to silence. This value is called the *level silence threshold*. If setDB is called with a value equal to or less than the level silence threshold, getLevel will return 0.0.

- After a call to setLevel(1.0), getDB returns a value for which larger values are not useful. This value is known as the *level maximum threshold*. If setDB is called with a value equal to or greater than the level maximum threshold, subsequent calls to get getLevel will return 1.0.

Listening for Changes to Gain Value

Often an object implementing the Control interface will need to inform an application of a change to its state. GainControl is a perfect example of such a Control. Whenever there is a change in the audio signal's gain, the Gain-Control posts a GainChangeEvent with all its listeners.

Any object that is interested in changes to a Player's gain must implement the GainChangeListener interface. It may then be passed as an argument to the addGainChangeListener method on the Player's GainControl object. As a GainChangeListener, an object's gainChange method will be invoked with a GainChangeEvent argument in response to each change in the GainControl's gain value.

To remove an object as a `GainChangeListener`, the `removeGain-ChangeListener` method is used. `addGainChangeListener` and `remove-GainChangeListener` are described in JMF API Synopsis 8.5.

JMF API Synopsis 8.5 *GainControl Listener Registration Methods*

Interface	`javax.media.GainControl`
Method	`addGainChangeListener`
Arguments	`javax.media.GainChangeListener`
Return	`void`
Description	Registers interest in `GainChangeEvents` on behalf of object passed as argument.
Method	`removeGainChangeListener`
Argument	`javax.media.GainChangeListener`
Return	`void`
Description	Removes object passed as argument from listener list of `GainControl` object.

Handling GainChangeEvents

A `GainChangeListener` implements a `gainChange` method. A `GainControl` object invokes the `gainChange` method of all its registered listeners each time there is a change in its gain value.

JMF API Synopsis 8.6 *GainChangeEvent Handler Method*

Interface	`javax.media.GainChangeListener`
Method	`gainChange`
Arguments	`javax.media.GainChangeEvent`
Return	`void`
Description	Handles a `GainChangeEvent`.

An excerpt from a typical `gainChange` method written by the parents of a typical teenager appears below.

(5)
```
public void gainChange(GainChangeEvent e) {
    float level = e.getLevel();
    // Do some level-dependent processing...
    if (level > 0.5f) {
        System.out.println("Please turn the music down!");
    }
}
```

From [5] you see that the `GainChangeEvent` contains the current gain level, accessible using the `getLevel` method. In all, four pieces of information can be extracted from the `GainChangeEvent`. The methods for getting this information are summarized in JMF API Synopsis 8.7.

JMF API Synopsis 8.7 *GainChangeEvent Methods*

Class	`javax.media.GainChangeEvent`
Method	`getSourceGainControl`
Arguments	`void`
Return	`javax.media.GainControl`
Description	Returns the `GainControl` object from which the `Gain-ChangeEvent` originated. This method is equivalent to the `getSource` method that `GainChangeEvent` implements by virtue of extending the `MediaEvent` interface.
Method	`getLevel`
Arguments	`void`
Return	`float`
Description	Returns the new level value for the `GainControl`.
Method	`getDB`
Arguments	`void`
Return	`float`
Description	Returns the new decibel value for the `GainControl`.
Method	`getMute`
Arguments	`void`
Return	`boolean`
Description	Returns `true` if `GainControl` is muted, `false` otherwise.

There is nothing earth-shaking here since three of the four methods replicate functionality of the `GainControl` object itself. If you need to manipulate the `GainControl`, you can retrieve it from the `GainChangeEvent` using the `getSourceGainControl`.

For example, a more, shall we say, interventionist parent of a typical teenager may write a `gainChange` method that looks like:

```
public void gainChange(GainChangeEvent e) {
    float level = e.getLevel();
    // Do some level-dependent processing...
    if (level > 0.5f) {
        GainControl gc = e.getSourceGainControl();
        gc.setLevel(0.1f);
    }
}
```

(6)
(7)

After testing the gain level and finding it way too high, the overwrought parent takes it upon himself to walk down to the basement, reach for the volume dial on the stereo [6] and turn down Cake's cover of Gloria Gaynor's "I Will Survive" by setting a new, lower gain level [7].

If this particular overwrought parent were an electrical engineer, he might prefer instead:

```
public void gainChange(GainChangeEvent e) {
    GainControl gc = e.getSourceGainControl();
    float db = e.getDB();
    gc.setDB(db - 6.0f);
}
```

(8)

In this case, the decibel scale is manipulated using the `setDB` [8] method. In accordance with (EQ 5), decrementing the current decibel value by 6dB will halve the signal strength.

Before we consider more serious possibilities for our typical teenager, let the record show that the `GainChangeEvent` is *not* a `ControllerEvent`. `javax.media.GainChangeEvent` extends directly from `Object`. Further, it is the `GainControl` that fires the event, not the `Controller`. Finally, the event is fired by invoking `gainChange` on a `GainChangeListener`, not `controllerUpdate` on a `ControllerListener`. This all may sound obvious but let it not be said that it goes without saying.

Finally, if you are a typical teenager reading this and you want to know just how bad it could get in the days of vinyl records, listen to the WAV file `$EJMF_HOME/classes/media/ruinrcrd.wav` using a `Player`.

Muting an Audio Signal

Our typical teenager could have suffered a worse fate, but his parents did not know anything about the setMute method. The setMute method can be used to totally suppress the audio signal produced by a GainControl object.

JMF API Synopsis 8.8 *Setting GainControl Muted State*

Interface	`javax.media.GainControl`
Method	`setMute`
Arguments	`boolean`
Return	`void`
Description	If the `boolean` argument to setMute is `true`, the audio signal is suppressed, otherwise a signal is produced.

A call to setMute(true) in [7] above would have meant that our typical teenager could not have had his Cake and heard it too.

Manipulating the muted state of a GainControl is entirely independent of the gain level. If the mute value is `true`, no audio signal is produced. If the mute value is `false`, a signal is produced and the current gain value is applied to it.

setMute has a companion method to test the muted state of a GainControl. Can you guess its name?

JMF API Synopsis 8.9 *Accessing GainControl Muted State*

Interface	`javax.media.GainControl`
Method	`getMute`
Arguments	`void`
Return	`boolean`
Description	Returns `true` if the audio signal is suppressed, `false` otherwise.

That was a good guess! The functionality of the GainControl is now complete. Let's turn now to the CachingControl.

Caching Control

Beyond the `GainControl` interface, the JMF offers one other standard `Control` extension. The `javax.media.CachingControl` interface extends the `Control` interface to provide a way to monitor the download of media by a `Controller`. It is used primarily to indicate that a time-consuming download is in progress, allaying any fears that the `Controller` is broken or stalled, or that the end of civilization as we know it is imminent.

User Control

One of the chief elements of a `CachingControl` is its `getProgressBar-Component` method. Through this method, the `CachingControl` provides a `java.awt.Component` that will graphically illustrate the download of the media. This allows a user of the JMF to tell how much of the media has been downloaded, and approximate the time remaining until the download is complete.

The `getProgressBarComponent` method is described in JMF API Synopsis 8.10.

JMF API Synopsis 8.10 *Accessing CachingControl Components*

Interface	`javax.media.CachingControl`
Method	`getProgressBarComponent`
Arguments	`void`
Return	`java.awt.Component`
Description	Gets a `java.awt.Component` to display the progress of the media download.

As a `Control`, the `CachingControl` also supports the `getControlCom-ponent` method. This method provides a `Component` to allow a user to affect some level of external `Control` over the media download. An example of this might be a "Pause Download" button which temporarily stops media download. As with all `Controls`, this method may return `null`, indicating that no such `Component` is provided.

Programmatic Control

In addition to providing graphical `Components` for the user's benefit, the `CachingControl` interface provides several methods to programmatically query the progress of the media download. These methods are described in JMF API Synopsis 8.11

JMF API Synopsis 8.11 *Querying Media Progress*

Interface	`javax.media.CachingControl`
Method	`isDownloading`
Arguments	`void`
Return	`boolean`
Description	Returns a `boolean` indicating whether or not the media is currently downloading.
Method	`getContentLength`
Arguments	`void`
Return	`long`
Description	Gets the total number of bytes of media data to be downloaded.
Method	`getContentProgress`
Arguments	`void`
Return	`long`
Description	Gets the number of bytes of media data that have been downloaded so far.

Using these methods, a program can determine from the `CachingControl` the exact details of the media download. If the length of the media data is unknown, as in the case of push media, the static final `LENGTH_UNKNOWN` is returned by the `getContentLength` method.

Caching Events

Unlike the `GainControl` interface, the `CachingControl` interface provides no internal mechanism to notify any interested parties of changes in its status. Instead, since the download of media data unconditionally involves a `Controller`, it relies on the downloading `Controller` to post updates of its download status.

This notification is done via a `CachingControlEvent` sent to all of the `Controller`'s registered `ControllerListeners`. As a `ControllerEvent`, the `CachingControlEvent` provides a reference to the downloading `Controller` with the `getSourceController` method.

The CachingControlEvent also specifies the associated CachingControl, as well as the current progress of the media download. This information is retrieved using the following methods

JMF API Synopsis 8.12 *Querying a CachingControlEvent*

Class	javax.media.CachingControlEvent
Method	getCachingControl
Arguments	void
Return	javax.media.CachingControl
Description	Gets the CachingControl object associated with this media download.
Method	getContentProgress
Arguments	void
Return	long
Description	Gets the number of bytes of media data that have been downloaded so far.

The latter method, getContentProgress, is equivalent to calling getCachingControl().getContentProgress(). Since it is logically the most common query of a CachingControl, it is provided by the CachingControlEvent interface as a convenience.

Monitoring Media Download: An Example

Figure 8.2 shows a typical caching control component employed by a JMF application monitoring a Controller's media download.

Figure 8.2 *CachingControl Component*

As you can see, the `CachingControl` involved in this media download provides both a progress bar `Component` and a control `Component`. These `Components` are used by the application in its GUI layout. Using information from the `CachingControl`, the application is also able to display the number of bytes expected and the number of bytes received throughout the download.

This download-monitoring application appears in the *Essential JMF* example source in the `$EJMF_HOME/src/ejmf/examples/cachingplayer` directory. The command to run this example is shown below.

• User Input   **Running the CachingPlayer Example**

```
% java ejmf.examples.cachingplayer.CachingPlayer \
       $EJMF_HOME/classes/media/hello.miv
```

The relevant source of the `CachingPlayer` example begins with the `controllerUpdate` method, shown in Listing 8.2.

Listing 8.2 *Monitoring Media Download*

```
     public void controllerUpdate(ControllerEvent event) {
(9)  if( event instanceof CachingControlEvent ) {

         CachingControlEvent cEvent =
             (CachingControlEvent)event;

(10)     final CachingControl cache =
             cEvent.getCachingControl();
```

```
                    Runnable r = new Runnable() {
                        public void run() {
(11)                        updateCacheMonitor(cache);
                        }
                    };

                    SwingUtilities.invokeLater(r);
                }


            ...
            }

        public void updateCacheMonitor(
            CachingControl cache)
        {

(12)    if( firstCachingEvent ) {

(13)        Component progressBar =
                    cache.getProgressBarComponent();

            if( progressBar != null ) {
(14)        addProgressBar(progressBar);
            }

(15)        Component progressControl =
                    cache.getControlComponent();

            if( progressControl != null ) {
                addProgressControl(progressControl);
            }

(16)        long length = cache.getContentLength();

(17)        if( length == cache.LENGTH_UNKNOWN ) {
                setExpectedBytes("Unknown");
            } else {
                setExpectedBytes(length);
            }

            firstCachingEvent = false;
        }

(18)        long received = cache.getContentProgress();

(19)        setReceivedBytes(received);
        }
```

When a `CachingControlEvent` is sent to the `controllerUpdate` method [9], the associated `CachingControl` is retrieved using the `get-CachingControl` method [10]. This `Control` is then sent as an argument to the `updateCacheMonitor` method [11], which constructs or updates the GUI download-monitoring window.

Within the `updateCacheMonitor` method, a check is first made to see if the current `CachingControlEvent` is the first to be received [12]. If so, the graphical components of the monitor must be obtained from the `Caching-Control` and added to the GUI layout.

The `CachingControl`'s progress bar is first acquired with the `getProgressBarComponent` method [13]. If it is not null, then it is added to the monitoring layout with the `addProgressBar` method. This method is purely GUI-oriented, and thus adds nothing to the understanding of media download monitoring. For this reason it, along with other GUI methods, will not be discussed here.

A similar process is then done for the `CachingControl`'s control component, acquired with the `getControlComponent` method [15].

In line [16], the media length is determined with the `CachingControl`'s `getContentLength` method. After checking to see that it is a known value [17], it is then set in the appropriate text field within the download monitor.

Finally, after the monitor window has been constructed, the current download progress is retrieved [18] and updated in the GUI [19]. This is the only step that is performed every time a `CachingControlEvent` is posted. Again, since the `setReceivedBytes` method is purely GUI-oriented and lends nothing to our discussion, it will not be discussed here.

CachingControlEvents: Reality Check

`CachingControlEvents` may seem like a great way to monitor the progress of a `Controller`'s media download. However, in reality neither Sun's nor Intel's JMF implementations currently generate this type of event. The reasons for this omission are unknown, since the `CachingControl` interface and `CachingControlEvents` are an integral part of the JMF API. Perhaps it was seen as an expendable feature in a time of tight deadlines and hasty release cycles. However, we may yet see full support for this in future JMF releases, at which point you will be fully prepared.

In Chapter 19 we will continue our discussion of the `CachingControl` as we develop a custom media `Player`. There we will implement the `Caching-Control` interface and provide support for `CachingControlEvent` generation.

Summary

The `Control` interface is provided by the JMF API so that implementations of `Controller` and `Player` have a way of providing the user access to their complete functionality if that functionality expands on what is specified by the API. If an implementation of a `Player`, for instance, supports an operation not comprehended by the API, there needs to be a way of making that operation accessible to the user of the `Player`. That is the intent of the `Control` interface and, specifically, its ability to provide a GUI component. Failing any general way to perform specialized operations, the API places the burden of providing a control mechanism on the `Player` implementation in the form of a GUI component.

Two common control needs are provided explicitly by the JMF API. A `GainControl` is associated with a `Player`, providing both a programmatic and visual interface for manipulating `Player` gain and mute state.

The `CachingControl` is also specified by the API and may be implemented by `Player` whose media may require extended download times. Again, because the `CachingControl` is part of the API, there is a programmatic interface that can be used without rendering an application non-portable across different `Player` implementations.

In this chapter we laid out the fundamentals of the `Control` interface and looked at the standard `Controls` provided by the API. There is still quite a bit more on `Controls` to come. In Chapter 20, "Creating Control Panel Controls" we will see custom `Controls` built and then in Chapter 21, "Creating a Custom Control Panel," we will see custom `Controls` built for custom control panels.

Chapter 9   *SYNCHRONIZING MULTIPLE PLAYERS*

Introduction

Imagine for a minute you are an aspiring rock star. You are sort of a rebel (like all *aspiring* rock stars) and you want to make it on your own. You eschew the big record labels and you plan to distribute your own material. The way you are going to do this involves a web site. You know the web is where all the rebels disenchanted with the commodification of their dissent hang out. It is the perfect medium to promote your latest single: "The Battle of Who Could Care Less."[1]

After laying down a perfect rendition of your future hit, you create a fifteen second clip in AIFF format. You are ready to go with your multimedia web site. But, wait, you think, why not a mini-video in the spirit of MTV?

You grab your film student friend and rush down to Starbucks and film people drinking really expensive coffee, *Wired* magazine spread out on the table next to their cell phones. It is the perfect backdrop for your cynical lyrics.

You take the video to your buddy's Macintosh and create an MPEG file of the scene where the guy smashes his first on the table after hearing from his

---

1. A tip of the hat to Ben Folds Five.

broker on his cell phone that Microsoft stock just plummeted in response to having lost their anti-trust law suit, spilling his Iced Caffè Americano over his magazine open to the article entitled "Consumerism IS Revolutionary."[2]

Now you have your content. You are ready to whip together that "rad" web page. However, since a Player can playback only a single media source at a time, you are going to need a way to coordinate the operation of two Players. The synchronization capabilities of the JMF Player are just what you need. You can take your AIFF file and your MPEG file, create two Players and synchronize those Players so that the audio and video start at the same time, nicely blending your hot music with the high culture of Starbucks.

In this chapter we will look at two ways to synchronize the operation of multiple Players using the JMF Player API.

The first approach involves more explicit effort to keep the coordinated Players synchronized. As with most things in life that are hard, there is some payoff. For a little extra work on your part, your application maintains direct control over each of the Players you are synchronizing. This approach requires that your program call setTimeBase and syncStart.

The second approach we will cover relieves the programmer of much of the burden of synchronizing multiple Players. By taking advantage of the Player method addController, your program need not worry about each of the individual Players. Instead, control of all the Players is directed through a *master* Player.

Explicit Synchronization: The Building Blocks

As you might imagine, the Clock interface figures centrally in the synchronization of multiple Players. If you recall from Chapter 5, starting the Clock moves the Player into the Started state. The idea behind synchronizing multiple Players is that you will want them to begin rendering their media at the same time. In order for two media streams to start playing at the same time, three conditions have to be met:

1. The synchronized Players must share a notion of what time it is, that is, they must share a TimeBase, and

2. The time-base time at which their media time starts to tick must be adjusted to accommodate their different start latencies.

3. All Players to be synchronized must be in Prefetched state before syncStart can be called.

Meeting these three conditions is sufficient to synchronize the starting of multiple Players. Often, however, it is not enough to simply start your Players at the same time. You may also need to coordinate the stopping,

---

2. Not the title of an article but the actual words of Kevin Kelly, Executive Editor of *Wired*.

rewinding and restarting your `Players`. These requirements impose some additional responsibilities on your application:

4. A `ControllerListener` must track state changes for each `Player`.

Finally, and optionally:

5. Each `Player`'s rate, media time and stop time may be set.

Item (1) translates into the use of `getTimeBase` and `setTimeBase`. Item (2) is accomplished using the `Controller` method `getStartLatency`. Item (3) is self-explanatory. Item (4) requires the use of the `Controller` method `addControllerListener`. Item (5) uses the `Clock` methods `setRate`, `setMediaTime` and `setStopTime` seen in Chapter 5.

Let's take a closer look at all of these conditions.

Sharing a TimeBase

In "Time Base Time" from Chapter 5 we were introduced to the two `Clock` methods, `getTimeBase` and `setTimeBase`. Here we will see them at work synchronizing `Players`.

Recall the scenes from the old *Mission Impossible* television show. After reviewing the dossiers of his crack agents, Peter Graves would gather the select few in a room and describe the dangers that awaited them. At the end of the briefing, Graves would say with all the gravity he could muster: "Synchronize your watches." For the rest of the show, every move of the IMF team was executed with precise timing.

The role of `getTimeBase` and `setTimeBase` is to allow JMF `Controllers` to "synchronize their watches" so that they all have the same notion of what time it is. When a request is made of a group of `Controllers` to do something at a specific time, you want to make sure all the `Controllers` are looking at the same clock to see when that time arrives. By setting the time-base time of two `Controllers` to the same `TimeBase` object, you are like Peter Graves telling his agents to synchronize their watches.

Only with a common `TimeBase` will `Controllers` be able to synchronize their activities. The following code segment illustrates sharing a single `Time-Base`. It is a little more complex than the simple example from Chapter 5 since it takes advantage of the *Principle of TimeBase Incompatibility Asymmetry*: Just because `Player` A cannot use `Player` B's `TimeBase` does not mean `Player` B can't use `Player` A's `TimeBase`.

The following code segment exploits this principle by trying all different combinations of `TimeBase` sharing between two `Players`.

```
Player p0 = Manager.createPlayer(mediaURL0);
Player p1 = Manager.createPlayer(mediaURL1);

//...realize both Players

try {
    p1.setTimeBase(p0.getTimeBase());
} catch (IncompatibleTimeBaseException e0) {
    try {
        p0.setTimeBase(p1.getTimeBase());
    } catch (IncompatibleTimeBaseException e1) {
        try {
            TimeBase sysTb = Manager.getSystemTimeBase();
            p0.setTimeBase(sysTb);
            p1.setTimeBase(sysTb);
        } catch (IncompatibleTimeBaseException e2) {
            System.err.println("No luck with setTimeBase");
        }
    }
}
```

(1) (next to `p1.setTimeBase(p0.getTimeBase());`)
(2) (next to `p0.setTimeBase(p1.getTimeBase());`)
(3) (next to `p0.setTimeBase(sysTb);`)
(4) (next to `p1.setTimeBase(sysTb);`)

The above code segment attempts to tie the Clocks of two different Players to the same TimeBase object, first at [1], then at [2]. Since it is not relevant which TimeBase is shared, both TimeBases are attempted. If the second attempt fails at [2], a third attempt is made whereby the two Players to be synchronized both try to use the system TimeBase at [3] and [4]. The third attempt, although legal, will fail in the case where either p0 or p1 uses the system time-base as its default time-base.[3]

The exception handling is required because not all Players are capable of being driven from an arbitrary TimeBase. Intel is explicit in stating that a setTimeBase call on a Player from its implementation may only use a TimeBase object obtained from another Player from Intel's implementation. Any other implementation of TimeBase will be rejected with an IncompatibleTimeBaseException.

In spite of the *Principle of TimeBase Incompatibility Asymmetry*, it is usually sufficient to test setting the TimeBase in one direction.

With setTimeBase and getTimeBase, we have the tools to satisfy condition (1) above. To meet the second condition, we must learn more about the Controller method getStartLatency.

---

3. Sun's JMF 1.0 does use the system time base as the default time-base for its Player implementation. If this code reaches the third try statement it will fail.

Accommodating Start Latency

The start latency for a JMF `Controller` is the time required for it to prepare media for rendering. When a `Controller` is started, the sequence of the stages it passes through is thus:

i. The `Controller` moves from the `Prefetched` state to the `Started` state. At this point, the `Clock` is also in the `Started` state.

ii. The `Controller` spends a small increment of time preparing its media.

iii. The first frame of the media is rendered.

The "small increment of time" referred to in (ii) is the `Controller`'s *start latency*. This is the amount of time after the `Clock` moves to the `Started` state and before the media is rendered. Start latency is reported by the `Controller` method `getStartLatency` which is described in JMF API Synopsis 9.1 below.

JMF API Synopsis 9.1 *getStartLatency*

Interface	`javax.media.Controller`
Method	`getStartLatency`
Arguments	`void`
Return	`javax.media.Time`
Description	Returns the amount of time spent in `Started` state before media actually starts playing. Returns LATENCY_UNKNOWN if the latency cannot be determined.

Once again, a VCR provides a nice analogy. On many older VCRs, you would drop in a tape, push the start button and wait a second or two while listening to whirs, whines and clicks before the tape starting moving and *Ernest Goes To Camp* started playing. The time between the push of the button and the appearance of the first frame on your screen is the start latency.

When your application needs to synchronize multiple `Players` using `syncStart`, each `Player`'s start latency needs to be taken into consideration so that the various media streams are rendered precisely at the expected time. In the general case, each `Player` will have a different start latency. The basic strategy is to defer synchronizing media time with time-base time until some time-base time increment greater than the maximum start latency across all the `Players`. A picture will help explain this.

Start Latency in Pictures

Suppose `Player p0` has a start latency of 1.1 seconds, `Player p1` has a start latency of 1.6 seconds and `Player p2` has a start latency of 2.4 seconds. Assume further that each `Player` will start playing at the beginning of its respective medium. In other words, assume a previous call to `setMediaTime` with a zero `Time` value.

In order that all media are rendered at the same time, you will want all the `Players` to synchronize media time and time-base time at some time greater than the current time plus 2.4 seconds, the greatest latency of the three `Players`. Figure 9.1 illustrates this idea.

Figure 9.1 *Synchronizing Multiple Players*

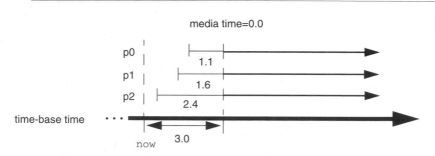

To give all the `Players` time to prepare their media, a synchronization point 3.0 seconds in the future is chosen. This choice is arbitrary as long as it is greater than the maximum latency of the `Players` being synchronized. Since each of the three `Players` has a start latency less than 3.0 seconds, calling `syncStart(now+3.0)` will ensure that each `Player` has enough time to prepare its media for rendering at the given time. Calling `syncStart` with a time-base time less than the current time plus the greatest start latency would result in the `Players` not properly synchronizing. If, for instance, `syncStart(now+2.0)` were called on each of the `Players`, then p2 would not be able to render its first frame of media until 0.4 seconds after p0 and p1 had begun rendering their media.

Start Latency, Media Time and Duration

It is important to understand the relationship between duration, start latency, and the progression of media time, as well as the sequence of events that transpire when the `syncStart` method is called. Figure 9.2 illustrates this relationship.

Figure 9.2 *Starting the Controller*

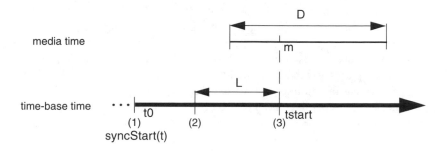

The process of starting the `Controller` begins at (1) in Figure 9.2, as the `syncStart` method is called at time-base time *t0* with the time-base start time of *tstart*. Immediately, regardless of the start time, the `Controller` is placed into the `Started` state. It is worth noting that since `Controller` extends `Clock`, the `Clock` is also moved to the `Started` state. However, the media time does not yet progress.

In (2) in Figure 9.2, the media rendering process is started at the time-base time *tstart − L*, where *L* is the `Controller`'s start latency. This value, returned by the `getStartLatency` method, represents the time-base time needed to prepare the media for rendering.

Finally, at (3) in Figure 9.2, when the time-base start time *tstart* is reached, the first frame of data is rendered and the media time begins progressing. The media is rendered starting at that frame that corresponds to media time *m*.

Note that

$$tstart − t0 > L \qquad\qquad \text{(EQ 6)}$$

This is an important criterion to meet when attempting to synchronize multiple `Players`. It ensures that all `Controllers` are ready to render their first frame at *tstart*. In practice, then, the three stages of `Player` start-up defined at the beginning of "Accommodating Start Latency" on page 141 expand to the four stages described below when using `syncStart` to synchronize `Players`.

i.   The `Controller` moves from the `Prefetched` state to the `Started` state.

ii. The `Controller` waits until *tstart - L*.

iii. The `Controller` spends the latency period *L* preparing its media.

iv. The first frame of the media is rendered at *tstart*.

The amount of time spent in stage (ii) is variable across `Controllers`. It is the time spent waiting *before* it starts its media rendering preparation. In Figure 9.2, it is the time between (1) and (2). Waiting for this amount of time will ensure that a `Player` will render its first frame at the time-base time sent as an argument to `syncStart`.

Recall that media time is not maintained directly by any timer, but rather is derived from the time-base time using the transformation (EQ 1) on page 56. The media time does not start moving forward until the time-base start time has been reached. This explains how a `Controller` can be in the `Started` state, preparing to render the media, without the media time progressing.

Note that the duration (D) of the media is purely a function of the media time. It represents the length of the media when played from start to finish at the default rate. The start latency, on the other hand, is a function of time-base time and has nothing to do with the duration of the media.

Coding for Start Latency

Returning to Figure 9.1 for example start latency values, the following sequence of `syncStart` calls would be performed in order that all three `Players` will render their media at the same time.

```
double su10, su11, su12;

// ...realize Players

try {
    p1.setTimeBase(p0.getTimeBase());
    p2.setTimeBase(p0.getTimeBase());
} catch (IncompatibleTimeBaseException tbe) {
    // do exception handling
}
// ...prefetch Players...
Time now = p0.getTimeBase().getSeconds();
p2.startSync(new Time(now + 3.0));
p1.startSync(new Time(now + 3.0));
p0.startSync(new Time(now + 3.0));
```

Of course a more general solution is needed for an arbitrary number of `Players`. As mentioned above, one approach is simply to calculate the maximum start latency across all the `Controllers` and add this value to the current time, using the result as an argument to `syncStart`. At its heart, it is a simple piece of code but it is provided nonetheless in the *Essential JMF* Toolkit.

Listing 9.1 *Calculating Maximum Start Latency for Multiple Controllers*

```
package ejmf.toolkit.util;

public static Time getMaximumLatency(Controller[] ctrls) {
    Time    maxLatency = new Time(0.0);
    Time    thisTime;
    double  maxSeconds = 0.0;

    for (int i = 0; i < ctrls.length; i++) {
        if (ctrls[i].getState() < Controller.Realized ||
            (thisTime = ctrls[i].getStartLatency())
                        == Controller.LATENCY_UNKNOWN) {
            continue;
        }
        double thisSeconds = thisTime.getSeconds();
        if (thisSeconds > maxSeconds)
            maxLatency = thisTime;
    }
     return maxLatency;
}
```

(5)
(6)

Two idiosyncrasies of dealing with a `Controller`'s start latency are taken care of by the `static` method `Utility.getMaximumLatency` from the `ejmf.toolkit.util` package.

Line [5] ensures that only the latency value of those `Controllers` in the `Realized` state contribute to the calculation of maximum latency. It is illegal to call `getStartLatency` on an unrealized `Controller`; a `NotRealized-Error` will be thrown. It is up to the caller of `getMaximumLatency` to ensure all the input `Controllers` are realized upon invocation of the method.

A `Controller` may report that its latency is unknown. This is tested for at [6]. Any `Controller` that reports `LATENCY_UNKNOWN` is skipped when computing the maximum start latency. This is a decision you may want to reconsider in your own implementation of `getMaximumLatency`. If you find a `Player` with an unknown start latency, you may want to return `LATENCY_UNKNOWN`. However, you are still left to contemplate what that means when attempting to synchronize this `Player` with others. As implemented, we will effectively ignore any uncooperative `Players`.

With the introduction of `getStartLatency` we have enough information to meet condition (2) on page 138.

It is now time to turn our attention to condition (4) on page 139.

Tracking State Changes

The standard way an object tracks state changes to a `Player` is by implementing the `ControllerListener` interface and registering as a listener on that

`Player`. We saw how this was done with `controllerUpdate` and `add-ControllerListener` in Chapter 3.

The important thing to keep in mind when synchronizing `Players` using `syncStart` is that each `Controller` will generate an event for each relevant change in its status. To track all `Controllers`, your application will have to register as a `ControllerListener` on each one. This will meet condition (4) on page 139.

Rate, Media Time, Stop Time and Explicit Synchronization

A brief discussion of the `setRate`, `setMediaTime` and `setStopTime` methods will suffice to further explain condition (5) on page 139.

Whether `setRate` is used to play synchronized `Players` at the same rate is optional. Typically, synchronized `Players` will play at the same rate. However, a few things need to be said about `setRate` in the context of synchronizing `Players`:

- `setRate` *will not* affect when time-base time gets mapped to media time. In other words, if two `Players` share the same `TimeBase` and are started with the same `Time` value to `syncStart`, they will start at the same time.

- `setRate` *will* affect the stop time of two synchronized `Players`. If two `Players` playing at the same rate are set to stop at the same media time, they will reach the stop time at different points in real-time.

Both of these points follow directly from the fact that a `Clock`'s rate comes into play only *after* media time and time-base time have been synchronized.

When using the explicit approach to synchronize multiple `Players`, setting the media time and stop time must be done on each `Player` separately. For example, to rewind all the `Players`, `setMediaTime(new Time(0.0))` would need to be called on each `Player`. Likewise, to stop the `Players` five seconds into their media stream, `setStopTime(new Time(5.0))` would be called on each `Player`.

Explicit Synchronization: An Example

We will now pull together what we have learned about synchronizing multiple `Players` using `syncStart`. The following application takes an arbitrary number of media file names or URLs on the command line, creates a `Player` for each and displays that `Player`'s visual component in its own Swing `JFrame`.

This example is rather long so we will discuss it in pieces. The central piece is the `XSync` class. It constructs and displays the `Players`, initializing them for synchronization. Two listener classes, a `ControllerListener` and an `ActionListener`, respond to `ControllerEvents` and a start button action, respectively.

XSync: A Class for Explicit Synchronization

We will look at the `main` method of `XSync` first. It appears in Listing 9.2.

Listing 9.2 *XSync: Explicit Synchronization of Multiple Players*

```
     public class XSync implements ControllerListener {
(7)      private static Player[]               players;
         private static JFrame                 frame;
(8)      private static int                    stopped;
         private static StandardControlPanel   cp;

         public static void main(String args[]) {
             if ( args.length == 0 ) {
                 System.out.println(
                     "Specify at least one media URL/file");
                 return;
             }

             Vector v = new Vector();

             for (int i = 0; i < args.length; i++) {
                 try {
(9)                  Player p = Manager.createPlayer(
                         Utility.appArgToMediaLocator(args[i]) );
(10)                 new StateWaiter(p).blockingRealize();
(11)                 v.addElement(p);
                 } catch(Exception e) {
                     System.out.println(
                         "Could not create Player: " + args[i]);
                     e.printStackTrace();
                 }
             }

             players = new Player[ v.size() ];
(12)         v.copyInto(players);
(13)         new XSync(players);
         }
     ...
```

We will run this example as an application, so the `main` method is called first. It is responsible for creating an array of `Players` to pass to the constructor of `XSync`.

Using the *Essential JMF* Toolkit utility, each argument to `main` is converted to a `MediaLocator` before being passed to `createPlayer`. After each `Player` is created [9], it is realized [10]. Recall that a `Player` must be realized to access its `TimeBase` which is the first step in synchronizing two `Players`.

As the `Players` are being created, they are placed in a `Vector` [11] which is copied into an array [12] before being passed to the constructor of `XSync` [10]. Listing 9.3 contains the constructor code.

Listing 9.3 *The XSync Constructor*

```
          public XSync(Player[] players) {
              this.players = players;
(14)          int master = 0;
(15)          TimeBase masterTB = players[master].getTimeBase();
(16)          for (int i = 0; i < players.length; i++) {
                  if ( i != master ) {
                      try {
(17)                      players[i].setTimeBase(masterTB);
(18)                  } catch(IncompatibleTimeBaseException e) {
                          System.out.println(
                              "Incompatible TimeBase, skipping..." );
                      }
                  }
(19)              new StateWaiter(players[i]).blockingPrefetch();
              }

(20)          Time msl = Utility.getMaximumLatency(players);
(21)          double latency = msl.getSeconds();

              for (int i = 0; i < players.length; i++) {
                  frame = new JFrame();
                  Container pane = frame.getContentPane();
                  pane.setLayout( new BorderLayout() );

                  Component vis =
                          players[i].getVisualComponent();

                  if ( vis != null ) {
                      pane.add(vis, BorderLayout.CENTER);
                  }

(22)              players[i].addControllerListener(
                      new XSListener());
```

```
                    if ( i == master ) {
                        frame.setTitle("Master Player");
(23)                    cp = new StandardControlPanel(players[i],
                            AbstractControlPanel.USE_START_BUTTON);

(24)                    cp.setStartButton(
                            cp.getStartButton(),
(25)                        new StartListener(players, latency));

                        pane.add(cp, BorderLayout.SOUTH);
                    } else {
                        frame.setTitle("Managed Controller");
                    }

                    if ( pane.getComponentCount() != 0 ) {
                        Runnable r = new Runnable() {
                            public void run() {
                                frame.pack();
                                frame.setVisible(true);
                            }
                        };
                        SwingUtilities.invokeLater(r);
                    }
                }
            }
        }
```

Sharing a TimeBase

The first job of the constructor is to assign the same TimeBase to all the Players. At [14] an arbitrary choice of master Player is made and its TimeBase is retrieved at [15]. With the master TimeBase in hand, the for loop at [16] applies it to each of the Players [17] except the master. If any Player has an incompatible TimeBase, it is skipped [18]. After the shared TimeBase is set, each Player is moved to the Prefetched state [19], a requirement imposed by the use of syncStart.

Accommodating Start Latency

The other requirement imposed by the use of syncStart is the need to calculate a start time that accommodates all the Player's start latency. Using the utility just introduced in Listing 9.1 on page 145, the maximum start latency across all the Players is calculated [20] as a Time object. The seconds representation of that object is used as the latency [21]. This value will reappear when we get around to starting the Players.

Tracking State Changes

In order to keep all the `Players` in the expected state, a `ControllerListener` must be register for each `Controller`. This is done at [22]. An instance of `XSListener` acts as the listener. We will look at `XSListener` in just a bit.

Custom Control Panel

The remainder of the constructor code is predominantly GUI work but, none-theless, germane to our discussion. The problem it solves is the inability to control multiple `Players` from a single control panel when those `Players` are not coordinated using `addController`. The control panel component returned by a call to `getControlPanelComponent` on a `Player` is "hard-wired" to that `Player`. Under normal circumstances, pressing the start button will start only that `Player`. Likewise, pressing the pause button will pause only that `Player`.

Given this tight coupling between the operation of a `Player` and its control panel component, the default control panel will not be of any help if we want the user to be able to manipulate the operation of a group of `Players` synchronized with `syncStart`.

To solve this problem we introduce the `ejmf.toolkit.gui.StandardControlPanel` class. This control panel is configurable in that different semantics can be assigned to its buttons. You will get the complete story on `StandardControlPanel` in Chapter 21, "Creating a Custom Control Panel," but we need it here, so we are going to use it here.[4]

The `StandardControlPanel` is created at [23], requesting that it display only the start button. The start button is then customized at [24], adding an instance of `StartListener` [25] as its `ActionListener`. `StartListener`, as we shall see, is written to start all the `Players` that are to be synchronized.

This completes the discussion of the `XSync` class. Two topics still need addressing. What does the `ControllerListener` code look like? and what does the `StartListener` code look like? Let's turn first to the `ControllerListener`.

XSListener: A ControllerListener for Explicit Synchronization

Recall at [22] on page 148 we added an instance of `XSListener` as the `ControllerListener` for each `Player`. `XSListener` is an inner class of `XSync` and relies on two of its static data fields, `players` [7] and `stopped` [8].

---

4. Linearity went out of style with the invention of HTML.

Listing 9.4 *ControllerListener for Multiple Players*

```
class XSListener implements ControllerListener {

    public void controllerUpdate(ControllerEvent event) {
        Controller c = event.getSourceController();
        if (event instanceof EndOfMediaEvent) {
            c.setMediaTime(new Time(0));
            stopped++;
            if (stopped == players.length) {
                stopped = 0;
            }
        }
    }
}
```

(26)
(27)
(28)
(29)
(30)

XSListener listens for EndOfMediaEvents [26] and rewinds the Player [27] when they are seen. It also tracks how many Players have been stopped [28] and, when it sees all the Players [29], resets it counter [30].

The moral of the story is that when synchronizing Players using the explicit approach, ControllerEvents are seen from every Controller. The implication of this is that a ControllerListener must be installed on each Controller to properly track its state.

Starting Multiple Players with syncStart

We have seen in "Coding for Start Latency" on page 144 the mechanics of starting multiple Players using syncStart to accommodate their different start latencies. Here analogous code appears in the ActionListener registered on the start button of our control panel.

Listing 9.5 *Start Button Listener*

```
class StartListener implements ActionListener {
    private Player[]       players;
    private double         latency;
    private static final double FUDGE = 0.1;

    public StartListener(Player[] players, double latency)
    {
        this.players = players;
        this.latency = latency;
    }
```

```
public void actionPerformed(ActionEvent event) {
    double now;
    TimeBase mtb = players[0].getTimeBase();
    now = mtb.getTime().getSeconds();
    for (int j = 0; j < players.length; j++) {
        players[j].syncStart(
            new Time(now + latency + FUDGE));
    }
}
```

(31)

(32)

This listener is created with the array of `Players` that it will be responsible for starting and the latency to use with `syncStart`.

Once the current time is fetched [31], each `Player` is started [32], adding a fudge factor to account for the overhead in the multiple invocations of `syncStart`.

This code is not ground-breaking in that we discussed the technique in "Coding for Start Latency." The relevant point is that if you want to use `syncStart` to start multiple `Players` from a control panel, you will need to build your own and provide a start button with an `ActionListener` similar to `StartListener`.

An Augmented SyncStartStrategy?

`XSync` provides a fairly simple example of explicit synchronization. For instance, we only use `setMediaTime` on a `Player` after it has played its entire media. Allowing arbitrary use of `setMediaTime` would make it more difficult to keep the `Players` synchronized.

If the `Players` are started and `setMediaTime` is called, some `Player` may need to move to the `Prefetching` state to buffer the appropriate media data. Those `Players` that do may take a different amount of time, and so when they move back through the `Prefetched` state into the `Started` state, they will no longer be synchronized with each other, not to mention with those `Players` that did not need to buffer new media data.

To handle this scenario, your application would have to stop all `Players` before `setMediaTime` was called on each of them; you would need to get the `Players` to a known state. Your application would then have to track which `Players` reverted to the `Prefetching` state and wait for them to post `PrefetchCompleteEvent` before restarting all the `Players`.

This is not an impossible task but it has already been done for us in the JMF `Player`. Instead of reinventing the proverbial wheel, let's take advantage of available functionality in developing another strategy for synchronizing multiple `Players`. After we see how to run the `XSync` example, we will look at `addController`.

Running XSync

The `XSync` example source is located in `$EJMF_HOME/src/ejmf/exam-ples/xsync`. The following sample command line shows how to run the `XSync` application.

◀ **• User Input**   **Running XSync Application**

```
% java ejmf.examples.xsync.XSync \
        $EJMF_HOME/classes/media/safexmas.mov \
        $EJMF_HOME/classes/xmas.avi
```

Synchronization Using addController

The JMF `Player` API defines a method that greatly simplifies the synchronization of multiple `Player`s. To avoid the complexity of having to manage multiple `Player`s individually, the `Player` method `addController` is used.

`addController` provides a means for bringing multiple `Controller`s under the control of a single `Player`. The `Player` object on which `addController` is invoked is considered the master `Player`. `addController` takes a single `Controller` argument and adds it to a list of `Controller`s the invoking `Player` is said to *manage*. A synopsis of the `addController` method, and its companion `removeController`, appears below.

JMF API Synopsis 9.2 *The addController Method*

Interface	`javax.media.Player`
Method	`addController`
Arguments	`javax.media.Controller`
Returns	`void`
Description	Brings the `Controller` passed as an argument under the management of the invoking `Player`. An `IncompatibleTimeBaseException` is thrown if the `Controller`'s time base cannot be set to the `Player`'s time base.
Method	`removeController`
Arguments	`javax.media.Controller`
Returns	`void`
Description	Removes the `Controller` passed as an argument out from under control of the invoking `Player`.

Since much goes on as a result of either of these calls, further explanation is in order.

Adding a Controller

The managing `Player` must at least be in the `Realized` state, and not started, before its `addController` method can be called. When a `Controller` is added to a `Player`'s managed `Controller` set, the managing `Player` performs the following operations:

- Sets the time base of the managed `Controller` to its own time base using `setTimeBase`.

- Sets the media time, rate and stop time of the managed `Controller` to the respective values of the master `Player`.[5]

- Recomputes its duration based on the duration of the managed `Controller`. If the `Player` and all its managed `Controllers` have a known duration, the duration of the master `Player` is the maximum of all of its managed `Controllers`. If either the master `Player` or any of the managed `Controllers` has an unknown duration, the `Player`'s `getDuration` will be `Controller.DURATION_UNKNOWN`. If either the master `Player` or any of its managed `Controllers` reports an unbounded duration, the `Player`'s `getDuration` method will return `Controller.DURATION_UNBOUNDED`. An unknown duration will always trump an unbounded duration. If some managed `Controllers` have an unknown duration and others an unbounded duration, the managing `Player` will return `Controller.DURATION_UNKNOWN` in response to `getDuration`.

- Recomputes its latency. The start latency reported by a `Player` managing multiple `Controllers` is the maximum latency across all the `Controllers`, including the master `Player`. On Intel's implementation, if the managing `Player` or any of its managed `Controllers` has an unknown latency, the aggregate latency will be `LATENCY_UNKNOWN`.

- Adds itself as a `ControllerListener` for the managed `Controller`.

As a side-effect of any of these operations, `ControllerEvents` may be fired by the master `Player`. For example, a change to the `Player`'s duration resulting from an addition of a `Controller` with a longer duration, will generate a `DurationUpdateEvent`. In general, any change to the `Player` or its managed `Controllers` that would normally cause a `ControllerEvent` to be fired will also cause a `ControllerEvent` to be fired as a result of the call to `addController`.

---

5. Sun's JMF 1.0 does not implement these operations and is therefore not in compliance with the API specification.

Restrictions on the Managed Controllers

The above activity imposes the following restrictions on the managed `Controller`:

- It must not be in the `Started` state, or a `ClockStartedError` is thrown when its time base is set.

- It must be at least in the `Realized` state, or a `NotRealizedError` is thrown.

- Its time base must be compatible with the time base of the master `Player`, otherwise an `IncompatibleTimeBaseException` is thrown.

Resultant Master Player Transitions

It is possible that adding a `Controller` to a `Player` will result in state transition events. Exactly what events are generated depends on which implementation of the JMF you are using. The `Player` API states:

When a Controller is added to a Player the Player does not transition the added Controller to a new state, nor does the Player transition itself forward. The Player either transitions back to the Realized state if the added Controller is Realized or Prefetching or it stays in the Prefetched state if both the Player and the added Controller are in the Prefetched state.

Since Sun and Intel implement this requirement a bit differently, a `ControllerListener` attached to the managing `Player` will see different events on each of the different implementations.

With Sun's `Player` implementation, if `addController` is called on a `Prefetched` `Player` with a `Controller` that is not yet in the `Prefetched` state, `addController` forces the `Player` to revert to the `Realized` state by calling `deallocate` on the `Player`. This will generate a `DeallocateEvent` as the `Player` moves to the `Realized` state. When `addController` returns, the `Player` is in the `Realized` state.

The Intel developers will be forgiven if they interpreted the above run-on sentence differently and ended up implementing `addController` a bit differently than Sun. Intel's `addController` makes a decision to affect a state transition solely on the current state and target state of the managing `Player`. If the `Controller`'s target state is the `Prefetched` state, but is not yet there, `addController` calls the managing `Player`'s `prefetch` method. There is no movement back to the `Realized` state; instead there is a possible forward transition. When `addController` returns, the managing `Player` is either `Prefetching` or `Prefetched`.

The point of this discussion is that the state of the managing `Player` may be different coming out of `addController` than it was going in. More importantly, it may be different across different implementations the `Player`.

Your best bet for consistent behavior across `Player` implementations is to add `Controllers` to a managing `Player` when both the `Player` and the managed `Controllers` are known to be in the same static state, either `Realized` or `Prefetched`. In this case, no state transition events will be fired.

JMF TIP: Using addController

For consistent results across different implementations of the JMF only use addController on a Player that is known to be in the Realized or Prefetched state and add only Controllers that are known to be in the same state.

Managing Slave Controllers

Once a `Controller` is being managed by a `Player`, you should no longer directly invoke its methods. The managing `Player` becomes responsible for affecting state changes in its managed `Controllers`, and setting the rate, start and stop time, etc. The general rule is that any operation you perform on the master `Player` gets dispatched to all of its slave `Controllers`.

The managing `Player` also bundles `ControllerEvents` from its managed `Controllers`. Consider a `Player` that is, along with all of its managed `Controllers`, in the `Realized` state. When the application invokes `prefetch` on the master `Player`, `prefetch` is also called on all of the managed `Controllers`. The master `Player` then waits until all of its `Controllers` have reported in with a `PrefetchCompleteEvent` before passing on a single `PrefetchCompleteEvent` to its listeners.

This arrangement does not constrain a listener from registering with one of the managed `Controllers`. Some third party object may observe the activity of a managed `Controller`. It should not, however, try to manipulate that `Controller` directly. The results, as they say, are unpredictable. If you are going to register a `ControllerListener` on a slave `Controller`, you should write the listener's `controllerUpdate` function to be "read-only" with respect to the managed `Controller`.

Removing a Controller

The removeController operation is fairly simple. The Controller is removed from the list of a Player's managed Controllers and its effect on the group reversed, namely:

- The managing Player removes itself as a listener on the Controller.
- The managing Player's start latency is recalculated, no longer taking the removed Controller into consideration.
- The managing Player's duration is recalculated, no longer taking the removed Controller into consideration.
- The Controller reverts back to its original time base.

The managing Player must be Stopped when removing a Controller. If it is not, a ClockStartedError is thrown.

addController Synchronization: An Example

The ACSync will provide an example of synchronizing multiple Players using addController. The structure of ACSync is borrowed from XSync. In our discussion of ACSync we will gloss over its similarities with XSync and, instead, focus on what is different and germane to the use of addController.

The code for ACSync appears in Listing 9.6.

Listing 9.6 *ACSync: Synchronizing Multiple Players Using addController*

```
public class ACSync {

public static void main(String args[]) {
    if ( args.length == 0 ) {
        System.out.println(
            "Specify at least one media URL/file");
        return;
    }

    Vector v = new Vector();

    for (int i = 0; i < args.length; i++) {
        try {
            Player p = Manager.createPlayer(
                Utility.appArgToURL(args[i]));
            new StateWaiter(p).blockingRealize();
            v.addElement(p);
        } catch(Exception e) {
            System.out.println(
```

```
                        "Could not create Player: " + args[i]);
                        e.printStackTrace();
                }
        }

        Player[] players = new Player[v.size()];
        v.copyInto(players);
(33)    int master = Utility.pickAMaster(players);

        for (int i = 0; i < players.length; i++) {
            if (players[i] != players[master]) {
                try {
(34)                players[master].addController(players[i]);
(35)            } catch(IncompatibleTimeBaseException e) {
                    System.out.println(
                        "Incompatible TimeBase, skipping..." );
                }
            }
        }

(36)    players[master].addControllerListener(
                            new PlayerListener());

        for (int i = 0; i < players.length; i++) {
            Frame f = new Frame();
            f.setLayout(new BorderLayout());

            Component vis =
                players[i].getVisualComponent();

            if (vis != null) {
                f.add(vis, BorderLayout.CENTER);
            }
            if (i == master) {
                f.setTitle("Master Player");
                f.addWindowListener(new WindowAdapter() {
                    public void windowClosing(WindowEvent e) {
                        System.exit(0);
                    }
                });
(37)            Component cont =
                    players[i].getControlPanelComponent();

                if (cont != null) {
                    f.add(cont, BorderLayout.SOUTH);
                }
            } else {
                f.setTitle("Managed Controller");
            }
```

```
            if (f.getComponentCount() != 0) {
                f.pack();
                f.setVisible(true);
            }
        }
    }
```

(38)
```
    class PlayerListener implements ControllerListener {
        public void controllerUpdate(ControllerEvent event) {
            Controller c = event.getSourceController();
            if (event instanceof EndOfMediaEvent) {
```
(39)
```
                c.setMediaTime(new Time(0.0));
            }
        }
    }
```

The crux of the ACSync class is line [34]. Here is where all of the managed Controllers are brought under the management of the master Player. The master Player is determined with the help of pickAMaster [33], a helper method for selecting which Player will be master. We will look at pickA-Master in the next section.

At [35], any IncompatibleTimeBaseException is caught. This is highlighted to emphasize that there is nothing magic about addController. Just as we saw in the XSync example, all synchronized Players have to share a common TimeBase. In the XSync code, we did it explicitly. Here addController takes care of it; specifically, it calls setTimeBase on the Controller passed as an argument. If the newly managed Controller cannot accept the managing Player's TimeBase, an exception is thrown. Hence the need for catching the IncompatibleTimeBaseException.

Moving to line [36], we see that only the master Player has a listener registered with it. Recall that all ControllerEvents are funneled through the master Player so there is no need to listen to all the managed Controllers. The controllerUpdate method appears at [38]. When it rewinds the Controller that reports the EndOfMediaEvent [39]—always the master— it indirectly rewinds all the managed Controllers. There is no need for iterating over the entire collection as was necessary in the XSync example.

Likewise, all operations performed on the master are delegated to the managed Controllers. That is why, at [37], we can get away with using the master's control panel component. Though it is hard-wired to the master Player, the master Player will take care of passing on to the managed Controllers any operations initiated by user interaction with the control panel component.

Which Control Panel?

When you are synchronizing media using the addController approach, you will need to give some thought to what you use for a control panel Component. The control panel supplied by an invocation of getControlPanelComponent on the master Player is an obvious choice. It is the only one among all the synchronized Players that is capable of starting and stopping all the Players. If you mistakenly display the control panel from one of the slave Controllers, you will only be controlling that slave and no others.

Depending on your requirements, though, there may be a problem with using the control panel supplied by the master Player. The problem arises if you are synchronizing a media source containing *only* video with another media source with an audio track. In this case, if the video source is used as the master Player, its control panel will not provide any way to manipulate the volume of the audio source. The situation is avoided by making the Player with the audio track the master and using its control panel. This argues for a helper method pickAMaster to select a master Player from the collection of Players to be synchronized. One implementation of pickAMaster is shown in Listing 9.7.

Listing 9.7 *Determining Master Player*

```
public static int pickAMaster(Player[] players) {
    for (int i = 0; i < players.length; i++) {
        GainControl gc = player[i].getGainControl();
        if ( gc != null &&
            gc.getControlComponent() != null) {
            return i;
        }
    }
    return 0;
}
```

If getGainControl returns null when invoked on a Player, the control panel for that Player will not display volume control buttons. pickAMaster simply returns the index of the first Player it finds with a GainControl. If none of the Players has a GainControl, pickAMaster returns zero.

As an alternative to having to decide upon a master that has a GainControl, you could explicitly display the GainControl component returned by GainControl.getControlComponent from your audio Player. The problem with this approach is that is does not scale well. If you have more than one audio-only Player, displaying the GainControl component from any one of them will not be enough to control the volume of all the Players as a group. On the other hand, if you want to control each Player's volume separately, then you will want to display the GainControl component from each one.

Running ACSync

The `ACSync` example source is located in `$EJMF_HOME/src/ejmf/examples/acsync`. The following sample command line shows how to run the `ACSync` application.

 **Running ACSync Application**

```
% java ejmf.examples.acsync.ACSync \
        $EJMF_HOME/classes/media/safexmas.mov \
        $EJMF_HOME/classes/xmas.avi
```

A Discussion of Trade-Offs

What would a programming book be without a discussion of trade-offs? Now that we have seen two different ways to synchronize multiple `Players`, let's look at them side by side.

As has been mentioned, when synchronizing `Players` using `addController`, you forfeit much control over the individual `Players`. Let's consider some of the specific areas in which you are limited.

- All `Players` must start at the same media time.

  You cannot, for example, start one `Player` at media time zero and another at media time equal to 2.0 seconds.

- All `Players` must play at the same rate.

  In the simplest cases, this is not a serious deficiency.

- Only a single `EndOfMediaEvent` will be seen.

  This is a specific statement of the more general condition of seeing only a single, aggregate `ControllerEvent` for all the managed `Players`. An example, however, shows how an aggregate `EndOfMediaEvent` has implications for even a simple and not unlikely application. Consider starting two `Players` at the same time and having one play end-to-end while the other loops continuously. If you are managing the looping `Controller` by the other `Player`, you would not have access to the `EndOfMediaEvent` of the looping `Controller`. Technically, you could register a `ControllerListener` on the looping `Controller`, listen for the `EndOfMediaEvent`, and restart it as necessary, but the API explicitly recommends against this in its discussion of `addController`.

- Using `setStopTime` affects all `Players`. You cannot let one `Player` run for 5.0 seconds and another run for 10.0 seconds.

None of these shortcomings undermines the utility of the `addController` approach for synchronizing the start of multiple `Players`. `addController` was designed to solve a simple and common problem, and it does that well. The simplicity of the `ACSync` class is testimony to that.

Explicitly managing a group of `Players` has its own problems. Generally stated, the application shoulders additional responsibility for ensuring all `Players` are in the state appropriate for a particular operation. This can be especially tricky when setting a new media time with `setMediaTime`. `setMediaTime` may force a backward transition if a `Player` in its role as `Controller` has to buffer additional media data, leaving it in the `Realized` state. Before the `Player` can be restarted with `syncStart`, it has to be prefetched. There is no magic involved with getting this right, but it is additional work and certainly unnecessary if the `addController` approach will do the job.

Another drawback of the explicit approach to `Player` coordination is the inability to use the standard control panel supplied by a `Player`. You can think of the start button, for example, as hard-wired to a particular `Player`'s `start` method. If you intend to start multiple `Players` with the press of a single button, you will need to customize the control panel interface so that the start button invokes an action that starts all your `Players`. We saw this in `XSync` where a `MouseListener` attached to our start button had the responsibility of starting the entire collection of `Players`.

Of course, the complexity of explicitly managing multiple `Players` can also be an advantage. One man's ceiling is another man's floor after all. In Chapter 24, "A Simple Mixer," we will undertake an example of a simple media mixer that requires the flexibility and fine control of `syncStart` and explicit management of multiple `Players`.

Summary

In this chapter we saw two different ways media can be synchronized. The first way requires explicit management of each `Controller`. The second way relies on the `Player` API method `addController` and relieves the application of much of the burden of tracking multiple `Controllers`.

The two approaches were compared. The explicit approach is generally more complex but offers complete freedom in the control of all `Players`. The `addController` approach, the "built-in" way of synchronizing multiple media streams, solves very nicely the simple problem of getting two `Players` to start at the same time. For any more complex coordination of multiple `Players`, you will most likely end up managing the associated `Players` directly. After all, that is what Peter Graves had to do.

Chapter 10   *LOCATING THE PLAYER*

Introduction

Throughout this book, we have used the `javax.media.Manager` class to create a `Player` based on a particular medium. This was done using the `Manager` method `createPlayer`, which takes a URL, `MediaLocator`, or `DataSource` object and returns a `Player` capable of rendering the given medium.

In this chapter we will look at the algorithm that the `createPlayer` method follows to locate and instantiate an appropriate `Player`. We will also address the reasons why `createPlayer` may throw an exception and fail. Understanding the reasons for a possible failure, you will be better able to diagnose and remedy a given error. After chapters of blindly accepting the `createPlayer` functionality, it is time to discuss the complete algorithm for locating a `Player` installed on your system.

The `Manager` class is part of the JMF API. Like anything in the `javax.media` or `javax.media.protocol` packages, the `Manager` class implementation, including the `createPlayer` algorithm, is the same across all distributions of the JMF. The algorithms discussed here will be the same regardless of the JMF implementation.

Stepping Stones to a Player

The creation of a Player depends on the successful creation of several other objects along the way. As we learned in chapter Chapter 7, "The Player," a Player depends on a DataSource to provide it with its media data. This object, as you recall, is a protocol-specific mechanism used to deliver data to a Player. Without a DataSource, a functional Player cannot be created.

As a Player depends on a DataSource, the creation of a DataSource in turn depends on a MediaLocator object. This object is similar to a URL in that it specifies the protocol and location of the media data. Unlike a URL, however, a MediaLocator does not restrict its protocol to only those with a corresponding URLStreamHandler. As a convenience, a URL may be used to define a MediaLocator object.

The process for creating a Player is described in Figure 10.1. Note that the createPlayer method may enter this process at a different stage depending on the type of argument passed to it.

Figure 10.1 *Stepping Stones to a Player*

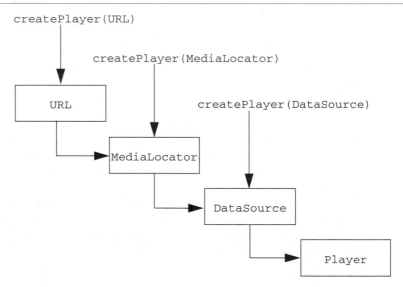

The three flavors of `createPlayer` are described in JMF API Synopsis 10.1.

JMF API Synopsis 10.1 *Creating a Player*

Class	`javax.media.Manager`
Method	`createPlayer`
Arguments	`java.net.URL`
Return	`javax.media.Player`
Description	Creates a `Player` for the media specified by the given `URL`.
Method	`createPlayer`
Arguments	`javax.media.MediaLocator`
Return	`javax.media.Player`
Description	Creates a `Player` for the media specified by the given `MediaLocator`.
Method	`createPlayer`
Arguments	`javax.media.protocol.DataSource`
Return	`javax.media.Player`
Description	Creates a `Player` for the media encapsulated by the given `DataSource`.

Each of these methods may throw a `javax.media.NoPlayerException` if a suitable `Player` cannot be located for the given media. Additionally, a `java.io.IOException` may be thrown if the `Player`'s `DataSource` cannot connect to the media data.

What constitutes a "suitable" `Player`? Let's look at the `createPlayer` algorithm and find out.

createPlayer: The Complete Algorithm

Depending on the argument passed to the `createPlayer` method, the algorithm to locate an appropriate `Player` may differ slightly. Let's start by looking at the first of these invocations depicted in Figure 10.1.

Creating a Player from a URL

The algorithm for creating a `Player` from a URL is quite simple. It defers the majority of its functionality to the version of `createPlayer` that takes a `MediaLocator` argument.

1. Create a `MediaLocator` from the given URL.
2. Call `createPlayer` with the new `MediaLocator` as an argument.

Creating a Player from a MediaLocator

The algorithm for creating a `Player` from a `MediaLocator` is much more complicated.

1. Using the `MediaLocator.getProtocol` method, get the protocol from the `MediaLocator`.
2. Using the `Manager.getDataSourceList` method, get a list of `Data-Source` classes that support the protocol.
3. For each `DataSource` class name in the list:
   a. Instantiate the `DataSource` using the `MediaLocator` passed to `createPlayer`.
   b. Call the `DataSource`'s `connect` method to connect to the media. This may result in an `IOException` if there are I/O problems when connecting. If this occurs, return to step (a) and try the next `Data-Source` in the list.
   c. Call `createPlayer` with the new `DataSource` as an argument. If this produces a `Player`, return it and skip all remaining steps. Otherwise, return to step (a) and try the next `DataSource` in the list.
4. If no `Player` has been found and returned, get the URL from the `MediaLocator` using the `MediaLocator`'s `getURL` method. If a URL cannot be created from the `MediaLocator`, throw a `NoPlayerException` and skip all remaining steps.
5. Instantiate a `javax.media.protocol.URLDataSource` using the URL just created. Connect to the source as in step (b) and call `createPlayer` with this `URLDataSource` as an argument. If this fails, the resulting exception will be propagated back to the original invocation of `createPlayer`. Otherwise, a `Player` will be returned.

The first priority of this algorithm is to create a `DataSource` object that can deliver the media to a `Player`. To do this, it systematically instantiates each `DataSource` that appears to support the given protocol. When it finds one that can successfully connect to the media, it calls a third invocation of `createPlayer` with this `DataSource` as an argument. This invocation of `createPlayer` is the subject of the next section. If it cannot find a `Player` for the given `DataSource`, the next `DataSource` in the list is tried.

If the `DataSource` list is exhausted without a `Player` being located, a `NoPlayerException` is thrown. Otherwise, the first `Player` that is successfully created is returned.

Creating a Player from a DataSource

To create a `Player` from a given `DataSource`, the `Manager` class takes the following steps.

1. Using the `DataSource`'s `getContentType` method, get the media's content-type.
2. Using the `Manager.getHandlerClassList` method, get a list of `MediaHandler` classes that support the media's content-type.
3. For each `MediaHandler` class name in the list:

   a. Instantiate the `MediaHandler` using its no-argument constructor.

   b. Call the `MediaHandler`'s `setSource` method to attach the `DataSource` to the `MediaHandler`. This may result in an `IncompatibleSourceException`. If this occurs, return to step (a) and try the next `MediaHandler` in the list.

   c. If the `MediaHandler` is a `Player`, return the new `Player` and skip all remaining steps.

   d. If the `MediaHandler` is a `MediaProxy`, obtain a new `DataSource` from the `MediaProxy` using the `MediaProxy`'s `getDataSource` method. Call `createPlayer` with this `DataSource` as an argument. If this produces a `Player`, return it and skip all remaining steps. Otherwise, return to step (a) and try the next `DataSource` in the list.

4. If no `Player` could be found for the content type returned from the `DataSource`'s `getContentType` method, then return to step (2) using the content type "unknown."

5. If no `Player` could be found, throw a `NoPlayerException`.

In this algorithm, the `createPlayer` method searches for an appropriate `Player` class based on the content-type of the media. If one is found, it is returned. Otherwise, the `createPlayer` method attempts to locate a `Player` for the content-type "unknown." This last-ditch effort may result in a "default" `Player` that can handle multiple types of media.

As you may have noticed, this algorithm does not specifically search for a `Player` object. Instead, it searches for an object that implements the `MediaHandler` interface. Recall from Chapter 7 that a `MediaHandler` is defined by its sole method, `setSource`. This method is called in step (b).

There are only two types of `MediaHandlers` in the JMF. The first, `Player`, is the object of our search. If the `createPlayer` method locates and successfully attaches a `DataSource` to a `MediaHandler` of this type, then it is returned immediately (c). The second, `javax.media.MediaProxy`, is a type of `MediaHandler` that has heretofore been unmentioned. It is discussed in the next section.

The MediaProxy Interface

A `MediaProxy` is used to produce a `DataSource` based on the content of another `DataSource`. It is typically used to read configuration information from a centralized location, describing how to make a connection to the actual media data. Using this information, it creates a `DataSource` that is then used to create a `Player`. It is, in essence, a way to dynamically define the media to be played.

The `MediaProxy` interface defines only one method. This method is used to retrieve the `MediaProxy`'s dynamically-created `DataSource`.

JMF API Synopsis 10.2 *Obtaining the DataSource from a MediaProxy*

Interface	`javax.media.MediaProxy`
Method	`getDataSource`
Arguments	`void`
Return	`javax.media.protocol.DataSource`
Description	Gets the `DataSource` object created by this `MediaProxy` based on the `DataSource` originally passed to its `setSource` method.

Using a `MediaProxy` class, an aspiring JMF developer could change the media to be played by remote applications by simply changing a line in a text file on a central server. This approach would require no recompilation of Java code, and thus could function as an efficient media solution in a fully-distributed environment.

The PackageManager Class

Within the `createPlayer` algorithms, we saw the `Manager` methods `getDataSourceList` and `getHandlerClassList` used to return a list of fully-qualified class names for candidate `DataSources` and `MediaHandlers`, respectively. These lists are based on the JMF's internal database of package prefixes, managed by the `javax.media.PackageManager` class.

The `PackageManager` class consists of several methods that provide programmatic control over the internal storage of the `DataSource` and `MediaHandler` package prefix lists. These lists, called the *protocol* and *content* prefix lists, determine the available `DataSource` and `MediaHandler` classes on the system. Each list consists of some number of `String` objects representing standard Java package prefixes.

Locating a DataSource

The protocol prefix list identifies the Java packages installed on the system which contain `DataSource` classes. For each package prefix in the list, the `Manager` class searches for a `DataSource` of the form

package-prefix`.media.protocol.`*protocol*`.DataSource`

As you can see, the package name of a `DataSource` class indicates the protocol that the `DataSource` supports. When searching for a `DataSource`, the `Manager` class gets the protocol portion of the package name from the `MediaHandler` or `URL` passed to the `createPlayer` method. With protocol in hand, it then methodically iterates through the `PackageManager`'s protocol prefix list searching for a `DataSource` that can serve the given media.

Suppose, for example, you wished to find a `DataSource` for the media referenced by the URL `http://www.broncos.com/media/elway.avi`. If the protocol prefix list consisted of the `javax`, `com.sun`, and `mypackages.sources` package prefixes, then the `Manager` class would attempt to find the following `DataSource` classes:

```
javax.media.protocol.http.DataSource
com.sun.media.protocol.http.DataSource
mypackages.sources.media.protocol.http.DataSource
```

Of these classes, the `Manager` class will instantiate and use the first one that exists, and will not throw an `IOException` when its `connect` method is called.

Locating a MediaHandler

The process for locating an appropriate `MediaHandler` is similar to that of locating a `DataSource`. Using the `PackageManager`'s content prefix list, the `Manager` class searches for `MediaHandler` classes of the form

package-prefix`.media.content.`*content-type*`.Handler`

Similar to the `DataSource` class, the fully-qualified class name of a `MediaHandler` reflects the content-type of the media it supports. The content-type, as you recall, is obtained from the `DataSource` using its `getContentType` method. It returns a `String` that generally reflects the MIME type of the media data.

Again, suppose the `Manager` were looking for a `Player` for the URL in the example above. After locating an appropriate `DataSource` for the HTTP protocol, the `Manager` would call the `DataSource`'s `getContentType` method. This method, depending on the `DataSource`, would most likely return `video.x_msvideo`, the MIME-type of the AVI video format. Supposing the content prefix list consisted of the `javax`, `com.sun`, and `mypack-ages.players` package prefixes, then the `Manager` class would attempt to find the following `MediaHandler` classes:

```
javax.media.content.video.x_msvideo.Handler
com.sun.media.content.video.x_msvideo.Handler
mypackages.players.media.content.video.x_msvideo.Handler
```

The `createPlayer` method will instantiate and return the first of these classes that exists and does not throw an `IncompatibleSourceException` when its `setSource` method is called. If none of these classes fits these criteria, a `NoPlayerException` is thrown.

Retrieving the Package Prefix Lists

The `PackageManager` class provides two `static` methods to retrieve the protocol and content package prefix lists. These lists are returned in the form of a `Vector` of `Strings`.

JMF API Synopsis 10.3 *Retrieving Prefix Lists from the PackageManager*

Class	`javax.media.PackageManager`
Method	`getProtocolPrefixList`
Arguments	`void`
Return	`java.util.Vector`
Description	Gets the JMF's internal protocol package prefix list.
Method	`getContentPrefixList`
Arguments	`void`
Return	`java.util.Vector`
Description	Gets the JMF's internal content package prefix list.

These methods, as discussed above, are used by the `Manager` class to determine where to look for installed `DataSources` and `MediaHandlers`.

The default values for the protocol and content package prefix lists may vary depending on the JMF distribution you are using. However, most likely they will contain the prefixes of the base packages that accompany the distribution.

Manipulating the Package Prefix Lists

The JMF provides the ability to augment or modify the protocol and content package prefix lists. In essence, this provides a programmatic way to extend the protocols and media types supported by the JMF. By changing these lists to reference new `Player` and `DataSource` packages, it provides the ability to enhance or override the default media support.

The protocol and content package prefix lists are manipulated with the following `static PackageManager` methods.

JMF API Synopsis 10.4 *Manipulating the Package Prefix Lists*

Class	`javax.media.PackageManager`
Method	`setProtocolPrefixList`
Arguments	`java.util.Vector`
Return	`void`
Description	Sets the JMF's internal protocol package prefix list.
Method	`setContentPrefixList`
Arguments	`java.util.Vector`
Return	`void`
Description	Sets the JMF's internal content package prefix list.

Any changes that these methods affect on the package prefix lists remain in effect only throughout the duration of the Java program. To make these changes persistent across invocations, use the following `static` methods.

JMF API Synopsis 10.5 *Making Changes to the Prefix Lists Persistent*

Class	`javax.media.PackageManager`
Method	`commitProtocolPrefixList`
Arguments	`void`
Return	`void`
Description	Makes the JMF's current internal protocol package prefix list persistent.
Method	`commitContentPrefixList`
Arguments	`void`
Return	`void`
Description	Makes the JMF's current internal content package prefix list persistent.

These methods write the current values of the package prefix lists to the `jmf.properties` file located in the `lib` directory of the JMF distribution. Every time a JMF application is started, this file is read to initialize the package prefix lists.

Since these methods affect a change to a system file, some applications or applets may not have permission to use them. If they are invoked by a Java program with insufficient permissions, a `java.lang.SecurityException` will be thrown.

Registering JMF Extensions: An Example

The `PackageManager` methods are intended to be used to extend the JMF's media and protocol support. A typical third-party extension might register its packages as in the following example.

```
Vector v;

// Register DataSource extensions
v = PackageManager.getProtocolPrefixList();
v.addElement("com.specialsauce.sources");
PackageManager.setProtocolPrefixList(v);
PackageManager.commitProtocolPrefixList();

// Register Player extensions
v = PackageManager.getContentPrefixList();
v.addElement("com.specialsauce.players");
PackageManager.setContentPrefixList(v);
PackageManager.commitContentPrefixList();
```

In this example the SpecialSauce Corporation registers its extension packages with the local JMF distribution. Typically, this code would be run only when the third-party packages are first installed.

More from the EJMF Toolkit

As always, the *Essential JMF* Toolkit exists to simplify your life as a JMF developer. Within the `ejmf.toolkit.install` package, the `PackageUtility` class provides the following `static` methods to simplify the addition and removal of package prefixes to the protocol and content package prefix lists.

EJMF Toolkit Synopsis 10.1 *Adding and Removing Package Prefixes*

Class	`ejmf.toolkit.install.PackageUtility`
Method	`addProtocolPrefix`
Visibility	`public`
Arguments	`java.lang.String`
	`boolean`
Return	`void`
Description	Adds the given element to the protocol package prefix list. Makes the list persistent based on the given `boolean` argument.
Method	`removeProtocolPrefix`
Visibility	`public`
Arguments	`java.lang.String`
	`boolean`
Return	`void`
Description	Removes the given element to the protocol package prefix list. Makes the list persistent based on the given `boolean` argument.
Method	`addContentPrefix`
Visibility	`public`
Arguments	`java.lang.String`
	`boolean`
Return	`void`
Description	Adds the given element to the content package prefix list. Makes the list persistent based on the given `boolean` argument.
Method	`removeContentPrefix`
Visibility	`public`
Arguments	`java.lang.String`
	`boolean`
Return	`void`
Description	Removes the given element from the content package prefix list. Makes the list persistent based on the given `boolean` argument.

In addition to providing the ability to easily add and remove package prefixes, the above methods ensure that no duplicate entries occur in a list.

The implementation of the addProtocolPrefix and removeProtocol-Prefix methods is shown in Listing 10.1. The corresponding methods for the content package prefix list are identical save the name of the list.

Listing 10.1 *Adding and Removing Package Prefixes*

```
public static void addProtocolPrefix(
    String prefix, boolean commit)
{
    Vector packagePrefix =
        PackageManager.getProtocolPrefixList();

    if( ! packagePrefix.contains(prefix) ) {
        packagePrefix.addElement(prefix);
        PackageManager.setProtocolPrefixList(
            packagePrefix);
        if( commit ) {
            PackageManager.commitProtocolPrefixList();
        }
    }
}

public static void removeProtocolPrefix(
    String prefix, boolean commit)
{
    Vector packagePrefix =
        PackageManager.getProtocolPrefixList();

    if( packagePrefix.contains(prefix) ) {
        packagePrefix.removeElement(prefix);
        PackageManager.setProtocolPrefixList(
            packagePrefix);
        if( commit ) {
            PackageManager.commitProtocolPrefixList();
        }
    }
}
```

Listing markers (1)–(5) appear on lines for getProtocolPrefixList [1], the if contains check [2], addElement [3], setProtocolPrefixList [4], and commitProtocolPrefixList [5].

Within the addProtocolPrefix method, the first step is to obtain the current protocol package prefix list [1]. Once this is done, a check is made to see if the given prefix is already in the list [2]. If it is not, the prefix is added to the list [3] and set with the PackageManager class [4]. Finally, if the new list is to be made persistent, the commitProtocolPrefixList method is called [5].

The implementation of the removeProtocolPrefix method is similar enough to be self-explanatory.

Summary

In this chapter we looked at a key part of the JMF, the `Manager.cre-atePlayer` algorithm. This algorithm made clear that the creation of a `Player` depends on several other prerequisite classes. Most notably, a suitable `DataSource` must be found that can handle the specified protocol and deliver the media to the `Player`.

Locating a `DataSource` and a `Player` for a given medium is dependent on the protocol and content package prefix lists. Managed by the `PackageM-anager` class, these lists can be augmented to allow support for new protocols and media formats. The `ejmf.toolkit.install.PackageUtility` class enhances the standard methods found in the `PackageManager` class, allowing for quick and easy registration of JMF extensions.

This chapter gave a preview of what is to be found in Part II, "Extending the Java Media Framework." There we will develop custom `Players` and `DataSources`, and ultimately register and use them with the JMF.

Part II

EXTENDING THE JAVA MEDIA FRAMEWORK

Chapter 11 *INTRODUCTION*

In Part II of this book we will look at how to extend the *Java Media Frame-work*. As we will see, new Players can be developed to provide support for a new or unsupported media format. Similarly, new DataSources can be developed to augment the list of protocols supported by the JMF. Finally, the user-interaction of a Player can be extended by providing custom Controls or a custom control panel Component for the Player.

An overview of each chapter in Part II follows.

Designing an Abstract Player Framework

Chapter 12, "Designing an Abstract Player Framework," introduces the process of creating a custom Player. Here we look at some of the issues surrounding the implementation of a custom Player, and design a framework to handle the majority of the overhead involved in implementing the Player interface.

Implementing the Clock Interface

In Chapter 13, "Implementing the Clock Interface," we begin the process of creating a custom `Player` by implementing the `Clock` interface. This interface is the most basic part of the `Player` interface and plays the key role in the timing of the media playback.

Implementing the Controller Interface

In Chapter 14, "Implementing the Controller Interface," the `Controller` interface is implemented. Extending the `Clock` interface implemented earlier, this interface provides a `Player` with a state machine that is used to track the "readiness" of the `Player` to play its media.

Implementing the Controller Transitions

Chapter 15, "Implementing the Controller Transitions," builds on the previous chapter by implementing the methods that transition a `Controller` between states. This chapter will show how a `Controller` progressively progresses to the `Started` state.

Implementing the Player Interface

In Chapter 16, "Implementing the Player Interface," the `Player` interface is implemented, paying special attention to the `Controller`-management capabilities of the `Player`. Several methods discussed in earlier chapters are re-implemented here to accommodate this functionality.

Implementing the Player Transitions

In Chapter 17, "Implementing the Player Transitions," we will begin to extend the `Controller` transition methods implemented in previous chapters. These methods will be extended to provide support for the `Player`'s managed `Controllers`. Any transition invoked on the `Player` will consequently be propagated on to each of its managed `Controllers`.

Creating a Custom Player

In Chapter 18, "Creating a Custom Player," we finally put to use the *Abstract Player Framework* (APF) implemented in the chapters that appear earlier. Here we implement two custom players. The first is for a known media format. The second is for an unknown media format that must be "registered" with the JMF.

Creating Custom Controls

Chapter 19, "Creating Custom Controls," introduces us to the capabilities provided to the `Player` by the `Control` interface. Here we will learn how to customize the interaction between a user and a `Player`, and we will look at some of the standard `Control`s defined by the JMF.

Creating Control Panel Components

Chapter 20, "Creating Control Panel Controls," will build on the previous chapter by creating `Control`s that can appear in a custom control panel. These controls will provide a user-interface for functionality common to all `Player`s.

Creating a Custom Control Panel

In Chapter 21, "Creating a Custom Control Panel," we will take the `Control`s developed in the previous chapter and place them in a control panel `Component` of our own design. We will also develop a unique and colorful control panel that offers a more interesting alternative to the standard control panel developed earlier.

Creating a Custom DataSource

In Chapter 22, "Creating a Custom DataSource," we will develop a `Data-Source` to support a new protocol. This protocol will be used to retrieve media from a Network News server. Here we will utilize a `Player` developed in Chapter 18.

Chapter 12 — DESIGNING AN ABSTRACT PLAYER FRAMEWORK

Introduction

The first part of this book has introduced you to the *Java Media Framework* and has shown you how your web-page, career, and life can be enhanced by Java multimedia. You are convinced that JMF is the wave of the future. You have put mpeg video on your home page. You have synchronized a video of your company's product with the theme to *Mission Impossible*. You are a Java machine. There is only one more frontier to conquer.

Your company has created its own media format and is anxious to deliver it to the masses. You can't wait to integrate this format into the JMF and impress your vice-president. You have gotten the nod from the pointy-haired individual responsible for inspiring you and you are ready to develop some kick-ass Java.

Fortunately for you, the JMF provides a (conceptually) simple way to support new media formats. Following a few guidelines, JMF will allow you to:

- Create a `Player` for a new media format.

- Create a `Player` for an existing format that does not yet have JMF support.

- Create a `Player` to replace the default `Player` for a particular media format.

In short, this is accomplished by implementing the entire `javax.media.Player` interface and registering your new `Player` with the JMF. While this may sound simple, we will soon see that it can be a time-consuming and difficult task at best. To assist you in this endeavor, we will implement here as much of the `Player` interface as possible, leaving you with only the most media-specific functionality to implement.

Player Methods

As you may imagine, the biggest step towards supporting a new media format is to implement the 32 not-so-trivial JMF `Clock`, `Duration`, `Controller`, `MediaHandler`, and `Player` methods that make up the `javax.media.Player` interface. Table 12.1 shows these methods.

Table 12.1 *Java Media Interface API Methods*

Clock
setTimeBase
getTimeBase
getRate
setRate
setMediaTime
getMediaTime
getMediaNanoseconds
mapToTimeBase
syncStart
stop
getSyncTime
setStopTime
getStopTime

Duration

```
getDuration
```

Controller

```
getState
getTargetState
addControllerListener
removeControllerListener
getControls
getControl
realize
prefetch
deallocate
close
getStartLatency
```

MediaHandler

```
setSource
```

Player

```
getVisualComponent
getGainControl
getControlPanelComponent
start
addController
removeController
```

When implementing these methods, it is important to stay within the guidelines of the JMF API. The API not only dictates what methods need to be implemented, but when and in what fashion they should execute. There are several caveats and fine points of implementation that need to be observed. If you do not follow each and every requirement when developing your `Player`, you will subject it to non conformance with the API and will have created a `Player` that may not work seamlessly with the JMF.

Why Interfaces?

When Sun and its partners designed the JMF, they were more interested in designing an API than an easily-extended `Player` framework. That is why virtually every piece of the `Player` architecture is an interface as opposed to a Java class. As we will see throughout this section, some of the numerous methods required by the `Player` interface could have been implemented in a generic fashion and included with the JMF. Sun's design could have included an abstract implementation of a `javax.media.Player` and left only the media-specific details to the average developer. Instead they chose to leave all details to the `Player` implementor, forcing Sun, Intel, and any other `Player` designers to worry about API compliance.

This philosophy has led to several inconsistencies between implementations of the JMF. In places where the API is vague, Sun and Intel have been forced to improvise, often resulting in differing functionality. And for individuals without a staff of highly-paid Java developers at their disposal, extending the JMF can be a difficult task at best. Neither Sun's nor Intel's abstract `Player` implementation is part of the public API, so Joe Developer is forced to start from scratch, just like Sun and Intel.

A Solution

In the first few chapters of Part II, we will develop an abstract implementation of the `javax.media.Player` interface, so that Joe and other aspiring multimedia developers can easily extend the JMF. We will discuss the fine points of the API, and point out and resolve any obscurity that we encounter. In places where Sun's and Intel's interpretation of the API differ, we will discuss what each has done and determine the best interpretation for our own implementation.

In developing this `Player` implementation, we will see that multiple classes are needed to offer complete JMF support. These classes, together with our abstract `Player` implementation, will constitute an *Abstract Player Framework* (APF) that will allow for easy extension of the JMF. To be sure, this section is not intended for the casual developer, and could be interpreted as a "Porter's Guide to the JMF." Readers who are interested only in quickly creating a custom `Player` may skip to Chapter 18, "Creating a Custom Player"—there we will put into use the framework that is developed here.

Framework Structure

Recall the JMF `Player` class diagram on page 40 in . Figure 12.1 reproduces that diagram without the `DataSource` and `TimeBase` member data.

Figure 12.1 *The JMF Player Class Diagram (partial)*

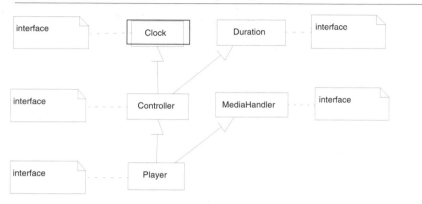

Since the ultimate goal is to provide an abstract `Player` implementation, we could, if we were so inclined, implement all five interfaces in one large class. However, for the purpose of maintainable code, as well as to allow for future extensibility, it makes sense to split up the implementation into functional groupings.

A large division of functionality exists between a `Controller` and a `Player`. While a `Controller` is only responsible for the management of one medium, a `Player` must be able to manage any number of `Controllers`. Much of the functionality that is easily implemented for a single `Controller` requires careful consideration when implementing for several managed `Controllers` and the `Player` itself.

A further division of functionality exists between a `Controller` and a `Clock`. A `Clock` has only two possible states: `Started` and `Stopped`. A `Controller`, on the other hand, divides the `Stopped` state into five more precise states: `Unrealized`, `Realizing`, `Realized`, `Prefetching`, and `Prefetched`. With these additional states come tighter restrictions on some of the `Clock` methods. Whereas the `Clock` interface, for example, may require the `Clock` to be in the `Stopped` state to execute a particular method without error, the `Controller` interface may further require that the `Controller` be in the `Realized` state.

For these reasons the `Clock` interface will be implemented in an `AbstractClock` class, and the `Controller` and `Duration` interfaces in an `AbstractController` class. The remaining interfaces, `MediaHandler` and `Player`, will be implemented in an `AbstractPlayer` class. Mirroring the JMF `Player` interface hierarchy, the `AbstractPlayer` class will extend from the `AbstractController` class, which, in turn, will extend from the `AbstractClock` class.

You may wonder why these classes are `abstract`. Obviously not all functionality can be implemented for every `Clock`, `Controller`, or `Player`. The portions of the class that render the media, or report on some aspect of the media that cannot be known beforehand, must be implemented by their subclasses. In general, the `AbstractClock`, `AbstractController`, and `AbstractPlayer` classes will implement as much of the `Clock`, `Controller`, and `Player` functionality as can be done without knowing about the details of a given media format. Subclasses of these classes will need to implement the rest.

The resulting class diagram appears in Figure 12.2.

Figure 12.2 *Abstract Player Framework and JMF Player Architecture*

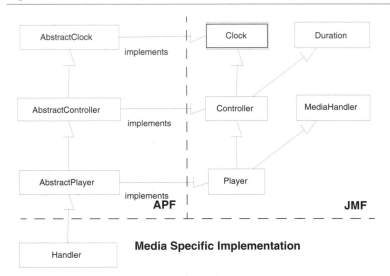

In developing the `abstract` classes, we will find the need to develop several helper classes as well. These classes may provide, for example, multithreaded support, support for event handling, or new `Controls` or `Media-Events`. Together with the `abstract` classes, these classes will comprise an APF that will provide for easy creation of a JMF `Player`. All classes derived in the next few chapters can be found in the `ejmf.toolkit.media` package that comes with the *Essential JMF* Toolkit.

Requirements for JMF API Compliance

At first glance it may appear that implementing a few methods to satisfy the `javax.media.Player` interface isn't all that difficult. But consider some of the requirements necessary for API compliance. All `Players`, if they are to comply with the JMF API, must contain the following functionality:

Maintaining a State Machine

A `Player`'s state must reflect the level of "readiness to play" as it progresses towards playing its media. It must keep track of what state it is currently in and what state (if any) it is trying to reach. Using the terminology introduced in Chapter 6, "The Controller," when a forward transition method is called, a `Player` must set its current state to a *transient* state and its target state to a *static* state. When a backward–transitioning method is called, the `Player` must set only its target state to a *static* state. When the forward or backward transition has completed, the `Player` must set its current state to its target state.

Checking State Requirements

As we saw in Table 6.3 on page 95, many methods require the executing `Clock/Controller/Player` to be in a particular state before the method can be executed. The `syncStart` method, for example, requires that the `Controller` be at least `Realized` but not `Started`.

Error Notification

When an error condition occurs through incorrect usage of the JMF API, as when a `Controller` method's state requirements are   not met (above), a `MediaError` should be thrown. A `MediaError` should reliably identify the situation in which the error has occurred.

Posting ControllerEvents

In Chapter 6 we learned that a `Controller` must dispatch a `Controller-Event` whenever its status changes in a significant way. As a `Controller`, a `Player` must notify all of its `ControllerListeners` of changes in its status.

Managing Media Time

As an extension of `javax.media.Clock`, a `Player` must reliably support the timing functionality needed to track media and time-base time. The `Player` must be able to play the media at an arbitrary time (within the media's duration), and return the current media time when requested. Support for automatically stopping or starting the media at a particular time must be included, and a `Player` must be able to report these values when requested. Finally, a `Player` must support a default `TimeBase`.

Asynchronous Execution of Forward Transitions

The API requires that the forward-transitioning methods realize, prefetch, syncStart and start be asynchronous. Care should be taken to coordinate and handle multiple, possibly simultaneous, invocations of these methods. Similarly, the backward-transitioning methods stop and deallocate should be synchronous, and should be able to stop the progression of the asynchronous forward–transitioning methods. In a multi-threaded environment, there are any number of issues that must be considered when implementing this functionality. Race conditions and thread collisions should be feverishly avoided. Above all, the Player must be kept in a known state at all times.

Managing "Slave" Controllers

When implementing a Player, multiple-Controller management is required by the API. This means that a Player must support the addition and removal of managed Controllers. All transitions, rate changes, and Clock routines called on the Player must be propagated on to each of the Player's managed Controllers. Each Controller must be kept in the same state as the managing Player, and a precise synchronization of the Controllers with each other and with the managing Player must occur when the Player is started. Finally, all ControllerEvents posted by the managed Controllers must be "funneled" through the Player, resulting in a single ControllerEvent posted by the Player.

Implementing all of this functionality reliably can certainly be a foreboding task![1] At best it is a hindrance to creating a custom Player. At worst, it is an invitation to cut corners and create a non-compliant Player, since even the most basic of Players cannot be considered API-compliant without several hundred lines of code and multiple threads of execution.

The purpose of the APF is to take as much of this burden as possible off the shoulders of the Player implementor. The framework that we develop here will separate all of the aforementioned overhead of API-compliance from the media-specific details of the Player, so that a Player implementor can make quick work of developing a fully-compliant JMF Player.

---

1. ...But we did it anyway.

A Framework Model

How is this done? Within the APF you will see several *action/doAction* pairs, where *action* is a JMF method required (often indirectly) by the javax.media.Player interface, and *doAction* is an abstract method defined by our APF. Generally these methods will have the same Java signature and will have an identical API description. The difference will be that as much of the API compliance functionality mentioned above will be implemented in the *action* method of the APF, leaving the implementor of the abstract *doAction* to concern himself only with the media-specific functionality.

This model allows for an easy separation of abstract and concrete functionality. Figure 12.3 shows this relationship.

Figure 12.3 *Relationship Between APF Method and JMF Method*

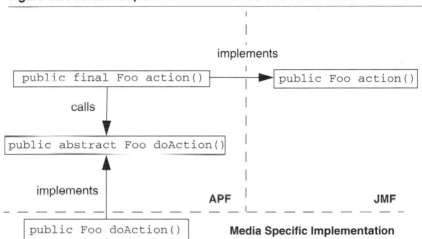

For a given *action* method defined by the JMF API, The APF implements *action*, possibly as a final method. The APF also defines the abstract method *doAction*, which is called by the *action* implementation. Finally, an implementation of the APF implements the *doAction* method to provide media-specific functionality.

Implementing the Model

How are the *action/doAction* methods linked? The following example shows a typical implementation. From AbstractPlayer.java:

```
public class AbstractPlayer {
    ...
    public void action(int blah, Foo fooObject) {
        if(state == Started) {
            throw new ClockStartedError(
                "Cannot do action() on a Started Clock");
        }
        doAction(blah, fooObject);
        postEvent(new FooEvent(this));
    }

    public abstract void doAction(int blah, Foo fooObject);
    ...
}
```

(1)

(2)
(3)

(4)

From `MyPlayer.java`:

```
public MyPlayer extends AbstractPlayer {
    ...
    public void doAction(int blah, Foo fooObject) {
        //  Do some media-specific functionality
        ...
    }
    ...
}
```

(5)

As you can see, the *action* method, representing a method from a JMF interface, is implemented in the APF. Within this method, the APF implements as much API-compliant behavior as possible (lines [1] and [3]), and calls *doAction* [2], an `abstract` method defined in line [4]. This method is later implemented [5] by a subclass to provide media-specific functionality.

If you consider Figure 12.3 in conjunction with Figure 12.2, the relationship between a method defined by the JMF API and an implementation of a `Player` using the APF is quite easy to see. Consider the `prefetch` method defined by the `Controller` API. The APF's `AbstractController` implements `Controller` and defines a `prefetch` method. In addition, it declares an `abstract` method `doPrefetch`. Any media-specific implementation of a `Controller` would then extend `AbstractController` and implement a `doPrefetch` method.

That is the structure of the relationship between the JMF and the APF but there are also some guidelines regarding the semantics of the *doAction* methods. Let's turn our attention to those now.

Model Assumptions

It is worthwhile to point out here that an implementation of the `abstract` *doAction* method can make a few assumptions when it is executed. Based on the above section on API compliance, some of these assumptions are as follows:

1. The APF will correctly set the current and target states. If there is a state change that occurs as a result of *doAction*, then implementations can rely on *action* to set the correct states.

   Corollary: Implementations should not set the `Controller`'s current or target states within the *doAction* method.

2. The `Controller` is in a legal state for this particular *action* operation. If the `Controller` were not in the correct state, then the APF would have posted a `MediaError` and the *doAction* method would not have been called.

   Corollary: Implementations do not need to check the `Controller` to ensure the correct state.

3. If the *action* operation requires that a *transition* or *change* `ControllerEvent` be posted, then the APF will post it when the *doAction* method returns. Since close events generally are posted when there is a catastrophic error with the `Controller`, their occurrence is unpredictable and therefore any code that posts them must be part of the media-specific implementation.

   Corollary: Implementations should not post any *transition* or *change* `ControllerEvents`. If there is a catastrophic error within the *doAction* method, then implementations should post a *close* `ControllerEvent` and return.

4. If the *action* operation affects the media time of the `Clock`, then the APF will make the appropriate adjustments.

   Corollary: Implementations do not need to explicitly start or stop the `Clock`. It will be started and stopped automatically.

5. If the *action* operation is required to be asynchronous, then the APF will invoke *doAction* on a separate thread.

   Corollary: Implementations do not need to execute this operation asynchronously.

6. No work is needed to perform the *action* operation on any managed `Controllers`. The APF is responsible for keeping all of the `Controllers` synchronized.

   Corollary: Implementations should not attempt to directly invoke an *action* operation on any managed `Controller`.

   In the next few chapters we will become better acquainted with this model as we put it into practice in developing our APF.

Summary

This chapter has considered some of the extensive requirements for implementing a custom `javax.media.Player`. Although the JMF provides an API for media players, it does not provide a public abstract implementation allowing for easy extension.

To solve this problem, we have taken it upon ourselves to design and implement an APF. This framework will implement as much API-compliant functionality as possible, allowing users of the framework to create a custom `Player` quickly and easily. To facilitate its use, the *action/doAction* model has been devised to allow for convenient integration into the APF.

In the next chapter we will begin our `AbstractClock` implementation by looking at the `javax.media.Clock` routines. Subsequent chapters will explore the details of implementing the single-media support of a `Controller`, and then later on, the multiple-`Controller` support of a `Player`. When we have completed the development of our APF, we will put it into practice by creating two fully-functional custom Players: one for a known format, and another for our own home-grown format.

Chapter 13   *IMPLEMENTING THE CLOCK INTERFACE*

Introduction

Since the `Clock` is at the root of the `Player` interface hierarchy, it makes sense to begin the development of our framework by implementing the `javax.media.Clock` methods in the `AbstractClock` class. These methods are implemented here purely to satisfy the requirements of the `javax.media.Clock` API. Later development of the `AbstractController` class will augment many of these methods in the context of implementing the `javax.media.Controller` interface.

Table 13.1 summarizes the methods defined by the `javax.media.Clock` API.

Table 13.1 *javax.media.Clock Methods*

Name	Description
setTimeBase	Set the TimeBase
getTimeBase	Get the TimeBase
setRate	Set the rate
getRate	Get the rate
setMediaTime	Set the media time
getMediaTime	Get the media time
getMediaNanoseconds	Get the media time in nanoseconds
mapToTimeBase	Map a media time to a time-base time
syncStart	Start the Clock
stop	Stop the Clock
getSyncTime	Get the time until the media time is synchronized with its time-base time
setStopTime	Set the stop time
getStopTime	Get the stop time

Subsequent sections of this chapter will look at each of these methods in detail. All code listings shown are reproduced from the `AbstractClock` class, the source for which is located in `$EJMF_HOME/src/ejmf/toolkit/media/AbstractClock.java`.

Selecting a TimeBase

The first methods to look at are the `TimeBase` methods. A listing of `setTimeBase` and `getTimeBase` appears in Listing 13.1.

Listing 13.1 *TimeBase Methods*

```
(1)  private TimeBase systemtimebase =
                       Manager.getSystemTimeBase();
(2)  private TimeBase timebase      = systemtimebase;

     public synchronized void setTimeBase(TimeBase timebase)
(3)            throws IncompatibleTimeBaseException {
         if (isStarted) {
(4)          throw new ClockStartedError(
                 "Cannot set time base on a Started Clock");
         }
         if (timebase == null) {
(5)          this.timebase = systemtimebase;
         } else {
(6)          this.timebase = timebase;
         }
     }
     public synchronized TimeBase getTimeBase() {
(7)      return timebase;
     }
```

From Chapter 5, "The Clock," you know that a TimeBase object is used to maintain the "real time" of a javax.media.Clock. A reference to this object is maintained within the AbstractClock [2], along with a default TimeBase [1]. In this case the default will be the system TimeBase, provided by the static method Manager.getSystemTimeBase.

The javax.media.Clock API requires that the Clock not be started when its TimeBase is set within the setTimeBase method. The reason for this is obvious: if the TimeBase were to change on a started Clock, then the Clock would have no way of determining the current media time. If this condition is not met a ClockStartedError is thrown [4].

Line [5] implements a feature of setTimeBase required by the API: when null is used as the TimeBase argument, the Clock's TimeBase is set to its default value. Otherwise, the AbstractClock's TimeBase is set to the given TimeBase argument [6].

Notice that there are no criteria for acceptance of the TimeBase, so an IncompatibleTimeBaseException [3] is never thrown. Subclasses may override the setTimeBase method to refine the acceptance criteria for a new TimeBase.

The getTimeBase method returns the TimeBase being used by the Clock [7]. Unlike setTimeBase, there are no state restrictions on the invocation of this method.

Clock Rate

Setting and getting the Clock's rate resembles the corresponding operations for the Clock's TimeBase. Listing 13.2 shows the implementations of the javax.media.Clock methods setRate and getRate.

Listing 13.2 *Rate Methods*

```
public synchronized float setRate(float rate) {
    if (isStarted) {
(8)         throw new ClockStartedError(
            "Cannot set rate on a Started Clock");
    }
(9)     if (rate != 0.0F) {
(10)        this.rate = rate;
    }
(11)    return this.rate;
}
public synchronized float getRate() {
(12)    return rate;
}
```

The setRate method holds few surprises. Line [8], as dictated by the javax.media.Clock API, imposes the same state requirement on setRate as is imposed on setTimeBase: if the Clock is started, a ClockStarted-Error is thrown. To set a Clock's rate, the Clock must be stopped. As we will see shortly, this requirement facilitates the calculation of the Abstract-Clock's media time.

Line [9] enforces the sole acceptance criterion of the rate property: it must be non-zero. Besides the obvious need for this requirement, it is also necessary to avoid "divide-by-zero" errors in the Clock calculations. We will see in the next chapter how we can augment this criterion.

If the rate is non-zero, the AbstractClock's rate property is set to the new rate [10]. Otherwise, no change is made. In either case, in accordance with the javax.media.Clock API, the actual rate set is returned in line [11].

getRate shows to be even more simple, returning the AbstractClock's rate property [12].

Media Time

The TimeBase and rate methods are about the most easily implemented that we will encounter in the Clock interface. Setting the media time is similar. However, unlike the rate and TimeBase, there is some additional overhead surrounding getting the media time. This is because the media time of a Clock is constantly changing when the Clock is started.

We will first look at how the media time is set.

Setting The Media Time

Listing 13.3 shows the AbstractClock's implementation of the setMedia-Time routine.

Listing 13.3 *Setting the Media Time*

```
public synchronized void setMediaTime(Time t) {
    if (isStarted) {
        throw new ClockStartedError(
            "Cannot set media time on a Started Clock");
    }
    mediaStartTime = t;
}
```

(13)

(14)

The implementation of setMediaTime is quite similar to that of setRate. Line [13] enforces the same Clock state requirement that we saw in the setRate implementation, throwing a ClockStartedError if the Clock is started. As with setRate, the reason for this requirement is to facilitate calculation of the media time within the getMediaTime method.

After this state requirement is enforced, the media time property is set to the given Time argument [14]. Note that it is assigned to a variable called mediaStartTime. This makes sense because the Clock is guaranteed to be stopped, forcing any changes in the media time to actually affect the point in the media where the Clock will be started.

Getting The Media Time

The *Java Media Framework* does not require that a Clock implementation actually "tick-off" each passing (nano-) second, but it does require it to implement the getMediaTime routine so that the current media time can always be calculated.

Before we look at the implementation of this method, a discussion of the time-tracking algorithm is in order. Recall the definitions of the time-related terms introduced in Chapter 5.

Media Time The point in the media that is currently playing (if the Clock is started), or the point it is scheduled to begin playing (if the Clock is stopped).

Time-Base Time The monotonically-increasing "real" time, independent of the media.

Media Start Time The media time when the Clock is started.

Time-Base Start Time The time-base time when the Clock is started.

In the simplest case of computing the current media time (M_c), it is simply the amount of time that has passed since the clock was started, i.e. the current time-base time (T_c) minus the time-base start time (T_s).

$$M_c = (T_c - T_s) \qquad \text{(EQ 7)}$$

(EQ 7) is depicted by Figure 13.1

Figure 13.1 *Simple Calculation of Media Time*

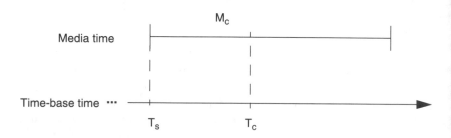

If the rate at which the media is playing is not 1.0, then (EQ 7) must be adjusted to accommodate a non-unity rate, resulting in (EQ 8).

$$M_c = (T_c - T_s) * rate \qquad \text{(EQ 8)}$$

Figure 13.2 shows the relationship between media time and time-base time when rate is taken into account.

Figure 13.2 *Calculation of Media Time Accounting for Rate*

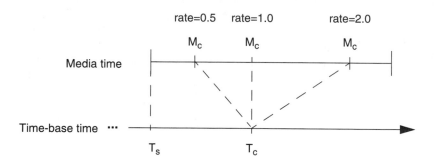

Depending on the rate, then, the elapsed media time could be more or less than the elapsed time-based time. Only if the clock's rate is 1.0 are these values equal.

One more variable comes into play when calculating the current media time. If the clock did not start the media from the beginning, then the initial media start time (M_s) must be added as an offset, resulting in (EQ 9).

$$M_c = (T_c - T_s) * rate + M_s \qquad \textbf{(EQ 9)}$$

Figure 13.3 illustrates the effect of a media start time that is not at the beginning of the media.

Figure 13.3 *Calculation of Media Time Accounting for Rate and Initial Offset*

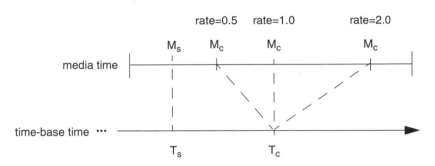

This suggests a fairly straightforward algorithm to calculate the current media time: When the Clock is started, save the time-base and media start times, and then later on use these values, plus the current rate and the current time-base time, to calculate the media time.

But what happens if the media time or rate is changed while the Clock is started? Then our equation will give us erroneous results. For this reason the Clock API requires that the Clock be stopped when either the rate or media time is set.

Listing 13.4 shows the private method calculateMediaTime that calculates the current media time for a started Clock, based on (EQ 9). This method is not part of the JMF API, but will be called by getMediaTime in the *Abstract Player Framework*.

Listing 13.4 *Media Time Calculation for a Started Clock*

```
       private synchronized Time calculateMediaTime() {
(15)       long tbCurrent = timebase.getNanoseconds();
(16)       long tbStart = timeBaseStartTime.getNanoseconds();

(17)       if(tbCurrent < tbStart) {
(18)           return mediaStartTime;
           }
(19)       long mStart = mediaStartTime.getNanoseconds();
(20)       long mCurrent = (long)((tbCurrent - tbStart) *
                                         rate + mStart);
(21)       return new Time(mCurrent);
       }
```

As you can see, this method follows equation (EQ 9) precisely. Lines [15] and [16] convert the current and starting time-base times into nanoseconds. If the current time is less than the starting time [17], then we can assume that the Clock has been scheduled to start with the syncStart method but has not actually started yet. In this situation, in accordance with the Clock API, the media start-time is returned immediately [18]. Otherwise, the current media time must be calculated. Line [19] converts the media start time into nanoseconds. The current media time is then calculated [20] and returned as a Time object [21].

With the calculateMediaTime method defined, getMediaTime becomes a simple matter to implement:

Listing 13.5 *Getting the Media Time*

```
public synchronized Time getMediaTime() {
    if (!isStarted) {
        return mediaStartTime;
    } else {
        return calculateMediaTime();
    }
}
public long getMediaNanoseconds() {
    return getMediaTime().getNanoseconds();
}
```

(22) appears beside `return mediaStartTime;`
(23) appears beside `return calculateMediaTime();`
(24) appears beside `public long getMediaNanoseconds() {`

If the Clock is stopped, then the media time is simply the media start time and this value is returned [22]. Otherwise, calculateMediaTime is called at [23] to calculate the media time on the started Clock.

Line [24] implements the convenience method getMediaNanoseconds to provide the current media time in nanoseconds instead of as a Time object.

Overriding getMediaTime

(EQ 9) may seem like a roundabout way to calculate something that may be known inherently just by looking at the time encoding in the media data itself. You may wonder why you can't just override getMediaTime and query the media itself for the correct media time. While this may be tempting and seem logical, consider some of the problems with this approach:

- If the media has stalled or cannot be rendered as fast as it should, then N seconds in the started state will result in less than N seconds of media being played. Thus getMediaTime would report a value smaller than the actual media time.

- If getMediaTime is overridden in each Controller being managed by a Player, then each Controller could report a different media time due to discrepancies in the time-encoding of each Controller's media.

- Other Clock routines within our framework that rely on a consistent implementation of getMediaTime could be compromised.

Besides each of these reasons, it's just easier to let the APF handle all aspects of timing.

Mapping Media Time to TimeBase Time

We have seen how the calculateMediaTime method essentially converts a time-base time (the current time) into a media time using (EQ 9). The javax.media.Clock interface defines the mapToTimeBase method to reverse this process, allowing the user to determine the time-base time at which a particular media time will occur.

By solving (EQ 9) for the current time-base time T_c, we can determine the time-base time that corresponds to a particular media time:

$$T_c = (M_c - M_s) / rate + T_s \qquad \text{(EQ 10)}$$

This is the equation used by the mapToTimeBase method. Listing 13.6 shows the complete implementation of mapToTimeBase.

Listing 13.6 *Mapping a Media Time to TimeBase Time*

```
public synchronized Time mapToTimeBase(Time t)
                   throws ClockStoppedException {
    if(!isStarted) {
        throw new ClockStoppedException(
            "Cannot map media time on a stopped Clock");
    }
    long mCurrent = t.getNanoseconds();
    long mStart = mediaStartTime.getNanoseconds();
    long tbStart = timeBaseStartTime.getNanoseconds();
    long tbCurrent =
            (long) (((mCurrent - mStart)/rate) + tbStart));
    return new Time(tbCurrent);
}
```

(25)

(26)

If the Clock is stopped, then there is no way to project when a particular point in the media time will pass. For this reason the Clock must be started when this method is invoked. If it is not, a `ClockStoppedException` is thrown [25]. After converting all times to nanoseconds, line [26] calculates the return value using equation (EQ 10).

Starting and Stopping the Clock

Starting the `Clock` is as easy as calling `syncStart(startTime)`, where `startTime` is the time-base time at which the `Clock` is to start. Stopping the clock is accomplished with the `stop` routine. Listing 13.7 shows the `AbstractClock`'s implementation of the `syncStart` and `stop` routines:

Listing 13.7 *Starting and Stopping the Clock*

```
public synchronized void syncStart(Time t) {
    if(isStarted)
(27)        throw new ClockStartedError(
            "Cannot call syncStart() on a started Clock");
(28)    isStarted = true;
    long now = getTimeBase().getNanoseconds();
    long start = t.getNanoseconds();
    if (start - now > 0) {
(29)        this.timeBaseStartTime = new Time(start);
    } else
(30)        this.timeBaseStartTime = new Time(now);
}
public synchronized void stop() {
(31)    if (isStarted) {
(32)        mediaStartTime = calculateMediaTime();
(33)        isStarted = false;
    }
}
```

Recall that the `javax.media.Clock` interface does not define a clock in the traditional sense. The `Clock` does not continuously "tick," as does a wall clock or wrist watch or even the system time-base. What it does is record a time-base start-time, and then, when requested, calculates the current media time based on the `Clock`'s `TimeBase`.

Line [27] enforces the requirement that the `Clock` be stopped for the `syncStart` method to execute. Line [28] effectively starts the `Clock`, setting the `isStarted` variable to true. Lines [29] and [30] set the time-base start-time based on the `Time` argument passed to `syncStart`. If the `Time` argument is in the future, then the time-base start-time is set to this value [29]. If, however, the `Time` value has already passed, then the time-base start-time is set to the current time [30].

Stopping the `Clock` is a trivial operation. The `javax.media.Clock` API dictates that any calls to the `stop` method on a stopped `Clock` be ignored [31]. If the `Clock` is in fact started, then the media start-time is set to the current media time [32] and the `Clock` is stopped [33]. The current media time, as we have seen before, is calculated in the `calculateMediaTime` method.

Time-Base Synchronization Time

The `javax.media.Clock` interface provides a method to determine the amount of time remaining until the `Clock` synchronizes to its `TimeBase`. If the `Clock` is started, the `getSyncTime` method returns the time remaining until the time-base start-time is reached. If the time-base start time has already been reached, or if the `Clock` is not started, `getSyncTime` returns the `Clock`'s media time.

Listing 13.8 shows the `AbstractClock`'s implementation of `getSync-Time`.

Listing 13.8 *Getting the Time-Base Synchronization Time*

```
public synchronized Time getSyncTime() {
    long startNano;
    long nowNano;
    if(isStarted) {
        startNano = timeBaseStartTime.getNanoseconds();
        nowNano = getTimeBase().getNanoseconds();
        if (startNano >= nowNano) {
            return new Time((long)(nowNano - startNano));
        }
    }
    return getMediaTime();
}
```

(34) is at `if(isStarted) {`
(35) is at `if (startNano >= nowNano) {`
(36) is at `return new Time((long)(nowNano - startNano));`
(37) is at `return getMediaTime();`

Line [34] checks to see if the `Clock` is started. If it is, the current time-base time is compared to the time-base start-time. If time-base start-time has not yet been reached [35], then time remaining is returned [36]. Otherwise, the current media time is returned [37].

It is important to note that `getSyncTime` returns a *negative* countdown until the time-base start-time. This is so that there will be no ambiguity from the return value. If `getSyncTime` returns a negative time, then the `Clock` is started but the time-base start-time has not been reached. If the return value is positive, then the `Clock` is stopped or the time-base start-time has already passed.

Interpretation of getSyncTime API

Unfortunately the `getSyncTime` specification in the JMF API is somewhat vague and subject to various interpretations. As of JMF 1.0, the Sun implementation consistently returns `Time(0)` as the `Clock`'s sync time. The Intel implementation, on the other hand, returns a `Time` value equal to the difference of the return of `getMediaTime` and a countdown value. Currently both

Sun and Intel have open bugs regarding their respective implementations of getSyncTime.

While getSyncTime is not a widely-used method in the Clock interface, it is important nevertheless to justify our own interpretation of the API. The following description of getSyncTime is excerpted from the API.

> *Get the current media time or the time until this Clock will synchronize to its TimeBase. The getSyncTime method is used by Players and advanced applet writers to synchronize Clocks.*
>
> *Like getMediaTime, this method returns the Clock's current media time, which is based on its TimeBase and rate. However, when syncStart is used to start the Clock, getSyncTime performs a countdown to the time-base start-time, returning the time remaining until the time-base start-time. Once the TimeBase reaches the time-base start-time, getSyncTime and getMediaTime will return the same value.*

The AbstractClock implementation follows this definition precisely. If the time-base start-time has been reached, getSyncTime returns the current media time. If the Clock is started but the time-base start-time has not yet been reached, then a "countdown" to the start-time is returned. The only point of contention is whether this "countdown" is to be negative or positive. Since getSyncTime returns positive Time values when it returns the current media time, making this "countdown" negative eliminates ambiguity about the return value.

Stop Time

The final pieces of the javax.media.Clock interface left to implement are the setStopTime and getStopTime methods. As we learned in Chapter 5, a stop time may be specified so that a Clock will stop automatically at a particular point in the media.

As we will see, setting the stop time of a Clock is much easier than reliably stopping the Clock at that time. For this reason, here we will focus only on setting and getting the stop time. In the next chapter, when we look at the javax.media.Controller interface, we will implement a way to enforce the stop time, stopping the Controller at the desired time.

Listing 13.9 shows the AbstractClock's implementation of the setStopTime methods.

Listing 13.9 *Stop Time Methods*

```
(38)    private Time mediaStopTime = Clock.RESET;
        public synchronized void setStopTime(Time mediaStopTime) {
            if( isStarted && this.mediaStopTime != RESET ) {
(39)            throw new StopTimeSetError(
                    "Stop time already set on Started Clock");
            }
(40)        this.mediaStopTime = mediaStopTime;
        }

        public Time getStopTime() {
(41)        return mediaStopTime;
        }
```

The `javax.media.Clock` API states that resetting the stop time of a `Clock` can be done by calling `setStopTime` with the `static final` `Clock.RESET` variable. This value is used to initialize the `AbstractClock`'s `mediaStopTime` variable [38].

The API also states that the stop time may only be set once on a started `Clock`. This requirement, according to the API, exists because it would be impossible to guarantee when the `Clock` would stop if a new stop time were set while the `Clock` was already approaching a previously-set stop time. In accordance with this rule, if the `Clock` is started and the stop time is already set, a `StopTimeSetError` is thrown [39]. Otherwise, the given stop time is committed [40] and the method returns.

The implementation of the `getStopTime` method is unremarkable. As there are no state requirements for this method, it simply returns the current value of the media stop time [41].

Summary

In this chapter we began the development of the APF. At the root of this framework is the `AbstractClock` class, which provides a media-independent implementation of the `javax.media.Clock` interface. This class contains methods for `TimeBase`, rate, and media time manipulation, as well as methods to stop and start the `Clock`. We derived the equation to use when calculating the media time, and implemented several `Clock` methods that use it.

In the next section we will extend the functionality of the `AbstractClock` class with the `AbstractController` class. This class will use all the methods developed here, and will implement most of the `javax.media.Controller` interface.

Chapter 14

IMPLEMENTING THE CONTROLLER INTERFACE

Introduction

Continuing with the development of the *Abstract Player Framework* (APF), we now turn to implement the `javax.media.Controller` interface. Where a `Clock` is only concerned with the management of a two-state machine, a `Controller` must manage six separate states and provide the ability to smoothly transition forward and backward through these states. The `Controller` must maintain a list of `ControllerListeners` so that all interested parties may be notified of any change in the `Controller`'s status. It may also provide a mechanism for allowing a finer level of external control over some aspect of its operation.

To this end we will develop an `AbstractController` class that will implement the `javax.media.Controller` interface. To satisfy the `javax.media.Clock` functionality required by the `Controller` interface the `AbstractController` will extend from the `AbstractClock` class, developed in the last chapter. Many of the methods developed there will be extended here to accommodate a multi-state machine.

A table of the `javax.media.Controller` methods follows.

Table 14.1 *javax.media.Controller Methods*

Method	Description
getState	Gets the current state of the Controller
getTargetState	Gets the target state of the Controller
getStartLatency	Gets the start latency of the Controller
addControllerListener	Adds a ControllerListener to listen for ControllerEvents from this Controller
removeControllerListener	Removes a ControllerListener from this Controller
realize	Realizes the Controller
prefetch	Prefetches the Controller
deallocate	Deallocates the Controller
close	Closes the Controller
getControls	Gets the supported Controls for this Controller
getControl	Gets a specific Control for this Controller

This chapter will focus on the parts of the `javax.media.Controller` interface that do not play an explicit role in transitioning the `Controller` between states. The state-transition methods (`realize`, `prefetch`, `syncStart`, `stop`, and `deallocate`) will be discussed in the next chapter. Here we will concentrate on the supporting methods that will eventually make these transitions possible.

State Manipulation

At the heart of the `javax.media.Controller` is the concept of the *current*, *previous*, and *target* states. These represent where the `Controller` is, was, and is heading, respectively. When a transition method is called, it uses this information to ensure that its state requirements are met. When the transition is complete, a `TransitionEvent` containing these states is posted.

The only state methods the `javax.media.Controller` API specifies are `getState` and `getTargetState`. However, in order to provide a more robust `Controller` implementation, three more methods will be added to the `AbstractController` class. These are shown EJMF Toolkit Synopsis 14.1.

EJMF Toolkit Synopsis 14.1 *State Manipulation Methods*

Class	`cjmf.toolkit.media.AbstractController`
Method	`setState`
Visibility	`protected`
Arguments	`int`
Return	`void`
Description	Sets the current and previous states of the `Controller` using the `static final` state variables defined in the `javax.media.Controller` interface.
Method	`setTargetState`
Visibility	`protected`
Arguments	`int`
Return	`void`
Description	Sets the target state of the `Controller` using the `static final` state variables defined in the `javax.media.Controller` interface.
Method	`getPreviousState`
Visibility	`public`
Arguments	`void`
Return	`int`
Description	Gets the previous state of the `Controller` as one of the `static final` state variables defined in the `javax.media.Controller` interface.

The first two methods, `setState` and `setTargetState`, provide the ability to set the state information within the `Controller`. These methods are declared `protected` so that only subclasses and classes within the package may invoke them. Allowing only these trusted classes to call these methods helps to ensure that state information for the `AbstractController` is accurate. The third method, `getPreviousState`, provides an accessor for the `Controller`'s previous state. This method is declared `public`, much like its counterparts `getState` and `getTargetState`.

Notice that there is no `setPreviousState` method. This functionality is handled by the `setState` method as shown in Listing 14.1.

Listing 14.1 *State Manipulation Methods*

```
(1)      private int previousState;
(2)      private int currentState;
(3)      private int targetState;

         public int getPreviousState() {
             return previousState;
         }

         public int getState() {
             return currentState;
         }

         public int getTargetState() {
             return targetState;
         }

(4)      protected synchronized void setState(int state) {
             if (state == currentState)
                 return;
             previousState = currentState;
             currentState = state;
         }

(5)      protected void setTargetState(int state) {
             targetState = state;
         }
```

The implementation of each of these methods is straightforward. Lines [1]-[3] define the `private` data that will store the `Controller`'s state information. For each of these properties, a `public` accessor method has been provided. The `setState` method [4] sets the `Controller`'s current and previous states. The `setTargetState` method [5] sets the `Controller`'s target state.

We will see these methods used frequently in the coming sections.

Event Handling

The `javax.media.Controller` interface supports the JDK 1.1 event handling model. When a significant change occurs within the `Controller`, the `Controller` API requires that a `ControllerEvent` describing the change be dispatched to all `ControllerListeners`. These `ControllerListeners` are registered with the `Controller` using the `addControllerListener` method and removed using the `removeControllerListener` method.

The implementation of these methods is shown below.

Listing 14.2 *Maintaining ControllerListeners*

(6)
```
private Vector listeners = new Vector();

public void addControllerListener(
            ControllerListener listener) {
    synchronized(listeners) {
        if(! listeners.contains(listener) ) {
            listeners.addElement(listener);
        }
    }
}
public void removeControllerListener(
            ControllerListener listener) {
    synchronized(listeners) {
        listeners.removeElement(listener);
    }
}
```

(7)

(8)

The `ControllerListeners` are maintained within a `java.util.Vec-tor` object [6]. When a `ControllerListener` is added to the `Controller` [7], it is only added to the list if not previously added. When a `Controller-Listener` is removed [8], no check is needed. In both cases it is necessary to first lock the `Vector` with the `synchronized` keyword so that it cannot change while it is being modified.

Dispatching ControllerEvents

Maintaining a list of `ControllerListeners` is the easy part of event handling. Dispatching the `ControllerEvents` is slightly more involved. Following the JDK 1.1 event model, `ControllerEvents` are posted asynchronously so that the thread that posts the `ControllerEvent` can continue executing while each `ControllerListener` is notified.

The `ControllerEventQueue` class provides a mechanism to post `Con-trollerEvents` easily. As its name suggests, it serves as a "queue" to which `ControllerEvents` can be added arbitrarily. As a `java.lang.Thread`, the `ControllerEventQueue` monitors its internal queue asynchronously, dispatching `ControllerEvents` soon after they are added to the queue.

A `ControllerEventQueue` is constructed as shown in EJMF Toolkit Synopsis 14.2.

EJMF Toolkit Synopsis 14.2 *ejmf.toolkit.media.ControllerEventQueue*
Constructor

Class	`ejmf.toolkit.media.ControllerEventQueue`
Constructor	`ControllerEventQueue`
Visibility	`public`
Arguments	`java.util.Vector`
Description	Creates a `ControllerEventQueue` that will dispatch `ControllerEvents` to all `ControllerListeners` contained in the given `Vector`.

Once constructed, `ControllerEvents` can be added to the `ControllerEventQueue` using the `postEvent` method.

EJMF Toolkit Synopsis 14.3 *Posting a ControllerEvent*

Class	`ejmf.toolkit.media.ControllerEventQueue`
Method	`postEvent`
Visibility	`public`
Arguments	`javax.media.ControllerEvent`
Return	`void`
Description	Posts the given `ControllerEvent` to the `ControllerEventQueue`'s internal queue.

Listing 14.3 shows the source for the `ControllerEventQueue` class.

Listing 14.3 *ControllerEventQueue.java*

```
        public class ControllerEventQueue extends Thread {
(9)         Vector eventQueue = new Vector();
(10)        Vector listeners;
(11)        public ControllerEventQueue(Vector listeners) {
                super();
                this.listeners = listeners;
                setDaemon(true);
(12)            start();
            }

(13)        public synchronized void postEvent(
                                ControllerEvent event) {
(14)            eventQueue.addElement(event);
(15)            notify();
            }
```

```
        private void monitorEvents() {
            Vector v;
            while(true) {
                synchronized(this) {
(16)                while( eventQueue.size() == 0 ) {
                        try {
                            wait();
                        } catch(InterruptedException e) {}
                    }
(17)                v = (Vector)eventQueue.clone();
(18)                eventQueue.removeAllElements();
                }
                for (int i = 0; i < v.size(); i++) {
                    ControllerEvent event =
                        (ControllerEvent)v.elementAt(i);
(19)                dispatchEvent(event);
                }
            }
        }

        private void dispatchEvent(ControllerEvent event) {
            Vector l;
            synchronized(listeners) {
                l = (Vector)listeners.clone();
            }
            for (int i = 0; i < l.size(); i++ ) {
                Object o = l.elementAt(i);
                if( o instanceof ControllerListener ) {
                    ControllerListener listener =
                        (ControllerListener)o;
                    try {
(20)                    listener.controllerUpdate(event);
(21)                } catch(Exception e) {
                        System.err.println(
                            "Exception during event dispatching");
                        e.printStackTrace();
                    }
                }
            }
        }

        public void run() {
(22)        monitorEvents();
        }
    }
```

The first thing this class does is declare two `Vector` objects. The first, at [9], holds the `ControllerEvents` that are posted. The second, at [10], maintains a list of `ControllerListeners` to notify. The `Vector` of `Controll-`

erListeners is initially passed into the constructor at line [11]. Note that by virtue of the java.util.Vector class being mutable,[1] changes made to this Vector from outside of the ControllerEventQueue class are still reflected here.

Once the ControllerEventQueue has been constructed, the thread that monitors the event queue is started [12] and ControllerEvents can be posted using the postEvent method [13]. When this method is called, the given ControllerEvent is added to the internal queue [14] and the monitoring thread is notified [15].

When started, the monitoring thread calls the monitorEvents method [22]. This thread runs in an infinite loop, waiting until a ControllerEvent has been posted. When a ControllerEvent has been added to the queue, the monitor thread wakes up and verifies that the queue is no longer empty [16]. Still within a synchronized block, the monitor thread copies [17] and reinitializes [18] the event queue so that new ControllerEvents can be posted while the current ones are being dispatched.

After leaving the synchronized block, each ControllerEvent within the copied Vector object is dispatched with dispatchEvent [19]. This method simply calls controllerUpdate [20] on each ControllerListener in the listeners Vector. Exceptions that occur during this call are caught [21] so that no single ControllerListener can disrupt the event-handling process.

Using the ControllerEventQueue

The AbstractController class maintains a ControllerEventQueue and provides its own postEvent method to access it. EJMF Toolkit Synopsis 14.4 describes postEvent.

EJMF Toolkit Synopsis 14.4 *Posting a ControllerEvent*

Class	ejmf.toolkit.media.AbstractController
Method	postEvent
Visibility	protected
Arguments	javax.media.ControllerEvent
Return	void
Description	Calls postEvent on the AbstractController's internal ControllerEventQueue.

---

1. Not be confused with the mute button on a Player's control component.

The `AbstractController` class in turn provides several convenience methods that utilize `postEvent` to automatically create and post `ControllerEvents`. Each of these protected methods takes no arguments and uses the `AbstractController`'s properties to construct the appropriate `ControllerEvent`.

EJMF Toolkit Synopsis 14.5 describes the event–posting methods.

EJMF Toolkit Synopsis 14.5 *Event-Posting Methods*

Class	`ejmf.toolkit.media.AbstractController`
Method	`postControllerClosedEvent`
Visibility	`protected`
Arguments	`void`
Return	`void`
Description	Creates and posts a `ControllerClosedEvent`.
Method	`postTransitionEvent`
Visibility	`protected`
Arguments	`void`
Return	`void`
Description	Creates and posts a `TransitionEvent` with the `Abstract-Controller`'s previous, current, and target states. This method is indicates whether the `Controller` is realizing or prefetching.
Method	`postRealizeCompleteEvent`
Visibility	`protected`
Arguments	`void`
Return	`void`
Description	Creates and posts a `RealizeCompleteEvent` with the `AbstractController`'s previous, current, and target states.
Method	`postPrefetchCompleteEvent`
Visibility	`protected`
Arguments	`void`
Return	`void`
Description	Creates and posts a `PrefetchCompleteEvent` with the `AbstractController`'s previous, current, and target states.
Method	`postStartEvent`
Visibility	`protected`
Arguments	`void`
Return	`void`
Description	Creates and posts a `StartEvent` with the `AbstractController`'s previous, current, and target states, media start time, and time-base start time.

EJMF Toolkit Synopsis 14.5 *Event-Posting Methods*

Class	`ejmf.toolkit.media.AbstractController`
Method	`postDeallocateEvent`
Visibility	`protected`
Arguments	`void`
Return	`void`
Description	Creates and posts a `DeallocateEvent` with the `Abstract-Controller`'s previous, current, and target states, and current media time.
Method	`postStopByRequestEvent`
Visibility	`protected`
Arguments	`void`
Return	`void`
Description	Creates and posts a `StopByRequestEvent` with the `AbstractController`'s previous, current, and target states, and current media time.
Method	`postStopAtTimeEvent`
Visibility	`protected`
Arguments	`void`
Return	`void`
Description	Creates and posts a `StopAtTimeEvent` with the `Abstract-Controller`'s previous, current, and target states, and current media time.
Method	`postEndOfMediaEvent`
Visibility	`protected`
Arguments	`void`
Return	`void`
Description	Creates and posts a `EndOfMediaEvent` with the `Abstract-Controller`'s previous, current, and target states, and current media time.
Method	`postRestartingEvent`
Visibility	`protected`
Arguments	`void`
Return	`void`
Description	Creates and posts a `RestartingEvent` with the `Abstract-Controller`'s media time, previous, current, and target states.

An example of the usage of these routines comes from the realize method, discussed in the next chapter.

```
        public void realize() {
(23)        setState( Realizing );
(24)        setTargetState( Realized );
(25)        postTransitionEvent();
            //... Do the actual realizing
(26)        setState( Realized );
(27)        postRealizeCompleteEvent();
        }
```

When the realize method is called, the Controller is placed in the Realizing state by setting the current [23] and target [24] states as appropriate. Once the states are set, a TransitionEvent is created and posted within the postTransitionEvent method [25] to indicate that the Controller is realizing. This TransitionEvent is automatically populated with the correct Controller and state information. Later on, after the Controller has finished realizing, a similar process occurs to place the Controller in the Realized state. After the current state is set in [26], a RealizeCompleteEvent is created and posted [27] to indicate that the transition is complete.

In general, subclasses of the AbstractController should use these methods to ensure that the information contained in the ControllerEvent is correct.

Clock Methods

As mentioned earlier, the javax.media.Controller API places additional state requirements on some of the javax.media.Clock methods. The most common requirement is that the Controller be at least in the Realized state, since an unrealized Controller knows nothing about the timing information related to its media.

Selecting a TimeBase

The setTimeBase and getTimeBase methods are examples of this common requirement. Listing 14.4 shows the TimeBase methods as implemented in the AbstractController class.

Listing 14.4 *TimeBase Methods*

```
public synchronized void setTimeBase(TimeBase timebase)
                throws IncompatibleTimeBaseException {
    if (currentState == Unrealized ||
        currentState == Realizing) {
        throw new NotRealizedError(
        "Cannot set TimeBase on Unrealized Controller.");
    }
    super.setTimeBase(timebase);
}

public synchronized TimeBase getTimeBase() {
    if (currentState == Unrealized ||
                currentState == Realizing){
        throw new NotRealizedError(
          "Cannot get TimeBase from Unrealized Controller");
    }
    return super.getTimeBase();
}
```

Both methods enforce the requirement that the Controller be realized when the method is called. If it is not, a NotRealizedError is thrown. Otherwise, the work is delegated to the AbstractClock superclass. Note that the superclass version of setTimeBase will still throw a ClockStarted-Error if the Controller is in the Started state.

Controller Rate

Some Clock methods providing support for a Controller involve more than just enforcing a state requirement and calling the superclass method. Consider the setRate method shown in Listing 14.5.

Listing 14.5 *Rate Methods*

```
public synchronized float setRate(float newRate) {
    if( currentState == Unrealized ||
                currentState == Realizing ) {
        throw new NotRealizedError(
          "Cannot set rate on an Unrealized Controller.");
    }

    float oldRate = getRate();
    float superRate = super.setRate(newRate);
    float subRate = doSetRate(superRate);
```

(28)

(29)
(30)

```
          if( newRate != 1.0F && superRate != subRate ) {
              superRate = super.setRate(subRate);
              if( superRate != subRate ) {
(31)              return setRate(1.0F);
              }
          }
          if(newRate != oldRate) {
(32)          postEvent( new RateChangeEvent(this, newRate) );
          }
(33)      return newRate;
      }

(34)  public abstract float doSetRate(float rate);
```

The setRate method is much more complicated than its superclass equivalent. Line [28] imposes the same state requirement as we saw with setTimeBase, throwing a NotRealizedError if the Controller is not yet realized. Line [29] sets the rate in the AbstractClock superclass. As we saw in the last chapter, this method throws a ClockStartedError if the Clock is started. After some delegated functionality in lines [30]-[31], setRate checks to see if the new rate is different than the current rate, and posts a RateChangeEvent [32] if it has changed. Then, in accordance with the API, it returns the actual rate set [33], which may differ from the requested rate.

Line [30] is the first time we see the *action-doAction* delegation model introduced in "A Framework Model" on page 191. Recall that while *action* implements general API-compliant functionality, *doAction* is responsible for implementation-specific functionality. The setRate method follows this model perfectly. After checking that the Controller is in the correct state [28], it delegates the actual rate-setting functionality to doSetRate [30], defined in line [34]. Subclasses should implement this method to set and return a rate suitable for the implementation. When the doSetRate method has returned, setRate takes the responsibility of checking the need for and posting a RateChangeEvent.

Because setRate (and doSetRate) are not required to support the exact rate given, there is a possibility that the superclass setRate and the subclass doSetRate never agree on a given rate. To avoid this deadlock, a rate of 1.0, the only rate guaranteed by the JMF API to be supported, is set all around [31] if super.setRate and doSetRate do not return the same value.

Since there are no additional state requirements for the getRate method, no Controller-specific implementation of it is needed.

Media Time

Like `setRate`, the `AbstractClock` methods `setMediaTime` and `getMediaTime` must be extended to provide support for the `AbstractController`. These methods are shown in Listing 14.6.

Listing 14.6 *Setting and Getting the Media Time*

```
       public synchronized void setMediaTime(Time t) {
(35)       if (currentState == Unrealized ||
               currentState == Realizing) {
             throw new NotRealizedError(
               "Cannot set media time on Unrealized Controller");
           }
           long nano = t.getNanoseconds();
           Time duration = getDuration();
           if( duration != DURATION_UNKNOWN
               && duration != DURATION_UNBOUNDED ) {
               long limit = duration.getNanoseconds();
(36)           if ( nano > limit ) {
                   t = new Time(limit);
               }
           }
(37)       super.setMediaTime(t);
(38)       doSetMediaTime(t);
(39)       postEvent( new MediaTimeSetEvent(this, t) );
       }
(40)   public synchronized Time getMediaTime() {
           Time mediaTime = super.getMediaTime();
           Time duration = getDuration();
           if ( duration != DURATION_UNKNOWN &&
                   duration != DURATION_UNBOUNDED &&
                   mediaTime.getNanoseconds() >
                           duration.getNanoseconds()) {
(41)           return duration;
           }
           return mediaTime;
       }

(42)   public abstract void doSetMediaTime(Time t);
```

As with the other revisited `Clock` routines, the `setMediaTime` method enforces the `Realized` state requirement immediately [35]. Line [37] sets the media time in the `AbstractClock` superclass. As with `setRate`, this method will throw a `ClockStartedError` if the `Clock` is started.

Line [38] calls `doSetMediaTime` to execute the implementation–specific functionality, following the same *action-doAction* delegation model used by `setRate`. The abstract `doSetMediaTime` method, defined on line [42], should be implemented by subclasses of `AbstractController` to carry out the actual media-time change. Continuing with the model, line [39] posts a `MediaTimeSetEvent` to indicate that a new media time has been set. Note that while a `MediaTimeSetEvent` is posted whenever `setMediaTime` is called, a `RateChangeEvent` is only posted if the call to `setRate` actually *changes* the rate of the `Clock`.

Line [36] employs functionality provided by the `javax.media.Duration` interface. By virtue of the `Controller` interface extending from the `Duration` interface, the `Controller` may utilize the `getDuration` method to constrain its media time. If the media time to be set extends beyond the `Controller`'s duration, then the actual media time set is the duration itself. A check is first made to ensure that the duration is both bounded and known. While this comparison with the `Controller`'s duration is not required by the API, it provides a logical convenience to the `setMediaTime` method.

A similar comparison is done by the `getMediaTime` method defined in line [40]. If the media time returned by the superclass does not fall within the media's duration, then the duration itself is returned [41]. More on the `Controller`'s duration will be discussed later.

Stop Time

The `AbstractController` implementation of the `setStopTime` method is similar to that of the `setRate` method.

Listing 14.7 *Setting the Stop Time*

```
       public synchronized void setStopTime(Time mediaStopTime) {
(43)       if (currentState == Unrealized
               || currentState == Realizing) {
             throw new NotRealizedError(
               "Cannot set stop time on Unrealized Controller");
           }
           Time oldStopTime = getStopTime();
(44)       if ( mediaStopTime.getNanoseconds() !=
                       oldStopTime.getNanoseconds()) {
(45)           super.setStopTime(mediaStopTime);
(46)           postEvent(new StopTimeChangeEvent(this,
                                       mediaStopTime) );
           }
       }
```

After ensuring that the `AbstractController` is realized [43], the `setStopTime` method checks to see if the new stop time is different from the old [44]. If it is, the stop time is set in the `AbstractClock` superclass [45] and a `StopTimeChangeEvent` is posted [46] to indicate a change in the stop time. Note that the superclass `setStopTime` method may throw a `Stop-TimeSetError` if the `Clock` is `Started` and the stop time is already set.

As with the `getRate` method, no `Controller`-specific implementation of the `getStopTime` method is required by the `javax.media.Controller` API.

Enforcing the Stop Time

As was discussed in "Stop Time" on page 206 from Chapter 13, setting a `Clock`'s stop time is fairly simple. Enforcing the stop time, however, is slightly more complicated. To reliably stop the `Clock` at a given time, a separate thread must be created to monitor the progression of the `Clock`.

Monitoring an AbstractController

The `StopTimeMonitor` class provides a mechanism to stop an `Abstract-Controller` at a particular media time. When the stop time is set, the `Stop-TimeMonitor` will calculate how long until the stop time will occur, wait for the appropriate amount of time, and stop the `AbstractController` upon waking up. This wait period is calculated based on the `AbstractControl-ler`'s stop time, rate and media time. If any of these properties changes within the `AbstractController`, the `StopTimeMonitor` will automatically recalculate the time until the `AbstractController` should be stopped.

A `StopTimeMonitor` is constructed as shown in EJMF Toolkit Synopsis 14.6.

EJMF Toolkit Synopsis 14.6 *ejmf.toolkit.media.StopTimeMonitor Constructor*

Class	`ejmf.toolkit.media.StopTimeMonitor`
Constructor	`StopTimeMonitor`
Visibility	`public`
Arguments	`ejmf.toolkit.media.AbstractController`
Description	Creates a `StopTimeMonitor` that will monitor the given `AbstractController` and stop it at its media stop time.

Once constructed, a `StopTimeMonitor` will register with the `Abstract-Controller` as a `ControllerListener` so that it will be notified of any change in the `AbstractController` that affects the stop time. If such a change occurs, the `StopTimeMonitor` will recalculate when to stop the `AbstractController`.

Listing 14.8 shows the methods from the `StopTimeMonitor` class necessary for this process.

Listing 14.8 *Monitoring the AbstractController*

```
                   public class StopTimeMonitor extends Thread
(47)                           implements ControllerListener {

                   private AbstractController controller;
                   private boolean wokenUp;

                   public StopTimeMonitor(AbstractController controller) {
                       super();
                       this.controller = controller;
(48)                   controller.addControllerListener(this);
                       setDaemon(true);
(49)                   start();
                   }

                   public void run() {
(50)                   monitorStopTime();
                   }

(51)               public synchronized void controllerUpdate(
                                              ControllerEvent e) {
                       if( e instanceof StopTimeChangeEvent ||
                           e instanceof RateChangeEvent ||
                           e instanceof MediaTimeSetEvent ||
                           e instanceof StartEvent ||
                           (e instanceof StopEvent &&
(52)                         !(e instanceof DeallocateEvent) ) ) {

                           wokenUp = true;
(53)                       notifyAll();
                       }
                   }
                       //  ...
                   }
```

Implementing the ControllerListener interface [47], the StopTimeMonitor registers itself [48] with the AbstractController passed to its constructor. It then starts the thread responsible for calculating when to stop the AbstractController [49].

As we have seen before, the controllerUpdate method [51] is the mechanism by which ControllerListeners are notified of any significant changes in a Controller. In this case, the StopTimeMonitor is interested in StopTimeChangeEvents, RateChangeEvents, and MediaTimeSetEvents. These are the events that require a recalculation of when to stop the AbstractController. When such an event occurs, the StopTimeMonitor notifies a separate thread [53] that does this calculation.

The `controllerUpdate` method also listens for `StartEvents` and `StopEvents` so that the `StopTimeMonitor` can keep track of whether the `AbstractController` is started or stopped. The reason for this is obvious, since the `StopTimeMonitor` need only enforce the stop time on a `Started` `AbstractController`. Notice that `DeallocateEvents` are explicitly filtered out of the list of significant `ControllerEvents` [52], since it is the only `StopEvent` that does not indicate a transition out of the `Started` state.

Stopping the AbstractController

When the `StopTimeMonitor` thread is started at [49] in Listing 14.8, the `monitorStopTime` method is called [50]. Within this method the `StopTimeMonitor` enters an infinite loop, recalculating the stop time when necessary and stopping the `AbstractController` at the appropriate time. The `monitorStopTime` method is shown in Listing 14.9.

Listing 14.9 *Stopping the AbstractController*

```
          private synchronized void monitorStopTime() {
              Time stopTime;
              long waittime;
              while(true) {
(54)              while (controller.getState() != Controller.Started
(55)                  || (stopTime = controller.getStopTime())
                                                   == Clock.RESET ) {
                      try {
(56)                      wait();
                      } catch(InterruptedException e) {}
                  }
(57)              wokenUp = false;
                  try {
(58)                  waittime = getWaitTime(stopTime);
(59)              } catch(ClockStoppedException e) {
                      continue;
                  }
                  if( waittime > 0 ) {
                      try {
(60)                      wait( waittime );
                      } catch(InterruptedException e) {}
                  }
(61)              if (!wokenUp) {
(62)                  controller.stopAtTime();
(63)                  controller.setStopTime(Clock.RESET);
                  }
              }
          }
```

The first thing that the StopTimeMonitor thread does is wait until the AbstractController is started [54], and the stop time is set [55]. Until both of these conditions have occurred, the StopTimeMonitor has nothing to do and goes to sleep [56]. When it is woken up by the controllerUpdate method at [53] from page 226, it again checks to see if these conditions are met before continuing.

Once the StopTimeMonitor thread has determined that the Abstract-Controller is started and the stop time is set, it calls the getWaitTime method [58]. This method, which will be examined shortly, determines how long to sleep until the stop time occurs. If the value returned from the getWaitTime method is greater than zero, i.e. the stop time has not yet occurred, the StopTimeMonitor sleeps for the appropriate amount of time [60]. Upon waking up, the StopTimeMonitor checks the wokenUp variable [61] to see if it was woken up due to a change in the AbstractController. This variable, originally set to false at [57] before calling getWaitTime, is set to true by controllerUpdate right before it notifies the StopTime-Monitor thread of a change at [53] from page 226.

If the StopTimeMonitor thread determines that it has not been "woken up" prematurely, it then calls the AbstractController method stopAt-Time [62]. This method, as we will see in the next chapter, simply calls stop and posts a StopAtTimeEvent. At this point, in accordance with the javax.media.Clock API, the stop time is reset [63] so that subsequent re-starts of the AbstractController will not cause it to stop immediately.

After stopping the Clock and resetting the media stop time, the StopTi-meMonitor thread returns to the beginning of the loop and again waits for the AbstractController to start and the stop time to be set.

Calculating the Wait Time

The getWaitTime method referenced by the StopTimeMonitor thread determines the amount of time to sleep until the media stop time occurs. This method is shown below.

Listing 14.10 *Getting the Time Until the Media Stop Time*

```
private long getWaitTime(Time stopTime)
                    throws ClockStoppedException {
    long stop = controller.mapToTimeBase(
                    stopTime).getNanoseconds();
    long now = controller.getTimeBase().getNanoseconds();
    return (stop - now) / 1000000;
}
```

(64)
(65)
(66)

Using the mapToTimeBase method, the media stop time is transformed to a time-base time and converted into nanoseconds [64]. As we saw in the last chapter, the mapToTimeBase method will, given the current media time and rate, calculate the corresponding time-base time for a given media time. Note that this method will correctly calculate the corresponding time-base time even if the `Clock`'s rate is negative.

After the current time-base time is also converted to nanoseconds [65], the difference between the two is converted to milliseconds and returned [66]. Note that if the media stop time has already occurred, the value returned by this method will be negative, in which case the `StopTimeMonitor` will stop the `AbstractController` immediately.

If the `Clock` has stopped when `getWaitTime` is called, a `ClockStoppedException` will be thrown by the `mapToTimeBase` method [63] from page 227. Within the `monitorStopTime` method, this exception is caught at [59] from page 227 and the `StopTimeMonitor` returns to the beginning of its loop.

Note that this routine returns the number of *time-base* milliseconds remaining until the media stop time. This value is used by `wait` to sleep until the appropriate time. What this means is that the `AbstractController`'s `TimeBase` must be monotonically increasing at the same rate as the system clock for the `StopTimeMonitor` to work. Otherwise, the value returned by `getWaitTime` may not reflect the actual number of real-time milliseconds to sleep.

Whoa Nelly!

The StopTimeMonitor class will not reliably stop an AbstractController whose TimeBase does not share the same rate as the system clock. While it is unlikely that such a TimeBase will be used, the JMF API does not constrain a Clock's TimeBase in this way.

For those `Clock`s whose `TimeBase` does not conform to this restriction, it is up to the `Clock` developer to provide an alternate mechanism to stop the `Clock` at a particular time.

Duration Methods

In addition to extending the `javax.media.Clock` interface, the `javax.media.Controller` interface extends the `javax.media.Duration` interface. This interface is not large, and in fact we've already seen its only method used in the `javax.media.Clock` methods `getMediaTime` and `setMediaTime`.

Table 14.2 *javax.media.Duration Methods*

Method	Description
getDuration	Gets the duration of the media represented by this object.

In the context of a javax.media.Controller, the getDuration method simply returns a Time object representing the length of the Controller's media. If the length of the media is unknown, the static final Duration.DURATION_UNKNOWN is returned. If the media is unbounded, as in the case of push media, the static final Duration.DURATION_UNBOUNDED is returned.

Although the name might suggest otherwise, a Controller's *duration* does not indicate how long it will take the media to play. Such a value might vary with changes in the Controller's rate and media time. Instead, the getDuration routine always returns the *length* of the media, or the time it would take to play the media from start to finish at the default rate. A more accurate name for the getDuration routine might be getMediaLength.

Listing 14.11 shows the AbstractController's token implementation of the getDuration routine.

Listing 14.11 *Getting the Controller's Duration*

```
public Time getDuration() {
    return DURATION_UNKNOWN;
}
```

Since the AbstractController, by virtue of being an abstract class, does not know anything about the media it manages, it returns DURATION_UNKNOWN as the duration of the media. Media-specific subclasses of the AbstractController may wish to override this method to provide a more accurate representation of the media's duration. In Chapter 16, "Implementing the Player Interface," we will see the AbstractPlayer class do exactly this.

Control Methods

As we learned in Chapter 6, the javax.media.Controller interface provides a way to give the user a fine level of control over some aspects of the Controller's operation. Through use of the Control interface, Controller developers can provide GUI components that allow the user to interact with the Controller in a manner not otherwise provided by the JMF API. An example of such a Control is a color Control for video media, or an equalizer Control for audio media.

Controls may also be non-interactive, or read-only. A Control that constantly displays the media time, or displays the format of the media upon request, would qualify as such a Control.

Obtaining a Controller's Controls

The Controller interface provides two methods to obtain the Controls supported by the Controller. The getControls method returns all of a Controller's supported Controls, while the getControl (no "s") method allows the user to obtain a specific Control.

The AbstractController's implementation of these methods is shown below.

Listing 14.12 *Obtaining a Controller's Controls*

```
(67)    private Vector controls = new Vector();

        public Control[] getControls() {
            Control[] array;
            synchronized(controls) {
                array = new Control[ controls.size() ];
(68)            controls.copyInto(array);
            }
            return array;
        }

(69)    public Control getControl(String forName) {
            Class c;
            try {
(70)            c = Class.forName(forName);
            } catch(Exception e) {
(71)            return null;
            }
            synchronized(controls) {
                for (int i = 0, n = controls.size(); i < n; i++) {
                    Control control =
                            (Control)controls.elementAt(i);
                    if( c.isInstance(control) ) {
(72)                    return control;
                    }
                }
            }
(73)        return null;
        }
```

The AbstractController stores its list of Controls in a java.util.Vector object [67]. When the getControls method is called, this Vector is copied into an array [68] and returned.

Unlike the getControls method, the getControl method returns a specified Control. This request is made in the form of a class name [69] passed as an argument to getControl. If there is no such class, null is returned immediately [71]. Otherwise, this class name is converted into a Class object [70]. The AbstractController then iterates through its list of Controls until it finds an instance of this class. If none is found, null is returned [73].

Adding and Removing Controls

Because the controls variable is private to the AbstractController class, two methods are provided to manipulate it. The addControl and removeControl methods are described in EJMF Toolkit Synopsis 14.7.

EJMF Toolkit Synopsis 14.7 *Control List Manipulation*

Class	ejmf.toolkit.media.AbstractController
Method	addControl
Visibility	public
Arguments	javax.media.Control
Return	void
Description	Adds the given Control object to the AbstractController's list of Controls.
Method	removeControl
Visibility	public
Arguments	javax.media.Control
Return	void
Description	Removes the given Control object from the AbstractController's list of Controls.

The implementation of these methods is very basic, as we might expect.

Listing 14.13 *Adding and Removing Controls*

```
public void addControl(Control newControl) {
    synchronized(controls) {
        if(! controls.contains(newControl) ) {
            controls.addElement(newControl);
        }
    }
}

public void removeControl(Control oldControl) {
    controls.removeElement(oldControl);
}
```

(74)

(75)

As in maintaining any list in a multi-threaded environment, the `Vector` is first synchronized before it is manipulated. Duplicate entries are avoided [74], and entries are removed without question [75].

Integrating a Custom Control

The `javax.media.Controller` interface does not specify any default `Controls` for the `Controller`. If a `Control` is to be provided, it is up to the `Controller` implementation to create it.

Note that the `AbstractController`'s `addControl` and `removeControl` methods are not part of the JMF API. By virtue of being `public`, they effectively allow any class with a reference to an `AbstractController` to add a custom `Control` for that `AbstractController`. This differs from the JMF API, where only the `Controller` itself can provide its `Controls`.

An Example: Integrating the Rate Control

In "Rate Control" on page 341 we will develop a custom rate control, `RateControl`. Within its constructor, a `RateControl` object associates itself with a `Controller`. `addControl` is then used as follows to add the `Control` to the `AbstractController`'s list of `Controls`.

```
addControl( new RateControl(this) );
```

Once this `Control` is added to the `AbstractController`'s list, it can be explicitly retrieved with the `getControl` method:

```
Control control = controller.getControl(
    "ejmf.toolkit.media.controls.RateControl");
Component c = control.getControlComponent();
```

In Chapter 18, "Creating a Custom Player," when we create a fully-functional `Player`, we will put the `RateControl` to use. In Chapter 19, "Creating Custom Controls," we will look at building the `RateControl` and other custom `Controls`.

Summary

This chapter introduced the `AbstractController` class, an abstract implementation of the `javax.media.Controller` interface. This class extends the `AbstractClock` class developed in Chapter 13. Many of the methods developed for the `AbstractClock` class were extended here to enforce state restrictions imposed by the `Controller` interface.

In addition to extending the `javax.media.Clock` methods, we implemented methods to track the previous, current, and target states of the `AbstractController`. We added support for notifying a list of `ControllerListeners` of any important changes within the `AbstractController`, and created several convenience methods for posting `ControllerEvents`. Finally, we looked at how to provide to the user a higher level of external control over various aspects of the `AbstractController`'s operation.

In this chapter we took a big step towards providing an APF from which fully-functional API-compliant `Players` can be derived. In the next section, we will continue with the development of the `AbstractController`, implementing the state-transition methods `realize`, `prefetch`, `syncStart`, `stop`, and `deallocate`.

Chapter 15

IMPLEMENTING THE CONTROLLER TRANSITIONS

Introduction

Now that we are thoroughly immersed in the intimate details of the `javax.media.Controller` API, it is time to move on to the most important part of the `Controller`. Recall that the greatest piece of functionality that a `javax.media.Controller` brings to the *Java Media Framework* is the division of the `javax.media.Clock`'s `Stopped` state into five more precise and descriptive states. Together with the `Clock`'s `Started` state, the `Controller`'s `Unrealized`, `Realizing`, `Realized`, `Prefetching`, and `Prefetched` states provide six degrees of "readiness to play" its media.

In the last chapter we implemented methods to track the `Controller`'s states, post `ControllerEvents`, and enforce state restrictions on `Clock` methods. To complete our `Controller` implementation, we must now provide the ability to transition the `Controller` forward and backward through these states.

Forward vs. Backward Transitions

As we learned in Chapter 6, the `realize`, `prefetch`, and `syncStart` methods transition the `Controller` forward, while the `stop` and `deallocate` methods transition the `Controller` backward. These methods are summarized in Table 15.1.

Table 15.1 *Transition Methods*

Method	Transition	Resulting State
`realize`	Forward	`Realized`
`prefetch`	Forward	`Prefetched`
`syncStart`	Forward	`Started`
`stop`	Backward	`Prefetched` or `Realized`
`deallocate`	Backward	`Realized` or `Unrealized`

While each of the forward transition methods moves the `Controller` to a definite target state, the resulting state of the backward transitioning methods depends on the state the `Controller` is in when they are invoked.

To Thread or Not to Thread

The JMF makes a procedural distinction between forward and backward transitions of a `Controller`. Specifically, the `javax.media.Controller` API requires all forward transitions to execute asynchronously, and all backward transitions to execute synchronously. What this means is that `realize`, `prefetch`, and `syncStart`, as forward transition methods, must spawn a separate thread to transition the `Controller`, while `stop` and `deallocate` must transition the `Controller` on the same thread on which they are invoked. While the forward transition methods return immediately after spawning a new thread, the backward methods do not return until the transition is complete.

The reasoning behind this distinction stems from the amount of time generally taken by each type of transition. The forward transitions, as you have seen, may take quite some time to complete, while the backward transitions are generally much faster. Because of this time difference, the forward transition methods are executed on a separate thread so that the invoking thread can continue on to execute other code. The backward transition methods, since they generally require less time to complete, can be executed synchronously by the invoking thread.

Asynchronous Forward Transitions

As an illustration of the convenience that asynchronous behavior brings to the forward transitions, consider the following example. Suppose you write an applet that, among other things, displays a media clip using the JMF. Within the applet `init` method, a `javax.media.Player` is created to display the media. Ideally, while the media is loading and the `Player` is being constructed, you would like the rest of the applet to continue to load so that by the time the media has finished loading the applet will be ready to run. Fortunately for you, since the `realize` and `prefetch` methods are asynchronous, the `init` method will continue on while the `Player` is preparing to play on a separate thread.

The asynchronous behavior of the `syncStart` method is likewise beneficial. When calling `syncStart` with a time-base time in the future, there may be a substantial amount of time to wait until the media playback begins. Since the `syncStart` method is asynchronous, this waiting is done on a separate thread so that the thread that invoked `syncStart` can continue on.

Synchronous Backward Transitions

Unlike the `Controller`'s forward transition methods, the backward transition methods rarely require time-consuming operations. The `stop` method, for example, simply stops the playback of the media and moves the `Controller` into the `Prefetched` state. Unlike its counterpart, `syncStart`, there is no waiting involved in this transition. The other backward transition method, `deallocate`, likewise generally takes little time to complete. As you may imagine, resources that may have taken some time to acquire in the `realize` or `prefetch` methods can usually be released quickly by the `deallocate` method. Often this is done simply by setting a `Controller` property to `null`, allowing the *Java Virtual Machine* to garbage-collect the resource.

Because these methods generally complete quickly, the backward transitions are executed on the same thread on which they are invoked.

Changing the Default Thread Behavior

In practice, the default thread behavior of the `Controller` transitions may not be appropriate for a particular JMF application. In such cases, as discussed in "The StateWaiter Class" in Chapter 6, the thread behavior can be explicitly changed. Using the `StateWaiter` class, applications can block the current thread until an asynchronous forward transitions completes. This effectively makes an asynchronous transition synchronous. Similarly, using the `AsynchStopper` class, applications can run the backward transition methods on a separate thread. This effectively makes a synchronous transition asynchronous.

Both the `StateWaiter` and `AsynchStopper` classes are part of the `ejmf.toolkit.util` package from the *Essential JMF* Toolkit. They are discussed in greater detail in Chapter 6, "The Controller."

Playing It (Thread-)Safe

Because the `AbstractController` is transitioned in a threaded environment, it is necessary to take precautions against multiple threads attempting to transition it at the same time. Imagine, for example, what might happen if two threads simultaneously attempted to transition a `Controller` forward. Each thread might attempt to acquire the same resources, possibly resulting in deadlock or failure. Equally serious, consider the consequences of one thread attempting to transition the `Controller` forward while another attempted to transition it backward. In such scenarios, the behavior of the `AbstractController` would be unpredictable.

The first step in enforcing thread-safe transitions is to declare the `realize`, `prefetch`, `syncStart`, `stop`, and `deallocate` methods synchronized. By doing this, we can ensure that only one transition method is run at a time. However, since the `realize`, `prefetch`, and `syncStart` operations are asynchronous, and thus return before the transition is completed, we need to further restrict how and when the forward transitions occur.

Synchronizing the Forward Transitions

As discussed earlier, the JMF API dictates that the forward transition methods spawn a separate thread and return immediately. Since the actual work of transitioning the `Controller` is done on these threads, we must ensure that no two of these threads are run simultaneously.

To that end we will create a `ThreadQueue` class that will allow only one forward transition thread to run at a time. This class will act as a thread "buffer," storing threads and running them one at a time in the order in which they were added. Only when the currently-running thread has completed will the next thread in the queue be started.

The complete source to the `ThreadQueue` class is shown in Listing 15.1.

Listing 15.1 *Queuing the Forward Transition Threads*

```
     public class ThreadQueue extends Thread {
(1)      private Vector queue = new Vector();
(2)      private Thread running;

         public ThreadQueue() {
             super();
             setDaemon(true);
             start();
         }

(3)      public synchronized void addThread(Thread t) {
(4)          queue.addElement(t);
(5)          notify();
         }

(6)      public void run() {
             while(true) {
(7)              synchronized(this) {
                     while ( queue.size() == 0 ) {
                         try {
(8)                          wait();
                         } catch(InterruptedException e) {}
                     }
(9)                  running = (Thread)queue.elementAt(0);
(10)                 queue.removeElementAt(0);
                 }
(11)             running.start();
                 while(true) {
                     try {
(12)                     running.join();
                         break;
                     }
(13)                 catch(InterruptedException e) {}
                 }
             }
         }
         public synchronized void stopThreads() {
             if ( running != null ) {
(14)             running.stop();
             }
             for (int i = 0, n = queue.size(); i < n; i++) {
                 Thread t = (Thread)queue.elementAt(i);
(15)             t.stop();
             }
(16)         queue.removeAllElements();
         }
     }
```

As a Thread itself, the ThreadQueue has a run method [6] that performs an infinite loop, monitoring additions made to the thread queue [1]. These additions are made via the addThread method [3], which simply adds a thread to the queue [4] and notifies the queue-monitoring thread [5].

Within the run method, the monitoring thread waits to be notified of an addition to the queue [8]. When it awakens, it sets the running Thread [2] to be the thread at the front of the queue [9]. It then removes this thread from the queue [10].

Before starting the running thread, the monitoring thread exits the synchronized block [7] so that the addThread method can run and new threads can be added to the queue. After starting the new thread [11], the monitoring thread blocks until the running thread has completed [12]. Even if the running thread is interrupted [13], the monitoring thread will continue to block until the running thread has completed. Once the running thread has completed, the process begins again.

The stopThreads method is provided so that the running thread, as well as any that are queued to run, can be stopped at any time. Within this method, each thread is stopped ([14] and [15]) and removed from the queue [16]. As we will see, this method will be used when implementing the Controller methods stop and deallocate.

Using the ThreadQueue Class

The ThreadQueue class provides the basis for synchronizing the Abstract-Controller's forward transitions. When a forward transition method is called, it will create a thread to carry out the transition. This thread will then be added to the ThreadQueue, where it will be started when all threads added before it have completed. Because this thread will be run at an indefinite time in the future, it must take responsibility for deciding whether or not the transition is still necessary by the time it is started.

An example of this idea is in order. Suppose the prefetch method is called while the AbstractController is in the process of realizing. After creating a thread to asynchronously prefetch the AbstractController, the prefetch method will add the thread to the queue and return. Since a separate thread is already realizing the AbstractController, the prefetch thread will wait in the queue for the realizing thread to complete. After the realizing thread has completed, the prefetching thread will be started, where it will first check the AbstractController's current state to determine if the prefetching operation is still necessary. Since the current state will only be realized, the prefetching thread will prefetch the Abstract-Controller.

This process will become more clear as the realize, prefetch, and syncStart methods are implemented in the coming sections.

Synchronizing the Backward Transitions

The JMF API dictates that the backward transition methods `stop` and `deallocate` stop any currently-running forward transitions before moving the `AbstractController` backward. As mentioned earlier, this is done by calling the `stopThreads` method within the `ThreadQueue` class. This will stop not only the currently-running forward transition thread, but any other forward transition threads waiting in the queue.

Since the transition methods are all declared synchronized, the backward transition methods can complete without any other transition methods executing. This will ensure that the `AbstractController` is in a known state at all times.

action/doAction Revisited

When implementing the `javax.media.Controller` transition methods, we will again utilize the *action/doAction* model introduced in "A Framework Model" in Chapter 12. This model, as you recall, allows the APF to implement as much API-compliance functionality as possible, leaving only the media-specific details to the implementation. Both the forward and backward transition methods will make use of this model.

In addition to the guidelines set forth in "Model Assumptions" on page 192, the following rules must be observed when implementing the transition *doAction* methods.

1. Do not return until the transition is complete. Once the transition is complete, return as soon as possible.

2. Return true if successful. If unsuccessful, post an appropriate `Control-lerErrorEvent` and return false.

3. The *doAction* methods should not call one another. They will be called in the correct order at the correct time, with the `AbstractController` in the correct state.

The first rule is required so that the appropriate `TransitionEvent` can be posted by the *Abstract Player Framework* at the correct time. What this rule says essentially is that the *doAction* methods should not spawn separate threads to do the actual work of transitioning the `AbstractController`. Or, if such a thread is spawned, the *doAction* method should not return until the thread has completed.

Consider the following example to illustrate why Rule (1) is necessary: Before the APF invokes the `doRealize` method, it sets the `AbstractCon-troller`'s state to `Realizing` and posts a `TransitionEvent` to indicate the impending transition. When the `doRealize` method returns, the APF sets the `AbstractController`'s state to `Realized` and posts a `Realize-`

CompleteEvent. If the doRealize method returns before the transition is complete, then this state change will be premature and possibly inaccurate.

The second rule provides a way to gauge the success of the *doAction* methods. Because the APF knows nothing about the details of a specific Controller implementation, it cannot tell if the transition is successful unless the media-specific implementations gives an indication. If the transition is successful, the *doAction* method returns true. Otherwise, it returns false. In the latter case, it is the responsibility of the *doAction* method to post a ControllerErrorEvent if one is necessary. The APF cannot take this responsibility as there is no way of knowing the exact reason for the failure.

The APF uses the return value of *doAction* to determine how to proceed. If the *doAction* method succeeds in transitioning the AbstractController, then the AbstractController's state is changed and a TransitionEvent is posted to reflect this. If it fails, the state returns to its previous value and no TransitionEvent is posted.

The third rule serves as a reminder of the fine level of control that the APF maintains over the Controller's transitions. When a *doAction* method is called, it can be certain that the AbstractController is in the appropriate state, and that there is no need to invoke other *doAction* methods at that time.

By following these guidelines as well as those laid out in Chapter 12, subclasses of the AbstractController can avoid all but the most media-specific of implementation details.

Realizing the AbstractController

Now that a general transition model has been introduced, we can turn our attention towards implementing the specific Controller transition methods.

The AbstractController's implementation of the realize method is shown in Listing 15.2.

Listing 15.2 *Realizing the AbstractController Asynchronously*

```
(17)    private ThreadQueue threadqueue = new ThreadQueue();

(18)    protected ThreadQueue getThreadQueue() {
            return threadqueue;
        }
        public final synchronized void realize() {
(19)        if ( currentState >= Realized ) {
(20)            postRealizeCompleteEvent();
                return;
            }
            if( targetState < Realized ) {
(21)            setTargetState(Realized);
            }
(22)        Thread thread = new Thread() {
                public void run() {
(23)                if ( getState() < Realized ) {
(24)                    synchronousRealize();
                    }
                }
            };
(25)        threadqueue.addThread(thread);
        }
```

The `AbstractController`'s `ThreadQueue` object is defined at line [17]. This object will be used throughout the life of the `AbstractController` to queue and run the forward transition threads. A protected accessor method [18] is provided so that subclasses of the `AbstractController` can use the `ThreadQueue` as well.

The first step that the `realize` method takes is to check to see if the `AbstractController` is already in the `Realized` state [19]. If it is, in accordance with the `javax.media.Controller` API, a `Realize-CompleteEvent` is posted [20] and the `realize` method returns.

If the `AbstractController` has not yet been realized, the `realize` method instead sets the target state to `Realized` [21] and creates a thread to asynchronously `realize` the `AbstractController` [22].

Within the `run` method of this thread, the `synchronousRealize` method is called [24] to do the actual transition. Since this thread may be run by the `ThreadQueue` at some indefinite point in the future, it must ensure that the transition is still necessary before calling the `synchronousRealize` method. It does this by making sure the `AbstractController` has not yet reached the `Realized` state [23].

After the thread has been created, it is added to the thread queue [25] and the `realize` method returns.

The synchronousRealize Method

Once the thread created by the `realize` method is started by the thread queue, the `synchronousRealize` method is executed. This method is shown in Listing 15.3 below.

Listing 15.3 *Realizing the AbstractController Synchronously*

```
          protected void synchronousRealize() {
(26)          setState( Realizing );
(27)          postTransitionEvent();
(28)          if ( doRealize() ) {
(29)              setState( Realized );
(30)              postRealizeCompleteEvent();
(31)              setRate(1);
(32)              setMediaTime( new Time(0) );
          } else {
(33)              setState( Unrealized );
(34)              setTargetState( Unrealized );
          }
          }

(35)      public abstract boolean doRealize();
```

When `synchronousRealize` method is called, the realizing process is officially underway. To reflect this, the `AbstractController`'s state is set to `Realizing` [26] and a `TransitionEvent` is posted [27].

Following the *action/doAction* model, the abstract `doRealize` method declared in line [35] is invoked [28]. This method should acquire any non-exclusive resources that the `Controller` will need to render its media. In compliance with Rule (2) on page 241, this method should return `true` if it is successful, and false otherwise. In the latter case, the current and target states of the `AbstractController` are reset to `Unrealized` ([33] and [34]), and no transition event is posted. In the event of such a failure, the `doRealize` method should post a `ControllerErrorEvent` before returning.

If the `doRealize` method was successful, the state is set to `Realized` [29] and a `RealizeCompleteEvent` is posted [30]. Then, before returning, the `AbstractController`'s rate [31] and media time [32] are initialized to their default values.

As you can see, the APF takes care of as much of the work of realizing the `Controller` as possible. By implementing the `doRealize` method, subclasses can take care of the rest.

Prefetching the AbstractController

As you will see, the process used to prefetch the AbstractController parallels the realizing process described above. The prefetch method is shown in Listing 15.4.

Listing 15.4 *Prefetching the AbstractController Asynchronously*

```
        public final synchronized void prefetch() {
(36)        if ( currentState >= Prefetched ) {
(37)            postPrefetchCompleteEvent();
                return;
            }
            if ( targetState < Prefetched ) {
(38)            setTargetState(Prefetched);
            }
(39)        Thread thread = new Thread() {
                public void run() {
(40)                if ( getState() < Prefetched ) {
(41)                    synchronousPrefetch();
                    }
                }
            };
(42)        threadqueue.addThread(thread);
        }
```

Like the realize method, the prefetch method first checks to see if the AbstractController has already reached the desired state [36]. If it has, a PrefetchCompleteEvent is posted [37] and the method returns.

If the AbstractController has not yet been prefetched, the prefetch method sets the target state to Prefetched [38] and creates a thread to asynchronously prefetch the AbstractController [39].

Within the run method of this thread, the synchronousPrefetch method is called [41] to do the actual transition. As with the realizing thread discussed in the last section, the current state of the AbstractController is checked when the thread is started to ensure that the AbstractController should still be prefetched [40].

After the thread has been created, it is added to the thread queue [42] and the prefetch method returns.

The synchronousPrefetch Method

The synchronousPrefetch method is similar to the synchronousRealize method. It is shown in Listing 15.5.

Listing 15.5 *Prefetching the AbstractController Synchronously*

```
      protected void synchronousPrefetch() {
(43)      if ( currentState < Realized ) {
(44)          synchronousRealize();
          }
(45)      setState( Prefetching );
(46)      postTransitionEvent();
(47)      if ( doPrefetch() ) {
(48)          setState( Prefetched );
(49)          postPrefetchCompleteEvent();
          } else {
(50)          setState( Realized );
(51)          setTargetState( Realized );
          }
      }
(52)  public abstract boolean doPrefetch();
```

The `javax.media.Controller` API states that the `prefetch` method will `realize` the `Controller` if it is not already in the `Realized` state. The `synchronousPrefetch` method checks for this possibility [43] and realizes the `Controller` if necessary [44]. Note that `realize` is not called in line [44] because the `synchronousPrefetch` method is already running asynchronously.

When the `AbstractController` is ready to be prefetched, its state is set to `Prefetching` [45] and a `TransitionEvent` is posted [46] to reflect that the prefetching process has begun.

Again utilizing the *action/doAction* model, the abstract `doPrefetch` method declared in line [52] is invoked [47]. This method should acquire any exclusive resources that the `Controller` will need to render its media. It may also buffer the media data or perform other start-up processing. If it is successful, the `AbstractController`'s state is set to `Prefetched` [48] and a `PrefetchCompleteEvent` is posted [49]. Otherwise, the current and target states of the `AbstractController` are reset to `Realized` ([50] and [51]), and no transition event is posted. In the event of such a failure, the `doPrefetch` method should post a `ControllerErrorEvent` before returning.

SyncStarting the AbstractController

Starting the `AbstractController` differs slightly from the other forward transitions. Whereas the `realize` and `prefetch` methods can be invoked regardless of the `Controller`'s current state, the `syncStart` method may only be run when the `Controller` is in the `Prefetched` state. If it is run in any other state, the `syncStart` method will throw a `MediaError`.

The `syncStart` method also differs from the others in that it takes a `Time` argument specifying the time-base time when the transition is to occur. In contrast, the `realize` and `prefetch` operations take place as soon as possible after their respective methods are called.

The `syncStart` implementation appears in Listing 15.6.

Listing 15.6 *SyncStarting the AbstractController Asynchronously*

```
public final synchronized void syncStart(final Time t) {
    if (currentState == Started) {
        throw new ClockStartedError(
            "Cannot call syncStart() on a started Clock");
    }
    if (currentState != Prefetched) {
        throw new NotPrefetchedError(
            "Controller not prefetched");
    }
    setTargetState(Started);
    Thread thread = new Thread() {
        public void run() {
            if ( getState() < Started ) {
                synchronousSyncStart(t);
            }
        }
    };
    threadqueue.addThread(thread);
}
```

- **(53)** at `throw new ClockStartedError(`
- **(54)** at `throw new NotPrefetchedError(`
- **(55)** (at `setTargetState(Started);`
- **(56)** at `Thread thread = new Thread() {`
- **(57)** at `synchronousSyncStart(t);`
- **(58)** at `threadqueue.addThread(thread);`

Line [53] enforces a state restriction imposed by the `javax.media.Clock` API. As you recall from Table 6.3 on page 95, this restriction requires the `Controller` to be stopped when the `syncStart` method is called. If it is not, a `ClockStartedError` is thrown. In line [54], this restriction is further narrowed by requiring the `Controller` to be in the `Prefetched` state. This requirement is imposed by the `javax.media.Controller` API. If it is violated, a `NotPrefetchedError` is thrown. In Chapter 16, "Implementing the Player Interface," we will see that both of these restrictions are relaxed by the `javax.media.Player` interface's start method.

After the `AbstractController`'s state has been verified as `Prefetched`, the target state is set [55] and a thread is created to `syncStart` the `AbstractController` [56]. This thread is similar to those of the `realize` and `prefetch` methods. The start time, first passed in as a parameter to the `syncStart` method, is propagated on to the `synchronousSyncStart` method [57].

Once the thread has been created, it is added to the thread queue [58] and the method returns.

The synchronousSyncStart Method

As vexing as this method sounds, it plays a key role in starting the Abstract-Controller. Like its asynchronous counterpart, the synchronousSync-Start method takes a Time object as an argument, indicating the time-base time at which the AbstractController is to start. The synchro-nousSyncStart implementation is shown in Listing 15.7.

Listing 15.7 *SyncStarting the AbstractController Synchronously*

```
          protected void synchronousSyncStart(Time t) {
(59)          setState( Started );
(60)          postStartEvent();
              long latency;
(61)          Time latencyTime = getStartLatency();
              if ( latencyTime == LATENCY_UNKNOWN ) {
(62)              latency = 0;
              } else {
(63)              latency = latencyTime.getNanoseconds();
              }
(64)          long start = t.getNanoseconds();
(65)          long now = getTimeBase().getNanoseconds();
(66)          long earliest = now + latency;
(67)          if (start < earliest)
(68)              t = new Time(earliest);
(69)          super.syncStart(t);
(70)          if ( !doSyncStart(t) ) {
(71)              setState( Prefetched );
(72)              setTargetState( Prefetched );
              }
          }
(73)      public Time getStartLatency() {
              if (currentState == Unrealized ||
                  currentState == Realizing) {
                  throw new NotRealizedError(
                      "Controller must be realized");
              }
              return LATENCY_UNKNOWN;
          }

(74)      public abstract boolean doSyncStart(Time t);
```

As with the other forward transitions, the first step to take is to set the AbstractController's current state to indicate that the transition is under-way. Since there is no intermediate starting state, the synchronousSync-Start method immediately places the AbstractController in the Started state [59]. A StartEvent is then posted [60] to notify all ControllerListeners of the transition in progress.

At this point the `synchronousSyncStart` method must ensure that the time-base start time given as an argument is valid. To be considered valid, it must occur some time after the earliest possible time that the media could be rendered. This value depends entirely on the start latency of the `Controller`, as determined by the `getStartLatency` method.

Consider the following diagram as an illustration of this point.

Figure 15.1 *Calculating the Earliest Possible Time-Base Start Time*

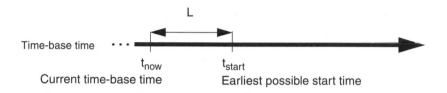

On the time-base time line, t_{now} represents the current time-base time and L represents the `Controller`'s start latency. As discussed in "Accommodating Start Latency" on page 141 in Chapter 9, the start latency is the amount of time needed by the `Controller` to prepare the first frame of media to be rendered. With these values, t_{now} and L, the `synchronousSyncStart` method can determine t_{start}, the earliest possible time that the media could be rendered.

$$t_{start} = t_{now} + L \qquad \text{(EQ 11)}$$

This time, t_{start}, is effectively the time-base time that the media would be rendered if it were started immediately. If the given start time, t, occurs before the earliest possible start time, t_{start}, then t must be set to t_{start}. This process is described below.

In line [61] of the `synchronousSyncStart` method, the `AbstractController`'s start latency is obtained using the `getStartLatency` method. This method, defined by the `javax.media.Controller` API, returns the `Controller`'s start latency in the form of a `javax.media.Time` object. If the latency cannot be determined, then the static final `LATENCY_UNKNOWN` should be returned. A default implementation of this method [73] is provided by the `AbstractController` class, throwing a `NotRealizedError` if the `Controller` is not realized and returning `LATENCY_UNKNOWN` otherwise. Subclasses of the `AbstractController` should override this method to provide a more precise estimate of the `Controller`'s start latency.

After getting the start latency, the `synchronousSyncStart` method converts it to a form suitable for numerical comparison. If `LATENCY_UNKNOWN` is returned by the `getStartLatency` method, then it is assumed that there is no latency involved in starting the `AbstractControl-`

ler [62]. Otherwise, the latency `Time` object is converted to nanoseconds [63]. The same is done for the given start time [64] and the current time-base time [65], before the earliest possible start time [66] is calculated.

If the given time-base start time occurs before the earliest possible start time [67], then the former is reset to the value of the latter [68]. This ensures that the media will begin rendering precisely at the `Controller`'s time-base start time.

Once the time-base start time has been validated, it is set in the `Abstract-Clock` superclass [69]. This value is used by several of the `javax.media.Clock` routines.

Finally, in line [70], the `doSyncStart` method is invoked to do the actual work of starting the media playback. This abstract method, declared in line [74], should be overridden by subclasses of the `AbstractController` to start the process of rendering the media. If this method is not successful, it returns false and the `AbstractController`'s current and target states are reset to the `Prefetched` state ([71]-[72]). As always, in such a failure, the `doSyncStart` method should post a `ControllerErrorEvent` before returning. If the `doSyncStart` method is successful, the `AbstractController` remains in the `Started` state and the method returns.

Blocking the Current Thread Until the Playback Start Time

Recall from "Accommodating Start Latency" in Chapter 9 that given a start time t_{start} and a start latency L, the `Controller` should start the media playback at the time-base time $t_{start} - L$. When implementing the abstract `doSyncStart` method in a media-specific subclass of the `AbstractController`, it may often be useful to block the current thread until this time has been reached. The `blockUntilStart` method, described in EJMF Toolkit Synopsis 15.1, serves just this purpose.

EJMF Toolkit Synopsis 15.1 *Blocking Until the Controller Start Time*

Class	`ejmf.toolkit.media.AbstractController`
Method	`blockUntilStart`
Visibility	`public`
Arguments	`javax.media.Time`
Return	`void`
Description	Based on the given time-base start time and the `AbstractController`'s start latency, blocks the current thread until the media playback should begin.

A typical use of the `blockUntilStart` method is as follows.

```
public boolean doSyncStart(Time t) {
    blockUntilStart(t);
    //... Start mechanism to render media
    return true;
}
```

If the time-base time t_{start} - L has already passed by the time the blockUntilStart method has been called, the method will return immediately.

The implementation of blockUntilStart is shown in Listing 15.8.

Listing 15.8 *Blocking Until the Controller Start Time*

```
public void blockUntilStart(Time t) {
    Time latencyTime = getStartLatency();
    long latency;
    if ( latencyTime == LATENCY_UNKNOWN ) {
        latency = 0;
    } else {
        latency = latencyTime.getNanoseconds();
    }
    long start = t.getNanoseconds();
    long now = getTimeBase().getNanoseconds();
    long delay = (start - latency - now)/1000000;
    if ( delay > 0 ) {
        try {
            Thread.sleep(delay);
        } catch(InterruptedException e) {}
    }
}
```

(75)
(76)
(77)

(78)

The first part of this method is similar to parts of the synchronousSyncStart implementation. As in synchronousSyncStart, if the value returned by getStartLatency is LATENCY_UNKNOWN, the start latency for the Controller is assumed to be zero. This may not be accurate, but it is the best estimation that can be made with an unknown start latency.

After the latency has been resolved, the given start time [75] and the current time-base time [76] are converted to nanoseconds. Since this method is to block until the time-base time start - latency, then the amount of time necessary to wait is start - latency - now. This value is calculated and converted to milliseconds in line [77], so that the current thread can sleep [78] for the appropriate amount of time before returning.

Note that this routine calculates the number of *time-base* milliseconds until the playback start time, and then uses this value as an argument to Thread.sleep. What this means is that the AbstractController's Time-Base must be monotonically increasing at the same rate as the system clock for the blockUntilStart method to work. Otherwise, the time that is spent sleeping may not reflect the actual number of real-time milliseconds until the playback start time, and the method may return before or after the appropriate time.

Stopping the AbstractController

Now that the Controller's forward transition methods have been discussed, we can move on to the backward transition methods. The first method we will look at is the stop routine. This method transitions the Controller from the Started state back to the Prefetched state.

Listing 15.9 *The Stop Method*

```
         public final void stop() {
(79)          if ( stopController() ) {
(80)              postStopByRequestEvent();
             }
         }
```

Within the implementation of the stop method, the entire stopping process is done in the protected method stopController [79]. This method returns true if the AbstractController is successfully stopped and false otherwise. If it is successful, a StopByRequestEvent will be posted upon its return [80].

The stopController method is shown in Listing 15.10.

Listing 15.10 *Stopping the Controller*

```
(81)     protected synchronized boolean stopController() {
(82)         threadqueue.stopThreads();
             switch(currentState) {
(83)             case Unrealized:
                 case Realized:
                 case Prefetched:
                     setTargetState(currentState);
                     return true;
(84)             case Realizing:
                     setState(Unrealized);
                     setTargetState(Unrealized);
                     return true;
(85)             case Prefetching:
                     setState(Realized);
                     setTargetState(Realized);
                     return true;
             }
```

```
(86)        if(! doStop() ) {
                return false;
            }
(87)        super.stop();
(88)        setState(Prefetched);
(89)        setTargetState(Prefetched);
            return true;
        }

(90)    public abstract boolean doStop();
```

Although the stop method is generally used to transition a Controller out of the Started state, the javax.media.Controller API states that the stop method may be called at any time, regardless of the current state of the Controller. If the Controller is in the Unrealized, Realized, or Prefetched state, then it remains in its current state and the method returns. Otherwise, if it is Realizing, Prefetching, or Started, then it is transitioned back to the previous static state.

Upon being invoked, the stopController method first stops any forward transition that may be running [82]. The ThreadQueue.stopThreads method, as you recall, kills the currently-running forward transition thread as well as any other threads stored in the queue. This ensures that no other thread will attempt to transition the AbstractController forward for the duration of the stopController method. Since the stopController method is synchronized [81], no other Controller transition method can execute until this method completes.

After stopping any forward transition threads that may be running or queued, the AbstractController must be stabilized and returned to a known state. If the AbstractController is in one of the static states [83], then the target state is reset to the current state to indicate that no transition is in progress. If, however, the AbstractController was in the middle of a forward transition when the stopThreads method was called, then the current state will be one of the two transient states. If it was in the process of realizing [84], then both the current and target states are reset to Unrealized. If the AbstractController was prefetching, then the states are reset to Realized [85].

At this point, unless the AbstractController is in the Started state, the stopController method returns. Otherwise, the routine continues and the doStop method is called [86]. This abstract method, declared in line [90], should be implemented to stop the playback of the Controller's media. Like the *doAction* methods of the other Controller transitions, the doStop method returns true if successful and false otherwise. In the latter case, a ControllerErrorEvent detailing the reason for the failure should be posted by doStop before returning.

If doStop is successful, then the stopController method continues. In line [87], the Clock is stopped within the AbstractClock superclass. As you recall from Chapter 5, this simply stops the media time from progressing and returns the Clock to the Stopped state.

Finally, before returning, both the current and target states of the AbstractController are returned to the Prefetched state at [88] and [89].

More Than One Way to Stop

As we saw in the stop method, if the stop operation is successful, a StopBy-RequestEvent is posted. This StopEvent indicates that the user has specifically requested that the Controller be stopped. However, there are other reasons to stop the Controller. The AbstractController provides the following methods to handle two such circumstances.

EJMF Toolkit Synopsis 15.2 *Alternate Stopping Mechanisms*

Class	ejmf.toolkit.media.AbstractController
Method	stopAtTime
Visibility	protected
Arguments	void
Return	void
Description	Stops the AbstractController and posts a StopAtTimeEvent if successful.
Method	stopInRestart
Visibility	protected
Arguments	void
Return	void
Description	Stops the AbstractController and posts a RestartingEvent if successful.

The first of these methods, stopAtTime, posts a StopAtTimeEvent after stopping the AbstractController. Unlike the StopByRequestEvent, the StopAtTimeEvent signals a scheduled stop of a Controller. We saw this method used by the StopTimeMonitor class developed in the last chapter.

The stopInRestart method posts a RestartingEvent after stopping the AbstractController. Although a RestartingEvent may not sound like it indicates a stopped Controller, it is indeed a StopEvent and is intended to be posted when the Controller must stop temporarily to make internal changes or gain resources. We will see this method used in Chapter 16, when we implement the javax.media.Player interface.

The implementation of these methods is shown in Listing 15.11.

Listing 15.11 *Alternate Stopping Mechanisms*

```
protected void stopAtTime() {
    if ( stopController() ) {
        postStopAtTimeEvent();
    }
}

protected void stopInRestart() {
    if ( stopController() ) {
        postRestartingEvent();
    }
}
```

As you can see, these methods are nearly identical to the stop method shown in Listing 15.9. The only difference is the type of StopEvent that is posted after successfully stopping the AbstractController.

The Last Stop: End of Media

There is one other StopEvent that has not been discussed. When the end of the media has been reached, the Controller must transition out of the Started state and post an EndOfMediaEvent. This StopEvent indicates that the Controller has rendered the entirety of its media and has moved back into the Prefetched state. A typical response to an EndOfMediaEvent is to reset the Controller's media time to Time(0).

Recall the guidelines from "Model Assumptions" on page 192 regarding the implementation of the *doAction* methods. According to Rule (3), the media–specific implementation of the APF should not directly post TransitionEvents. However, since the media-specific implementation is the only piece of code that knows when the end of media has been reached, it must take responsibility for notifying the APF of this change.

To this end the AbstractController defines the endOfMedia method, to be called by a media-specific subclass of the AbstractController when the end of media is reached. This method is described in EJMF Toolkit Synopsis 15.3.

EJMF Toolkit Synopsis 15.3 *Indicating the End of the Media*

Class	`ejmf.toolkit.media.AbstractController`
Method	`endOfMedia`
Visibility	`protected`
Arguments	`void`
Return	`void`
Description	Stops the `AbstractController` and posts an `EndOfMediaEvent`.

The source for the `endOfMedia` method is shown in Listing 15.12.

Listing 15.12 *End of Media*

```
protected synchronized void endOfMedia()
            throws ClockStoppedException              {
        if ( currentState != Started ) {
(91)        throw new ClockStoppedException();
        }
(92)    super.stop();
(93)    setState(Prefetched);
        setTargetState(Prefetched);
(94)    postEndOfMediaEvent();
}
```

The `endOfMedia` method is intended to be called while the `Abstract-Controller` is still in the `Started` state. If it is not, a `ClockStopped-Exception` is thrown [91]. If the `AbstractController` is indeed `Started`, the `Clock` is stopped [92], the current and target states are reset [93], and an `EndOfMediaEvent` is posted [94].

Failure to call this method when the end of the media has been reached will result in the `AbstractController` remaining in the started state. This will result in incorrect media time calculations by the `AbstractClock` routines, and will keep `ControllerListeners` from being notified of this important change in the `AbstractController`.

This last point is important enough to be added to the list of rules developed on page 241 regarding the implementation of the transition *doAction* methods.

4. When the end of the media has been reached, call `endOfMedia`.

This will post an `EndOfMediaEvent` and set the `Controller` states appropriately. Do not post an `EndOfMediaEvent` in any other way.

Deallocating the AbstractController

The remaining Controller transition method to implement is the deallocate method. Like stop, the deallocate method stops any forward transitions and moves the AbstractController backward. It is generally used to move the Controller from the Prefetched to the Realized state, stopping any resource-consuming activity that may be running and releasing any exclusive-use resources that the Controller has acquired.

The deallocate method appears in Listing 15.13.

Listing 15.13 *Deallocating the AbstractController*

```
        public final synchronized void deallocate() {
            int state;
            if ( currentState == Started ) {
(95)            throw new ClockStartedError(
                    "Can not deallocate Started Controller");
            }
(96)        threadqueue.stopThreads();
(97)        if ( doDeallocate() ) {
                if ( currentState == Unrealized ||
                    currentState == Realizing ) {
(98)                state = Unrealized;
                } else {
(99)                state = Realized;
                }
                setState(state);
                setTargetState(state);
(100)           postDeallocateEvent();
            }
        }

(101)   public abstract boolean doDeallocate();
```

If deallocate is called while the Controller is Started, a Clock-StartedError is thrown [95]. This requirement is necessary so that resources are not relinquished while the Controller is rendering the media.

As in the implementation of the stop method, the deallocate method stops and dequeues any current or queued forward transitions [96] so that the AbstractController can be transitioned backwards safely.

In [97], the abstract method doDeallocate, declared in [101], is called to execute the implementation-specific deallocation functionality. Within this method, subclasses should release any exclusive-use resources held by the Controller, and stop any resource acquisition in progress. If this method is successful, it should return true. Otherwise, as always, it should return false after posting a ControllerErrorEvent detailing the reason for its failure.

If doDeallocate is successful, then the AbstractController must be transitioned back to the previous state. If the AbstractController had not yet been realized when the deallocate method was called, it is moved back into the Unrealized state [98]. Otherwise, it is moved back to the Realized state [99]. This behavior is specified by the javax.media.Controller API. As you recall, once a Controller has been realized, there is no way to move it back to the Unrealized state.

Once the current and target states of the AbstractController have been set, a DeallocateEvent is posted [100] and the method returns.

Closing the AbstractController

The final Controller method to implement is the close method. Unlike the other methods discussed in this chapter, the close method does not affect a state transition within the Controller. Instead, it shuts down the Controller and releases as many resources held by the Controller as possible. Once a Controller has been closed, it ceases all activity and should not be used again. According the javax.media.Controller API, methods invoked on a closed Controller are not guaranteed to work and may throw errors.

The AbstractController's implementation of the close method is shown in Listing 15.14.

Listing 15.14 *Closing the AbstractController*

```
         public final synchronized void close() {
(102)        stop();
(103)        doClose();
(104)        controls = null;
             threadqueue = null;
(105)        postControllerClosedEvent();

(106)}   public abstract void doClose();
```

Immediately upon being invoked, the close method stops any Controller transitions in progress [103]. It then calls the abstract doClose method [103] declared in line [106]. This method should be overridden to release as many Controller resources as possible. Unlike the Controller transition *doAction* methods, the doClose method does not return a boolean indicating its success. In this case, the success of the doClose method is irrelevant since the Controller is closing anyway.

After releasing implementation-specific resources, the close method sets two of its member data objects to null [104]. Unless they are referenced by another class, this process flags the objects for garbage collection by the *Java*

Virtual Machine, freeing memory and ultimately rendering the AbstractController inoperative.

Before the close method returns, it posts a ControllerClosedEvent [105] to indicate to its listeners that the AbstractController is no longer being used.

Summary

This chapter completes the implementation of the AbstractController class introduced in the last chapter. As a javax.media.Controller, the AbstractController can be in one of six states, and must provide the methods necessary to transition forward and backward through them.

Early in this chapter we developed a model to asynchronously transition the AbstractController forward. This model utilized the ThreadQueue class, which allowed us to "buffer" the forward transitions. Using this class we can ensure that only one forward transition is executed at a time, and provide the ability to move the AbstractController forward asynchronously.

Since the backward Controller transitions are executed synchronously, no special transition "buffering" was needed. However, we did need to take precautions to ensure that no forward transitions were executed while the AbstractController moved backward. To this end, we utilized the stopThreads method from the ThreadQueue class, and declared all of the Controller transition methods to be synchronized.

The *action/doAction* model, first introduced in Chapter 12, was again used to implement the media specific portions of the Controller transitions. In addition to the guidelines set forth early on, four more rules were created to constrain its use when applied to the Controller transitions.

Finally, each of the five Controller transitions, as well as the close operation, were implemented in the appropriate Controller methods. These implementations followed the specifications laid out in the JMF API.

Having completed development of the AbstractController class, we now have a fully API-compliant abstract javax.media.Controller implementation. To provide a functional media-specific Controller, subclasses of the AbstractController need only implement the abstract *doAction* methods introduced herein. In the next chapter, we will begin implementation of the javax.media.Player interface, which will allow us to take the final step towards creating and using a custom Player.

Chapter 16

IMPLEMENTING THE PLAYER INTERFACE

Introduction

You need to straighten your posture and suck in your gut. We have implemented two of the three major interfaces necessary to create a custom media Player. There is only one more to go. The last one, the javax.media.Player interface, provides the final pieces of the puzzle needed to make your custom Player fully compliant with the *Java Media Framework* API. If you want to have media, you've got to build Players.[1]

Why a Player?

In the last few chapters we worked to develop the AbstractController class, an abstract implementation of the javax.media.Controller interface. This class implements all but the most implementation-specific functionality necessary to create a working Controller.

Although the Controller interface provides a media-based state machine, a timing mechanism, and an instrument to create and dispatch media events, it does not provide a complete media-rendering solution. Within the

---

1. You *can* have your Cake and a JMF Player, too.

`Controller` interface, there is no mechanism specified to load the media into the `Controller`, display the media, or provide explicit external control over the playback of the media.

The `Player` interface, among other things, fills the functional gaps not addressed by the `Controller` interface. Building on the foundation of the `Controller`, the `Player` takes the final steps necessary to retrieve and render an arbitrary medium.

Continuing with the *Abstract Player Framework*, in this chapter we will develop the `AbstractPlayer` class. This class, as its name suggests, will extend the `AbstractController` class to provide an abstract implementation of the `Player` interface. As with the abstract classes developed in previous chapters, as much API-compliant functionality as possible will be implemented here, leaving only the implementation-specific details to its subclasses.

Player Functionality

The `Player` interface consists of the following methods.

Table 16.1 *javax.media.Player Methods*

Method	Description
`getVisualComponent`	Get the visual component, if any, for this `Player`.
`getControlPanelComponent`	Get the control panel component, if any, for this `Player`.
`getGainControl`	Get the gain control, if any, for this `Player`.
`start`	Start this `Player` as soon as possible. `Prefetch` this `Player` if necessary.
`addController`	Place a Controller under the control of this `Player`.
`removeController`	Remove a `Controller` from control of this `Player`.

Although there are only a handful of methods in the `Player` interface, it is by no means trivial to implement. Among other things, the `Player` interface provides the following functionality:

- Visual and control panel components
- Support of a `DataSource`
- Relaxation of state restrictions on `setMediaTime` and `setRate`
- Introduction of the `start` method
- Synchronization of multiple `Controllers`

Let's look at each of these in depth.

Visual and Control Panel Components

The `Player` interface provides an easy way to display and allow user interaction with a `Player` and its media. If a `Player` supports video media, the `getVisualComponent` method provides the visual `java.awt.Component` on which the media is rendered. If the `Player` supports audio media, the `getGainControl` method provides the `GainControl` object to control the volume of the media. This object, in turn, provides a gain control component if one is available. Finally, through use of the `getControlPanelComponent` method, the `Player` provides a control panel component that allows the user to control different aspects of the playback of the media.

Support of a DataSource

The `Player` interface extends the `MediaHandler` interface, allowing the `Player` to read media data through a `DataSource` object. Using the `setSource` method, the `Manager` class sets the `DataSource` of the `Player` when it is first created. This object delivers the media data to the `Player` throughout the life of the `Player`.

Relaxation of Restrictions on setMediaTime and setRate

The `Controller` API specifies that the `Controller` may not be in the `Started` state when the `setMediaTime` and `setRate` methods are called. The `Player` interface relaxes this restriction by stopping the `Player` before the media time and rate are set, and restarting it afterwards.

Introduction of the start Method

The `start` method offers some advantages over the `syncStart` method. First, it relaxes the requirement that the `Controller` be in the `Prefetched` state when it is started. If the `Player` has not been prefetched, the `start` method will prefetch it before attempting to render the media. Second, if the

Player is already in the Started state when the start method is called, the start method will return without throwing a ClockStartedError.

Unlike the Controller.syncStart method, the start method does not take a Time argument specifying the time-base start time. Instead, the start method simply starts the Player as soon as possible.

Synchronization of Multiple Controllers

Easily the most extensive feature of the Player interface is the ability to manage and synchronize multiple Controllers. Using the addController method, Controllers can be placed under the control of a master Player. From that point on, all actions invoked on the master Player, including Clock methods and Controller transitions, are propagated on to each managed Controller. Conversely, all ControllerEvents posted by the managed Controllers are funneled through the master Player.

This feature has greater implications than any other for our Abstract-Player implementation. In addition to the new methods introduced by the Player interface to support this functionality, many of the operations implemented in the AbstractClock and AbstractController classes will need to be extended here to accommodate managed Controllers.

Augmenting the action/doAction Model

When developing the AbstractController in previous chapters, we allowed for extended functionality in many of the methods by utilizing the *action/doAction* model introduced in Chapter 12, "Designing an Abstract Player Framework." In order to provide support for management of multiple Controllers within the AbstractPlayer class, we will implement each of the abstract *doAction* methods introduced in the AbstractController.

Since we must still provide a way for subclasses of the AbstractPlayer to implement media-specific functionality, we will introduce a third tier to our *action/doAction* model. Following the same rules as their *doAction* counterparts, the abstract *doPlayerAction* methods will be introduced in this chapter to augment the now-implemented *doAction* methods. Subclasses of the AbstractPlayer will need to implement the *doPlayerAction* methods to effect behavior specific to their own implementation.

The *doPlayerAction* methods will follow the same rules and guidelines set forth for the *doAction* methods in Chapter 12 and "action/doAction Revisited" on page 241. Like the *doAction* methods, they will have the same Java signature and will have an identical API description as the *action* method specified in the JMF.

If a picture is a thousand words and a class diagram worth two thousand (See "Controller Events Class Hierarchy" on page 87), then the following high-level architectural drawing is worth at least three thousand. On that assumption, Figure 16.1 should help greatly to describe this amended model.

Figure 16.1 *The action/doAction/doPlayerAction Model*

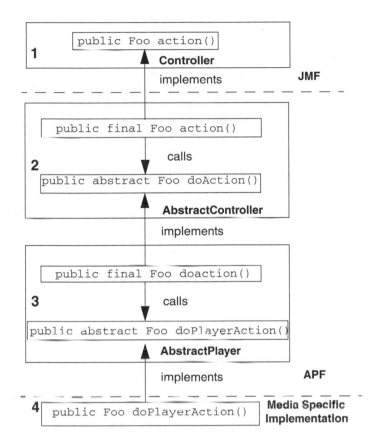

As you can see, the abstract *doPlayerAction* methods will be called from the *doAction* methods implemented in the `AbstractPlayer` class. These methods, as we have already seen, are called by the `Controller` methods implemented in the `AbstractController` class.

Each part of the chain adds functionality to the original method declared in the JMF. In step (1), the *action* method is declared in the `Controller` interface. This method is then implemented in the `AbstractController` class (2) to provide API-compliant `Controller` functionality. In step (3), the *doAction* method is implemented in the `AbstractPlayer` class, adding `Player`-specific functionality to the `Controller` implementation. Finally, in step (4), a subclass of the `AbstractPlayer` implements the *doPlayerAction* method to provide functionality specific to the media it supports.

We will see step (4) in *action* in Chapter 18, "Creating a Custom Player" as we create a custom `Player` using the `AbstractPlayer` class developed here. For now, let's concentrate on step (3) and the rest of the `Abstract-Player` class.

Player Components and Controls

As mentioned above, the `Player` interface provides methods to return the visual and control panel `java.awt.Component`s used when rendering its media. If the `Player` implementation supports audio media, a `GainControl` object may also be provided to control the volume of the media. This object may contain a visual component to allow for external control of the media volume.

The Visual Component

The first of the `Player`'s components, the visual component, is returned by the `getVisualComponent` method. The `AbstractPlayer` implementation of this method is shown in Listing 16.1.

Listing 16.1 *Getting/Setting the Visual Component*

```
(1)    private Component visualComponent;

       public Component getVisualComponent() {
           int currentState = getState();

           if(currentState == Unrealized ||
              currentState == Realizing){
(2)            throw new NotRealizedError(
                       "Player must be realized");
           }
(3)        return visualComponent;
       }

(4)    protected void setVisualComponent(Component c) {
           visualComponent = c;
       }
```

The `getVisualComponent` method requires that the `Player` be realized for the visual component to be obtained. The rationale for this requirement is that the `Player` may not know enough about its media to provide a visual component until the media has been at least partially loaded in the realizing stage. If this requirement is not met, a `NotRealizedError` is thrown [2]. Otherwise, the visual component, declared in line [1], is returned [3].

Since the visual component property of the `AbstractPlayer` is declared `private`, a `protected setVisualComponent` method is provided [4] so that its value can be set from outside of the `AbstractPlayer`. It is declared protected so that only subclasses of the `AbstractPlayer` and classes within the `ejmf.toolkit.media` package can set the visual component. It is intended that this method be called while the `AbstractPlayer` is realizing, so that once the `AbstractPlayer` has reached the `Realized` state its visual component can be acquired.

The `setVisualComponent` method, although simple, is described in EJMF Toolkit Synopsis 16.1.

EJMF Toolkit Synopsis 16.1 *Setting the Player's Visual Component*

Class	`ejmf.toolkit.media.AbstractPlayer`
Method	`setVisualComponent`
Visibility	`protected`
Arguments	`java.awt.Component`
Return	`void`
Description	Sets the visual component of the `AbstractPlayer`. This method should be called within the `realize` method of media-specific implementations of the `AbstractPlayer`.

If the `AbstractPlayer` does not support visual media, the `setVisual-Component` method need not be called. In such an event, the `getVisual-Component` method will return `null`, indicating that there is no visual component for this `Player`.

The Control Panel Component

The `Player` interface provides for a control panel component that will allow the user of the `Player` to affect different aspects of the playback of the media. This control panel component is obtained using the `getControlPanelComponent` method. Its implementation in the `AbstractPlayer` class is shown in Listing 16.2.

Listing 16.2 *Getting/Setting the Control Panel Component*

(5)
```
private Component controlPanelComponent;

public Component getControlPanelComponent() {
    int currentState = getState();

    if(currentState == Unrealized ||
       currentState == Realizing)
    {
```
(6)
```
        throw new NotRealizedError(
            "Player must be realized to get control panel");
    }
```
(7)
```
    return controlPanelComponent;
}
```
(8)
```
protected void setControlPanelComponent(Component c) {
    controlPanelComponent = c;
}
```

As with the `getVisualComponent` method, a `NotRealizedError` will be thrown [6] if the `Player` has not yet been realized when the `getControl-PanelComponent` method is invoked. This is because the control panel, in response to user input, may invoke methods such as `setMediaTime` and `setRate`, that require the `Player` to be realized. If this condition is met, the control panel component, declared in line [5], is returned [7].

To specify the control panel, subclasses of the `AbstractPlayer` should use the `setControlPanelComponent` method defined in line [8]. As with `setVisualComponent`, this method should be called when the `Player` is realizing so that the control panel component is available once the `Player` reaches the `Realized` state.

The `setControlPanelComponent` method is described below.

EJMF Toolkit Synopsis 16.2 *Setting the Player's Control Panel Component*

Class	`ejmf.toolkit.media.AbstractPlayer`
Method	`setControlPanelComponent`
Visibility	`protected`
Arguments	`java.awt.Component`
Return	`void`
Description	Sets the control panel component of the `AbstractPlayer`. This method should be called within the `realize` method of media-specific implementations of the `AbstractPlayer`.

If no control panel component is specified by the `AbstractPlayer` implementation, then the `getControlPanelComponent` method will return `null`, indicating that no control panel is available for this `Player`.

The GainControl

If a `Player` supports the playback of audio data, it may wish to provide a `javax.media.GainControl` object to allow control over the audio signal gain. As discussed in "Gain Control" on page 122, this class provides a programming interface to control the volume of the audio data. Additionally, through the `getControlComponent` method, the `GainControl` class may also provide a graphical user interface allowing external control over the volume of the media.

The `AbstractPlayer` implementation of the `getGainControl` method is shown in Listing 16.3.

Listing 16.3 *Getting/Setting the GainControl*

```
(9)     private GainControl gainControl;

        public GainControl getGainControl() {
            int currentState = getState();

            if(currentState == Unrealized ||
               currentState == Realizing)
            {
(10)            throw new NotRealizedError(
                        "Player must be realized");
            }
(11)        return gainControl;
        }

(12)    protected void setGainControl(GainControl c) {
            if( gainControl != null ) {
(13)            removeControl(gainControl);
            }
(14)        addControl(c);
(15)        gainControl = c;
        }
```

As you have come to expect, a `NotRealizedError` is thrown [10] if the `AbstractPlayer` is not realized when the `getGainControl` method is called. This is because a `Player` may not know whether a `GainControl` is necessary until it is examined the media in the realizing stage. If the `AbstractPlayer` has been realized, the `GainControl` object declared in line [9] is returned [11].

The `setGainControl` method [12] provided by the `AbstractPlayer` class differs slightly from its visual and control panel counterparts. In addition to setting the gainControl property, the setGainControl adds the given GainControl object to the list of Controls maintained by the Abstract-Controller class. This list, as you recall, is manipulated with the addControl and removeControl methods introduced in "Control Methods" on page 230.

When the setGainControl method is called, it first removes any previously-set GainControl from the AbstractController's list of Controls [13]. After adding the new GainControl to this same list [14], the gainControl property is set [15].

The setGainControl method is described in EJMF Toolkit Synopsis 16.3.

EJMF Toolkit Synopsis 16.3 *Setting the Player's Gain Control*

Class	ejmf.toolkit.media.AbstractPlayer
Method	setGainControl
Visibility	protected
Arguments	javax.media.GainControl
Return	void
Description	Sets the GainControl object for this AbstractPlayer. This method should be called within the realize method of media-specific implementations of the AbstractPlayer.

If the AbstractPlayer subclass does not support audio data, or if the audio gain should not change, the setGainControl method need not be called. The default null value will be returned by the getGainControl method, indicating that no GainControl is available for this Player.

Acquiring the Media: DataSource Support

As mentioned previously, the Controller API specifies no standard way to locate or load its media data. The Player remedies this matter by extending the javax.media.MediaHandler interface, which provides support for a javax.media.protocol.DataSource object. As discussed in "The Data-Source Interface" on page 44, the DataSource class provides a protocol-specific mechanism to fetch the media from a variety of sources.

As shown in Table 16.2, the MediaHandler interface consists of only one method.

Table 16.2 *javax.media.MediaHandler Methods*

Method	Description
setSource	Sets the DataSource to be used to acquire the media data.

Its sole method, setSource, allows a DataSource to be set within the MediaHandler. If the MediaHandler cannot use the DataSource specified, the setSource method will throw an IncompatibleSourceException.

As a MediaHandler, the Player interface uses this feature as a "litmus test" of whether it can support a particular DataSource. When the javax.media.Manager class locates a Player class for a specific medium, it instantiates the Player and calls its setSource method with a DataSource referencing the media data. If the Player is not equipped to handle that particular DataSource, it will throw an IncompatibleSourceException and the Manager class will continue to look for a suitable Player.

The AbstractPlayer implementation of setSource is shown in Listing 16.4.

Listing 16.4 *Setting the DataSource*

(16)
```
private DataSource source;

public void setSource(DataSource source)
    throws IncompatibleSourceException
{
    if( this.source != null ) {
```
(17)
```
        throw new IncompatibleSourceException(
            "Datasource already set");
    }
```
(18)
```
    this.source = source;
}

public DataSource getSource() {
    return source;
}
```

The only requirement that the AbstractPlayer places on acceptance of a DataSource is that it has not already been set. This requirement is intended to limit the Player to exactly one medium throughout its life. Changing a Player's media after it had already been set would require the Player to return to the Unrealized state, an *action* which is explicitly forbidden in the Controller API.

If the DataSource has already been set, the setSource method throws an IncompatibleSourceException [17]. Otherwise, the AbstractPlayer source property, defined in line [16], is set to the given DataSource object [18].

Subclasses of the AbstractPlayer may wish to extend the acceptance criteria for a DataSource by overriding the AbstractPlayer's setSource routine. A common requirement is that the DataSource be specifically a PushDataSource or a PullDataSource. We will see an example of this in Chapter 18 when we implement a fully-functional custom Player.

In line [19], the AbstractPlayer method getSource is defined. This method, described in EJMF Toolkit Synopsis 16.4, simply returns the AbstractPlayer's DataSource.

EJMF Toolkit Synopsis 16.4 *Getting the Player's DataSource*

Class	ejmf.toolkit.media.AbstractPlayer
Method	getSource
Visibility	public
Arguments	void
Return	javax.media.protocol.DataSource
Description	Returns the DataSource object for this AbstractPlayer. If the DataSource has not yet been set with setSource, this method returns null.

The getSource routine is an obvious addition to the *APF*. Its omission from the JMF is regrettable, since the DataSource of a Player is often a useful reference to maintain. If, for example, given a Player object, you wished to know the original URL associated with the Player's media, you would need to reference the DataSource object providing the media data to the Player. This object, through its getLocator method, would return the MediaLocator object containing the media URL. Although a reference to the DataSource is not required to manage a Player, the AbstractPlayer provides it as a convenience to its implementors.

Relaxed Restrictions on Clock Methods

The `Player` API not only extends the functionality of the `Clock` and `Controller` interfaces, but also relaxes some of the state restrictions imposed by the `Clock` API. Specifically, whereas the `Clock` API requires that the `Clock` not be started when the media time or rate of the `Controller` is set, the `Player` interface relaxes this restriction and allows these properties to be set even when the `Player` is started.

A More Flexible setMediaTime

The first of the methods to be revisited is the `setMediaTime` method. Its implementation in the `AbstractPlayer` is shown below.

Listing 16.5 *Relaxed Restriction on setMediaTime*

```
        public synchronized void setMediaTime(Time t) {
(19)        boolean isStarted = (getState() == Started);

            if(isStarted) {
(20)            stopInRestart();
            }

(21)        super.setMediaTime(t);

            if(isStarted) {
(22)            start();
            }
        }
```

As you can see, the requirement that the `Clock` be stopped is not overridden or ignored, but simply circumvented. In line [19], it is first determined whether the `Player` is started or not. If it is, it is temporarily stopped [20]. The media time is then set in the `AbstractController` superclass [21]. Then, the `Player`, if it needed to be stopped initially, is restarted [22] before the method returns.

Several points need to be made regarding this implementation. First, the `Player` is stopped using the `stopInRestart` method [20] defined in the `AbstractController` interface and discussed in "More Than One Way to Stop" on page 254. As you recall, this method stops the `AbstractController` and posts a `RestartingEvent`. This event, a subclass of `StopEvent`, indicates that the `Controller` has temporarily moved from the `Started` to the Prefetched state, but intends to return to the `Started` state as soon as possible.

Secondly, notice that there is no check within this method to ensure that the `Player` has been realized. As you recall, the `Controller` interface requires that the `Controller` be realized before the media time can be set. This requirement is enforced in line [21], when the `setMediaTime` method calls into the `AbstractController` superclass to set the media time. Within the superclass, if the `Controller` has not been realized, a `NotRealizedError` is thrown and the media time will not be set.

Finally, there is no `MediaTimeSetEvent` explicitly posted within this method. As with the realized `Controller` restriction, this functionality is implemented in the superclass. After the media time has been set, the `AbstractController` posts a `MediaTimeSetEvent` before returning.

A More Flexible setRate

Setting the rate of the `AbstractPlayer` is nearly equivalent to setting its media time. The `setRate` method, implemented to relax the same restriction on stopped `Clocks`, is shown in Listing 16.6.

Listing 16.6 *Relaxed Restriction on setRate*

```
          public synchronized float setRate(float rate) {
(23)          boolean isStarted = (getState() == Started);

              if(isStarted) {
(24)              stopInRestart();
              }

(25)          float newRate = super.setRate(rate);

              if(isStarted) {
(26)              start();
              }

(27)          return newRate;
          }
```

Like `setMediaTime`, the `setRate` method first determines whether the `AbstractPlayer` is currently `Started` [23]. If it is, it is temporarily stopped [24] before the rate is set in the `AbstractController` superclass [25]. After the superclass `setRate` returns, the `Player` is restarted [26] and the new rate, returned from the superclass in line [25], is returned [27].

Again mirroring the `setMediaTime` implementation, the requirement that the `Controller` be realized is enforced within the `AbstractController` superclass. Also within the superclass, as we saw in "Controller Rate" on page 221, a `RateChangeEvent` is posted if the rate has changed as a result of this invocation.

Further Relaxation: The start Method

Recall that the `syncStart` method has two restrictions on its use. If called while the `Player` is started, the `Clock` API requires that a `ClockStarted-Error` be thrown. If called without the `Player` being prefetched, the `Controller` API requires that a `NotPrefetchedError` be thrown. Together, both of these state restrictions require the `Player` to be precisely in the `Prefetched` state when `syncStart` is invoked.

The `Player` API does not redefine `syncStart` to relax these state restrictions. Instead, it defines the `start` method, which ensures that the `Player` is in the `Prefetched` state before starting it. It is, in effect, a "wrapper" around the `Controller.syncStart` method.

The `start` method, as implemented in the `AbstractPlayer` class, is shown in Listing 16.7.

Listing 16.7 *Starting the AbstractPlayer*

```
         public final synchronized void start() {
             int state = getState();
             int target = getTargetState();

             if( state == Started ) {
(28)             postStartEvent();
                 return;
             }

             if( target < Started ) {
(29)             setTargetState(Started);
             }

(30)         Thread thread = new Thread() {
                 public void run() {
(31)                 if( getState() < Started ) {
(32)                     synchronousStart();
                     }
                 }
             };

(33)         getThreadQueue().addThread(thread);
         }
```

The `start` method resembles the `AbstractController`'s realize, prefetch, and `syncStart` implementations discussed in Chapter 15. When the `start` method is invoked, in accordance with the `Player` API, a `StartEvent` is posted [28] and the method returns if the `AbstractPlayer` is already in the `Started` state. Otherwise, the `Player`'s target state is set to `Started` [29] and the method continues.

Like `realize`, `prefetch`, and `syncStart`, the `start` method is executed asynchronously. Accordingly, a `Thread` object is created in line [30]. Within the `run` method of this thread, the `synchronousStart` method is called [32] to do the actual transition. As with the forward transitions implemented in the `AbstractController` class, this thread is added to the `AbstractController`'s `ThreadQueue` object [33] and executed when all forward transitions queued before it have completed. At that point, the `start` thread will ensure that the transition is still necessary by checking to see if the `AbstractPlayer` has already reached the `Started` state [31].

The synchronousStart Method

Once the thread created by the `AbstractPlayer`'s start method is started by the thread queue, the `synchronousStart` method is executed. This method is shown in Listing 16.8 below.

Listing 16.8 *Starting the AbstractPlayer Synchronously*

```
       protected void synchronousStart() {
           if( getState() < Prefetched ) {
(34)           synchronousPrefetch();
           }

(35)       Time t = getTimeBase().getTime();

(36)       synchronousSyncStart(t);
       }
```

This method is short and simple. As promised, if the `AbstractPlayer` has not yet been prefetched, then the `synchronousPrefetch` method, defined in the `AbstractController` class, is called [34]. Since the transition is executed synchronously, this method will not return until the `AbstractPlayer` has been prefetched.

After the `AbstractPlayer` has been prefetched, it must be started as soon as possible. In media terms, "as soon as possible" is defined as the current time-base time, retrieved in line [35]. Maintaining its synchronous nature, the `synchronousSyncStart` method is then called [36], moving the `AbstractPlayer` to the `Started` state and posting a `StartEvent`.

To reiterate, the `start` method is simply a wrapper around the prefetch and `syncStart` transitions implemented in the `AbstractController` class. All of the actual work of transitioning the `AbstractPlayer`, including setting the states, invoking the media-specific behavior, and posting the appropriate `TransitionEvents`, is done in the `AbstractController` superclass.

Adding a Managed Controller

As mentioned above, the most significant piece of functionality that the `Player` interface offers is the ability to manage and synchronize multiple `Controllers`. When an *action* is invoked on a master `Player`, it is systematically propagated on to each of its managed `Controllers`. Conversely, the master `Player` takes the responsibility of posting the appropriate *transition* or *change* `ControllerEvent` when each of its managed `Controllers` has completed an operation. A managed `Controller` shares its master `Player`'s `TimeBase`, and affects the aggregate duration and start latency of the master `Player`.

Controllers are placed under the control of a master `Player` with the `Player`'s `addController` method. The algorithm that this method follows, as well as the restrictions that it imposes on both the master `Player` and the `Controller` to be managed, are discussed in detail in "Synchronization Using addController" on page 153. Its implementation in the `Abstract-Player` class is shown in Listing 16.9.

Listing 16.9 *Adding a Managed Controller*

(37)
```
private Vector controllers;

public synchronized void addController(
                          Controller newController)
    throws IncompatibleTimeBaseException
{
    if( controllers.contains(newController) ||
        this == newController )
    {
```
(38)
```
        return;
    }

    int currentState = getState();
```
(39)
```
    if( currentState == Unrealized ||
        currentState == Realizing )
    {
        throw new NotRealizedError(
                    "Player must be Realized");
    }
```
(40)
```
    if(currentState == Started) {
        throw new ClockStartedError(
            "Cannot add Controller to a Started Player");
    }

    int controllerState = newController.getState();
```

```
(41)        if( controllerState == Unrealized ||
                controllerState == Realizing )
            {
                throw new NotRealizedError(
                    "Cannot add Unrealized Controller to a Player");
            }

(42)        if (controllerState == Started) {
                throw new ClockStartedError(
                    "Cannot add Started Controller to a Player");
            }

(43)        newController.setTimeBase(getTimeBase());

(44)        stop();
(45)        newController.stop();
            currentState = getState();
            controllerState = newController.getState();

(46)        if( controllerState < Prefetched &&
                currentState > Realized )
            {
(47)            deallocate();
            }

(48)        newController.setMediaTime( getMediaTime() );

            float rate = getRate();
(49)        if( rate != newController.setRate(rate) ) {
                newController.setRate(1.0F);
                setRate(1.0F);
            }

(50)        newController.setStopTime(Clock.RESET);

(51)        controllers.addElement(newController
(52)        newController.addControllerListener(this);

(53)        updateDuration();
        }
```

When the `addController` method is invoked, the `AbstractPlayer` first checks to see if it is already managing the specified `Controller`. If it is, or if the given `Controller` is the `AbstractPlayer` itself, the `addController` method returns immediately [38].

After verifying that the `Controller` is not already under control of the `AbstractPlayer`, the `addController` method enforces several state restrictions on both the master `Player` and the given `Controller`. If either the AbstractPlayer or the Controller has not yet been realized ([39] and [41]), or is currently started ([40] and [42]), the Controller cannot be placed under the AbstractPlayer's control. The necessity for the former condition stems from the fact that an unrealized Controller knows nothing about its TimeBase, start latency, or duration, and thus these values cannot be set or compared between the two. The latter restriction is imposed because the AbstractPlayer cannot synchronize the start-up of a Controller if one of the two is already started. If either of these conditions are not met, an appropriate MediaError is thrown.

The final criterion for a Controller to be managed is that it must support the Player's TimeBase. If it does not, an IncompatibleTimeBaseException will be thrown by the Controller's setTimeBase method [43].

At this point the AbstractPlayer and the Controller need to be synchronized. The first step in this process is to stop any forward transition of either the AbstractPlayer [44] or the Controller [45]. Since the addController method is synchronized, no other forward transitions can occur until the addController method returns.

The Player API dictates the next step in the process of adding a Controller:

When a Controller is added to a Player, the Player does not transition the added Controller to new state, nor does the Player transition itself forward. The Player either transitions back to the Realized state if the added Controller is Realized or Prefetching, or it stays in the Prefetched state if the both the Player and the added Controller are in the Prefetched state.

This somewhat convoluted rule is implemented in lines [46]–[47]. If the AbstractPlayer has been prefetched but the Controller has not, then the AbstractPlayer is returned to the Realized state. Otherwise, both the AbstractPlayer and the Controller are left "as-is."

The next major step in the process is to set the Controller's media time, rate, and stop time to that of the master AbstractPlayer. In line [48], the AbstractPlayer's media time is retrieved and set in the Controller. The same is done for the AbstractPlayer's rate in line [49]. However, if the Controller cannot use the AbstractPlayer's current rate, then the rate for both the AbstractPlayer and the Controller are set to 1.0, the only rate guaranteed to be supported.

In line [50], the stop time of the Controller is set to Clock.RESET, indicating that no specific stop time is set for the Controller. This is done because the AbstractPlayer, using its own scheduled stopping mechanism, will stop the Controller at the correct time. In this case, the Abstract-Player, as an AbstractController, uses the StopTimeMonitor class introduced in "Enforcing the Stop Time" on page 225.

Finally, in line [51], the Controller is added to the AbstractPlayer's list of managed Controllers. This list is stored in a java.util.Vector object declared in line [37]. In line [52], the AbstractPlayer registers as a

ControllerListener to the new Controller. This will enable the AbstractPlayer to closely monitor and control the Controller's transitions.

As you recall from page 157, a Player's duration is the greater of its own and its managed Controller's durations. Before the addController routine returns, the duration of the Player must be recalculated to take account of the newly-added Controller [53]. The method used to do this, updateDuration, will be discussed later in this chapter.

Like the duration, the start latency of a Player is also dependent on that of its managed Controllers. However, unlike duration, the start latency of a Controller can change as the Controller moves closer to the Started state. For this reason, the start latency of the AbstractPlayer, in consideration of its managed Controllers, is calculated dynamically every time the getStartLatency method is called. The duration, on the other hand, is only recalculated when a Controller is added to or removed from the AbstractPlayer's list of managed Controllers.

Removing a Managed Controller

The process for removing a Controller from the control of a Player is essentially the opposite of that of adding the Controller. The removeController method, as implemented in the AbstractPlayer class, is shown in Listing 16.10.

Listing 16.10 *Removing a Managed Controller*

```
public synchronized void removeController(
                           Controller oldController) {
    int currentState = getState();

    if( currentState == Unrealized ||
        currentState == Realizing)
    {
        throw new NotRealizedError(
            "Player must be realized");
    }

    if(currentState == Started) {
        throw new ClockStartedError(
            "Player must not be Started");
    }

    if( controllers.indexOf(oldController) == -1 ) {
        return;
    }

    stop();

    controllers.removeElement(oldController);

    oldController.removeControllerListener(this);

    try {
        oldController.setTimeBase(null);
    } catch(IncompatibleTimeBaseException e) {}

    updateDuration();
}
```

The labels along the left margin of the listing are:
(54) (55) (56) (57) (58) (59) (60) (61)

Like the addController method, the removeController method
requires that the AbstractPlayer be realized for a Controller to be
removed. This requirement is academic; if a Player has not been realized,
then no Controller could have been added to it in the first place. However,
in the event that this method is called when the AbstractPlayer is unrealized, a NotRealizedError is thrown [54]. Similarly, if the Abstract-
Player is started when this method is invoked, a ClockStartedError is
thrown [55].

If the Controller to be removed is not actually managed by this
AbstractPlayer, then the removeController method returns [56].
Otherwise, the AbstractPlayer prepares to remove the Controller by
first stopping any currently-running transitions [57], thereby stabilizing its
state. This ensures that the Controller is not transitioned while it is

removed. At that point, the `Controller` is removed from the list of managed `Controllers` [58] and the `AbstractPlayer` removes itself as a `ControllerListener` of the `Controller` [59].

In line [60], the `Controller`'s `setTimeBase` method is called with a null argument. As you recall, this resets the `Controller`'s `TimeBase` to its default value.

Finally, before returning, the duration of the `AbstractPlayer` is recalculated to account for the `Controller` being removed [61].

Implications of Managed Controller Support

The `addController` and `removeController` methods do not in themselves provide complete support for `Controller` management. They are, in fact, only the tip of the iceberg. As we will see, many of the `Clock` and `Controller` methods implemented in previous chapters will need to be overridden or augmented here to provide support for managed `Controllers`.

Let's turn now to these augmented methods. For the remainder of this chapter, we will look at some of the simpler methods affected by the support of managed `Controllers`. In the next chapter, we will look at how the `Controller` transition methods are affected by support of managed `Controllers`.

Player Duration

As we saw in the `addController` and `removeController` implementations, the overall duration of the `Player` needs to be recalculated whenever there is a change in the `Player`'s list of managed `Controllers`. This is done in the `private` method `updateDuration`, which calculates the greatest duration among the `AbstractPlayer` and each of its managed `Controllers`. In order to make this calculation, however, a new method must be defined to return *only* the duration of the `Player`'s media.

To this end the `AbstractPlayer` defines the abstract method `getPlayerDuration`. This method has a Java signature identical to the `Player` `getDuration` method, and is intended to be overridden by subclasses of the `AbstractPlayer` to indicate the duration of the `Player`'s media.

Unlike `getDuration`, which returns the aggregate duration of the `Player` and all of its managed `Controllers`, the `getPlayerDuration` method returns the duration of this `Player`'s media only. Using this method on the master `Player`, and the `getDuration` method on each of the managed `Controllers`, the `Player`'s aggregate duration can be calculated by the `updateDuration` method. Let's look now at how this is done.

Calculating the Aggregate Duration

As discussed in "Adding a Controller" on page 154, the general rule for determining the aggregate duration of a `Player` and its `Controllers` is as follows:

1. If the `Player` or any of the `Controllers` has a duration of DURATION_UNKNOWN, then this will be the aggregate duration. Otherwise,

2. If the `Player` or any of the `Controllers` has a duration of DURATION_UNBOUNDED, then this will be the aggregate duration. Otherwise,

3. The aggregate duration is the maximum duration of the `Player` and each of its managed `Controllers`.

This algorithm is implemented in the `updateDuration` method, shown in Listing 16.11.

Listing 16.11 *Calculating the Aggregate Duration*

```
(62)    private Time duration;

        private synchronized final void updateDuration() {
(63)        Time duration = getPlayerDuration();

            if( duration != DURATION_UNKNOWN )
            {
(64)            for (int i = 0,
                    n = controllers.size(); i < n; i++)
                {
                    Controller c =
                        (Controller)controllers.elementAt(i);

                    Time d = c.getDuration();

                    if( d == DURATION_UNKNOWN ) {
                        duration = d;
                        break;
                    }

                    if( duration != DURATION_UNBOUNDED &&
                            (d == DURATION_UNBOUNDED ||
                            d.getNanoseconds() >
                            duration.getNanoseconds() ) )
                    {
                        duration = d;
                    }
                }
            }
        }
```

```
          boolean newDuration = false;

(65)      if (  duration      == DURATION_UNKNOWN   ||
                 duration      == DURATION_UNBOUNDED ||
                 this.duration == DURATION_UNKNOWN   ||
                 this.duration == DURATION_UNBOUNDED)
          {
(66)         if( this.duration != duration ) {
                 newDuration = true;
             }
          } else

(67)      if( duration.getNanoseconds() !=
              this.duration.getNanoseconds() )
          {
             newDuration = true;
          }

          if( newDuration ) {
(68)         this.duration = duration;
(69)         postEvent(
                 new DurationUpdateEvent(this,duration) );
          }
      }

(70)  public abstract Time getPlayerDuration();

      }
```

The first step that the updateDuration method takes is to call the abstract method getPlayerDuration [63]. To reiterate, this method, declared in line [70], should be overridden by subclasses of the AbstractPlayer to return the duration of the Player's media.

After getting the duration of the Player's media, the updateDuration method iterates through the AbstractPlayer's list of managed Controllers to find the maximum duration [64]. Following the rules set forth above, if any of the Controllers, or the Player itself, has a duration of DURATION_UNKNOWN or DURATION_UNBOUNDED, then the aggregate duration is set to this value.

Following this process, if the aggregate duration of the Player has changed since the last time it was calculated, a DurationUpdateEvent must be posted. To determine whether this is necessary, the newly-calculated duration is compared with the current value of the AbstractPlayer's duration property declared in line [62]. If either object is one of the static finals DURATION_UNKNOWN or DURATION_UNBOUNDED [65], then a strict object comparison is used [66]. Otherwise, the two durations are converted to nanoseconds and compared numerically [67]. If the duration has indeed changed, it is saved in the AbstractPlayer [68] and a DurationUpdateEvent is posted [69].

Getting the Aggregate Duration

Having implemented the updateDuration method, the implementation of the Player method getDuration is trivial.

Listing 16.12 *Getting the Player's Aggregate Duration*

```
public final synchronized Time getDuration() {
    if( duration == null ) {
(71)        updateDuration();
    }
(72)    return duration;
}
```

If the duration has not been calculated, the updateDuration method is called [71]. Otherwise, the AbstractPlayer's duration property is returned [72].

Player Start Latency

Like duration, the Player's start latency depends on both the latency required to present its own media, and the start latency of each of its managed Controllers. To obtain the former, the AbstractPlayer provides the abstract method getPlayerStartLatency.

Unlike getStartLatency, which returns the aggregate start latency of the Player and all of its managed Controllers, the getPlayerStartLatency method returns the start latency for the master Player and its media only. This method will be called by getStartLatency, as it dynamically calculates the aggregate start latency every time it is called.

Calculating the Aggregate Start Latency

There is some dispute over how the aggregate start latency of a Player and its Controllers should be determined. In the Intel version of the JMF, the algorithm is as follows:

1. If the Player or any of the Controllers has a start latency of LATENCY_UNKNOWN, then this will be the aggregate start latency. Otherwise,

2. The aggregate start latency is the maximum start latency of the Player and each of its managed Controllers.

In the Sun version of the JMF, the algorithm is brilliantly avant-garde:

1. Return LATENCY_UNKNOWN.

Okay, so perhaps Sun's implementation of getStartLatency leaves something to be desired. Namely, it ignores start latency calculation for both the Player and its managed Controllers.

The AbstractPlayer's implementation of the getStartLatency follows an algorithm that is similar, but not identical, to Intel's implementation:

1. If the Player and each of the Controllers has a start latency of LATENCY_UNKNOWN, then this will be the aggregate start latency. Otherwise,

2. The aggregate start latency is the maximum start latency of the Player and each of its managed Controllers.

Essentially, this algorithm produces the maximum known start latency among the Player and its managed Controllers. The philosophy of this algorithm stems from the AbstractController's implementation of the syncStart method. Recall from "SyncStarting the AbstractController" on page 246 that this implementation uses the start latency to determine whether the given time-base start time is sufficiently in the future for the Controller's media to be rendered at the given time. In this calculation, if the latency returned by the Controller is LATENCY_UNKNOWN, it is assumed to be zero.

In the case of a Player with multiple Controllers, it is better that syncStart use a known start latency, if possible, for this calculation. Consider the following example as an illustration of this point. Suppose a Player has five Controllers under its control. Together with the Player, there are six different start latencies to consider when determining an appropriate time-base start time. If one of the Controllers has a latency of LATENCY_UNKNOWN, then Intel's algorithm would return LATENCY_UNKNOWN as the collective start latency. With this value, the AbstractController's syncStart method would have no way to tell if the given time-base time is far enough in the future for the Player and the Controllers to be properly synchronized. This might result in the Player and its Controllers all starting at different times.

With the AbstractPlayer's start latency algorithm, however, the unknown latency of the single Controller is ignored, and the maximum known start latency is returned instead. Using this value, the syncStart method can, at the very least, ensure that all but the Controllers with the unknown latency begin rendering their media at the same time. It is, essentially, making the best of limited information.

Subclasses of the AbstractPlayer who do not agree with this philosophy may override the AbstractPlayer's getStartLatency routine in favor of a different algorithm.

Putting the Algorithm into Practice

Using the above mentioned algorithm for determining a Player's start latency, the AbstractPlayer's implementation of the getStartLatency method is shown in Listing 16.13.

Listing 16.13 *Calculating the Aggregate Start Latency*

```
public synchronized Time getStartLatency() {
    int currentState = getState();

    if( currentState == Unrealized ||
        currentState == Realizing )
    {
        throw new NotRealizedError(
            "Controller must be Realized");
    }

    Time latency = getPlayerStartLatency();

    for(int i = 0, n = controllers.size(); i < n; i++) {
        Controller c =
            (Controller)controllers.elementAt(i);
        Time l = c.getStartLatency();

        if( l == LATENCY_UNKNOWN ) {
            continue;
        }

        if( latency == LATENCY_UNKNOWN ||
            l.getNanoseconds() > latency.getNanoseconds() )
        {
            latency = l;
        }
    }

    return latency;
}

public abstract Time getPlayerStartLatency();
```

(73)

(74)

(75)

Following the requirements set forth by the Controller API, a NotRealizedError is thrown [73] if the AbstractPlayer has not been realized when the getStartLatency method is called. Otherwise, the calculation of the aggregate start latency begins by getting the Player's own start latency [74]. This value is obtained from the abstract method getPlayerStartLatency declared in line [75]. Subclasses of the AbstractPlayer should override this method to reflect the Player's individual start latency.

The rest of the getStartLatency method calculates the maximum start latency by iterating through the list of managed Controllers. Only if every Controller, including the master Player, has an unknown start latency will the getStartLatency method return LATENCY_UNKNOWN.

We've seen how the management of multiple Controllers can affect a Player's duration and start latency. Now let's take a look at how setting some of the Clock properties changes when the managed Controllers are taken into account.

Setting the Media Time

As we saw in "A More Flexible setMediaTime" on page 273, the Abstract-Player overrides the Clock method setMediaTime to provide for fewer restrictions on the Player's state. This implementation, as you recall, called the setMediaTime method in the AbstractController superclass after moving the Player out of the Started state.

In "Media Time" on page 223, we saw that the AbstractController's setMediaTime method implements as much API-compliant functionality as possible before setting the media time in the implementation-specific subclass. Through the use of the abstract method doSetMediaTime, subclasses of the AbstractController can set the media time in their own implementation without having to worry about much of the API-required overhead, such as enforcing state restrictions or posting a Media-TimeSetEvent.

As a subclass of the AbstractController, the AbstractPlayer implements the abstract doSetMediaTime method to provide support for the management of multiple Controllers. Within this method, the media time must be set in each of the managed Controllers, as well as in the Player itself.

The doSetMediaTime method appears in Listing 16.14.

Listing 16.14 *Setting the Media Time*

(76)
(77)

(78)

(79)

(80)

```
public synchronized final void doSetMediaTime(Time t) {
    for(int i = 0, n = controllers.size(); i < n; i++ ) {
        Controller c =
            (Controller)controllers.elementAt(i);

        c.setMediaTime(t);
    }
    doPlayerSetMediaTime(t);
}

public abstract void doPlayerSetMediaTime(Time t);

}
```

Having taken care of much of the API-compliant overhead in the `AbstractController`'s `setMediaTime` method, the `AbstractPlayer`'s `doSetMediaTime` implementation is fairly simple. Iterating through the list of managed `Controllers` [77], the media time is set using the `Controller` method `setMediaTime` [78]. Because this method is synchronized [76], this list of controllers cannot be changed while the media time is being set.

Once the media time has been set on each of the `Controllers`, the abstract method `doPlayerSetMediaTime` is called [79]. This method, declared in line [80], should be overridden to set the media time in media-specific subclasses of the `AbstractPlayer`.

The operation of setting the media time is the first example of the *action/doAction/doPlayerAction* model introduced earlier in this chapter. As we saw here, the bulk of the API-compliant functionality is taken care of in the `setMediaTime` method implemented in the `AbstractController` class. This method calls the abstract `doSetMediaTime` method, implemented by the `AbstractPlayer` class to provide support for managed `Controllers`. In turn, the `doSetMediaTime` method calls the `doPlayerSetMediaTime` method, setting the media time in specific implementations of the `Abstract-Player`.

We will see the *action/doAction/doPlayerAction* model used wherever the `AbstractPlayer` must augment the `Controller` or `Clock` methods to provide support for managed `Controllers`. Such is the case in the next section, as we look at setting the `Player`'s rate.

Setting the Rate

As with the media time, changes in the `Player`'s rate must be propagated on to each of the `Player`'s managed `Controllers`. With this goal in mind, the `AbstractPlayer` implements the `AbstractController` method `doSetRate` to provide support for managed `Controllers`.

The `doSetRate` implementation is shown in Listing 16.15.

Listing 16.15 *Setting the Rate*

```
(81)    public synchronized final float doSetRate(float rate) {
            float actual;

            for(int i = 0, n = controllers.size(); i < n; i++ ) {
                Controller c =
                    (Controller)controllers.elementAt(i);

(82)            actual = c.setRate(rate);

(83)            if( rate != 1.0F && actual != rate ) {
(84)                doSetRate(1.0F);
(85)                return 1.0F;
                }
            }

(86)        actual = doPlayerSetRate(rate);

(87)        if( actual != rate &&
(88)            ! controllers.isEmpty() )
            {
(89)            doSetRate(1.0F);
(90)            return 1.0F;
            }

(91)        return actual;
        }

(92)    public abstract float doPlayerSetRate(float rate);
```

The doSetRate method has the same function and Java signature as the Clock method setRate, taking a "requested rate" argument and returning the actual rate set. As with the doSetMediaTime method, the doSetRate method is synchronized [81] so that Controllers cannot be added or removed from the AbstractPlayer while the rate is being set.

Within an iterative loop, the rate is set on each of the AbstractController's managed Controllers [82]. If a Controller cannot use the given rate, it will return a value different from the desired rate. In such a case [83] the doSetRate method resets the rate on all of the Controllers to 1.0, the only rate guaranteed to be supported. This is done with a recursive call to doSetRate in line [84]. When this invocation returns, the universal rate is then returned in line [85].

If the given rate is successfully set on each of the Controllers, the abstract method doPlayerSetRate is called [86]. This method, declared in line [92], should be overridden to set the rate in subclasses of the Abstract-

`Player`. Like the `doPlayerSetMediaTime` method, this method follows the *action/doAction/doPlayerAction* model discussed earlier.

As with each of the `Controllers`, the actual rate returned from the `doPlayerSetRate` method may differ from the given rate [87]. If the `AbstractPlayer` has no managed `Controllers` [88], this is not an issue and the `doSetRate` method returns the actual rate used [91]. Otherwise, the rate is reset to `1.0` [89] and the `doSetRate` method returns [90].

Having augmented the media time and rate-setting operations, there is only one more method to be discussed before moving on to the `Player` transitions in the next chapter. This method is discussed below.

Getting the Managed Controllers

Subclasses of the `AbstractPlayer` may wish to perform an operation on each of its managed `Controllers`. To provide these `Controllers`, the `AbstractPlayer` provides the `getControllers` method, described in EJMF Toolkit Synopsis 16.5.

EJMF Toolkit Synopsis 16.5 *Getting the Managed Controllers*

Class	`ejmf.toolkit.media.AbstractPlayer`
Method	`getControllers`
Visibility	`protected`
Arguments	`void`
Return	`java.util.Vector`
Description	Returns a `Vector` containing the `Controllers` managed by this `AbstractPlayer`.

The implementation of this routine simply clones the controllers `Vector`.

Listing 16.16 *Getting the Managed Controllers*

```
protected Vector getControllers()
    return (Vector)controllers.clone();
}
```

It is important to note that the `AbstractPlayer`'s list of `Controllers` may change after the `getControllers` method has been called. Methods that need to ensure this list does not change should synchronize on the `AbstractPlayer` object so that the `addController` and `removeController` methods will block until the operation has completed.

Summary

In this chapter we began to implement the Player interface in the AbstractPlayer class. Extending from the AbstractController class, this class inherits all of the Clock and Controller functionality developed in previous chapters.

The Player interface offers several points of extended functionality over the Controller interface. It provides visual and control panel components for displaying the media, a DataSource object to read the media, and relaxes several of the state restrictions imposed by the Controller API.

The most extensive feature of the Player interface is the ability to synchronize and manage multiple Controllers. This provides an enormous convenience to the user but requires a fair amount of work to implement. Within this chapter, we provided routines to add and remove Controllers from our AbstractPlayer class, and began to augment some of the Controller methods developed in earlier chapters. In the next chapter, we will complete the AbstractPlayer implementation by augmenting the Controller transition methods to transition the managed Controllers as well as the Player itself.

Chapter 17   *IMPLEMENTING THE PLAYER TRANSITIONS*

Introduction

In the last chapter we began to develop the AbstractPlayer class, the final piece of our *Abstract Player Framework*. This class extended the Abstract-Controller class to provide, among other things, support for Controller management. In this chapter we will complete the AbstractPlayer implementation by augmenting the AbstractController's transition methods to support the AbstractPlayer's managed Controllers. Once we have completed this task, the APF will be complete and we can move on to creating our custom Players.

Player Transition Model

As with any process involving the coordination of multiple objects and threads, the transition of the AbstractPlayer and its managed Controllers requires some design before it can be implemented.

In accordance with the javax.media.Player API, a Player cannot officially report a successful transition until each of its managed Controllers has done the same. It is for that reason that the Player registers itself as a `ControllerListener` when a `Controller` is placed under its control. By monitoring its `Controllers` in this way, a `Player` can tell when to post a `TransitionEvent` to indicate that the aggregate transition is complete. Conversely, if a `Controller` transition fails, the `Player` will be notified and the aggregate transition will fail.

As a `ControllerListener`, the `AbstractPlayer` implements the `controllerUpdate` method to receive `ControllerEvents` from its managed `Controllers`. This method, along with some of the `private` methods used to handle errors, is shown in Listing 17.1.

Listing 17.1 *Monitoring Managed Controllers with controllerUpdate*

(1)
```
private ControllerErrorEvent controllerError;

public final void controllerUpdate(ControllerEvent e) {
    synchronized(controllers) {
        if( e instanceof TransitionEvent ) {
```
(2)
```
            controllers.notifyAll();
        } else

        if( e instanceof ControllerErrorEvent ) {
```
(3)
```
            setControllerError((ControllerErrorEvent)e);
```
(4)
```
            controllers.notifyAll();
        }
    }
}
```

(5)
```
private void setControllerError(ControllerErrorEvent e) {
    this.controllerError = e;
}
```

(6)
```
private ControllerErrorEvent getControllerError() {
    return controllerError;
}
```

(7)
```
private void resetControllerError() {
    setControllerError(null);
}
```

If a managed `Controller` begins or completes a transition, the `controllerUpdate` method notifies any threads waiting on the list of managed `Controllers` [2]. If one of the `Controllers` posts a `ControllerErrorEvent` indicating that it has failed in an operation, then the error is saved [3] before the master `Player` is notified [4].

The `setControllerError` method [5], called by `controllerUpdate`, simply saves the given `ControllerErrorEvent` to the `controllerError` member data field declared in line [1]. This property can be retrieved using the getControllerError method declared in line [6]. As a convenience, the resetControllerError method [7] sets the controllerError property to null. This is called by the Player transition thread before a transition is invoked on its Controllers, so that it can ensure that any ControllerErrorEvent that is saved is a direct result of the requested transition.

One more method is used by the AbstractPlayer to track its Controllers' states. The isStateReached method, shown in Listing 17.2, iterates through the AbstractPlayer's list of managed Controllers and checks to see if a given state has been reached.

Listing 17.2 *State Query of Managed Controllers*

```
private boolean isStateReached(int state) {
    synchronized(controllers) {
        for(int i = 0, n = controllers.size(); i < n; i++) {
            Controller controller =
                (Controller)controllers.elementAt(i);
            if( controller.getState() < state ) {
                return false;
            }
        }
        return true;
    }
}
```

(8)

If any of the Controllers has not yet reached the given state [8], the isStateReached method returns false. Otherwise, it returns true, indicating that each of the managed Controllers has reached the given state.

Managing Controller Transition Failure

When the controllerUpdate method notifies the Player transition thread that a ControllerErrorEvent has occurred, the Player itself is required to post a ControllerErrorEvent. This is done within the postManagedControllerErrorEvent method, appearing in Listing 17.3.

Listing 17.3 *Handling ControllerErrorEvents*

```
private void postManagedControllerErrorEvent() {
    Controller c = controllerError.getSourceController();
    String message =
        "Managing Player " + getClass().getName() +
        " received ControllerErrorEvent from " +
        c.getClass().getName();

    postEvent( new ManagedControllerErrorEvent(
        this, controllerError, message ) );

    resetControllerError();
}
```

(9)

(10)

(11)

Within this method, an `ejmf.toolkit.media.event.ManagedControllerErrorEvent` is created and posted. This class, itself a `ControllerErrorEvent`, indicates that a transition of a managed `Controller` has failed, resulting in the failure of the transition of the `Player` and its `Controllers` as a whole.

After creating a suitable error message string [9], the `ManagedControllerErrorEvent` is created and posted [10]. Before returning, the `controllerError` property is cleared [11].

The ManagedControllerErrorEvent Class

The `ManagedControllerErrorEvent` class consists of two constructors and a single method. The two constructors are described in EJMF Toolkit Synopsis 17.1.

EJMF Toolkit Synopsis 17.1 *ManagedControllerErrorEvent Constructor*

Class	`ejmf.toolkit.media.` `    ManagedControllerErrorEvent`
Constructor	`ManagedControllerErrorEvent`
Visibility	`public`
Arguments	`javax.media.Player` `javax.media.ControllerErrorEvent`
Description	Creates a `ManagedControllerErrorEvent` given a master `Player` and a `ControllerErrorEvent` posted by one of its managed `Controllers`.

EJMF Toolkit Synopsis 17.1 *ManagedControllerErrorEvent Constructor (Continued)*

Class	`ejmf.toolkit.media.` `ManagedControllerErrorEvent`
Constructor	`ManagedControllerErrorEvent`
Visibility	`public`
Arguments	`javax.media.Player` `javax.media.ControllerErrorEvent` `java.lang.String`
Description	Creates a `ManagedControllerErrorEvent` given a master `Player`, a `ControllerErrorEvent` posted by one of its managed `Controllers`, and a `String` describing the failure.

The single method is described in EJMF Toolkit Synopsis 17.2

EJMF Toolkit Synopsis 17.2 *Getting a ControllerErrorEvent*

Class	`ejmf.toolkit.media.` `ManagedControllerErrorEvent`
Method	`getControllerErrorEvent`
Visibility	`public`
Arguments	`void`
Return	`javax.media.ControllerErrorEvent`
Description	Returns the `ControllerErrorEvent` for this `ManagedControllerErrorEvent`.

Now that a framework has been laid out to transition the `Player` and its `Controllers`, let's begin our discussion by looking at the most simple of the transition methods.

Realizing the Player

Per the augmented *action/doAction* model discussed in the last chapter, the `AbstractPlayer` implements the `AbstractController` method `doRealize` to transition itself and its managed `Controllers` to the `Realized` state. As you recall, this method is called by the `AbstractController` class as a result of the `realize` method being called. It is shown in Listing 17.4.

Listing 17.4 *Realizing the Player*

```
public final boolean doRealize() {

        try {
(12)        source.start();
        }
        catch(IOException e) {
(13)        postEvent(
                new ResourceUnavailableEvent(this,
                    "Could not start DataSource") );
(14)        return false;
        }

(15)    if(! doPlayerRealize() ) {
            return false;
        }

(16)    updateDuration();

(17)    return true;
}

(18) public abstract boolean doPlayerRealize();
```

The first step in realizing a Player is to start the transfer of data from the DataSource. This is done with the DataSource's start method [12]. Note that it is not necessary to call the DataSource's connect method here, since this method was called by the javax.media.Manager class when the Player was first created.

If the call to start fails, a ResourceUnavailableEvent is posted by the AbstractPlayer [13]. This event is a subclass of the ControllerError-Event class and reflects a catastrophic failure of the Player. After reporting this failure, in accordance with the AbstractController API, the doRealize method returns false [14] to indicate that the realize operation failed.

In line [15], the AbstractPlayer calls the doPlayerRealize method declared in line [18]. This method should be implemented by subclasses of the AbstractPlayer to do the actual work of realizing the Player. This may include, among other things, acquiring any non-exclusive resources that the Player will need to render its media. As with doRealize, this method returns a boolean indicating its success.

Once the AbstractPlayer has been realized, the duration is updated [16]. The updateDuration method, discussed in the last chapter, simply determines the maximum duration between the AbstractPlayer and its managed Controllers. It is called here because realizing a Player usually will result in a more accurate estimation of the it's duration. After this method is called, the `doRealize` method returns true [17] to reflect the successful transition.

Note that in no part of this method does the `AbstractPlayer` reference any of its managed `Controllers`. The reason for this is simple: Since the `AbstractPlayer` has not yet been realized, the `addController` method could not yet have been called, and thus there are no `Controllers` to manage at this point. Furthermore, the `Controllers` themselves must be realized before they are added to a master `Player`, so in fact this method will never be called when the `AbstractPlayer` has `Controllers` under its control.

Let's look now at a transition that does require the `Player`'s managed `Controllers` to be considered.

Prefetching the Player

Prefetching the `AbstractPlayer` is slightly more involved than the realizing operation. When the `prefetch` method is called, the `Player` may have `Controllers` under its control. The `Player` must transition these `Controllers` along with it as the prefetching operation takes place.

Again following the augmented *action/doAction* model, the `Abstract-Player` implements the `AbstractController` method `doPrefetch` to prefetch the `Player`. This method, called from the `AbstractController` as a result of the prefetch operation, is shown in Listing 17.5.

Listing 17.5 *Prefetching the Player*

```
public final boolean doPrefetch() {

        resetControllerError();

        for(int i = 0; i < controllers.size(); i++) {
            Controller c =
                (Controller)controllers.elementAt(i);
            c.prefetch();
        }

        if(! doPlayerPrefetch() ) {
            return false;
        }

        synchronized(controllers) {
            while( controllerError == null &&
                    ! isStateReached(Prefetched) )
            {
                try { controllers.wait(); }
                catch(InterruptedException e) {}
            }
        }
```

(19)
(20)
(21)
(22)
(23)
(24)

```
          if( controllerError != null ) {
(25)          postManagedControllerErrorEvent();
              return false;
          }

(26)      updateDuration();

          return true;
       }

(27)   public abstract boolean doPlayerPrefetch();
```

In preparation for prefetching each of its managed `Controllers`, the `AbstractPlayer` first resets the `controllerError` property [19]. This ensures that any `ControllerErrorEvent` that is logged by the `controllerUpdate` method is a direct result of the forthcoming prefetching operation.

The next step in the process is to prefetch each of the `AbstractPlayer`'s managed `Controllers` [20]. This is done within an iterative loop through the `AbstractPlayer`'s `controllers` `Vector`. It may seem necessary to synchronize this `Vector` while we are referencing it, but in fact there is no chance of it being modified throughout the duration of this method. Recall that the only methods that manipulate the `controllers` `Vector`, `addController` and `removeController`, stop any forward transitions before making any changes. In such a case, this prefetching thread would be stopped before the list of `Controllers` is changed.

After the prefetching operation is started asynchronously on each `Controller`, the `Player` itself is prefetched in the `abstract` method `doPlayerPrefetch` [21]. This method, declared in line [27], should be implemented by subclasses of the `AbstractPlayer` to acquire any exclusive resources that the `Player` will need to render its media. It may also buffer the media data or perform other start-up processing. Like `doPlayerRealize`, the `doPlayerPrefetch` method returns true if successful and false otherwise.

After the `AbstractPlayer` itself is prefetched, it must wait for each of its `Controllers` to finish prefetching. As discussed above, when any of the `Controllers` post a `TransitionEvent` or a `ControllerErrorEvent`, the `controllerUpdate` method notifies any waiting threads. In line [24], the prefetching thread waits for such notifications. Each time it is woken up, it checks to see if an error has occurred [22] or if the transition is complete [23]. If either of these conditions is true, the `AbstractPlayer` leaves the waiting loop.

If one of the `Controllers` fails to prefetch, the `postManagedControllerErrorEvent` method is called [25]. This method, discussed earlier, posts an event indicating that the collective transition has failed.

As with `doRealize`, the prefetching operation may result in a more accurate estimate of media duration. If the `AbstractPlayer` and all of its `Controllers` were prefetched successfully, the duration is updated [26] and the `doPrefetch` method returns.

Starting the Player

The `doSyncStart` method, called by the `AbstractController` as a result of the `syncStart` method being called, is nearly identical to the `doPrefetch` method above. It is shown in Listing 17.6.

Listing 17.6 *Starting the Player*

```
public final boolean doSyncStart(Time t) {

    resetControllerError();

    for(int i = 0; i < controllers.size(); i++) {
        Controller c =
                    (Controller)controllers.elementAt(i);
(28)        c.syncStart(t);
    }

(29)    if( ! doPlayerSyncStart(t) ) {
        return false;
    }

    synchronized(controllers) {
        while( controllerError == null &&
              ! isStateReached(Started) )
        {
            try { controllers.wait(); }
            catch(InterruptedException e) {}
        }
    }

    if( controllerError != null ) {
        postManagedControllerErrorEvent();
        return false;
    }

    return true;
}

(30) public abstract boolean doPlayerSyncStart(Time t);
```

The only difference between this method and the `doPrefetch` method is the `javax.media.Time` argument passed in to indicate the time-base time at which the `Player` should begin rendering its media. Recall that this value is precisely calculated in the `AbstractController` method `synchronousSyncStart`. Taking the start latency of the `Player` into account, this value is guaranteed to be far enough in the future for the `Player` and each of its managed `Controllers` to begin rendering their media at the same time.

After passing the starting `Time` argument to each of the managed `Controllers` [28], the `Player` starts the rendering of its own media [29]. The `doPlayerSyncStart` method, declared in line [30], should be implemented by subclasses of the `AbstractPlayer` to asynchronously begin the process of rendering the `Player`'s media. When this method returns, the `Player`, on a separate thread, should be preparing the media to begin rendering at the given time-base time.

Error handling and successful transitions are handled identically to the `doPrefetch` method. The `doSyncStart` method returns true if successful and false otherwise. If a managed `Controller` cannot be started, a `ManagedControllerErrorEvent` is posted and the collective transition fails.

Now that the forward transitions have been implemented, let's look at the `Player`'s backward transitions.

Stopping the Player

Because the backward transitions are synchronous, the process for monitoring the managed `Controllers` differs somewhat from that of the forward transitions. This is evident in the `doStop` method, shown in Listing 17.7. This method, as you recall, is called by the `AbstractController` as a result of the `stop` method being called.

Listing 17.7 *Stopping the Player*

```
public final boolean doStop() {

        resetControllerError();

        int size = controllers.size();
        Thread[] threads = new Thread[size];
```

(31)

```
         for(int i = 0; i < size; i++) {
             final Controller c =
                 (Controller)controllers.elementAt(i);

(32)         threads[i] = new Thread() {
                 public void run() {
(33)                 c.stop();
                 }
             };
(34)         threads[i].start();
         }

(35)     if( ! doPlayerStop() ) {
             return false;
         }

         for(int i = 0; i < size; i++) {
(36)         try { threads[i].join(); }
             catch(InterruptedException e) {}
         }

         if( controllerError != null ) {
(37)         postManagedControllerErrorEvent();
             return false;
         }

         return true;
     }

(38) public abstract boolean doPlayerStop();
```

As with the forward transitions, the controllerError property is first reset [31] before stopping the Controllers. Again, this ensures that any ControllerErrorEvent reported by the controllerUpdate method is a result of a failed stop operation.

The AbstractPlayer then enters an iterative loop to stop each of its managed Controllers. Since the stop operation is synchronous, it could simply call stop on each of the Controllers, waiting until one has been stopped before stopping another. However, since we want each of the Controllers to be stopped essentially at the same time, the stop operation [33] is wrapped in a thread [32] and run asynchronously [34].

After the stop operation has been invoked on each Controller, the Player itself is stopped [35]. The abstract doPlayerStop method, declared in line [38], should be implemented to stop the media rendering and prepare the Player to be moved back into the Prefetched state. As with the other doPlayerTransition methods, this method should return true if success-ful and false otherwise.

Once the Player has been stopped, the doStop method waits for each of the previously-created stop threads to complete [36]. Once this is done, the doStop method checks to see if any of the Controllers could not be successfully stopped. If any of the Controllers has posted a Control-lerErrorEvent, a ManagedControllerErrorEvent is posted [37] to reflect the failure of the transition as a whole.

End of Media

As mentioned before, reaching the end of the Player's media is another way that the Player can be moved out of the Started state. The AbstractCon-troller API states that media-specific subclasses of the AbstractCon-troller should call the endOfMedia method when they reach the end of their media. This method, as discussed in "The Last Stop: End of Media" on page 255, simply stops the Clock, sets the state to Prefetched, and posts an EndOfMediaEvent.

The AbstractPlayer overrides the endOfMedia method to provide support for Controller management. Its implementation in the Abstract-Player class is shown in Listing 17.8.

Listing 17.8 *End of Media*

```
       protected void endOfMedia() throws ClockStoppedException {
           synchronized(controllers) {
(39)           while( ! areControllersStopped() )
               {
(40)               try { controllers.wait(); }
                   catch(InterruptedException e) {}
               }
           }
(41)       super.endOfMedia();
       }

(42)   private boolean areControllersStopped() {
           synchronized(controllers) {
               for(int i = 0, n = controllers.size(); i < n; i++) {
                   Controller controller =
                       (Controller)controllers.elementAt(i);
(43)               if( controller.getState() == Started ) {
                       return false;
                   }
               }
               return true;
           }
       }
```

When the `endOfMedia` method is called, the `AbstractPlayer` waits [40] until each of its managed `Controllers` has been stopped [39]. Whenever the `controllerUpdate` method notifies it of a `Controller` transition, it wakes up and calls the `areControllersStopped` method [42] to see if the `Controllers` have stopped. This method simply looks at each of the `Controllers`' states [43] and returns true only if none of the `Controllers` is in the Started state.

After ensuring that each of the managed `Controllers` has stopped, the superclass `endOfMedia` method is called to complete the transition [41].

Deallocating the Player

The process of deallocating the `Player` is similar to that of stopping it. The `doDeallocate`, as implemented in the `AbstractPlayer` class, is shown in Listing 17.9. It is called by the deallocate method within the `AbstractController`.

Listing 17.9 *Deallocating the Player*

```
public final boolean doDeallocate() {

    resetControllerError();

    int size = controllers.size();
    Thread[] threads = new Thread[size];

    for(int i = 0; i < size; i++) {
        final Controller c =
            (Controller)controllers.elementAt(i);

        threads[i] = new Thread() {
            public void run() {
                c.deallocate();
            }
        };
        threads[i].start();
    }

    if( ! doPlayerDeallocate() ) {
        return false;
    }
```

(44)

(45)

```
        for(int i = 0; i < size; i++) {
            try { threads[i].join(); }
            catch(InterruptedException e) {}
        }

        if( controllerError != null ) {
            postManagedControllerErrorEvent();
            return false;
        }

        return true;
    }
```

(46)   `public abstract boolean doPlayerDeallocate();`

The only differences between the `doDeallocate` and the `doStop` methods are the two calls made in lines [44] and [45]. After calling deallocate on each `Controller` [44], the `Player` itself is deallocated [45] in the abstract method `doPlayerDeallocate` declared on line [46]. This method should be implemented to release any exclusive resources that the `Player` holds. It may also release any buffered media data to save memory for other `Players`.

Once the `Player` has been deallocated, the `doDeallocate` method follows the same algorithm as the `doStart` routine. If the deallocation is successful, the `doDeallocate` method returns true. Otherwise, a `ControllerErrorEvent` is posted and the method returns false.

Closing the Player

Although the close operation is not technically a state transition, it is discussed here because it follows the same model as the `Player` transition methods. The `close` method, as you recall, is intended to shut down the `Player` and release as many resources as possible. As implemented in the `AbstractController` class, the `close` method calls the abstract method `doClose`. This method, implemented in the `AbstractPlayer` class, is shown in Listing 17.10.

Listing 17.10 *Closing the Player*

```
        public synchronized final void doClose() {
            Vector controllers = getControllers();
            for(int i = 0, n = controllers.size(); i < n; i++ ) {
                Controller c =
                    (Controller)controllers.elementAt(i);
(47)            c.close();
            }
            try {
(48)            source.stop();
                source.disconnect();
            }
            catch(IOException e) {}

(49)        doPlayerClose();
(50)        controllers = null;
            source = null;
            gainControl = null;
            duration = null;
            controllerError = null;
        }
(51)    public abstract void doPlayerClose();
```

In accordance with the `Player` API, the first step that the `doClose` method takes is to close each of its managed `Controllers` [47]. You may think this is a rather drastic step, and wonder why the `Player` doesn't just remove the `Controllers` instead of closing them. The answer is that the close operation, consistent with every other operation invoked on the `Player`, affects the same changes on a `Player`'s managed `Controllers` as it does on the `Player` itself. Suffice it to say, users who wish to spare a `Controller` from this fate should remove it before closing the `Player`.

Once the `Controllers` have all been closed, the `Player`'s `DataSource` is stopped and disconnected [49]. Any `IOException` that occurs as a result of this operation is ignored.

The next step taken is to call `doPlayerClose` [49]. This abstract method, declared in line [51], should be implemented by subclasses of the `Abstract-Player` to release as many resources as possible.

The final step in closing the `AbstractPlayer` is to set several of the `AbstractPlayer`'s member data to null [50]. When the `doClose` method returns, the `close` method in the `AbstractController` superclass posts a final `ControllerClosedEvent` to indicate that the `Player` is now closed and inoperable. Any operations invoked on the `Player` at that point, according to the `Controller` API, "might throw errors."

Summary

This chapter completes the APF by implementing the `Player` transitions in the `AbstractPlayer` class. Using the *action/doAction/doPlayerAction* model introduced in the last chapter, we implemented several of the `AbstractController`'s *doAction* methods to transition the `Abstract-Player`'s managed `Controllers`.

In the next chapter we will utilize the APF to create two custom `Players`. The first will be a `Player` for a known but unsupported media type, and the second will be a `Player` for a media type of our own design.

Chapter 18

CREATING A CUSTOM PLAYER

Introduction

In this chapter we will create our very own custom Players to extend the media support of the *Java Media Framework*. Using the *Abstract Player Framework* developed in earlier chapters, we will create two API-compliant Players to render two new types of media.

To follow this chapter, it is not necessary to have read and understood every part of the API development chapters. All that is required is that you understand how to *use* the framework. We will cover that in detail here.

The first custom Player that we create will be for a known media type. This Player will graphically display text-based media in a "ticker tape" format. It is a simple example that will help us understand the basics of creating a custom Player.

Our second custom Player will be slightly more complicated. It will provide support for a completely new, unsupported media type of our own design. This example will add video and timing information into the media equation. In addition to providing a Player for this new media format, we will look at how to make Java aware of this new media type.

Four Steps to a Custom Player

Before jumping into our first example, let's review the steps needed to create a custom `Player`. They are, in order:

1. Create a class called `Handler` that implements the `Player` interface.
2. Create a no-argument constructor for the `Handler` class.
3. Place the `Handler` class in the *package-prefix*.`media.` `content.`*content-type* package.
4. Register the package prefix with the `PackageManager` class.

Step (1), as you may suspect, is the most difficult and involved step in the process. It is one thing to implement the `Player` interface. It is quite another to fully comply with the API when doing so. Fortunately, the bulk of this is taken care of by the APF that we've spent numerous chapters developing. Following some simple rules, this step is reduced to extending the `ejmf.toolkit.media.AbstractPlayer` class and implementing a few abstract methods.

Step (2) is necessary because of the way the `Manager` class instantiates a `Player`. After locating an appropriate `Handler` class, the `createPlayer` algorithm calls the `Class` method `newInstance` to instantiate the `Handler`. This method calls the class's no-argument constructor to create a `Player` object. If no such constructor exists, a `java.lang.NoSuchMethodError` will be thrown and the `Player` will not be created.

Steps (3) and (4) were discussed in detail in Chapter 10, "Locating the Player." Recall that both of these steps are necessary for the `Manager` class to be able to locate the `Player` at run-time. After placing the `Player` in a package reflective of the media it supports, the package prefix must be added to the `PackageManager`'s *content* prefix list. This list is referenced by the `Manager` method `createPlayer` when a `Player` is being sought for a given medium.

With these four basic steps in mind, let's turn now to look at our first `Player`.

The Text Player

Our first custom `Player` will render text-based media data. It will serve as an example of how to provide support for a known, but unsupported, media type. In this case, the known media format is standard ASCII text. Our `Player` will simply display the contents of a text file in a graphical ticker tape, and provide all of the features that come with a fully-functional `Player`.

The TickerTape Component

If you have ever spent any length of time browsing the colorful, image-laden, neural-overload that is the World Wide Web, then you've inevitably run across the most common of all Java Applets, the ticker tape. This is the quintessential Java applet, the one invariably found in the back of every beginning Java book ever written. It's function is simple: Given a text string, scroll the text slowly across a Java `Component` so that a user can read a long message in a limited space. Most ticker tapes allow for multiple colors, shadow effects, variable fonts, or variable speeds of text. Ours is no exception.

The `ejmf.toolkit.gui.tickertape.Tickertape` class is a typical, feature-rich ticker tape implementation. Alone, it has no relation at all to the *JMF*. However, once it is integrated into our Text Player example, it will serve as the `Player`'s visual component.

The `TickerTape` class contains several methods, the following of which will be used by the Text Player.

EJMF Toolkit Synopsis 18.1 *TickerTape Methods*

Class	`ejmf.toolkit.gui.tickertape.Tickertape`
Method	`setMessage`
Visibility	`public`
Arguments	`javax.lang.String`
Return	`void`
Description	Sets the message to be displayed in the `TickerTape`.
Method	`setRate`
Visibility	`public`
Arguments	`int`
Return	`void`
Description	Sets the rate of the text animation in the `TickerTape`.
Method	`start`
Visibility	`public`
Arguments	`none`
Return	`void`
Description	Starts the `TickerTape`.
Method	`stop`
Visibility	`public`
Arguments	`void`
Return	`void`
Description	Stops the `TickerTape`.

Since the implementation of the `TickerTape` sheds no light on our understanding of the JMF, it will not be discussed here. However, if you wish to peruse the source to the `TickerTape` class, you can find it in the `$EJMF_HOME/src/ejmf/toolkit/gui/tickertape` directory of the example source available from the Prentice Hall `ftp` site for *Essential JMF*.

Implementing the Player Interface

Beginning with step (1) of the process outlined above, we will need to create a `Handler` class that implements the `Player` interface. As mentioned before, this is done by extending the `AbstractPlayer` class developed in earlier chapters. The `Handler` class for implementing the Text Player appears in Listing 18.1.

Listing 18.1 *Text Player Handler Class*

```
public class Handler extends AbstractPlayer {
    private PullSourceStream stream;
    private TickerTape tape;
    private boolean prefetchNeeded = true;

    public Handler() {
        super();
    }
...
```

As you recall, the `AbstractPlayer` class takes care of as much `Player` functionality as possible, leaving only a few abstract methods for its subclasses to implement. These methods generally begin with the *doPlayer-* prefix and have the same Java signature as their JMF counterparts. Let's now turn to look at these and other methods necessary to implement the Text Player.

Player Initialization

To begin, our `Handler` class provides no explicit constructor. However, the `AbstractPlayer` superclass provides a no-argument constructor, so step (2) is nevertheless satisfied.

Immediately after constructing a `Player`, the `Manager` class calls the `Player`'s setSource method with a candidate `DataSource`. If the `Player` cannot use the `DataSource`, the setSource method throws an `IncompatibleSourceException`. Otherwise, the `DataSource` is set in the `Handler` and the method returns without incident.

Listing 18.2 shows the Text Player's implementation of the setSource method.

Listing 18.2 *Setting the DataSource in the Player*

```
(1)   private PullSourceStream stream;

      public void setSource(DataSource source)
         throws IncompatibleSourceException
      {
         if(! (source instanceof PullDataSource) ) {
(2)         throw new IncompatibleSourceException(
               "Only PullDataSources supported" );
         }

(3)      PullSourceStream[] streams =
            ((PullDataSource)source).getStreams();

         if( streams == null || streams.length == 0 ) {
(4)         throw new IncompatibleSourceException(
               "Invalid SourceStream" );
         }

(5)      super.setSource(source);
(6)      stream = streams[0];
      }
```

The first requirement that the Handler class enforces is that the given DataSource be a PullDataSource. Recall from Chapter 2, "Why JMF?" that while push data transfers are instantiated by the media server, pull transfers are initiated by the client. In our case, since we wish to use standard pull protocols (HTTP, FTP, etc.), our setSource method will reject any DataSource that is not a PullDataSource [2].

After determining that the DataSource is of the correct type, the DataSource's array of SourceStreams is retrieved with the getStreams method [3]. If this array is null or empty, then no media data can be read and the Handler throws an IncompatibleSourceException [4].

In [5], the superclass setSource method is called. As we saw in Chapter 16, "Implementing the Player Interface," this method simply ensures that a DataSource has not been set with this Player already. If no exception is thrown, the PullSourceStream stream property, declared in [1], is set in [6]. This SourceStream will be used to read the media data throughout the life of the Player.

Realizing the Text Player

Transitioning the Text Player is a simple proposition with the majority of the overhead already implemented by the AbstractPlayer class. As you recall, each of the Controller transition methods has been reduced to a corresponding method in the AbstractPlayer class which returns a boolean indicating its success.

Let's begin implementing the `Controller` transitions by looking at the Text Player's `doPlayerRealize` method.

Listing 18.3 *Realizing the Text Player*

```
private TickerTape tape;

public boolean doPlayerRealize() {
    tape = new JMFTickerTape(this);
    setVisualComponent(tape);

    addControl( new FontControl(tape) );
    addControl( new ColorControl(tape) );

    return true;
}
```

(7)
(8)

(9)
(10)

(11)

This is about as simple a transition as could be expected. Recall that the *realizing* operation is intended to be used to secure any non-exclusive resources for the `Player`, and also to construct the `Player`'s visual and control panel `Components`.

In line [7] the `TickerTape` object is constructed. A subclass of `Ticker-Tape`, the `JMFTickerTape` class acts as a JMF wrapper around a normal `TickerTape` object. Its key feature is that it automatically posts an `EndOf-MediaEvent` when the display of the text media has completed. We will see more of this class later.

After constructing the `JMFTickerTape`, the `Handler` class sets it as the Text Player's visual `Component` [8]. This `AbstractPlayer` method, as you recall, simply sets the visual `Component` with the superclass.

In lines [9] and [10] a `FontControl` and a `ColorControl` are constructed and added to this `Player` using the `AbstractPlayer`'s `addControl` method. Specific to the Text Player, these `Controls` allow for external control over several aspects of the text display. They can be retrieved at runtime using the `Controller` method `getControls`. Their respective `Component` can be retrieved, as with any `Control`, using the `getControl-Component` method defined by the `Control` interface.

The `FontControl` and `ColorControl` classes live in the `ejmf.tool-kit.media.text.plain.controls` package. Instead of discussing them here, we will instead defer to a more general discussion of custom `Controls` in Chapter 19, "Creating Custom Controls."

Having completed the realizing process without error, the `doPlayerRe-alize` method returns `true` [11]. This is in compliance with the `Abstract-Player` API.

The Control Panel Component

The Text Player uses as its control panel Component an EjmfControlPanel object from the ejmf.toolkit.gui.controlpanel package. This class, which will be discussed in greater detail in Chapter 21, "Creating a Custom Control Panel,", provides a snazzy graphical control panel for our custom Players.

The EjmfControlPanel cannot be created until the Player is realized. So, instead of constructing it in the doPlayerRealize method, it is created when the getControlPanelComponent method is first called. This method is shown in Listing 18.4.

Listing 18.4 *Providing a Control Panel Component*

```
        public Component getControlPanelComponent() {
(12)        Component c =
                super.getControlPanelComponent();

            if( c == null ) {
(13)            c = new EjmfControlPanel(this);
(14)            setControlPanelComponent(c);
            }

(15)        return c;
        }
```

The first thing that this method does is call into its superclass [12]. This verifies that the Player has been realized, and throws a NotRealizedError if it has not. If the superclass getControlPanelComponent returns null, indicating that no control panel Component has been set, then a new Ejmf-ControlPanel is constructed [13]. It is then set in the superclass [14] and returned [15].

Prefetching the Text Player

When prefetching, the Player is intended to acquire any exclusive-use resources that it may need in order to play. This generally includes the media data itself.

In Listing 18.5, we see how the Text Player prefetches its media data.

Listing 18.5 ***Prefetching the Text Player***

```
     public boolean doPlayerPrefetch() {
        DataInputStream in = null;
        byte[] b;

        try {
(16)       PullSourceInputStream pull =
              new PullSourceInputStream(stream);

(17)       in = new DataInputStream(pull);

(18)       long length = stream.getContentLength();

           if( length != stream.LENGTH_UNKNOWN ) {
              b = new byte[(int)length];
(19)          in.readFully(b,0,(int)length);
           } else {
(20)          postEvent(
                 new ResourceUnavailableEvent(this,
                    "Could not get content length") );

              return false;
           }
        }

        catch(EOFException e) {
(21)       postEvent(
              new ResourceUnavailableEvent(this,
                 "Unexpected EOF reading data stream") );

           return false;

        }
        catch(IOException e) {
(22)       postEvent(
              new ResourceUnavailableEvent(this,
                 "I/O error reading data stream") );

           return false;
        }
        finally {
           try { in.close(); } catch(Exception e) {}
        }

(23)    tape.setMessage( new String(b,0,b.length) );
(24)    return true;
     }
```

The process for acquiring the media data from the `DataSource` is simple. To facilitate the transfer, a `PullSourceInputStream` is first constructed [16] from the `PullSourceStream` originally set in the `setSource` method in Listing 18.2. As part of the `ejmf.toolkit.io` package, this class bridges the gap between the standard `java.io` classes and the JMF `SourceStream` classes. Essentially, the `PullSourceInputStream` class is a `java.io.InputStream` wrapper around the somewhat unconventional I/O of the JMF `SourceStreams`.

Once an `InputStream` is created, a `DataInputStream` can be constructed [17] to facilitate the media transfer. This class provides the `read-Fully` method [19], which populates a `byte` array based on the length of the media [18]. Once this array is filled, it is converted to a `String` and set as the text message in the `TickerTape` object [23].

Several errors are possible throughout this process. If the `SourceStream` cannot provide its content length [18], a `ResourceUnavailableEvent` is posted [20]. Similarly, if the stream reaches the end of the media before its content length is reached, the resulting `EOFException` is caught and a `ResourceUnavailableEvent` is posted [21]. There are certainly ways to populate a `byte` array without knowing the length of the input stream, but this is left, as they say, as an exercise for the reader.

Finally, if an `IOException` is thrown by the `SourceStream` while the media is being read, the `doPlayerPrefetch` method again posts a `ResourceUnavailableEvent` [22]. On all errors, `false` is returned. Otherwise, upon successfully prefetching the media data, the method returns `true` [24] and the `Player` progresses to the `Prefetched` state.

JMF TIP: Media Decoding

The doPlayerPrefetch method is where Players of more sophisticated media formats might, if necessary, decode the media data. Suppose, for instance, that the data being prefetched were compressed using some standard compression algorithm. After downloading the data, the doPlayer-Prefetch method would take the necessary steps to decompress the data before returning. In the case of the Text Player, however, the media can be played "as is."

Starting the Text Player

Once the `Player` has been prefetched, it can be started with the `syncStart` method. This method, as we saw in previous chapters, indirectly calls the `doPlayerSyncStart` method, below.

Listing 18.6 *Starting the Text Player*

```
        public boolean doPlayerSyncStart(Time t) {
(25)        blockUntilStart(t);
(26)        tape.start();
(27)        return true;
        }
```

    The `AbstractPlayer` API says that no transition method may return until the transition is complete. So, given a time-base start time, the `doPlayer-SyncStart` method blocks the current thread until the `Player` is to be started [25]. This is done through the `blockUntilStart` method [25], defined in the `AbstractController` class and discussed in Chapter 15, "Implementing the Controller Transitions.". Once this method has returned, the `TickerTape` is started [26] and the method returns [27].

Stopping the Text Player

Stopping the Text Player is as simple as stopping the text animation in its `TickerTape` object.

Listing 18.7 *Stopping the Text Player*

```
        public boolean doPlayerStop() {
            tape.stop();
            return true;
        }
```

Stopping at End of Media

When the ticker tape's entire text message has been displayed, an `EndOf-MediaEvent` is posted. This is done by the `JMFTickerTape` class, a `TickerTape` subclass specifically designed for use with the JMF.

Listing 18.8 *Posting an EndOfMediaEvent*

```
        public class JMFTickerTape extends TickerTape {
            private Handler player;
(28)        public JMFMultiImageRenderer(Handler player) {
                super();
                this.player = player;
            }

            public void run() {
(29)            super.run();
(30)            player.endOfMedia();
            }
        }
```

The JMFTickerTape class is constructed with a Handler object argument [28]. This Handler is used to post an EndOfMediaEvent.

As a java.lang.Runnable object, the JMFTickerTape's run method is called indirectly when the ticker tape is started. Within this method, it immediately calls its superclass's run method [29]. When the text animation completes, this method returns and the AbstractController method endOfMedia is called [30]. This method, as we saw in Chapter 15, stops the Clock and posts an EndOfMediaEvent.

By design, if the JMFTickerTape is stopped before the end of the media is reached, the superclass's run method will never complete and an EndOf-MediaEvent consequently will not be thrown.

Deallocating the Text Player

Deallocating the Text Player is the most trivial of the Text Player transitions. Although the deallocation process is intended to release resources held by the Player, the Text Player holds no expensive resources. For this reason, the deallocate method is a no-op.

Listing 18.9 *Deallocating the Text Player*

```
public boolean doPlayerDeallocate() {
    return true;
}
```

Closing the Text Player

In closing the Text Player, the Handler class needs to release as many resources as possible.

Listing 18.10 *Closing the Text Player*

```
public void doPlayerClose() {
    tape = null;
    stream = null;
}
```

Here, both the TickerTape and the PullSourceStream are set to null, freeing memory and rendering the Player inoperable.

Implementing the Clock and Duration Operations

Since ASCII text is not a time-based media format, many of the Clock and Duration operations are trivially implemented here. Later, when we develop a custom Player for a time-based media format, many of these methods will have much more substantial implementations.

The Text Player's implementation of the AbstractPlayer's abstract Clock and Duration methods is shown in Listing 18.11.

Listing 18.11 *Clock and Duration Methods*

```
(31)    public float doPlayerSetRate(float rate) {
(32)        int intRate = Math.round(rate);
(33)        tape.setRate(intRate);
(34)        return (float)intRate;
        }

(35)    public void doPlayerSetMediaTime(Time t) {}

(36)    public Time getPlayerStartLatency() {
(37)        return new Time(0);
        }

(38)    public Time getPlayerDuration() {
(39)        return DURATION_UNKNOWN;
        }
```

Like all of the AbstractPlayer's abstract methods, the doPlayerSet-Rate method [31] behaves much in the same way as its JMF counterpart. Since the TickerTape's setRate method takes an integer argument, the float passed to the doPlayerSetRate method is first rounded [32] before being passed along to the TickerTape object [33]. This value, per the AbstractPlayer API, is then returned [34] in the same style as the Clock.setRate method.

The doPlayerSetMediaTime implementation [35] is empty, since setting the media time on a non-time-based medium is meaningless.

In line [36], the getPlayerStartLatency method is implemented. As we will see, when the Text Player is started, there is essentially no latency involved. For this reason the getPlayerStartLatency method returns a Time of zero latency [37].

Finally, the getPlayerDuration method is implemented in line [38]. Again, since our medium is not time-based, it is impossible to return a meaningful duration, and thus DURATION_UNKNOWN is returned [39].

Integrating the Text Player

Now that the Handler class has been implemented, steps (1) and (2) from "Four Steps to a Custom Player" on page 310 have been satisfied. Now we can move on to steps (3) and (4), which deal with "registering" the Player with the JMF.

The first part of this process involves placing the Handler class just created in a Java package that reflects the content-type of media supported. As mentioned in Chapter 10, the content-type of the media is determined by the DataSource class. After a DataSource has been constructed, its getContentType method is called to determine the media format, and ultimately, the Player that can render it.

The getContentType method returns, based on the media's file extension, the MIME-type of the media. This is simply a String of the form *type.subtype*, where *type* and *subtype* are general and specific classifications, respectively, of the media data. The MIME-type of MPEG video, for example, is video.mpeg, whereas the MIME-type of WAV audio is audio.x-wav.

In the case of the Text Player, the media type supported is ASCII text, or, more specifically, files of the MIME-type text.plain. Generally, this can include files with a .txt, .c, .cc, .h, or .java extension.

Following step (3), then, the Text Player's Handler class will be placed in the ejmf.toolkit.media.content.text.plain package. This means that the ejmf.toolkit package prefix, in accordance with step (4), must be added to the *content* prefix list maintained by the PackageManager class.

(40)   `Vector v = PackageManager.getContentPrefixList();`
(41)   `v.addElement("ejmf.toolkit");`
(42)   `PackageManager.setContentPrefixList(v);`
(43)   `PackageManager.commitContentPrefixList();`

After getting the existing *content* prefix list from the PackageManager class [40], the ejmf.toolkit prefix is added to the list [41] and set in the PackageManager class [42]. Finally, the commitContentPrefixList method is called [43] to make the addition persistent.

As a shortcut, the ejmf.toolkit.install.PackageUtility class can do all of the above with a single method call:

```
PackageUtility.addContentPrefix("ejmf.toolkit", true);
```

Finally, to make this change manually, you may use Sun's jmfconfig utility, described in Appendix C, "Configuring the Java Media Framework," or simply edit the jmf.properties file located in the lib directory of the JMF distribution. This tool works with all implementations since the jmf.properties file is always referenced when locating a Player.

Running the Text Player

Now that the Text Player has been implemented and registered with the JMF, it can be used as any other Player would be. Using the GenericPlayer class developed in earlier chapters, the Text Player can be displayed simply by specifying a text-based media file.

◀ **• User Input**   **Running the Text Player**

```
% java ejmf.examples.genericplayer.GenericPlayer \
     $EJMF_HOME/classes/media/helloworld.txt
```

The resulting `Player`, including its font and color `Controls`, is shown in Figure 18.1.

Figure 18.1 *The Text Player*

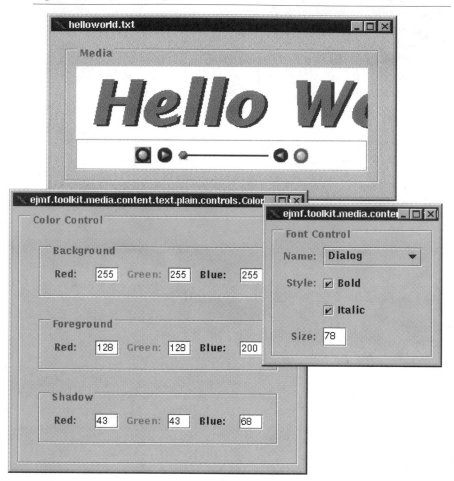

Moving On

The Text Player is a simple example of how to create a custom `Player`. However, it does not address some of the finer points of supporting a new format. Specifically, the ASCII text that the `Player` supports is not a time-based media format, and thus many of the `Clock` methods, as we saw, were trivially implemented.

The JMF was designed specifically with time-based media in mind. In our next example, we will look at how to support a time-based media format, as well as some of the other issues that the Text Player did not address.

The Multi-Image Video Player

In this section we will develop a `Player` for a time-based media format of our own design. This format, called the Multi-Image Video (MIV) format, will present video data consisting of Java-readable images concatenated into one source. These images will make up the frames of the video media and can be of any image format (GIF, JPEG, etc.) understood by the Swing `ImageIcon` class.

The MIV Format

The MIV format is specified in Table 18.1.

Table 18.1 *MIV Format Specification*

Bytes	Definition
1-4	A Java `int` (32 bits) describing the width of the largest image
5 - 8	A Java `int` (32 bits) describing the height of the largest image
9 - 16	A Java `long` (64 bits) describing the total duration of the video in nanoseconds
17 - end	One or more "image frames"

A MIV frame is defined as:

Table 18.2 *MIV Frame Specification*

Bytes	Definition
1-8	A Java `long` (64 bits) describing the length (in bytes) of the image
9 - 16	A Java long (64 bits) describing the time in nanoseconds to wait before displaying the next frame
17 - end	An image (GIF, JPEG, etc.) understood by the Swing `Image-Icon` class

Several MIV files can be found in the `$EJMF_HOME/classes/media` directory of the example source available from the Prentice Hall `ftp` site.

Creating Your Own MIV File

To make your own custom MIV media files, the `MakeMultiImage` class in the `ejmf.toolkit.gui.multiimage` package may be used. The syntax of this utility is as follows:

► • User Input   **Creating a MIV File**

```
% java ejmf.toolkit.gui.multiimage.MakeMultiImage\
     <out-file> <frame-delay-nanos> <in-files...>
```

The first parameter specified is the name of the MIV file to be created, followed by the number of nanoseconds to wait between frames. The remaining parameters specify the image files that will make up the individual frames of the video.

The MultiImageRenderer Component

The `ejmf.toolkit.gui.multiimage.MultiImageRenderer` class is a `Component` that can render MIV data. Alone, it is simply a `JLabel` that has no relation at all to the JMF. However, once it is integrated into our MIV `Player` example, it will serve as the `Player`'s visual `Component`.

Like the `TickerTape` class, the implementation of the `MultiImageRenderer` class will not be discussed here since it has no relevance to the JMF. However, a minimal subset of commands must be understood to work with the `MultiImageRenderer` class.

EJMF Toolkit Synopsis 18.2 *MultiImageRenderer Methods*

Class	`ejmf.toolkit.gui.multiimage.` `   MultiImageRenderer`
Method	`setFrames`
Visibility	`public`
Arguments	`ejmf.toolkit.gui.multiimage.` `   MultiImageFrame[]`
Return	`void`
Description	Sets the MIV frames to be displayed.
Method	`setImageSize`
Visibility	`public`
Arguments	`java.awt.Dimension`
Return	`void`
Description	Sets the size of the images to be displayed. This method is only necessary before the image frames are set. Once they are set, this value is determined automatically.
Method	`setRate`
Visibility	`public`
Arguments	`int`
Return	`void`
Description	Sets the rate of the MIV.
Method	`setMediaNanoseconds`
Visibility	`public`
Arguments	`long`
Return	`void`
Description	Sets the media time of the MIV in nanoseconds.
Method	`start`
Visibility	`public`
Arguments	`void`
Return	`void`
Description	Starts the MIV animation.

EJMF Toolkit Synopsis 18.2 *MultiImageRenderer Methods (Continued)*

Class	ejmf.toolkit.gui.multiimage. MultiImageRenderer
Method	stop
Visibility	public
Arguments	void
Return	void
Description	Stops the Multi-Image Video animation.

With these methods in hand, let's look at the MIV Player implementation.

Implementing the Player Interface

Like the Text Player developed earlier, the MIV Player will be implemented in a `Handler` class that extends the `AbstractPlayer` class. Many features of the MIV Player will mirror those of the Text Player.

Player Initialization

In accordance with step (2) from "Four Steps to a Custom Player" on page 310, the `Handler` class provides a no-argument constructor to create the `Player`. Its only duty is to set up the `Player`'s `CachingControl` object.

Listing 18.12 *Initializing the Handler*

```
private BasicCachingControl cache;

public Handler() {
    cache = new BasicCachingControl(this, 0);
}
```

As we saw in Chapter 8, "Player Controls," a `Player` may choose to support a `CachingControl`, allowing all interested parties to keep apprised of the `Player`'s download progress. By supporting this interface, `Caching-ControlEvents` are posted to each of the `Player`'s `ControllerListeners`, indicating to them how much of the media download has completed.

As we will see in Chapter 19, "Creating Custom Controls," the `ejmf.toolkit.media.BasicCachingControl` class provides a generic `CachingControl` implementation to be used by any `AbstractPlayer` subclass. Since the download of MIV data may take some time, the `Basic-CachingControl` will be used here to keep the `Player`'s `ControllerListeners` updated.

Setting the DataSource

As with the Text Player, the real initialization of the Handler class occurs in the setSource method.

Listing 18.13 *Setting the DataSource*

```
private PullSourceStream stream;

public void setSource(DataSource source)
    throws IncompatibleSourceException
{
    if(! (source instanceof PullDataSource) ) {
        throw new IncompatibleSourceException(
            "Only PullDataSources supported" );
    }

    PullSourceStream[] streams =
        ((PullDataSource)source).getStreams();

    if( streams == null || streams.length == 0 ) {
        throw new IncompatibleSourceException(
            "Invalid SourceStream" );
    }

    super.setSource(source);
    stream = streams[0];
}
```

(44)

(45)

As with the Text Player, the MIV Player accepts only PullDataSources [44], and throws an IncompatibleSourceException if the SourceStream array is null or empty [45].

Realizing the MIV Player

Whereas the Text Player did very little during the Realizing stage, the MIV Player has quite a bit more to do. Unlike the Text Player, the MIV Player must read the header information in the media data to prepare its visual Component and set its media duration.

The doPlayerRealize method is shown in Listing 18.14.

Listing 18.14 *Realizing the MIV Player*

```
        private long duration = 0L;
        private MultiImageRenderer mic;

        public boolean doPlayerRealize() {
(46)        mic = new JMFMultiImageRenderer(this);
            DataInputStream in = null;

            try {
(47)            in = new DataInputStream(
                    new PullSourceInputStream(stream) );

(48)            int w = in.readInt();
                int h = in.readInt();
(49)            mic.setImageSize( new Dimension(w,h) );

(50)            duration = in.readLong();
            }

            catch(EOFException e) {
(51)            postEvent(
                    new ResourceUnavailableEvent(this,
                        "Unexpected EOF reading data stream") );

                return false;
            }

            catch(IOException e) {
(52)            postEvent(
                    new ResourceUnavailableEvent(this,
                        "I/O error reading data stream") );

                return false;
            }

            finally {
                try { in.close(); } catch(Exception e) {}
            }

(53)        setVisualComponent(mic);
(54)        cache.reset( stream.getContentLength() );

(55)        return true;
        }
```

Again paralleling the design of the Text Player, the MIV Player extends its visual Component to provide a JMF-enabled implementation of the Multi-ImageRenderer. Like its TickerTape counterpart, the

JMFMultiImageRenderer class [46] provides a mechanism to automatically post EndOfMediaEvent events when the media playback is complete. More will be seen of this class later.

After creating the MultiImageRenderer, a DataInputStream is constructed to facilitate the reading of the media header [47]. As we saw earlier, it is constructed using the ejmf.toolkit.media.io.PullSource-InputStream class, an adapter between the java.io classes and the JMF.

Following Table 18.1, the first part of the media header is a Java int representing the width of the largest video frame. This is read in line [48], along with the image height. Together, these values are used to set the initial size of the MultiImageRenderer [49] Component.

JMF TIP: Creating the Visual Component

A Player's responsibilities in regard to its visual Component do not end when the Component is created. Once a Player has been realized, the Component should be the size that it will ultimately be when it is rendering video. This enables all GUI layout to be done immediately and reliably after the Realizing state.

Continuing with the media header, a Java long value indicating the nanosecond duration of the media is read and saved [50]. This value will be used in the getDuration method to return a Time object indicating the Player's duration. Once the header has been read, all that remains are the individual video frames. This portion of the data will be read in the Prefetching stage, covered in the next section.

Before returning, the visual Component is set [53] and the BasicCach-ingControl initialized [54] with the SourceStream's content length.

While reading the media header, two errors may occur. First, if the end of the media is unexpectedly encountered, an EOFException is thrown [51]. Secondly, if there is an I/O error, an IOException is thrown [52]. In either case the method posts a ResourceUnavailableEvent and returns false. Otherwise, the doPlayerRealize method returns true [55] and the Player advances to the Realized state.

The Control Panel Component

Like the Text Player, the MIV Player employs an EjmfControlPanel as its control panel Component. This Component is constructed the first time it is requested by the getControlPanelComponent method, below.

Listing 18.15 *Providing a Control Panel Component*

```
public Component getControlPanelComponent() {
    Component c =
        super.getControlPanelComponent();

    if( c == null ) {
        c = new EjmfControlPanel(this);
        setControlPanelComponent(c);
    }

    return c;
}
```

Again, the EjmfControlPanel class and its companions will be discussed in Chapter 21, "Creating a Custom Control Panel," when we look at creating a custom control panel Component.

Prefetching the MIV Player

Within the Prefetching stage, the MIV Player downloads the bulk of the media data, the individual video frames.

Listing 18.16 *Prefetching the MIV Player*

```
       public boolean doPlayerPrefetch() {
(56)       Vector frameVector = new Vector();
           DataInputStream in = null;

           try {
(57)           in = new DataInputStream(
                   new PullSourceInputStream(stream) );

               try {
                   while(true) {
(58)                   long length = in.readLong();
(59)                   long nanos = in.readLong();

                       byte[] b = new byte[(int)length];
(60)                   in.readFully(b,0,(int)length);

(61)                   cache.addToProgress(16 + length);

(62)                   ImageIcon icon = new ImageIcon(b);
(63)                   MultiImageFrame m =
                           new MultiImageFrame(icon, nanos);
(64)                   frameVector.addElement(m);
                   }
               }
```

```
               catch(EOFException e) {
(65)               cache.setDone();
               }
           }

           catch(IOException e) {
(66)           postEvent(
                   new ResourceUnavailableEvent(this,
                       "I/O error reading data stream") );

               return false;
           }

           finally {
               try { in.close(); } catch(Exception e) {}
           }

           MultiImageFrame[] frames =
               new MultiImageFrame[ frameVector.size() ];

           frameVector.copyInto(frames);
(67)       mic.setFrames(frames);

(68)       return true;
       }
```

The first step in downloading the video frames is to create a Vector object to hold them [56]. Then, as always, a DataInputStream is created [57] to facilitate reading the primitive Java data types. Using this DataInput-Stream, following the frame specification in Table 18.2, the length of the frame is retrieved [58] followed by the nanosecond display time of the image [59].

Once the length of the video frame is known, a byte array can be created and populated with the image data [60]. From this byte array, an ImageIcon can then be constructed [62], which in turn is used to construct an ejmf.toolkit.gui.multiimage.MultiImageFrame object [63]. This class, a functional grouping of an image and its display time, is used by the MultiImageRenderer class to initialize the MIV frames. Once it is created, it is added to the Vector created earlier [64].

As part of its CachingControl support, the MIV Player updates its CachingControl object every time a significant chunk of data has been downloaded. Using the addToProgress method [61], the CachingControl's progress bar Component is advanced to reflect the given number of bytes just downloaded. In this case, it is equal to 16 (two longs at eight bytes each) plus the length of the frame image.

When the end of the media data is reached, the downloading stops and the CachingControl is updated [65].

If an `IOException` is thrown during the media download, a `Resource-UnavailableEvent` is posted [66] and the method returns `false`. Otherwise, the frame `Vector` is converted to an array and set in the `MultiImageRenderer` object [67]. At this point, the `MultiImageRenderer` is fully prepared to display the video and the `doPlayerPrefetch` method returns [68].

Starting the MIV Player

The remaining `Controller` transitions are nearly identical to those of the Text Player. The `syncStart` operation, for example, is implemented as follows.

Listing 18.17 *Starting the MIV Player*

```
          public boolean doPlayerSyncStart(Time t) {
(69)          blockUntilStart(t);
(70)          mic.start();
(71)          return true;
          }
```

After waiting until the given time-base start time [69], the `MultiImageRenderer` is started [70] and the `doPlayerSyncStart` method returns `true` [71].

Stopping the MIV Player

Stopping the MIV Player is simply a matter of stopping the animation in the `MultiImageRenderer`.

Listing 18.18 *Stopping the MIV Player*

```
          public boolean doPlayerStop() {
(72)          mic.stop();
(73)          return true;
          }
```

After calling `stop` on the `MultiImageRenderer` [72], the `doPlayerStop` returns `true` [73] and the `Player` moves out of the `Started` state.

Stopping at End of Media

As mentioned earlier, the `MultiImageRenderer` class is extended by the `JMFMultiImageRenderer` class to provide support for `EndOfMedia-Events`. This class is shown in Listing 18.19.

Listing 18.19 *Posting an EndOfMediaEvent*

```
public class JMFMultiImageRenderer
    extends MultiImageRenderer
{
    private Handler player;

    public JMFMultiImageRenderer(Handler player) {
        super();
        this.player = player;
    }

    public void run() {
        super.run();
        player.endOfMedia();
    }
}
```
(74)
(75)

As a `java.lang.Runnable`, the `JMFMultiImageRenderer`'s run method is called indirectly when it is started. Therein, the superclass run method is called [74], and the animation begins. When it has completed, the superclass run method returns and the `AbstractController` method `endOfMedia` is called [75]. This method, as you recall, stops the `Clock` and posts an `EndOfMediaEvent`.

Deallocating the MIV Player

The final `Controller` transition to implement is the `deallocate` operation. Like the Text Player, however, this operation is a no op.

Listing 18.20 *Deallocating the MIV Player*

```
public boolean doPlayerDeallocate() {
    return true;
}
```

Recall that at this point the media data is effectively stored in the `Multi-ImageRenderer` class. Therefore, with no expensive resources to release, this method simply returns `true`.

Closing the MIV Player

When closing the MIV Player, the `Handler`'s object member data are all released, rendering the `Player` inoperable.

Listing 18.21 *Closing the Multi-Image Video Player*

```
public void doPlayerClose() {
    mic = null;
    stream = null;
    cache = null;
}
```

Implementing the Clock and Duration Operations

As a `Player` of time-based media, the MIV Player contains more substantive implementations of the `Clock` and `Duration` methods than the Text Player. These method implementations are shown below.

Listing 18.22 *Clock and Duration Methods*

```
        public float doPlayerSetRate(float rate) {
(76)        return mic.setRate(rate);
        }

        public void doPlayerSetMediaTime(Time t) {
(77)        mic.setMediaTime( t.getNanoseconds() );
        }

        public Time getPlayerStartLatency() {
(78)        return new Time(0);
        }

        public Time getPlayerDuration() {
            if( getState() < Realized ) {
(79)            return DURATION_UNKNOWN;
            } else {
(80)            return new Time(duration);
            }
        }
```

Because the `MultiImageRenderer` was designed for fine control over image animation, the `Clock` and `Duration` methods are short and sweet. In line [76], the `float` value sent to the `doPlayerSetRate` method is passed on without modification to the `MultiImageRenderer`. A similar step is taken in the `doPlayerSetMediaTime` method, as the given `Time` is converted to nanoseconds and passed on to the `MultiImageRenderer` [77]. In line [78], a `Time` value of zero is returned from the `getPlayerStartLatency` method, since the `MultiImageRenderer` effectively takes no measurable time to start.

For the `getPlayerDuration` method to return a meaningful value, the `Handler` must be `Realized`. If it is not, the `static final` `DURATION_UNKNOWN` is returned [79]. Otherwise, the duration returned is based on the `long` value read from the media header in the `Prefetching` state [80].

Integrating the MIV Player

Like the Text Player, the MIV `Handler` class needs to be placed in a Java package that reflects the type of media that it supports. Since the MIV media format is of our own design, we will arbitrarily choose the `.miv` extension for all of our media files. Unfortunately, like any unknown file type, the content-type of a `.miv` file is `unknown`. This leaves us with two possibilities for packaging our `Player`.

1. Place the `Handler` class in a *package-prefix*`.media.con-tent.unknown` package.

2. Register a new content-type with each `DataSource` that is likely to transport MIV media, and then place the `Handler` class in a more descriptive package reflecting this new content-type.

The first of these options is the easiest to implement, but also has several drawbacks. If the MIV `Handler` class is placed in a package reflective of the default `unknown` content-type, then every media file without a known content-type will be directed to this `Player`. This effectively places the burden of media classification on the `Player`, which, depending on its implementation, could keel over and die given an incompatible medium.

Creating a default `Player` for all unknown content-types does have its advantages, however. A `Player` that could handle multiple types of otherwise-unknown media would be a good candidate for a default `Player`. Placing this `Player` in an `unknown` package might eliminate `NoPlayerExceptions` for many media types, and provide a more graceful failure mechanism for others.

The bottom line on package naming is that placing a `Handler` in a package reflecting support of unknown media types is a risk, and should usually be done only if the `Player` in question can handle many types of unsupported media. At the very least, it must be able to determine within the `setSource` method whether it can support the media it is given. If the `setSource` method returns without error, then the `Player` is committed to reliably rendering the given media.

As an alternative to creating a `Player` for all unsupported media types, it is often better to register the new content-type with each `DataSource` that is likely to transport this type of media. Let's look at the second option for packaging a `Handler`.

Registering a New Content-type

As you recall, it is the `DataSource`'s responsibility to determine the content-type of the media when the `Manager` class is searching for an appropriate

`Player`. This is generally based on the extension of the media file. Most `DataSources` reference some sort of database or hash table that maps a file extension to a content-type. Others may go through a long string of `if-then-else` statements. Whatever the method, the key to making a new content-type known is to understand the `DataSource`'s algorithm.

The URLDataSource

As you may know, the most common transfer protocols (HTTP, FTP, FILE, etc.) are all handled by the `javax.media.protocol.URLDataSource` class. This `DataSource` transports the media data by simply using the built-in `java.net.URL` class.

The `URLDataSource` takes the following steps to determine the content-type of its media:

1. Call `openConnection` on the media `URL`. This returns a `java.net.URLConnection` object.

2. Call the `URLConnection`'s `getContentType` method. This method references the content-type database stored in the `$JDK_HOME/lib/content-types.properties` file.

3. If the extension of the media file is found in this database, then the corresponding MIME-type is returned as a `String`. Otherwise, "unknown" is returned.

From this algorithm, it is clear that adding an entry to the `$JDK_HOME/lib/content-types.properties` file would be sufficient to register the MIV content-type with the `URLDataSource` class. Entries from this file take the following form:

```
content-type: \
    description=descriptive-string \
    file_extensions=comma-delimited-list
```

Arbitrarily, we will choose the `video/multi-image` content-type to reflect the MIV media format. To register this type and associate it with the `.miv` extension, the following lines are added to the `$JDK_HOME/lib/content-types.properties` file:

```
video/multi-image: \
    description=Multi-image Video;\
    file_extensions=.miv
```

Hereafter, the `URLDataSource` will report the content-type of any media file with a `.miv` extension as `video.multi_image`. This string is produced by taking the original content-type and replacing / (forward slash) with . (period), and all other non-alpha-numeric characters with _ (underscore). This convention is based on the requirements placed on a Java package name.

Other DataSources

In most cases, making a new content-type known to the URLDataSource class is sufficient. Rarely are DataSources other than this one utilized. If, however, you are using a different DataSource to transfer media with an unconventional protocol, then you will likewise need to find a way to make it aware of the new content-type. This may be as easy as making an entry in a file, as we just did, or as involved as extending the DataSource and overriding its getContentType method.

Creating the Package

Now that the URLDataSource officially recognizes a .miv file as having a content-type of video.multi_image, the Handler class can be placed in the ejmf.toolkit.media.content.video.multi_image package. This follows the template laid out by the JMF API, and requires us to add the ejmf.toolkit prefix to the PackageManager's content prefix list.

```
PackageUtility.addContentPrefix("ejmf.toolkit", true);
```

This is the same step taken in "Integrating the Text Player" on page 320 when we integrated the Text Player into the JMF. If the ejmf.toolkit package prefix is already part of the content prefix list, then this step can be skipped.

Running the MIV Player

After implementing the Handler class, registering the video.multi_image content-type, associating the .miv extension with this content-type, placing the Handler class in an appropriate package, and adding the package prefix to the PackageManager's content prefix list, we can now play MIV media as transparently as any other media type. Again using the GenericPlayer class, the MIV Player can be displayed by specifying a MIV media file.

▶ **• User Input**   **Running the MIV Player**

```
% java ejmf.examples.genericplayer.GenericPlayer \
     $EJMF_HOME/classes/media/helloworld.miv
```

The resulting Player is shown in Figure 18.2.

Figure 18.2 *The Multi-Image Video Player*

Summary

In this chapter we culminated our multi-chapter effort to design and implement an API-compliant JMF `Player`. Using the APF developed earlier in Part II, we were able to create two fully-functional `Players`.

The first `Player` created rendered ASCII text in a standard ticker tape `Component`. This `Player` served as a simple example of how to support an existing media format. Because ASCII text is not a time-based media format, however, many of the `Clock` and `Duration` methods were trivially implemented.

The second `Player` created was one for a media format of our own design. This format rendered video as a series of image files. As a time-based media format with a significant media header, more consideration was needed to implement most of the `AbstractPlayer` methods.

Each `Player` created was placed in a package reflective of the media it supports. In the case of the MIV Player, an extra step was taken to register a new content-type with the `URLDataSource` class. Finally, the package prefix of both `Players` was added to the JMF's content prefix list using the `PackageManager` class.

This chapter showed that API-compliant `Players` can be relatively easy to create using the APF. In the next few chapters, we will look at how to enhance our `Players` with custom `Controls` and control panel `Components`.

Chapter 19   *CREATING CUSTOM CONTROLS*

Introduction

In Chapter 8, "Player Controls," the `Control` interface was discussed. Recall that the `Control` interface is a generic mechanism by which an application can affect control over a *Java Media Framework* `Player`.

Two interfaces which extend the `Control` interface are the `GainControl` and the `CachingControl`. These controls are sufficiently common and useful that they are specified by the JMF API. The `Control` interface, however, has a much more general application. Its real power lies in providing an API-compliant way to perform operations on a `Controller` *not* specified by the JMF API. It does this by defining a single method, `getControlComponent`, returning a GUI component through which the user can interact with the `Control`.

In this chapter we are going to develop generally useful custom controls. After a few words to address some design issues involved in the implementation of custom controls, we will look at a rate control, a full-blown caching control, and a read-only `Control` that displays media time.

Some Design Issues

The `Control` interface purposely defines very little about what a control should do. The designers of the JMF correctly left that definition to specific `Control` implementations. However, aware of the possible requirement of a user interacting with a `Control`, those prescient folks defined the `getControlComponent` method, effectively requiring a `Control` to present users an interface through which they can interact with it.

The job of building a custom `Control`, then, has as much to do with building a GUI component as it does with manipulating a `Controller`. Apart from the interface issues, there are some design issues that should be considered when building a `Control`.

- Does the `Control` even require a GUI component?

  Not all `Controls` require a GUI component. This is especially true with internal controls built into an implementation of the JMF. Both Sun and Intel have internal controls that return a `null` control component. This is not typical though, as most `Controls` will provide a GUI component.

  If a `Control` is to represent a property of the `Controller` and the `Control` component is to display that property, then the `Control` component must be automatically updated when the property changes. If the `Control` is to allow the user to modify a property of the `Controller`, then the `Control` component must be able to filter invalid input from the user and handle the resulting errors from the `Controller`.

- Are the actions of the `Control` dependent on the state of the `Controller`? If so, does the `Control` properly manage that state?

  Here a `Control` is no different than any other object interacting with a `Controller`. If it invokes any state-dependent methods, it will need to manage the `Controller` appropriately so that it is in the correct state for a given method.

- Does the `Control` need to track `Controller` state changes? What `ControllerEvents` does it need to field?

  If a `Control` is involved in reporting `Controller` state or acting in response to `Controller` events, it will need to implement the `ControllerListener` interface.

- Will the `Control` need to keep other objects informed of its status?

  The `GainControl` is an example of a `Control` upon which objects can register as listeners. If a `Control` needs to inform interested parties of changes to its state, it will want to supply methods for adding and removing listeners.

Just as the designers of the `Control` interface left open questions about the details of a `Control` implementation, these design questions will be left open here. Instead of answering them directly, we can see how they are addressed within the individual examples of Control implementations presented.

Rate Control

The RateControl monitors and sets a Controller's rate. A very basic Control, its AWT Component will consist simply of a text field to allow the user to specify the Controller's rate. Upon pressing the Enter key within the text field, the rate will be set in the Controller. When the Controller's rate is changed, whether it is due to this Control or not, the new rate will be reflected in the GUI component.

Since it will need to monitor user input within a text field, the RateControl class implements ActionListenerControl. Since it must also monitor the rate of the Controller, it will also implement the ControllerListener interface.

Let's start by looking at the constructor and member data for RateControl.

Listing 19.1 RateControl Constructor

```
public class RateControl implements ActionListener,
                      ControllerListener, Control {
(1)         private JPanel controlComponent = new JPanel();
(2)         private JTextField rateField = new JTextField(6);
(3)         private Controller controller;

            public RateControl(Controller controller) {
(4)             this.controller = controller;
(5)             setUpControlComponent();
(6)             loadRate();
(7)             rateField.addActionListener(this);
(8)             controller.addControllerListener(this);
            }
    ...
        private void loadRate() {
            rateField.setText(
                Float.toString(controller.getRate() ));
        }
}
```

The RateControl class first declares all the data it will need. The Component that will function as the control component is declared and initialized at [1]. Notice that it is a JPanel. It is the JTextField declared at [2] that will report the current Controller rate and receive input of desired rate values. The call to setUpControlComponent [5] does the work of initializing the control component. It is pure GUI work so we will spare you the details and instead refer you to `$EJMF_HOME/src/ejmf/toolkit/con-trols/RateControl.java`.

The `Controller` with which this `Control` is associated is defined at [3] and initialized at [4].

The initial rate value is written to the text field at [6]. Even though this call updates the text field component, it need not be called on the event-dispatching thread since the text field is not yet realized.

To track user changes to the text field, `RateControl` adds itself as a listener to the text field [7]. When the user types into this text field and hits Enter, the `RateControl`'s `actionPerformed` method will be invoked.

Finally, since the `Control` needs to update the text field in response to changes in the `Controller`'s rate, it adds itself as a `ControllerListener` on its associated `Controller` [8].

Once constructed, the `RateControl` can provide its `Component` to interested users. This is done in accordance with the API using `getControlComponent`.

Listing 19.2 *RateControl getControlComponent*

```
public Component getControlComponent() {
    return controlComponent;
}
```

In the hands of a client, the control component is presumably displayed and the `RateControl` needs to respond to input as well as changes in the `Controller`'s rate. It listens for `ActionEvents` from the text field and `RateChangeEvents` from the `Controller`. In response to `ActionEvents`, `actionPerformed` is executed.

Listing 19.3 *RateControl actionPerformed Method*

```
       public void actionPerformed(ActionEvent e) {
(9)         if( e.getSource() != rateField ) {
                return;
            }
            float rate;
            try {
(10)            String rateString = rateField.getText();
(11)            rate = Float.valueOf(rateString).floatValue();
(12)            controller.setRate(rate);
(13)        } catch(NumberFormatException ex) {}
(14)        rate = controller.getRate();
(15)        rateField.setText( Float.toString(rate) );
       }
```

After a validation check [9], the current value in the text field is retrieved [10] and converted from a `String` to a `float` [11]. Conversion exceptions are caught at [13]. Barring an exception, the `float` value is passed to the `set-Rate` method [12], updating the `Controller`.

At [14] the `Controller` is queried for its current rate. The current rate is then converted to a `String` and written to the text field [15].

While one of `RateControl`'s ears is trained on `ActionEvents`, its other is listening for `ControllerEvents`, specifically `RateChangeEvents`.

Listing 19.4 *RateControl controllerUpdate Method*

```
          public void controllerUpdate(ControllerEvent e) {
              if( e.getSourceController() == controller &&
(16)                e instanceof RateChangeEvent)
              {
(17)              SwingUtilities.invokeLater(new LoadRateThread());
              }
          }

(18)      class LoadRateThread implements Runnable {
              public void run() {
                  loadRate();
              }
          }
```

In response to `RateChangeEvents`, the `controllerUpdate` method does the Swing thing and runs a `LoadRateThread` on the event-dispatching thread. `LoadRateThread` is responsible for updating the value in the text field based on the current rate of the `Controller` with a call to `loadRate`.

The `RateControl Component` appears in Figure 19.1.

Figure 19.1 *The RateControl Component*

Recall that the `AbstractController` developed in Chapter 14 uses the `RateControl`.

TimeDisplay Control

The `TimeDisplayControl` displays media time. It is unusual in that it is a read-only `Control`.

The `TimeDisplayControl` works by creating a timer that "ticks" when the `Controller` is started. Whenever it "ticks," the `Control` queries the `Controller` for the current media time. After converting the time to a `String`, the `Control` displays it in its control component. So that it can start and stop the timer as the `Controller` starts and stops, the `TimeDisplay-Control` implements the `ControllerListener` interface.

The timer used by `TimeDisplayControl` is a `SourcedTimer` from the `ejmf.toolkit.util` package in the *Essential JMF* Toolkit. Since we will see this class again in Chapter 20, we will say a few words about it here.

A `SourcedTimer` maintains two notions of time. First, there is the unitless "ticking" that marks the passage of real-time. There is also the *source time*. The source time has units associated with it and is provided by a `Time-Source`. A `TimeSource` maintains some meaningful time value. In our case, the `TimeDisplayControl` itself is the `TimeSource` which reports the media time of its associated `Controller`. When the `SourcedTimer` "ticks," the source is asked for the correct time. The "ticks" are heard by objects registered as a `SourcedTimerListener`.

Let's look the implementation of `TimeDisplayControl` to see how this all works.

Listing 19.5 *TimeDisplayControl Constructor and Member Data Fields*

```
        public class TimeDisplayControl
(19)                    implements Control,
(20)                        SourcedTimerListener,
(21)                        TimeSource,
(22)                        ControllerListener {

(23)        private JLabel
                timerField = new JLabel("0:00:00", JLabel.RIGHT);
(24)        private JPanel          controlComponent = new JPanel();
(25)        private String          timeVal;
            private SourcedTimer    timer;
            private long            divisor;

            private Controller      controller;

            public TimeDisplayControl(Controller controller) {
                this.controller = controller;

(26)            timer = new SourcedTimer(this);
(27)            timer.addSourcedTimerListener(this);
(28)            divisor = timer.getConversionDivisor();

(29)            controller.addControllerListener(this);

(30)            setUpControlComponent();

(31)            timeVal = convertTime(getTime(), divisor);
(32)            loadTime();
        }
        ...
(33)        private void loadTime() {
                timerField.setText(timeVal);
            }

            class LoadTimeThread implements Runnable {
                public void run() {
                    loadTime();
                }
            }

(34)        public Component getControlComponent() {
                return controlComponent;
            }
        }
```

The first thing that jumps out from `TimeDisplayControl` is that it has a few interfaces to implement [19]-[22]. We will discuss the details of each interface after a close look at `TimeDisplayControl`'s constructor and member data.

`TimeDisplayControl` has a structure similar to that of `RateControl`. The control component is a `JPanel` [24] that contains a `JLabel` [23] for displaying the current media time. All the GUI work to title and border the control component, as well as to add the `JLabel` into the component's `JPanel`, is done in `setUpControlComponent` [30]. Finally, the `Component` is available from the very simple `getControlComponent` [34].

To write to the label displaying the current media time, the `loadTime` method [33] is used. The member datum `timeVal` [25] contains the `String` representation of the current media time.

The timer mechanism for `TimeDisplayControl` is set up starting at [26]. First, a `SourcedTimer` object is constructed [26] passing `this TimeDisplayControl` object as the `TimeSource` argument. This `TimeDisplayControl` object is then registered as a `SourcedTimerListener` [27]. Thus the `TimeDisplayControl` will both receive the "ticks" and provide the media time.

The `divisor` value retrieved in [28] represents the value the `TimeSource` value has to be divided by to convert it to seconds. This value is used by `convertTime` [31] when converting `TimeSource` units to a `String`.

The `TimeDisplayControl` needs to register as a `ControllerListener` so that starting and stopping of the `SourceTimer` can be coordinated with the `Controller`. This is done at [29].

Finally, the initial time is loaded into the text field at [32]. Since the text field has not been realized yet, there is no need to execute `loadTime` on the event-dispatching thread at this point.

Implementing ControllerListener

When the `Controller` starts, the `SourcedTimer` should start. Likewise, when the `Controller` stops or experiences an error, the `SourcedTimer` should stop. The `controllerUpdate` method performs this task.

Listing 19.6 *TimeDisplayControl controllerUpdate Method*

```
public void controllerUpdate(ControllerEvent e) {
    if (e instanceof StopEvent ||
        e instanceof ControllerErrorEvent) {
        timer.stop();
    } else if (e instanceof StartEvent ) {
        timer.start();
    }
}
```
(35)(36)(37)(38)

In response to a `StopEvent` or a `ControllerErrorEvent` [35], the timer is stopped [36]. In response to a `StartEvent` [37], the timer is started [38].

Let it be said that stopping the `SourcedTimer` is not a requirement. This is done so that `SourcedTimerEvents` are not generated when the `Controller` is stopped. Not doing this may cause the `JLabel` displaying the time to flicker.

Implementing SourcedTimerListener

To implement the `SourcedTimerListener` interface, `TimeDisplayControl` defines the `timerUpdate` method.

Listing 19.7 *TimeDisplayControl timerUpdate Method*

```
public void timerUpdate(SourcedTimerEvent e) {
    timeVal = convertTime(getTime(), divisor);
    SwingUtilities.invokeLater(new LoadTimeThread());
}
```
(39)
(40)

In response to a "tick" or, formally, a `SourcedTimerEvent`, the media time is retrieved using `getTime` and converted to a `String` [39]. Since the time label needs to be updated, and the text field is displayed, the `loadTime` method is run in the AWT event-dispatching thread [40].

The `getTime` call in [39] brings us to the final interface implemented by `TimeDisplayControl`.

Implementing TimeSource

Two methods need to be defined to implement the `TimeSource` interface.

Listing 19.8 *TimeDisplayControl getTime Method*

```
public long getTime() {
    return controller.getMediaNanoseconds();
}
```
(41)

```
public long getConversionDivisor() {
    return TimeSource.NANOS_PER_SEC;
}
```
(42)

The role of `getTime` is to return the current time as maintained by the `TimeSource`. Here that means returning the current media time in nanoseconds [41].

The second responsibility of the `TimeSource` is to tell its clients something about the units of its time value. Specifically, the `getConversionDivisor` [42] method returns a value such that:

`getTime()/getConversionDivisor()`

results in seconds.

That is enough looking at code. The previous forty-four or so lines of code are worth one picture. Figure 19.2 shows the `TimeDisplayControl` Component.

Figure 19.2 *The TimeDisplayControl Component*

To really see the `TimeDisplayControl` in action, run the following command.

 **Running the TimerPlayer Example**

```
% java ejmf.examples.timerplayer.TimerPlayer \
    $EJMF_HOME/classes/media/safexmas.mov
```

This command will bring up a `Player`'s visual and control components in one frame and the `TimeDisplayControl` as it appears in Figure 19.2 in another.

The `TimeDisplayControl` is interesting because it is a read-only `Control`. Implementing such functionality as a `Control` illustrates the general nature of the `Control` interface. It is also, perhaps, stretching the meaning "control." One generally thinks of a "control" as an active means of changing the behavior of some subject. To make `TimeDisplayControl` a control in that sense of the word, it could be modified to allow the user to set the media time. It is left as an exercise to the reader to make such changes.

Now let's revisit, from the ground-up, the `CachingControl`.

Caching Control

Long ago, in a chapter far away (Chapter 8, "Player Controls"), we looked at the `javax.media.CachingControl` API. In that chapter we saw an example of how to use the `CachingControl`. In this section, we will develop a working `CachingControl` for use with the `AbstractController` class developed in Chapter 14 and Chapter 15. In fact, the `CachingControl` we will develop has already been put to use in the MIV Player presented in Chapter 18.

Our `CachingControl` implementation, `ejmf.toolkit.media.Basic-CachingControl`, provides a complete implementation of the `CachingControl` interface, reviewed briefly in Table 19.1

Table 19.1 *CachingControl Interface Methods*

Method	Description
`getContentLength`	Gets the total number of bytes to download.
`getContentProgress`	Gets the total number of bytes downloaded so far.
`getControlComponent`	Gets the `Component` that provides "additional" download control.
`getProgressBarComponent`	Gets the `Component` that displays download progress.
`isDownloading`	Checks whether media is being downloaded.

The first thing to notice is that the `CachingControl` interface defines two methods for providing AWT `Components` for display. It treats the progress bar for displaying download progress separately than the usual `Component` returned by `getControlComponent`. This component is intended for "additional" control purposes.

`BasicCachingControl` uses this component to present a button that pauses the download activity on the `Controller`.

BasicCachingControl Constructor

Let's look at the constructor and member data for `BasicCachingControl` for a translation of this prose to Java.

Listing 19.9 *BasicCachingControl Constructor*

```
public class BasicCachingControl implements CachingControl
{
    private final static String PAUSEMESSAGE = "Pause";
    private final static String RESUMEMESSAGE = "Resume";

    private AbstractController controller;
    private boolean isPaused;
```

(43)
(44)
(45)

```
    private boolean isDownloading;
    private long length;
    private long progress;
```

(46)
(47)

```
    private JProgressBar progressBar;
    private JButton pauseButton;
```

```
(48)        public BasicCachingControl(AbstractController c,
                                       long length) {
(49)          controller = c;
(50)          progressBar = new JProgressBar();
              progressBar.setMinimum(0);
(51)          pauseButton = new JButton(PAUSEMESSAGE);

(52)          pauseButton.addActionListener(
                new ActionListener() {
                  public void actionPerformed(ActionEvent e) {
                    String label = pauseButton.getText();
(53)                if( isPaused() ) {
                      pauseButton.setText(PAUSEMESSAGE);
(54)                  setPaused(false);
                    } else {
                      pauseButton.setText(RESUMEMESSAGE);
(55)                  setPaused(true);
                    }
                    pauseButton.getParent().validate();
                  }
                }
              );

(56)          reset(length);
(57)          controller.addControl(this);
            }
        ...
        }
```

Starting at [48], we see that the BasicCachingControl constructor takes an AbstractController and a long as its arguments. The AbstractController is the Controller downloading media. The length argument is the length of the media in bytes. If the length of the media is unknown, the value of length should be CachingControl.LENGTH_UNKNOWN.

After recording its associated Controller at [49], the BasicCaching-Control sets about building the relevant GUI components. The progress bar is built at [50] while the stop toggle button is built at [51]. References to both of these components are maintained in member data at [46] and [47]. Since the pause button must respond to user input, an ActionListener is registered with it at [52]. The ActionListener tests whether the download activity is paused [53] and then toggles the paused state of the BasicCachingControl at [54] and [55].

With the components built, the reset method is called [56] to initialize the BasicCachingControls properties. Finally, the addControl method from the AbstractController is called [57] to add the BasicCachingControl to the list of Controls maintained by controller. To refresh your memory on the operation of addControl, refer back to "Adding and Removing Controls" on page 232.

Implementation of the CachingControl Interface

Returning to the top of Listing 19.9, lines [43]-[47], we see five member variables. These correspond directly to the five methods required to implement the CachingControl interface.

Listing 19.10 *BasicCachingControl Implementation of CachingControl*

```
public boolean isDownloading() {
    return isDownloading;
}

public long getContentLength() {
    return length;
}

public long getContentProgress() {
    return progress;
}

public Component getProgressBarComponent() {
    return progressBar;
}

public Component getControlComponent() {
    return pauseButton;
}
```

Nothing could be simpler. However, we must now turn to the pieces of the BasicCachingControl that do all the work to make sure these methods have the correct value to return.

BasicCachingControl: The Meat

We have seen the construction of the BasicCachingControl and its implementation of methods required by virtue of its extending CachingControl. That was certainly enjoyable and we learned a lot, but we have yet to take a bite into the meat of the BasicCachingControl. We will do that now as we look at how a BasicCachingControl is initialized, how download status is updated and how a pause in the download is affected.

Initializing the BasicCachingControl

The reset method invoked in the constructor initializes the BasicCaching-Control. This is a public method and can therefore be called by the Controller if it has to restart the download.

reset sets the `BasicCachingControl` properties to their appropriate initial values and posts a `CachingControlEvent` to mark the start of downloading. The source for `reset` appears in Listing 19.11.

Listing 19.11 *BasicCachingControl reset Method*

```
      public synchronized void reset(long length) {
(58)      this.length = length;
(59)      progress = 0;
(60)      progressBar.setValue(0);
(61)      setContentLength(length);
(62)      setDownLoading(false);
(63)      setPaused(false);
(64)      controller.postEvent(
              new CachingControlEvent(controller,
                                      this,
                                      progress) );
      }
```

`reset` first records the length of the media in the appropriate member variable [58] and sets the current number of bytes received to zero [59]. The progress bar is then initialized to zero at [60]. Lines [61]-[63] then set the `length`, `isDownloading` and `isPaused` properties.

Finally, a `CachingControlEvent` is posted [64]. This is the first `CachingControlEvent` that listeners registered with `BasicCachingControl` will see. `getContentProgress` invoked on this event will return zero. See "Caching Events" on page 131.

Besides being called from `reset`, `setContentLength` may be called by the `Controller` to initialize the length of the media after object construction.

Listing 19.12 *BasicCachingControl setContentLength*

```
      public synchronized void setContentLength(long length) {
          this.length = length;
(65)      if( length == LENGTH_UNKNOWN ) {
(66)          progressBar.setMaximum(0);
          } else {
(67)          progressBar.setMaximum((int)length);
          }
      }
```

If the value of the `length` argument passed to `setContentLength` is LENGTH_UNKNOWN [65], the progress bar's maximum value is set to zero [66]. This effectively disables the progress bar as it will not "fill" in response to `setValue` calls.

For any value other than LENGTH_UNKNOWN, the progress bar's maximum value is set to the value of the `length` argument [67].

Updating the Download Progress

setValue also makes an appearance in the setContentProgress method used to update the download progress.

Listing 19.13 *BasicCachingControl setContentProgress*

```
public synchronized void setContentProgress(long progress)
{
(68)        blockWhilePaused();
(69)        this.progress = progress;
(70)        setDownLoading(progress < length);
(71)        progressBar.setValue((int)progress);

(72)        controller.postEvent(
                new CachingControlEvent(controller,
                                        this,
                                        progress) );

}
```

The first thing setContentProgress does is to check the paused state of the BasicCachingControl and, possibly, block the current thread. This is done within the blockWhilePaused method [68] which we will see in a bit.

The current number of bytes that have been downloaded is then set [69]. The downloading state of the control is set [70] depending on whether the number of bytes already downloaded is less than the total number of bytes to be downloaded.

At [71] the progress bar is updated, followed by the posting of a Caching-ControlEvent [72].

Another way a Controller can update the BasicCachingControl as media is downloaded is with the addToProgress method. This method differs from setContentProgress in that it is used for incremental updates. As you see from Listing 19.14, addToProgress calls setContent-Progress.

Listing 19.14 *BasicCachingControl addToProgress*

```
public void addToProgress(long toAdd) {
    setContentProgress(progress + toAdd);
}
```

Pausing Download Progress

The user pauses the download by clicking on the pause button. As you saw in the ActionListener defined in constructor code in Listing 19.9 on page 349, successive clicks toggle the paused state of the BasicCachingControl by calling `setPaused`. `setPaused` is best understood alongside `block-WhilePaused`.

Listing 19.15 *setPaused and blockWhilePaused Methods*

```
public synchronized void blockWhilePaused() {
    while( isPaused ) {
        try {
            wait();
        } catch(InterruptedException e) {}
    }
}

protected synchronized void setPaused(boolean isPaused) {
    this.isPaused = isPaused;
    notifyAll();
}
```

(73)
(74)

(75)
(76)

The `blockWhilePaused` method tests whether the `isPaused` property is set [73]. If so, it calls `wait` and blocks [74]. Recall that `blockWhilePaused` is called by `setContentProgress` (see Listing 19.13 on page 353) when the `Controller` is reporting the download progress. By blocking the `Controller` within the `BasicCachingControl`, the `BasicCachingControl` affects the pause. This method is to be called by the thread that downloads the media data. If this method blocks, the downloading will be paused until the thread is notified.

A paused `Controller` is awakened by the user again pressing the pause button. The `ActionListener` calls the `setPaused` method which sets the paused state [75] and in turn calls `notifyAll` [76].

Completing the Download

The `Controller` can explicitly end the download with a call to `setDone`.

Listing 19.16 *BasicCachingControl setDone Method*

```
public void setDone() {
    setContentProgress(length);
}
```

`setDone` simply calls `setContentProgress` with the length of the media as its argument. This will completely fill the progress bar and set the downloading state of the `Control` to `false`, as well as post a `CachingControlEvent`. We saw the source for `setContentProgress` in Listing 19.13.

To view the `CachingControl` in action, refer back to Figure 8.2 on page 133.

Summary

The `Control` interface of the JMF API provides a very general interface for building objects which affect the operation of a `Controller`. This simple interface allows a very broad interpretation of what a `Control` can do. The only requirement the API places on `Control` designers is that they implement the `getControlComponent` method. The API even allows that method to return `null`.

The rationale for this design is that it gives the `Control` designer absolute freedom regarding how a `Control` will interact with the `Controller` while still preserving the ability for the user to interact with the `Control`.

In this chapter we took advantage of this broad API design to implement three different `Controls`. The `RateControl` provides a simple interface for manipulating and monitoring a `Controller`'s rate of play. The `TimeDisplayControl` is a read-only `Control` that provides a convenient way to display the media time of a `Controller`. Finally, the `BasicCachingControl` provides a GUI for monitoring the loading of media data. It can be used without modification by any `Controller` built from the `AbstractController`.

The next chapter will continue with custom `Controls` and focus on a set of `Controls` required for custom control panels. Would you like to come along?

Chapter 20   *CREATING CONTROL PANEL CONTROLS*

Introduction

Earlier in Part II we developed an *Abstract Player Framework* which implemented as much API-compliant Player functionality as possible without building a complete Player. In Chapter 18, "Creating a Custom Player," we saw two complete Players built from that framework for two custom media formats.

The observant reader may have noticed a slick, non-standard control panel accompanying those custom Players. The curious reader, fond of unusual sentence construction, may have asked "Whence come these fancy control panels?"

This chapter will begin to satisfy the curious reader's curiosity. A general framework for designing control panel Controls will be presented. From that general framework, we will implement the standard Controls available in a Player's control panel. In the next chapter, we will see those standard Controls brought together into a ready-to-use control panel.

A Custom Control Model

For the purposes of the model we will develop, you can think of each Control as having two pieces: a GUI component and some associated semantics. The two pieces are related but not tightly-bound to one another. They are related in that the semantics are implemented as a listener on the component. The specific listener responsible for implementing the Control's semantics is referred to as the *control listener*. This is to distinguish it from other listeners that may be registered with the control component, which the model does not preclude.

The control model has been designed so that you can change the component and the control listener independently of one another. The idea is to support the most common means of customization, changing the look of a control panel control, in a straightforward way.

An abstract class AbstractListenerControl defines the common functionality that we will see present in all of our custom controls. It does this by employing the *template method pattern*. A template method defines an algorithm in terms of abstract operations that subclasses must override.[1] All of the controls we build will be rooted, for our purposes, at the AbstractListenerControl class. These subclasses are Controls by virtue of AbstractListenerControl implementing the Control interface.

The model distinguishes the Controls based on the type of control listener their respective component requires. Extending from AbstractListenerControl are ActionListenerControl, MouseListenerControl and ChangeListenerControl. Figure 20.1 illustrates these relationships.

Figure 20.1 *Control Panel Controls Class Hierarchy*

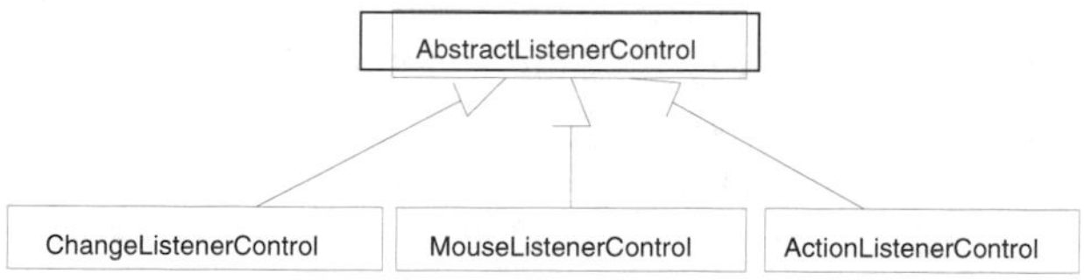

The direct subclasses of AbstractListenerControl are also abstract. AbstractListenerControl could be extended to support other types of listeners. The subclasses shown in Figure 20.1 are used in the further development of our concrete controls, which we will see when we extend these classes.

In the following sections we will proceed in a top-down fashion, starting with the AbstractListenerControl class. Unless noted, all of the classes discussed in this chapter reside in the ejmf.toolkit.controls package.

---

1. See *Design Patterns*, Gamma, et al., Addison-Wesley, 1995, pp. 325-330.

The AbstractListenerControl

All of the controls we will build are rooted, for our purposes, in the `abstract` class `AbstractListenerControl`. This `abstract` class imposes four functional constraints on its subclasses:

1. Its constructors enforce a uniform initialization policy.

2. It implements the `Control` interface, thereby providing a definition of `getControlComponent`.

3. It defines two `abstract` methods that supply it with a default control component and a default control listener, respectively.

4. It defines two `abstract` methods responsible for managing the association between the control component and a single control listener.

In addition to these constraints, the `AbstractListenerControl` provides `public` functionality that guarantees all of its subclasses support a minimal set of operations. This leads to:

5. It provides a `public` interface for determining whether a `Control` is operational.

6. It provides `public` methods for setting its control component, control listener and `Controller` member data fields.

AbstractListenerControl Class Diagram

Figure 20.2 shows a class diagram for `AbstractListenerControl`. Each instance maintains references to two `EventListeners`, a `Controller` and a `Component`.

Figure 20.2 *AbstractListenerControl Class Diagram*

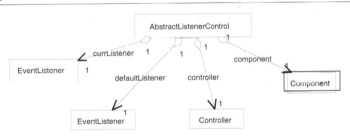

The `Component` represents the value returned by `getControlCompo-nent`, while the `Controller` is the JMF object with which this `Control` interacts. The `AbstractListenerControl` maintains two references to `EventListeners` which encapsulate the `Control` semantics. The `currL-istener` member field is the currently registered control listener. The `defaultListener` is the default control listener. A reference to it is maintained so the `Control` can be reset to the default listener if desired.

We will see these values manipulated in the following code excerpts from concrete `Control` classes that extend from `AbstractListenerControl`.

AbstractListenerControl Constructors

We will start by looking at `AbstractListenerControl`'s constructors. They are designed to ensure all control subclasses are properly initialized.

EJMF Toolkit Synopsis 20.1 *AbstractListenerControl Constructors*

Class	`ejmf.toolkit.controls.` `    AbstractListenerControl`
Constructor	`AbstractListenerControl`
Visibility	`protected`
Arguments	`void`
Description	Initializes `component` and `defaultListener` member data fields.
Constructor	`AbstractListenerControl`
Visibility	`protected`
Arguments	`javax.media.Controller`
Description	Initializes `component`, `defaultListener` and `controller` member data fields.

Each constructor is responsible for initializing the `private` member data that stores this `Control`'s `Component`, control listener and associated `Controller`.

Listing 20.1 excerpts from the `AbstractListenerControl` class source and shows the declaration of its member data fields and its constructors.

Listing 20.1 *AbstractListenerControl Constructor*

```
public abstract class AbstractListenerControl
                              implements Control {
(1)        private Component          component;
(2)        private EventListener      currListener;
(3)        private EventListener      defaultListener;
(4)        private Controller         controller;

(5)        protected AbstractListenerControl() {
(6)            component = createControlComponent();
(7)            initListener(createControlListener());
           }

(8)        protected AbstractListenerControl(
                       Controller controller) {
               this();
(9)            setController(controller);
           }
    ...
}
```

If the first form of the constructor [5] is used, a subsequent call to setController is necessary to associate the Control with a Controller. The second form of the constructor [8] will assign a Controller to this Control. Once a Control is associated with a Controller, it may not be associated with another.

The zero-argument constructor does most of the work. At [6], the component member data field declared at [1] is initialized using the value produced by createControlComponent, as implemented by one of AbstractListenerControl's subclasses. Likewise, at [7], a subclass provides a control listener by virtue of implementing createControlListener. This value is passed to the private method initListener, which simply sets the currListener and defaultListener member data fields declared at [2] and [3].

If the constructor is called with a Controller argument, setController is called [9] to set the controller member data field [4]. The description of setController appears in EJMF Toolkit Synopsis 20.2.

EJMF Toolkit Synopsis 20.2 *AbstractListenerControl setController Method*

Class	`ejmf.toolkit.controls.` `AbstractListenerControl`
Method	`setController`
Visibility	`public`
Arguments	`javax.media.Controller`
Return	`void`
Description	Associates a `Controller` with this `AbstractListener-` `Control`.

Before `setController` associates a `Controller` with an `AbstractListenerControl` two checks are performed. First, if a `Controller` has already been assigned to this `Control`, an `Illegal-` `ArgumentException` is thrown. A check is also made to ensure the `Con-` `troller` is realized. The source for `setController` appears in Listing 20.2.

Listing 20.2 *AbstractListenerControl setController Method*

```
       protected void setController(Controller controller)
                       throws IllegalArgumentException {
(10)       if (this.controller != null) {
(11)           throw new IllegalArgumentException(
                       "Controller already set on Control");
           }

(12)       if (controller.getState() < Controller.Realized) {
(13)           throw new NotRealizedError(
                       "Control requires realized Player");
           }
(14)       this.controller = controller;
(15)       setControllerHook(controller);
       }

(16)   protected void setControllerHook(Controller controller) {
           // no-op
       }
```

The requirement that a `Control` may only be associated with a `Control-` `ler` once is enforced at [10]. If there was a previous call to `setController`, an exception is thrown [11].

After ensuring that the control does not already have a `Controller` asso- ciated with it [11], `setController` checks to make sure its `Controller` argument is at least in the `Realized` state [12] and, if not, throws a `NotRealizedError` [13]. If the `Controller` is realized, the `controller` member data field is set at [14].

If a subclass of `AbstractListenerControl` needs to augment the operation of `setController` it should override and provide the guts to the *hook* method, `setControllerHook` [16]. As you see, `setControllerHook` is called by `setController` [15]. By default, it is a no-op; subclasses provide the code to make it meaningful. This arrangement relieves subclasses that need to extend `setController` from having to "remember" to invoke `super.setController` so that basic initialization is performed. We will see application of this more than once in subsequent discussions of the concrete subclasses of `AbstractListenerControl`.

As we will see, it is finally the concrete subclass that supplies the necessary implementations of `createControlComponent` and `createControlListener` that `AbstractListenerControl` relies upon in its constructors.

By enforcing the definition of these methods and using them in its constructors, `AbstractListenerControl` ensures all of its subclasses are initialized in a uniform manner, satisfying functional constraint (1) on page 359.

The Control Interface

That the `AbstractListenerControl` class is capable of implementing the `Control` interface should be obvious at looking at Listing 20.1. It maintains a `component` member field for all of its subclasses, relieving them of that responsibility.

The implementation of `getControlComponent` is left as an exercise for the user. Completing this exercise is no guarantee you will pass the Certified Java Developer test, but it will satisfy (2) on page 359.

Providing the Default Component and Listener

The responsibility for providing the control component and control listener resides with concrete subclasses of `AbstractListenerControl`. That responsibility is fulfilled by implementing the two `abstract` methods `createControlComponent` and `createControlListener`

EJMF Toolkit Synopsis 20.3 *Providing Component and Listener*

Class	`ejmf.toolkit.controls.` `    AbstractListenerControl`
Method	`createControlComponent`
Visibility	`protected`
Arguments	`void`
Return	`java.awt.Component`
Description	Creates and returns a `java.awt.Component` to serve as control component for this `Control` object.

EJMF Toolkit Synopsis 20.3 *Providing Component and Listener (Continued)*

Class	`ejmf.toolkit.controls.` `    AbstractListenerControl`
Method	`createControlListener`
Visibility	`protected`
Arguments	`void`
Return	`java.util.EventListener`
Description	Creates and returns the default control listener for this `Control` object.

It is the purpose of this design that it be easy to create custom controls for a `Player` control panel. All that is required to do so is the implementation of these two methods. We will look at implementations of these methods when we discuss concrete extensions to `AbstractListenerControl`.

The type of the `Component` returned by `createControlComponent` constrains the type of listener that may be returned by `createControlListener`. For example, if `createControlComponent` returns an `AbstractButton`, `createControlListener` must return an `ActionListener`.[2] These two methods are `protected` so that they are available only to subclasses. As defined, they are not type-safe. The assumption is made that a subclass knows to do the right thing.

Managing Component-Listener Association

A `java.awt.Component` can have multiple listeners associated with it. However, the design of the `AbstractListenerControl` is such that one and only one is treated as the control listener. The control listener implements the semantics of a particular control. A control listener is required to be registered for each `AbstractListenerControl`.

---

2. Granted, other types of listeners are legal but not so directly applicable to the needs of an `AbstractButton` within a control panel.

Subclasses must define the following methods to add and remove the control listener.

EJMF Toolkit Synopsis 20.4 *AbstractListenerControl Abstract Methods for Managing Control Listener*

Class	`ejmf.toolkit.controls.` `AbstractListenerControl`
Method	`addControlListener`
Visibility	`protected`
Arguments	`java.util.EventListener`
Return	`void`
Description	Adds the `EventListener` passed as an argument to the listener list of the control component.
Method	`removeControlListener`
Visibility	`protected`
Arguments	`java.util.EventListener`
Return	`void`
Description	Removes the `EventListener` passed as an argument from the listener list of the control component.

Certainly there may be multiple listeners associated with any `java.awt.Component`. However, to explicitly couple the control component with a specific listener, the `AbstractListenerControl` imposes a special interface for adding and removing that listener to the `Component`'s listener list. By identifying a particular listener as the control listener, the idea of substituting one semantic for another becomes more precise. This design also provides a general interface for manipulating different types of control listeners. As may be inferred from the names of the direct subclasses of `AbstractListenerControl`, as shown in Figure 20.1, each of these classes deals with a different type of `EventListener` and is responsible for ensuring the correct type. That `addControlListener` and `removeControlListener` are `protected` prevents an arbitrary client from trying to install the wrong type of listener, resulting in a run-time `ClassCastException`.

Determining Whether a Control Is Operational

A `Control` may not be operational based on some `Control`-specific conditions. For example, if a `Player` does not render an audio signal its control panel should not present any gain control GUI component.

`AbstractListenerControl` provides a method for setting the operational state and another for testing the operational state of a `Control`.

EJMF Toolkit Synopsis 20.5 *AbstractListenerControl Methods for Manipulating Operational State*

Class	ejmf.toolkit.controls. AbstractListenerControl
Method	setOperational
Visibility	protected
Arguments	boolean
Return	void
Description	Sets whether this Control is operational.
Method	isOperational
Visibility	public
Arguments	void
Return	boolean
Description	Returns true if this Control is operational.

The `setOperational` method is `protected` so that only subclasses can set the operational state of a `Control`. External objects do not know enough about a `Control` to be able to set its operational state.

What it means for a `Control` to be operational will differ for each `Control`. The gain control was mentioned above as a `Control` whose operation is dependent on an attribute of the `Player`. We will also see that the progress bar control will not be operational unless a `Controller` is able to report a known duration. All `AbstractListenerControls` are operational by default.

Setting the Component and Control Listener

`AbstractListenerControl` provides three `protected` methods for managing a control's GUI component and control listener in a uniform fashion. `AbstractListenerControl` implements these methods, so a subclass must override them to change their behavior.

EJMF Toolkit Synopsis 20.6 *AbstractListenerControl Methods*

Class	`ejmf.toolkit.controls.` `   AbstractListenerControl`
Method	`setControlListener`
Visibility	`protected`
Arguments	`java.util.EventListener`
Return	`void`
Description	Associates a new control listener with the component of this `Control`.
Method	`setComponent`
Visibility	`protected`
Arguments	`java.awt.Component`
Return	`void`
Description	Sets the GUI component associated with this `Control`.
Method	`setComponentAndListener`
Visibility	`protected`
Arguments	`java.awt.Component` `java.util.EventListener`
Return	`void`
Description	Associates both a `Component` and a control listener with this `Control`.

As you can see, these methods allow a user to independently set the control listener and control component, using `setControlListener` and `setComponent`. Additionally, the two control attributes can be set at the same time using `setComponentAndListener`.

Listing 20.3 *AbstractListenerControl Setter Methods*

```
(17)  protected void setComponentAndListener(
              Component component, EventListener listener) {
          this.component = component;
(18)      setControlListener(listener);
      }

(19)  protected void setComponent(Component component) {
          setComponentAndListener(component,
                                  getDefaultControlListener());
      }
```

```
(20)    protected void setControlListener(EventListener listener){
(21)        if (currListener != null) {
(22)            removeControlListener(currListener);
            }
(23)        addControlListener(listener);
(24)        currListener = listener;
        }
```

This code is fairly straightforward but there are a few things worth mentioning. setComponentAndListener [17] is used to set both the GUI component and control listener [18] on the Control. setComponent [19] relies on setComponentAndListener to set the component and install the default control listener on the Control.

In setControlListener [20], use is made of removeControlListener and addControlListener to change the single control listener associated with this Control. If the Control already has a control listener associated with it [21], this listener is removed from the Component's list of listeners [22]. In any case, the new control listener is installed by addControlListener [23].

It is important to note two more things about these methods. First, they are protected and, second, they provide no type-safety with respect to either the Component or EventListener arguments. If a subclass wants to make this functionality public, in a type-safe manner, it should provide public type-safe analogs to the methods in EJMF Toolkit Synopsis 20.6 that call those methods. Let's look at the direct subclasses of AbstractListenerControl to see the specifics of this strategy.

The ListenerControl Classes

Figure 20.1 on page 358 shows three direct subclasses of AbstractListenerControl. These classes are named to reflect the type of EventListener they impose upon their subclasses. Specifically, a control panel Control which employs an ActionListener will extend ActionListenerControl; a Control which employs a MouseListener will extend MouseListenerControl; and, a Control which employs a ChangeListener will extend ChangeListenerControl. Our discussion is limited to these three subclasses because that is what will be used in our custom control panel in Chapter 21. The design is not limited to supporting subclasses for only these types of listener.

These subclasses have the explicit requirement of defining addControlListener and removeControlListener. They may optionally make public the ability to modify an AbstractListenerControl's Component and control listener independently of one another, as discussed above.

Since the internals of our "listener controls" are quite similar, looking at one of them will suffice to explain all of them. Hence, we will direct our attention toward the `ActionListenerControl`. First, we will look at the implementation of `addControlListener` and `removeControlListener`. We will follow with `public` versions of `AbstractListenerControl`'s setter methods.

Managing the Control Listener

The `AbstractListenerControl` provides a uniform way of looking at a `Control` but it does so at the expense of type-safety. As defined by `AbstractListenerControl`, add- and `removeControlListener` require a generic `EventListener` as argument. However, subclasses require a certain type of listener depending on the type of their `Component`.

Both add- and `removeControlListener` must be written to accommodate that type of listener. A quick look at the source for these two methods will make this point clear.

Listing 20.4 *addControlListener from ActionListenerControl*

```
protected void addControlListener(EventListener listener)
{
     AbstractButton b;
(25)     b = (AbstractButton) getControlComponent();
(26)     b.addActionListener((ActionListener) listener);
}

protected void removeControlListener(
                         EventListener listener) {
     AbstractButton b;
(27)     b = (AbstractButton) getControlComponent();
(28)     b.removeActionListener((ActionListener) listener);
}
```

As you can see at [26] and [28], the `ActionListener`-specific method is used to add and remove the listener to and from the `Component`'s `ActionListener` list. Analogous operations are performed within `MouseListenerControl` and `ChangeListenerControl`.

Two related questions arise from this code. First, how is it that the casts to `AbstractButton` at [25] and [27] are known to be safe? Second, how is it that the casts to `ActionListener` at [26] and [28] are known to be safe?

There are two parts to the answer. When the control `Component` and control listener are first created with `createControlComponent` and `createControlListener`, these methods are counted on to provide objects of the appropriate type, as mentioned in "Providing the Default Component and Listener" on page 363. Subclass designers take heed!

Type-Safe Setters

The second part of the answer brings us back to the optional `public` setter functionality a listener `Control` may choose to implement.

Recall from EJMF Toolkit Synopsis 20.6, the `AbstractListenerControl` method `setComponentAndListener`. This method allows a subclass to modify both the `Component` and control listener associated with an `AbstractListenerControl`. When making such functionality public, a subclass may define a type-safe method that invokes its superclass's analog.

Listing 20.5 shows `ActionListenerControl`'s implementation of `AbstractListenerControl`'s setter functionality.

Listing 20.5 *ActionListenerControl Setter Methods*

```
public void setComponentAndListener(AbstractButton button,
                    ActionListener listener) {
    super.setComponentAndListener(button, listener);
}

public void setControlListener(ActionListener listener) {
    super.setControlListener(listener);
}

public void setComponent(AbstractButton button) {
    super.setComponent(button);
}
```

These `public` methods guarantee that when a client of an `ActionListenerControl` modifies either that control's listener or component, the correct type of object is supplied. This functionality can be used by a control panel to provide to users the ability to change the attributes of one of its controls in a type-safe manner. This type-safety applies only to clients, however. Designers of new subclasses of `AbstractListenerControl` are still responsible for providing the correct type of object to their implementations of `setComponentAndListener`, `setControlListener` and `setComponent`.

Now that we have seen the direct subclasses of `AbstractListenerControl`, we are ready to create some concrete classes implementing useful control panel `Controls`. In the next section we will describe what the `Controls` will do.

Control Panel Controls

In Chapter 18 the custom `Players` that were presented provided their own controls panels. In the next chapter, Chapter 21, "Creating a Custom Control Panel," we will see how these control panels were built. First, however, in this section we will build some of the pieces used to construct the custom control panel seen on the Text and Multi-Image Players. Specifically, we will build a set of standard controls that cover a wide range of control panel functionality. All of these controls will extend from the general model presented above.

The control panel `Controls` that will be implemented are described below. All of the classes that implement these `Controls` are in the `ejmf.tool-kit.controls` package of the *Essential JMF* Toolkit. These controls are the standard controls you would expect from a `Player`.

- Start Control – Start the media.
- Pause Control – Pause the media.
- Fast Forward Control – Play the media at twice the normal speed.
- Progress Slider Control – Display the progress of the media over time. Allow the user to position the media.
- Reverse Control – Play the media in reverse.
- Stop Control – Stop the media and reset the media to the beginning.
- Gain Control – Manipulate the volume of an audio signal associated with the media.
- Gain Meter Control – This control performs two jobs. First, it can be used to toggle and report the muted state of a `Player`. Second, it reports the level of the audio signal. It is not used to modify the audio signal.

For our purposes, the default control components associated with these controls are all rooted at `ejmf.toolkit.gui.controls.BasicControl-Button`. There are two exceptions.

1. The default progress `Control` component is a slider. In general, an object used as the component for the progress control must implement the `ejmf.toolkit.gui.control.ProgressBar` interface.

2. The default gain `Control` component is a `JPanel` containing two buttons. In general, an object functioning as the component for the gain control must extend from `ejmf.toolkit.gui.AbstractGainBut-tonPanel`.

There is also the further constraint on the gain meter control.

3. The default gain meter `Control` component must implement `ejmf.toolkit.gui.controls.GainMeter`. This interface defines methods for toggling the mute state as well as displaying different gain levels.

We will peek ahead and see what the standard `Controls` look like displayed in a control panel, but we will not build that control panel until next chapter.

Figure 20.3 *Standard Controls Displayed Within a Control Panel*

The control components appear from left to right in the order the Controls are described above.

The still observant reader may notice that this is not the control panel seen used with the custom Players in Chapter 18. Figure 20.3 displays an instance of the yet to be introduced StandardControlPanel. This class uses the standard controls developed in the next section.

The Standard Controls

With all the preliminaries out of the way, we will now look at the concrete classes that provide the final pieces of functionality for our control panel controls. As promised, because of all the work that has gone before, the Controls themselves will be very simple.

Our goal is to provide a standard set of controls, as listed on page 371, for the custom control panel to be built in Chapter 21. A naming convention is used to establish these controls. Each concrete class that defines a standard control begins with Standard, followed by the control name, followed by Control. For example, the Control for starting the Controller is StandardStartControl.

Start, Stop and Pause Controls

StandardStartControl, StandardStopControl, and StandardPauseControl all extend from ActionListenerControl. Figure 20.4 depicts these relationships.

Figure 20.4 *Controls Extending ActionListenerControl*

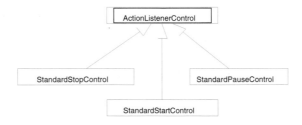

A class that extends ActionListenerControl is expected to provide an instance of an ActionListener as its control listener by implementing the ActionListener interface. We will look at each of the controls that extend ActionListenerControl, starting with the StandardStartControl. For this class, we will look at the entire class source, pointing out what is common to all standard controls. For subsequent standard controls, we will focus on the control listener, since that is where the interaction with the Controller resides, and attend to other details only in the exceptional case.

The StandardStartControl

The StandardStartControl starts the Controller. It is a very simple control, but we look at it in its entirety to illustrate how a concrete class can successfully implement an AbstractListenerControl.

Listing 20.6 *The StandardStartControl Class Source*

```
public class StandardStartControl
              extends ActionListenerControl {

(29)        public StandardStartControl(Controller controller) {
(30)            super(controller);
(31)            getControlComponent().setEnabled(true);
            }

(32)        public StandardStartControl() {
                super();
(33)            getControlComponent().setEnabled(true);
            }

(34)        protected Component createControlComponent() {
(35)            return new StartButton();
            }
    . . .
}
```

StandardStartControl defines two constructors ([29] and [32]), both of which call into the corresponding constructor in StandardStartControl's superclass. The constructor taking a Controller argument will always call super(controller) [30] to invoke the setController method of AbstractListenerControl.

In addition to invoking its superclass's constructor, this Control sets the initial enabled state of its control component in each of its constructors ([31] and [33]). In general, any Control-specific initialization is done in the constructors.

Recall that it is the responsibility of a subclass of AbstractListener-Control to supply a GUI component. AbstractListenerControl expects this component to be returned from the createControlComponent method.

At [34], `StandardStartControl` implements this method. It simply returns a new `StartButton` at [35], an instance of `ejmf.toolkit.gui.controls.StartButton`.

Since `createControlComponent` is called within the constructor of the `Control`'s superclass, all initialization of the `Control` component must be done from within this method. Initialization of non-static member data occurs when an instance of a class is created, that is, when the class's constructor is invoked. Since the superclass's constructor is invoked *before* the constructor of the class being instantiated, the following initialization of a `Control` component would result in a `NullPointerException` in `AbstractListenerControl`'s constructor.

```
JButton myControlComponent = new JButton("start");
...
public Component createControlComponent() {
    return myControlComponent;
}
```

This is because `myControlComponent` is not initialized until the constructor from the class of which it is a member is called. When `createControlComponent` is invoked by `AbstractControlListener`'s constructor, `myControlComponent` will be `null`.

This brings us to the `createControlListener` method. This method provides the control listener for this `Control` to the super class. The `StandardStartControl` provides an `ActionListener` [36].

Listing 20.7 *StandardStartControl createControlListener*

```
protected EventListener createControlListener() {
(36)    return new ActionListener() {
        public void actionPerformed(ActionEvent e) {
            Controller controller = getController();
            int state = controller.getState();
(37)        if (state == Controller.Started)
                return;

            if (state < Controller.Prefetched) {
                StateWaiter w = new StateWaiter(controller);
                w.blockingPrefetched();
            }
(38)        TimeBase tb = controller.getTimeBase();
(39)        controller.syncStart(tb.getTime());
        }
    };
}
```

This listener starts the `Controller` as soon as possible using `syncStart` [39] after ensuring that it is not already started [37]. "As soon as possible" is achieved by grabbing the current `TimeBase` time [38] and using that as an argument to `syncStart`.

The StandardStopControl

The `StandardStopControl` stops the `Controller` and sets the media time to 0.0, rewinding the media.

Listing 20.8 *StandardStopControl Control Listener*

```
protected EventListener createControlListener() {
    return new ActionListener() {
        public void actionPerformed(ActionEvent e) {
            Controller controller = getController();
            controller.stop();
            controller.setMediaTime(new Time(0.0));
        }
    };
}
```

`StandardStopControl` returns a `StopButton` as its control component. `StopButton` lives in the `ejmf.toolkit.gui.controls` package.

Listing 20.9 *StandardStopControl createControlComponent*

```
protected Component createControlComponent() {
    return new StopButton();
}
```

The StandardPauseControl

The `StandardPauseControl` stops the `Controller`. Unlike the stop control, it does not change the media time.

Listing 20.10 *The StandardPauseControl Control Listener*

```
protected EventListener createControlListener() {
    return new ActionListener() {
        public void actionPerformed(ActionEvent e) {
            getController().stop();
        }
    };
}
```

`StandardPauseControl` returns a `PauseButton` as its control component.

Listing 20.11 *StandardPauseControl createControlComponent*

```
protected Component createControlComponent() {
    return new PauseButton();
}
```

Fast Forward and Reverse Controls

StandardFastForwardControl and StandardReverseControl extend MouseListenerControl so that they can respond to both a mouse press and release. Both controls affect the Controller only when the control button remains depressed.

Figure 20.5 *Controls Extending MouseListenerControl*

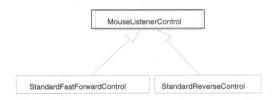

The StandardFastForwardControl

The StandardFastForwardControl plays the media forward at some rate greater than 1.0. The forward rate can be set when constructing a Standard-FastForwardControl. StandardFastForwardControl supports the two constructors inherited from AbstractListenerControl as well as the one for setting the rate, shown in Listing 20.12.

Listing 20.12 *StandardFastForwardControl Constructors*

```
public class StandardFastForwardControl
        extends MouseListenerControl {
(40)    private static final float DEFAULT_FF_RATE = 2.0f;
(41)    private float         fastForwardRate;

(42)    public StandardFastForwardControl(
                    Controller controller) {
            this(controller, DEFAULT_FF_RATE);
        }

(43)    public StandardFastForwardControl() {
            super();
            fastForwardRate = DEFAULT_FF_RATE;
            getControlComponent().setEnabled(true));
        }
```

```
(44)        public StandardFastForwardControl(
                      Controller controller, float rate) {
                super(controller);
(45)            fastForwardRate = (rate < 1.0f) ?
                              DEFAULT_FF_RATE: rate;
                getControlComponent().setEnabled(true);
            }


            . . .
        }
```

Both the standard constructors ([42] and [43]) use the default fast forward rate [40], while the third constructor [44] takes an additional `float` argument. The member data field `fastForwardRate` is set to this value [45] for later use in the control listener. If the `rate` argument value is less than 1.0, `fast-ForwardRate` is forced to the default rate.

The `StandardFastForwardControl` implements its control listener by extending `MouseAdapter` as shown in Listing 20.13.

Listing 20.13 *StandardFastForwardContol Control Listener*

```
protected EventListener createControlListener() {
    return new MouseAdapter() {
            private float   saveRate;
            private int     priorState;

            public void mousePressed(MouseEvent mouseEvent) {
                Controller controller = getController();
(46)            saveRate = controller.getRate();
(47)            priorState = controller.getState();
(48)            if (priorState == Controller.Started) {
(49)                controller.stop();
                }
(50)            controller.setRate(fastForwardRate);
                TimeBase tb = controller.getTimeBase();
(51)            controller.syncStart(tb.getTime());
            }

            public void mouseReleased(MouseEvent mouseEvent) {
                Controller controller = getController();
(52)            controller.setRate(saveRate);
(53)            if (priorState != Controller.Started) {
(54)                controller.stop();
                }
            }
        };
}
```

The fast forward control is enabled regardless of whether the `Controller` is stopped or started. However, when the control button is released, the control must return the `Controller` to its previous state and rate. To prepare for this, the current rate and state of the `Controller` are saved in member data fields ([46] and [47]). These values will be used later in the `mouseReleased` method to restore the `Controller` to the state it was in when the fast forward button was pressed

If the `Controller` is started [48], it must be stopped [49] since `setRate` cannot be called on a started `Controller`. At [50], the `Controller`'s rate is set to the value of the `fastForwardRate` variable. Finally, the `Controller` is started unconditionally [51] since it is known to be stopped at this point.

You will notice that there is no attempt to ensure the `Controller` is in the `Prefetched` state in the `mousePressed` method. With the exception of the start `Control`, which does `prefetch` to initially get the `Controller` to a known state, the `Controls` assume that they are the sole mechanism by which the `Controller` is being manipulated. As long as the `Control` GUI components are kept in the appropriate enabled state, the `Controller` will be in the correct state for a given `Control` operation. It is the responsibility of the `Control` panel to modify the `Control` components to correctly reflect the state of the `Controller`. We will see how this is accomplished in the next chapter.

As long as the control button is held down, the `Controller` will continue to play at the `fastForwardRate`. When the button is released, the `mouseReleased` method of the control listener is called. First, the previous rate saved at [46] is restored at [52]. Then, if the `Controller` was previously stopped [53], it is once again stopped [54].

`StandardFastForwardControl` returns an `ejmf.toolkit.gui.controls.FastForwardButton` as its control component.

Listing 20.14 *StandardFastForwardControl createControlComponent*

```
protected Component createControlComponent() {
    return new FastForwardButton();
}
```

The StandardReverseControl

The reverse control plays media in the reverse direction. Like the fast forward control, the `StandardReverseControl` is affected by selecting its component and holding the mouse button down.

As a subclass of `MouseListenerControl`, its control listener is implemented by extending `MouseAdapter`.

Listing 20.15 *StandardReverseControl Control Listener*

```
      protected EventListener createControlListener() {
          return new MouseAdapter() {
              private int       priorState;
              private float     saveRate;

              public void mousePressed(MouseEvent mouseEvent) {
(55)              if (isOperational()) {
                      Controller controller = getController();
(56)                  saveRate = controller.getRate();
(57)                  priorState = controller.getState();

(58)                  if (priorState == Controller.Started) {
(59)                      controller.stop();
                      }

(60)                  controller.setRate(-1.0f * saveRate);
                      TimeBase tb = controller.getTimeBase();
(61)                  controller.syncStart(tb.getTime());
                  }
              }

              public void mouseReleased(MouseEvent event) {
(62)              if (isOperational()) {
                      Controller controller = getController();
(63)                  controller.setRate(saveRate);
                      if (priorState != Controller.Started) {
(64)                      controller.stop();
                      }
                  }
              }
          };
      }
```

StandardReverseControl's control listener looks very similar to StandardFastForwardControl's. When the reverse control component is pressed, the current rate and state of the Controller are stored away in member data fields at [56] and [57].

In order to call setRate, the Controller must be stopped. At [58] the state of the Controller is checked and if started, it is stopped [59]. The rate is then set to be the negative of the current rate [60]. Finally, the Controller is started using syncStart [61].

Reverse play is terminated in the mouseReleased method. The previous rate of the Controller is restored [63], and the Controller stopped [64], if that was its previous state.

Note that the reverse control listener code is conditional on the isOperational method ([55] and [62]) returning true. It is not enough to disable the component since, if the client of `StandardReverseControl` has a reference to it, it can enable the component at will.

The operational state of the reverse control is set with a call to `setOperational`. This call is made in `StandardReverseControl`'s `setControllerHook` method. When the control is associated with a `Controller`, the control determines whether or not the `Controller` is capable of supporting negative rates.

Listing 20.16 *StandardReverseControl setControllerHook Method*

```
public void setControllerHook(Controller controller) {
    float saveRate = controller.getRate();
    float rate = controller.setRate(-1.0f);
    setOperational(rate < 0.0f);
    component.setEnabled(isOperational());
    controller.setRate(saveRate);
}
```

(65)
(66)
(67)

This simple piece of code attempts to set a negative rate for the `Controller` passed as an argument [65]. Whether or not this control is operational depends on whether the call to `setRate` returns a negative value [66]. The control component's enabled state is then set based on the `Control`'s operational state [67]. If the reverse control is not operational but the button has been enabled, the `mousePressed` and `mouseReleased` methods from its control listener are no-ops.

`StandardReverseControl` returns an `ejmf.toolkit.gui.controls.ReverseButton` as its control component.

Listing 20.17 *StandardReverseControl createControlComponent*

```
protected Component createControlComponent() {
    return new ReverseButton();
}
```

Progress Slider Control

The progress control displays a slider which shows the relative position of the media. As media progresses, the slider value changes and the slider "thumb" moves. Additionally, the "thumb" can be dragged to manually position the media time.

The `StandardProgressControl` is the single example of a subclass of `ChangeListenerControl`. This is because its component is a cheap imitation of the Swing `JSlider`.[3] As such, it fields mouse events and reports them to its listeners as change events.

---

3. There is just too much overhead associated with a `JSlider` to make it responsive enough in this context. Instead, much code was lifted from and much ignored in the source for `JSlider`.

Figure 20.6 *Controls Extending ChangeListenerControl*

The StandardProgressControl

The StandardProgressControl is a fairly sophisticated Control. In addition to extending ChangeListenerControl, it implements the following interfaces.

- ControllerListener

  StandardProgressControl must listen for ControllerEvents for two reasons. First, since some Controllers may not report a meaningful duration until they have reached the Prefetched state, the StandardProgressControl listens for the PrefetchCompleteEvent before making a final determination on its operational state.

  Second, since, as we will see, the StandardProgressControl is driven by its own timer, this timer needs to be started and stopped in response to StartEvents and StopEvents, respectively.

- TimeSource

  StandardProgressControl provides a getTime method that returns the current media time.

- SourcedTimerListener

  As a SourcedTimerListener, StandardProgressControl implements the timerUpdate method. Upon receipt of each timer event, StandardProgressControl queries the TimeSource for the current media time. Once the current media time is obtained, the slider is updated.

Additionally, the StandardProgressBar requires that its component implement the ProgressBar interface. This interface defines eight methods listed in Table 20.1. Their use will become clear in the subsequent discussion.

382 / Creating Control Panel Controls

Table 20.1 *ProgressBar Interface Methods*

Method	Description
getValue	Get the current value of the slider. The value will be between getMinimum and getMaximum.
setValue	Set the current value.
getMinimum	Get the minimum possible value.
setMinimum	Set the minimum possible value.
getMaximum	Get the maximum possible value.
setMaximum	Set the maximum possible value.
addChangeListener	Add a ChangeListener to this object's listeners.
removeChangeListener	Remove a ChangeListener from this object's listeners.

For a complete description of the ProgressBar interface see the *Essential JMF* Toolkit javadoc available with the example code from the Prentice Hall ftp site.

As its component, StandardProgressControl returns a Slider which implements the ProgressBar.

Listing 20.18 *StandardProgressControl createControlComponent*

```
protected Component createControlComponent() {
    return new Slider();
}
```

The StandardProgressControl is further complicated by the fact that a Controller's duration may not be definitely known until it has reached the Prefetched state. We have until now determined a standard control's operational state in the setControllerHook method. However, with Standard-ProgressControl, this task must be deferred until its associated Controller has been prefetched. Instead setControllerHook forces the operational state to false and installs itself as a listener on the Controller.

Listing 20.19 *StandardProgressControl setControllerHook Method*

```
public void setControllerHook(Controller controller) {
    setOperational(false);
    controller.addControllerListener(this);
}
```

(68)
(69)

StandardProgressControl's setControllerHook implementation forces the operational state to be false at [68] and, at [69], it registers as a ControllerListener on its Controller. When the controllerUpdate method sees a `PrefetchCompleteEvent`, the `Controller` will have complete information about its duration and will update its operational state.

The `controllerUpdate` method is shown in Listing 20.20

Listing 20.20 *StandardProgressControl controllerUpdate and init Methods*

```
private boolean        firstPrefetch = true;
private SourcedTimer   controlTimer;
private long           duration;

public void controllerUpdate(ControllerEvent event) {
(70)      if (isOperational()) {
              if (event instanceof StartEvent ||
                  event instanceof RestartingEvent) {
(71)              controlTimer.start();
              } else if (event instanceof StopEvent ||
                      event instanceof ControllerErrorEvent) {
(72)              controlTimer.stop();
(73)          } else if (event instanceof MediaTimeSetEvent) {
(74)              setValue(getTime());
              }
          } else {
(75)          if (firstPrefetch &&
                      event instanceof PrefetchCompleteEvent) {
(76)              init();
                  firstPrefetch = false;
(77)              SwingUtilities.invokeLater(
                          new EnableComponentThread());
              }
          }
}

class EnableComponentThread implements Runnable {
    public void run() {
        getControlComponent().setEnabled(isOperational());
    }
}
```

```
(78)      private void init() {
              Time d = controller.getDuration();
(79)          boolean flg = d != Duration.DURATION_UNBOUNDED &&
                            d != Duration.DURATION_UNKNOWN;

              if (flg) {
(80)              duration = d.getNanoseconds();
(81)              flg = (duration != 0L);
              }
(82)          setOperational(flg);
              if (flg) {
(83)              controlTimer = new SourcedTimer(this, TIMER_TICK);
(84)              controlTimer.addSourcedTimerListener(this);

                  Time mTime = controller.getMediaTime()
                  long mediaTime = mTime.getNanoseconds();
(85)              setValue(mediaTime);
              }
          }
```

The behavior of StandardProgressControl's controllerUpdate
method is dependent upon the return value of isOperational [70]. Since
we forced the operational state to false in [68] on page 382, the first time
controllerUpdate executes, it will start at [75]. Here if the Prefetch-
CompleteEvent is seen for the first time [75], the init method [76] is
called.

After init returns, isOperational will return an updated operational
status. Based on this status, the StandardProgressControl's component
will be enabled or disabled. In accordance with Swing programming rules,
this is done by a thread running on the AWT event queue [77].

The init method [78] is responsible for setting the operational state of the
Control. If the duration of Control's Controller is either unknown,
unbounded or zero, the slider will not be operational and the test at [79] will
fail. This test determines whether the duration is some known value. If it is,
the duration member field is set at [80], and at [81] a zero value is tested for.
By the time [82] is reached, the flg variable contains the correct operational
state of the Control where it is used as an argument to setOperational.

If the slider is operational, a timer must be created to drive its motion in
conjunction with the passing of media time. A SourcedTimer is created at
[83] and the StandardProgressControl registers itself as a SourcedTimerListener on this timer at [84]. A SourcedTimer contains both a *timer*
that "ticks" at a given interval and a time *source*. Whenever a "tick" occurs,
the source is queried for the time value. In the context of a StandardProgressControl, the source time is media time. See the *Essential JMF* Toolkit
javadoc for a complete description of both SourcedTimer and Sourced-
TimerListener.

Assuming the `Control` is operational, subsequent trips through the `controllerUpdate` method start [71] and stop [72] the timer depending on the `ControllerEvent` seen. Additionally, at [73], if a `Media-TimeSetEvent` is seen, the slider value is set based on the current time.

Returning to our discussion of the `init` method, we see that upon receipt of the first `PrefetchCompleteEvent` by `controllerUpdate` a call to `setValue` [85] initializes the slider. The source for `setValue` appears in Listing 20.21.

Listing 20.21 *StandardProgressControl setValue Method*

```
(86)    public void setValue(long mediaTime) {
            ProgressBar bar;

            if ( !isOperational() ) {
                return;
            }

            bar = (ProgressBar) getControlComponent();
(87)        long diff = bar.getMaximum() - bar.getMinimum();
(88)        int value = (int) ((diff * mediaTime) / duration);

(89)        SwingUtilities.invokeLater(
                new SetProgressSliderValueThread(bar, value));
        }

(90)    class SetProgressSliderValueThread implements Runnable {
            int              value;
            ProgressBar      bar;

            public SetProgressSliderValueThread(ProgressBar bar,
                                                int value)
                this.value = value;
                this.bar = bar;
            }

            public void run() {
(91)            bar.setValue(value);
            }
        }
```

`setValue` maps a media time into a slider value. It takes as input a media time [86], and based on the length of the slider track [87] and the `Control-ler`'s duration, calculated at [80] in Listing 20.20, it calculates the physical location of the thumb [88]. Finally, it creates a `SetProgressSliderValueThread` object and passes it to `invokeLater` [89]. This `Runnable` object, defined as an inner class at [90], directly calls the slider's `setValue` method at [91] to move the thumb to the right spot on the slider.

We have yet to see how the slider gets updated on an ongoing basis as media time progresses. Recall that `StandardProgressControl` implements a `SourcedTimerListener` and is registered to hear from a `SourcedTimer` at [84]. Every time a tick of the `SourcedTimer` occurs, `StandardProgressControl`'s `timerUpdate` method is called.

Listing 20.22 *StandardProgressControl timerUpdate Method*

```
public void timerUpdate(SourcedTimerEvent e) {
    setValue(getTime());
}
```

Each call to `timerUpdate` updates the slider value with a call to `setValue`. The value it sends to `setValue` is a media time value returned from its own `getTime` that it implements by virtue of implementing the `TimeSource` interface. This is a simple method also but worth looking at because it connects the movement of the slider thumb directly to the progression of media time.

Listing 20.23 *StandardProgressControl getTime*

```
public long getTime() {
    return controller.getMediaNanoseconds();
}
```

`getTime` returns the media time that is used as an argument to `setValue`. `setValue` maps the media time into slider track coordinates and calls the slider's `setValue` method.

Up to now, we have discussed the `StandardProgressControl` only in terms of how it is used to display the passing media time. The component of the `StandardProgressControl` can also be used to set the media time. This brings us back to our general control model and the role of `StandardProgressControl` as a subclass of `AbstractListenerControl`.

As an `AbstractListenerControl`, `StandardProgressControl` must provide a `createControlListener` method. This method is shown in Listing 20.24.

Listing 20.24 *StandardProgressControl Control Listener*

```
protected EventListener createControlListener() {
    return new ChangeListener() {
        public void stateChanged(ChangeEvent e) {
```
(92)
```
            ProgressBar s = (ProgressBar) e.getSource();
```
(93)
```
            int value = s.getValue();
```
(94)
```
            long mediaNanos = (long)((value * duration) /
                        (s.getMaximum() - s.getMinimum())));
            Controller controller = getController();
            int priorState = controller.getState();
            if (priorState == Controller.Started) {
                controller.stop();
            }
```
(95)
```
            controller.setMediaTime(new Time(mediaNanos));
            if (priorState == Controller.Started) {
                TimeBase tb = controller.getTimeBase();
                Time now = tb.getTime();
                controller.syncStart(now);
            }
        }
    };
}
```

Since StandardProgressControl extends directly from ChangeListenerControl, createControlListener returns an instance of a ChangeListener. A ChangeListener registered with a slider is intended to follow user changes to the location of the thumb. In this context, the user moves the slider thumb in order to set the current media time. The job, then, of the ChangeListener object returned by createControlListener is to convert a location on the slider track to a media time.

When stateChanged is called, the source slider is retrieved at [92] and cast to a ProgressBar. Methods from this interface are employed by stateChanged at [93] and [94].

Once the ProgressBar object is retrieved, the current value of the slider can be obtained [93] and used in the mapping of the slider value to media time in [94]. This newly calculated media time value is then used in a call to setMediaTime to update the control's associated Controller [95].

The above calculation of media time [94] only makes sense because the Controller is guaranteed to have a known duration at this point. If the Control were not operational, it would have been disabled and stateChanged never called.

Gain-Related Controls

There are two gain-related controls supported by the general control model. The first, StandardGainControl, is used to increase and decrease Player gain. The second, `StandardGainMeterControl`, is used to toggle a `Player`'s muted state, display that state, and display a `Player`'s gain level.

Both of these `Controls` are instances of `ActionListenerControl`. However, they extend directly from `AbstractGainControl`. `Abstract-GainControl` is itself an `abstract` class because it leaves `abstract` methods from `ActionListenerControl` unimplemented.

The relationship between `ActionListenerControl`, `AbstractGain-Control` and the concrete classes implementing the standard gain-related controls is shown in Figure 20.7.

Figure 20.7 *AbstractGainControl and The Standard Gain Controls*

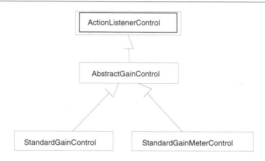

The AbstractGainControl Class

`AbstractGainControl` performs two functions for its subclasses. First, it determines the operational state of the `Control`. If a `Control` is going to manipulate gain, two conditions must be met.

1. The `Controller` associated with it must be an instance of a `Player`.

2. That `Player` must have a `GainControl`.

The checks for these conditions are made in `AbstractGainControl`'s `setControllerHook` method appearing in Listing 20.25.

Listing 20.25 *AbstractGainControl setControllerHook Method*

```
(96)  private GainControl          gc;
      ...
      public void setControllerHook(Controller controller) {
(97)      if (controller instanceof Player) {
(98)          gc = ((Player) controller).getGainControl();
(99)          setOperational(gc != null);
          } else {
(100)         setOperational(false);
          }
      }
```

Condition (1) above is tested for at [97]. If the `Controller` passed as an argument to `setControllerHook` is a `Player`, a reference to the `GainControl` is retrieved and saved at [98] into the `private` member data declared at [96].

Whether the `Player` has a `GainControl` determines whether this `Control` is operational. The test at [99] satisfies (2) above.

If the `Controller` is not an instance of a `Player`, the `Control` implemented by a concrete class extending `AbstractGainControl` will not be operational [100].

The second thing `AbstractGainControl` provides to its subclasses is access to the `GainControl` reference it derived from the `Controller` argument to `setControllerHook` [98]. This is achieved with the simple accessor method `getGainControl`.

Listing 20.26 *AbstractGainControl getGainControl*

```
protected GainControl getGainControl() {
    return gc;
}
```

Simple enough, but necessary since subclasses are going to need to access the associated `GainControl` object.

Let's look now at the two subclasses of `AbstractGainControl` that implement two standard controls.

The StandardGainControl

To understand the `StandardGainControl`, you first must understand a little bit about its component. The `StandardGainControl`'s component must be a subclass of `AbstractGainButtonPanel`.

Listing 20.27 *StandardGainControl createControlComponent Method*

```
protected Component createControlComponent() {
    return new StandardGainButtonPanel();
}
```

The `AbstractGainButtonPanel` extends `JPanel` and contains two buttons, one each for increasing and decreasing `Player` gain. `AbstractGainButtonPanel` defines two `public` methods for accessing these buttons.

Table 20.2 *AbstractGainButtonPanel Public Methods*

Method	Description
getGainIncreaseButton	Get the button component meant for increasing gain.
getGainDecreaseButton	Get the button component meant for decreasing gain.

That `AbstractGainButtonPanel` is a `java.awt.Container` has implications for adding and removing the control listener. Specifically, the buttons internal to the `AbstractGainButtonPanel` are the components that need to have a listener added to them. This requires that `StandardGainControl` override the `addController` and `removeController` methods from `ActionListenerControl` so that they do the right thing. `addControlListener` is reproduced in Listing 20.28 to make this clear.

Listing 20.28 *StandardGainControl addControlListener*

```
protected void addControlListener(
                                  EventListener listener) {
    if (listener instanceof ActionListener) {
        AbstractButton ab;
        AbstractGainButtonPanel p =
            (AbstractGainButtonPanel) getControlComponent();
        ab = p.getGainIncreaseButton();
        ab.addActionListener((ActionListener) listener);
        ab = p.getGainDecreaseButton();
        ab.addActionListener((ActionListener) listener);
    } else {
        throw new IllegalArgumentException(
                        "ActionListener required");
    }
}
```

(101)
(102)
(103)
(104)

The "right thing" involves extracting the buttons from the `Abstract-GainButtonPanel` at lines [101] and [103] and then adding the listener to these components at lines [102] and [104]. Analogous operations are required to remove the control listener.

Notice that the same listener is being attached to both buttons. That, of course, has implications for how the listener is written. From Listing 20.29 you can see that the source of the `ActionEvent` is tested to decide which path through the `ActionListener` code is taken.

Listing 20.29 *StandardGainControl Control Listener*

```
       protected EventListener createControlListener() {
          return new ActionListener() {
             public void actionPerformed(ActionEvent e) {
(105)           AbstractGainButtonPanel gbp =
                   (AbstractGainButtonPanel)
                                  getControlComponent();
(106)           GainControl gc = getGainControl();
(107)           float level = gc.getLevel();
(108)           if (e.getSource() ==
                              gbp.getGainIncreaseButton()) {
                   level += 0.1f;
(109)              gc.setLevel(level > 1.0f ? 1.0f : level);
(110)           } else if (e.getSource() ==
                              gbp.getGainDecreaseButton()) {
                   level -= 0.1f;
(111)              gc.setLevel(level < 0.0f ? 0.0f : level);
                }
             }
          };
       }
```

In [105]–[107] some preliminary work is done: the component is cast to a `AbstractGainButtonPanel`, the `Player`'s `GainControl` is retrieved and the current gain level is accessed.

At [108] and [110] the source component is tested against the components returned from the `AbstractGainButtonPanel`.

If the source component is the gain increase button [108], the gain level is incremented and then set [109], after ensuring that the maximum useful value is not exceeded. If the source is the gain decrease button [110], the gain level is decremented and then set [111], again after ensuring that the minimum useful level is not exceeded.

The `StandardGainControl` relies upon `GainChangeEvents` to set the enabled state of the gain increase and decrease buttons. From within `gainChange` [112], `setState` is called [114], via the `SetStateThread` thread [113], to update the state of the buttons.

Listing 20.30 *StandardGainControl gainChange Method*

```
(112)   public void gainChange(GainChangeEvent e) {
            SwingUtilities.invokeLater(
                        new SetStateThread(e.getLevel()));
        }

(113)   class SetStateThread implements Runnable {
            private float level;
            public SetStateThread(float level) {
                this.level = level;
            }
            public void run() {
(114)           setState(level);
            }
        }

(115)   private void setState(float level) {
            AbstractGainButtonPanel gbp =
                        (AbstractGainButtonPanel) component;
            gbp.getGainIncreaseButton().setEnabled(level < 1.0f);
            gbp.getGainDecreaseButton().setEnabled(level > 0.0f);
        }
```

setState [115] simply fetches the buttons from the AbstractGainButtonPanel and sets their enabled state based on the level value.

Since the StandardGainControl needs to be informed of gain changes to correctly maintain the state of its buttons, it needs to register as a GainChangeListener. This is done in the setControllerHook method.

Listing 20.31 *StandardGainControl setControllerHook*

```
        public void setControllerHook(Controller newController) {

(116)       super.setControllerHook(newController);

            GainControl gc;

(117)       if (isOperational()) {

(118)           gc = getGainControl();
(119)           setState(gc.getLevel());
(120)           gc.addGainChangeListener(this);

            }
        }
```

Recall that StandardGainControl's superclass, AbstractGainControl, takes care of setting the operational state of this Control. This is accomplished with the call to the superclass's `setControllerHook` method at [116]. If `isOperational` tests `true` [117], the `GainControl` is fetched from the `Player` associated with this `Control` [118]. After setting the initial state of the buttons [119], the `Control` adds itself as a `GainChangeListener` on the `GainControl` object [120].

The StandardGainMeterControl

The role of the `StandardGainMeterControl` is twofold. First, it is used to toggle the muted state of the `Player`'s audio signal. Second, it is used to display the level of the audio signal.

Because of its dual role, the control component for the `StandardGainMeterControl` must implement the `ejmf.toolkit.gui.controls.GainMeter` interface. The `GainMeter` interface provides four methods for manipulating the state of the gain meter button.

Table 20.3 *GainMeter Interface Methods*

Method	Description
`setLevel`	Set the display level of this component.
`setMute`	Set the muted state of this component.
`updateView`	Redraw the gain meter component.
`mapToMeterLevel`	Map a true gain level to meter "level."

An implementation of `GainMeter` is free to render the "level" as it wishes by mapping a gain level to a relevant meter level value. Likewise, the component determines what it means to display a particular muted state. A method for performing the mapping from gain level to meter level, and another for updating the meter display, are defined by the `GainMeter` interface.

For its Component, `StandardGainMeterControl` uses the `GainMeterButton`.

Listing 20.32 *StandardGainMeterControl createControlComponent*

```
protected Component createControlComponent() {
    return new GainMeterButton();
}
```

When necessary, `StandardGainMeterControl` delegates to its `GainMeterButton` to update the display state of the `Control`. We will see examples of this in the next two listings.

As a subclass of `ActionListenerControl`, `StandardGainMeterControl` functions in its first role. When the control component is toggled, its `actionPerformed` method is called and the `Control` changes the muted state of the `Player` associated with the `Control`. Listing 20.33 shows the implementation of `StandardGainMeterControl`'s `createControlListener`.

Listing 20.33 *StandardGainMeterControl Control Listener*

```
protected EventListener createControlListener() {
    return new ActionListener() {
        public void actionPerformed(ActionEvent e) {
            GainControl gc = getGainControl();
            boolean muted = gc.getMute();
            gc.setMute(!muted);
            setMute(!muted);
        }
    };
}
```

(121)
(122)
(123)

After getting the muted state from the `Player`'s `GainControl` [121], the muted state of the `Player` [122] and the display state of the control component [123] are toggled. The component display is toggled with a call to `setMute`. `setMute` and its companion `setLevel` appear in Listing 20.34. These methods are used to set the appropriate attribute on the gain meter component.

Listing 20.34 *StandardGainMeterControl setMute and setLevel Methods*

```
public void setLevel(float level) {
    ((GainMeter) getControlComponent()).setLevel(level);
}
public void setMute(boolean muted) {
    ((GainMeter) getControlComponent()).setMute(muted);
}
```

Both `setLevel` and `setMute` from `StandardGainMeterControl` rely on its component being an instance of `GainMeter`, calling the `setLevel` and `setMute` from that class.

The second role of the gain meter control requires it to track changes to the `Player`'s gain and, therefore, it must implement `GainChangeListener`. Listing 20.35 shows the implementation of `gainChange`.

Listing 20.35 *StandardGainMeterControl gainChange Method*

```
       public void gainChange(GainChangeEvent gce) {
           float level = gce.getSourceGainControl().getLevel();
(124)      SwingUtilities.invokeLater(new SetLevelThread(level));
       }

       class SetLevelThread implements Runnable {
           private float level;
           public SetLevelThread(float level) {
               this.level = level;
           }
(125)      public void run() {
(126)          setLevel(level);
           }
       }
```

In response to every change in gain, setLevel is called [126] by SetLevelThread's run method [125] which is scheduled to execute on the AWT event-dispatching thread by invokeLater [124].

Both the actionPerformed method of the default control listener and the gainChange method depend on the availability of a GainControl. The availability of a GainControl further determines the operational state of the StandardGainMeterControl. StandardGainMeterControl's operational state is determined in its superclass's setControllerHook method as we saw in Listing 20.25 on page 388. To properly set this value, StandardGainMeterControl's setControllerHook must first call super.setControllerHook.

Listing 20.36 *StandardGainMeterControl setControllerHook Method*

```
       public void setControllerHook(Controller newController) {
(127)      super.setControllerHook(newController);
(128)      if (isOperational()) {
               GainControl gc = getGainControl();
(129)          setLevel(gc.getLevel());
(130)          setMute(gc.getMute());
(131)          gc.addGainChangeListener(this);
           }
       }
```

The call to super.setControllerHook [127] sets the operational state correctly. If the Control is operational [128], the initial values of the gain meter component are set ([129] and [130]), and the Control adds itself as a GainChangeListener [131].

Summary

The Control interface of the JMF API provides a general interface for build-ing objects which affect the operation of a Controller. It defines a single method, getControlComponent. This simple interface allows a very broad interpretation of what a Control can do. The only requirement the API places on Control designers is that they implement getControlCompo-nent. The API even allows that method to return null.

In this chapter we took advantage of this broad API design to implement Controls that correspond to the operations performed on a Player through its control panel. In this chapter we built eight controls that can be dropped right into a control panel. These Controls were built by designing, and then extending, a general Control model. We will see these Controls used in the next chapter when we build a custom Control panel.

Chapter 21 — CREATING A CUSTOM CONTROL PANEL

Introduction

In the last chapter a lot of work went into designing `Controls` for use within a `Player`'s control panel. In this chapter we are going to collect those `Controls` for use within a custom control panel. In fact, we already saw one of the end products of this chapter in Chapter 18, "Creating a Custom Player."

Providing a control panel for a custom `Player` is only one reason that motivates the need for custom control panels. There are others.

First, since the *Java Media Framework* API does not specify what a control panel should look like, there is no guarantee that control panels across vendors will look the same. This does not bode well for a uniform look and feel for your applets. In fact, the control panel components from Sun and Intel do not look the same.

That would be enough to get you started thinking about building your own control panel, but there is more. For all practical purposes, the default control panels are black boxes. A `setBackground` call on either Sun's or Intel's control panel does not do anything meaningful. Additionally, there is no way to get at the individual components to either change or remove them if you do not want to provide a particular operation. Suppose, for instance, you did not want to display the progress bar. The JMF API does not specify how to remove the progress bar from the control panel. In fact, it does not guarantee that a control panel has a progress bar. If you were to look inside a control panel at its constituent components and attempt to identify the progress bar, you would immediately marry your code to a particular implementation of the JMF.

To avoid this particularly stifling form of monogamy, you may instead be drawn to the idea of building your own custom control panel. In this chapter we will start by looking at some reusable Java classes for doing just that.

The EJMF Toolkit Control Panel Package

The *Essential JMF* Toolkit provides four classes that supply varying degrees of control panel functionality. Two `abstract` classes provide a framework upon which you can build your own custom panels. Two additional concrete classes combine to provide a ready-to-use, configurable control panel.

The following class diagram shows the relationship between these four classes, as well as their relationship to a `Player`.

Figure 21.1 *Custom Control Panel Framework*

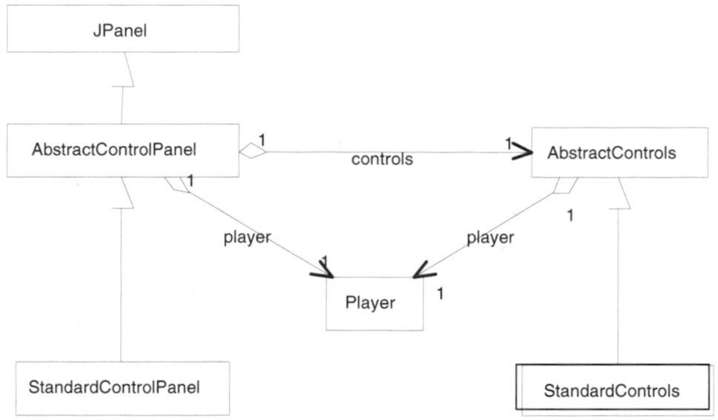

In addition, note that `AbstractControlPanel` extends `JPanel`. The two `abstract` classes, `AbstractControlPanel` and `AbstractControls`, constitute the custom control framework. The "panel" in control panel comes from the fact that `AbstractControlPanel` extends `JPanel`.

The `AbstractControls` class is a collection of `Controls`. It provides a familiar method for accessing each `AbstractListenerControl` by name (i.e. `getControl`) and a means of updating each component's display state based on the state of the associated `Player`. In this capacity it performs as a `ControllerListener`. The `AbstractControlPanel` class has a reference to `AbstractControls`. This object is responsible for laying out the control

Components. In addition, `AbstractControlPanel` provides a mechanism for replacing `Controls` within its layout.

We will look at these two classes before moving to the `StandardControlPanel` and `StandardControls` classes which, together, provide a ready-to-use control panel.

The AbstractControlPanel

The `AbstractControlPanel` supplies basic control panel functionality. It makes use of the *template method pattern*[1] to define `abstract` operations that are implemented by its concrete subclasses. The `abstract` methods are *template methods* that defer the details of implementation to a subclass.

As Figure 21.1 shows, an `AbstractControlPanel` object maintains an association with a `Player` and an instance of the `AbstractControls` class. That the `AbstractControlPanel` holds a reference to a `Player` should come as no surprise. Although we do not know yet what an `AbstractControls` object entails, for now it is enough to understand it as the collection of `Controls` whose component is displayed in the control panel.

`AbstractControlPanel` extends `JPanel` so that, in addition to maintaining these associations, the `AbstractControlPanel` manages control panel layout, including the addition and removal of controls. Finally, the `AbstractControlPanel` allows selective determination of which `AbstractListenerControl` components will appear in the control panel.

`AbstractControlPanel` places two requirements on its subclasses. First, a subclass must provide the `Controls`, in the form of an `AbstractControls` reference, that it supports. Second, the subclass must determine which of the components from that set of controls will be displayed within the control panel.

Both of these requirements are imposed by the declaration of `abstract`, or *template,* methods. A brief description of these methods appears in EJMF Toolkit Synopsis 21.1.

---

1. See *Design Patterns*, Gamma, et al., Addison-Wesley, 1995, pp. 325-330.

EJMF Toolkit Synopsis 21.1 *AbstractControlPanel Template Methods*

Class	`ejmf.toolkit.gui.controlpanel.` `   AbstractControlPanel`
Method	`createControls`
Visibility	`protected`
Arguments	`void`
Return	`ejmf.toolkit.gui.controlpanel.` `   AbstractControls`
Description	Creates an `AbstractControls` object for use by `AbstractControlPanel`.
Method	`addComponents`
Visibility	`protected`
Arguments	`int`
Return	`void`
Description	Adds `AbstractListenerControl` components to `AbstractControlPanel` based on the value of its input argument which is a mask identifying which control components are to be added.

We will look at the source for an implementation of these methods in a bit. For now, let's look at how they are used by `AbstractControlPanel`'s constructors.

AbstractControlPanel Constructor

The `AbstractControlPanel` constructors are available to subclasses to ensure proper initialization of all concrete classes. Each of the two constructors requires a `Player` argument.

The first constructor also takes an integer argument which is a mask defining what control components are to be presented by this control panel.

EJMF Toolkit Synopsis 21.2 *AbstractControlPanel Constructors*

Class	ejmf.toolkit.gui.controlpanel. AbstractControlPanel
Constructor	AbstractControlPanel
Visibility	protected
Arguments	javax.media.Player int
Description	Create a control panel and add components based on the value of the int argument.
Constructor	AbstractControlPanel
Visibility	protected
Arguments	javax.media.Player
Description	Create a control panel and add all possible components.

The source for both of the constructors from EJMF Toolkit Synopsis 21.2 appears in Listing 21.1.

Listing 21.1 *AbstractControlPanel Constructors*

```
(1)   private Player                player;
(2)   private AbstractControls      controls;

(3)   protected AbstractControlPanel(Player player) {
          this(player, 0xffffffff);
      }

(4)   protected AbstractControlPanel(Player player, int flags) {
(5)       setControlPanelLayout();
(6)       setControlPanelBorder();
(7)       this.player = player;
(8)       controls = createControls(player);
(9)       addComponents(flags);
      }
      . . .
```

Dispatching with the single argument constructor first [3], we see that it simply calls its companion with 0xffffffff as the second argument.

Turning to [4], we see that the two-argument constructor does all the work. The first thing it does is to assign a LayoutManager [5] and Border [6] to the control panel. The default LayoutManager is FlowLayout while the default border is EtchedBorder. Subclasses which desire to change these defaults should override setControlPanelLayout and setControlPanelBorder.

At [7], the associated `Player` is saved into the member data field defined at [1].

Next the constructor moves to the work defined by the template methods described in EJMF Toolkit Synopsis 21.1. `createControls` is invoked at [8], assigning to this `AbstractControlPanel` a set of controls defined by a subclass. A reference to this `AbstractControls` object is maintained at [2]. The components are then added to the `AbstractControlPanel` using the other template method [9]. Which control components are added are determined by the value of the `flags` argument to the constructor.

The value of the flags variable passed to the two-argument constructor should be the bit-wise OR of any number of the following `static final` values defined by `AbstractControlPanel`.

Table 21.1 *AbstractControlPanel Component Mask Values*

Name
USE_START_CONTROL
USE_STOP_CONTROL
USE_REVERSE_CONTROL
USE_PAUSE_CONTROL
USE_VOLUME_CONTROL
USE_FF_CONTROL
USE_PROGRESS_CONTROL
USE_GAINMETER_CONTROL

Referring back to "Control Panel Controls" on page 370, you will see that these names correspond to the `Controls` developed in Chapter 20. As an example of how these values are used, assume `MyControlPanel` extends `AbstractControlPanel`.

To create a control panel with a full complement of controls, the constructor for `MyControlPanel` would be called as follows.

```
myCP = new MyControlPanel(player);
```

To selectively display controls, `MyControlPanel`'s two argument constructor could be used.

```
myCP = new MyControlPanel(player,
            AbstractControlPanel.USE_START_CONTROL |
            AbstractControlPanel.USE_STOP_CONTROL);
```

Using a constructor as above builds a control panel displaying only the control components for the start and stop `Controls`.

Which control components are to be displayed is determined at object construction. However, the `AbstractControlPanel` also supports replacing control components after construction. We will defer discussing this feature until "Customizing StandardControlPanel" on page 419.

Layout Management Support

AbstractControlPanel implements a protected method for determining the LayoutManager used for the control panel.

EJMF Toolkit Synopsis 21.3 *AbstractControlPanel Layout Methods*

Class	ejmf.toolkit.gui.controlpanel. AbstractControlPanel
Method	setControlPanelLayout
Visibility	protected
Arguments	void
Return	void
Description	Sets the layout manager for the control panel.

The default layout for a control panel is a FlowLayout. Subclasses should override setControlPanelLayout to change the layout. Listing 21.2 shows the default implementation of setControlPanelLayout.

Listing 21.2 *AbstractControlPanel setControlPanelLayout Method*

```
protected void setControlPanelLayout() {
    FlowLayout flow = new FlowLayout();
    flow.setHgap(5);
    setLayout(flow);
}
```

Two additional methods are available to subclasses of AbstractControlPanel for replacing existing control components with new control components. These methods make it possible to change the look of a control panel component without changing the semantics of the control. We will see them put to use when we extend AbstractControlPanel.

EJMF Toolkit Synopsis 21.4 *AbstractControlPanel Layout Methods*

Class	`ejmf.toolkit.gui.controlpanel.` `AbstractControlPanel`
Method	`replaceControlComponent`
Visibility	`protected`
Arguments	`java.awt.Component` `java.awt.Component`
Return	`void`
Description	Removes the first component from the control panel and replaces it with the second component argument.
Method	`replaceControlComponent`
Visibility	`protected`
Arguments	`java.awt.Component` `int`
Return	`void`
Description	Replaces the component at the location within the control panel identified by the `int` argument with the component argument.

These methods rely on the `add`, `remove` and `getComponentCount` methods provided by `java.awt.Container`. As you can see, the first form of `replaceControlComponent` calls the second form.

These methods are fully-implemented in the `AbstractControlPanel` class to relieve subclasses of having to manage layout of the control panel `Components`.

Listing 21.3 *AbstractControlPanel Layout Management Methods*

```
protected void replaceControlComponent(
            Component existing, Component withComponent) {
(10)        if (existing == null || existing == withComponent) {
                return;
            }
(11)        int count = getComponentCount();
            for (int i = 0; i < count; i++) {
(12)            if (existing == getComponent(i)) {
(13)                replaceControlComponent(withComponent, i);
                    break;
                }
            }
        }
```

```
(14)   protected void replaceControlComponent(
                    Component withComponent, int atIndex) {
(15)        remove(atIndex);
(16)        add(withComponent, atIndex);
       }
```

After some initial checking for reasonable values [10], the number of components in the control panel `Container` is retrieved [11] and each component tested for a match with the `existing` argument [12]. If a match is found, the *other* `replaceControlComponent`, defined at [14], is called [13].

This method makes direct use of the `Container` methods `remove` [15] and `add` [16] to replace the component located at `atIndex` with the new component.

When overriding `AbstractControlPanel` and changing the default layout, these methods will have to be overridden.

Accessing Controls

`AbstractControlPanel` provides two simple helper methods for accessing the controls it manages. They are summarized briefly here because they both simply delegate to the `AbstractControls` reference [2] maintained by an `AbstractControlPanel`.

Table 21.2 *Accessing Controls Associated With an AbstractControlPanel*

Method	Description
getControl	Returns an `AbstractListenerControl` given a name.
getControls	Returns the `AbstractControls` reference.

In the next section, we will see the `AbstractControls`'s version of these methods.

This completes the discussion of the `AbstractControlPanel` and the functionality it provides to its subclasses. We still need to need follow the reference to an `AbstractControls` object maintained by the `AbstractControlPanel`.

The AbstractControls Class

The `AbstractControls` class maintains a collection, in the form of a `java.util.Hashtable`, of `Controls`. Its role is to provide a simple way of managing multiple `Controls`. In addition to maintaining a `Hashtable` of related `Controls`, the `AbstractControls` class implements `ControllerListener` so it can function as a central listener for its constituent `Controls`.

AbstractControls Constructor

`AbstractControls` defines a single constructor that requires a `Player` argument. EJMF Toolkit Synopsis 21.5 specifies this constructor.

EJMF Toolkit Synopsis 21.5 *AbstractControls Constructor*

Class	`ejmf.toolkit.gui.controlpanel.` `    AbstractControls`
Constructor	`AbstractControls`
Visibility	`public`
Arguments	`javax.media.Player`
Description	Creates an `AbstractControls` object and associates its constituent `Controls` with the `Player` passed as the input argument.

After making some initial checks to ensure the `Player` sent as an argument is in the appropriate state, the constructor relies on a template method, `make-Controls`, to actually build the `Controls`. Let's look at the source for `AbstractControls`' constructor.

Listing 21.4 *AbstractControls Constructor*

```
(17)    private Player player;

        protected AbstractControls(Player player) {
(18)        if (player.getState() < Controller.Realized) {
                throw new NotRealizedError(
                        "Player must be realized");
            }
(19)        this.player = player;
(20)        makeControls();
(21)        setControlsPlayer(player);
(22)        player.addControllerListener(this);
        }
```

A realized `Player` is needed by most of the `Controls` so, at [18], the constructor checks to make sure the `Player` is realized. The `Controls` themselves are then free to make the assumption that the `Player` is realized.

As Figure 21.1 shows, an `AbstractControls` object maintains a reference to a `Player`. This reference is maintained by a `protected` member data field [17] set at [19].

The primary role of `AbstractControls`'s constructor is to initialize its collection of `AbstractListenerControls`. It does this by calling the `makeControls` method defined by its subclass [20]. `makeControls` builds `Controls` and adds them to the `Hashtable` maintained by `AbstractCon-`

trols. Once the controls have been built, a call to `setControlsPlayer` [21] associates the `Player` passed as an argument with each of the controls. `setControlsPlayer` simply calls `setController` from EJMF Toolkit Synopsis 20.2 on page 362 on each of the `AbstractListenerControls` in its `Hashtable`.

Finally, the `AbstractControls` object adds itself as a `ControllerListener` on the `Player` [22].

Accessing Controls

`AbstractControls` provides two simple helper methods for accessing the `Controls` it manages. The first, `addControl`, is available to its subclasses for adding controls. The second, `getControl`, is `public` and mimics the `Controller getControl` method. These methods are described in EJMF Toolkit Synopsis 21.6.

EJMF Toolkit Synopsis 21.6 *AbstractControls addControl and getControl Methods*

Class	`ejmf.toolkit.gui.controlpanel.` `AbstractControls`
Method	`addControl`
Visibility	`protected`

Arguments	`java.lang.String`
	`ejmf.toolkit.gui.controls.`
	`AbstractListenerControl`

Return	`void`
Description	Adds an `AbstractListenerControl` to the `Abstract-` `Controls` object.
Method	`getControl`
Visibility	`public`
Arguments	`java.lang.String`
Return	`ejmf.toolkit.controls.` `AbstractListenerControl`
Description	Returns an `AbstractListenerControl` managed by `AbstractControls`. The input argument is a name that identifies that control. In accordance with the API, this name should be a fully-qualified class name.

We will see `addControl` used within the `makeControls` method implemented in subclasses of `AbstractControls`. Similarly, we will see `getControl` used by subclasses of `AbstractControlPanel`.

AbstractControls as a ControllerListener

The `AbstractControls` class implements the `ControllerListener` interface. In doing so it provides minimum functionality in response to some `ControllerEvents`. The main purpose of `AbstractControls`'s `controllerUpdate` method is to call `setControlComponentState` to appropriately update the enabled state of the control components based on the state of the `Controller`.

Listing 21.5 *AbstractControls controllerUpdate Method*

```
public void controllerUpdate(ControllerEvent event) {
    if (event instanceof StartEvent) {
        SwingUtilities.invokeLater(
           new ControllerEventThread(Controller.Started));
    } else if (event instanceof StopEvent ||
            event instanceof ControllerErrorEvent) {
        SwingUtilities.invokeLater(
            new ControllerEventThread(
                Controller.Prefetched));
    }
}

class ControllerEventThread implements Runnable {
    private int state;
    public ControllerEventThread(int state) {
        this.state = state;
    }
    public void run() {
        setControlComponentState(state);
    }
}
```

(23)
(24)
(25)

(26)

(27)

In response to a `StartEvent` [23], `controllerUpdate` relies on `invokeLater` to execute `setControlComponentState` [24] with `Controller.Started` as its argument. This signals that the `Controller` is started and, for example, certain buttons should be enabled and others disabled.

In response to either a `StopEvent` or a `ControllerErrorEvent` [25], the control components are forced to the "stopped" state by running `setControlComponentState` on the event-dispatching thread with `Controller.Prefetched` as its argument [26].

In either case, `setControlComponentState` is called from the `run` method [26] of a `Runnable` object passed to `invokeLater`.

`setControlComponentState` is an `abstract` method that must be defined by subclasses of `AbstractControls`. It is described in EJMF Toolkit Synopsis 21.7. In other words, subclasses decide what buttons are in what state, under what conditions. On the other hand, `AbstractControls`'s `controllerUpdate` method takes care of running `setControlCompo-nentState` in the AWT event-dispatching thread.

EJMF Toolkit Synopsis 21.7 *AbstractControls setControlComponentState Method*

Class	`ejmf.toolkit.gui.controlpanel.` `AbstractControls`
Method	`setControlComponentState`
Visibility	`protected`
Arguments	`int`
Return	`void`
Description	Sets the display state of the control components. Subclasses must define this method.

The intent of `controllerUpdate` is to provide default functionality, through the use of `setControlComponentState`, for manipulating the standard controls in response to `Controller` state changes. Generally speaking, whether a `Player` is stopped or started is all that is relevant for setting the state of the control panel components. If control panel components change in response to other `Controller` transitions, `controllerUpdate` should be overridden to accommodate this more complex behavior.

Building a Concrete Control Panel Class

Before we move to building a concrete class implementing a control panel, we will review the requirements for successfully subclassing `AbstractCon-trolPanel` and `AbstractControls`.

Extending AbstractControlPanel

1. A subclass's constructor *must* invoke either the single- or two-argument constructor defined by `AbstractControlPanel` (see EJMF Toolkit Synopsis 21.2 on page 401). This is a syntactical requirement imposed by the absence of a zero argument constructor.

2. A subclass of `AbstractControlPanel` *must* define the following methods.

   - `createControls`
   - `addComponents`

3. If a subclass of `AbstractControlPanel` wants to change the layout or border of a control panel, the following methods may be overridden.

- `setControlPanelLayout`
- `setControlPanelBorder`

4. If a subclass of `AbstractControlPanel` overrides `setControl-PanelLayout` to change the default layout, it may need to override the following methods.

- `replaceControlComponent`
- `removeControlComponents`

These methods both rely on the left-to-right indexing of the default `Flow-Layout`. They may have to be overridden to accommodate a new layout manager.

Extending AbstractControls

5. A subclass of `AbstractControls` *must* define the following methods.

- `makeControls`
- `setControlComponentState`

6. If a subclass of `AbstractControls` wants to monitor `Controller-Events` other than `StartEvent`, `StopEvent` and `ControllerErrorEvent`, it should override `controllerUpdate`.

With this review fresh in our heads, let's turn to `StandardControlPanel` and `StandardControls` and see how they apply these rules to derive a concrete control panel class.

The StandardControlPanel

We are now going to build a working control panel using AbstractControlPanel and AbstractControls. We are going to do this by extending AbstractControlPanel and AbstractControls according to the guidelines just discussed in "Building a Concrete Control Panel Class." When all is said and done, we will have built a control panel that looks like the one displayed in Figure 21.2.

Figure 21.2 *The StandardControlPanel Displaying All Components*

The control panel displayed above contains what the following treatment considers the "standard" controls. These are the controls developed in the last chapter.

Extending AbstractControlPanel

The StandardControlPanel extends AbstractControlPanel in accordance with the rules above. A quick look at StandardControlPanel's constructor confirms adherence to requirement (1) from page 409.

Listing 21.6 *StandardControlPanel Constructors*

```
public StandardControlPanel(Player p, int buttonFlags) {
    super(p, buttonFlags);
}

public StandardControlPanel(Player p) {
    this(p, 0xffffffff);
}
```

(28)

The requirement that the two-argument `super` constructor [28] be called ensures that the object is initialized correctly. It is this code that invokes `createControls` and `addComponents`.

The implementation of `createControls` is very simple. A `Standard-Controls` object is constructed and returned.

Listing 21.7 *StandardControlPanel createControls Method*

```
protected AbstractControls createControls(Player player) {
    return new StandardControls(player);
}
```

`createControls` leaves the real work of creating `AbstractListener-Control` objects to the `StandardControls` constructor, which we will see in a minute.

Once the `Controls` have been created, they need to be added to the `JPanel` from which the `StandardControlPanel` ultimately extends (see Figure 21.1 on page 398). This is the job of `addComponents`. `Standard-ControlPanel`'s implementation of `addComponents` appears in Listing 21.8.

Listing 21.8 *StandardControlPanel addComponents Method*

```
public void addComponents(int flags) {
    AbstractListenerControl c;
    String name;

    c = getControl(StandardControls.START_CONTROL);
    if ((c != null) && (flags & USE_START_CONTROL) != 0)
        add(c.getControlComponent());

    c = getControl(StandardControls.PAUSE_CONTROL);
    if ((c != null) && (flags & USE_PAUSE_CONTROL) != 0)
        add(c.getControlComponent());

    c = getControl(StandardControls.FF_CONTROL);
    if ((c != null)  && (flags & USE_FF_CONTROL) != 0)
        add(c.getControlComponent());
```

(29)
(30)
(31)

```
       c = getControl(StandardControls.PROGRESS_CONTROL);
       if ((c != null) && (flags & USE_PROGRESS_CONTROL) != 0)
          add(c.getControlComponent());

       c = getControl(StandardControls.REVERSE_CONTROL);
(32)   if ((c != null) &&
          (flags & USE_REVERSE_CONTROL) != 0 &&
          c.isOperational())
          add(c.getControlComponent());

       c = getControl(StandardControls.STOP_CONTROL);
       if ((c != null) && (flags & USE_STOP_CONTROL) != 0)
          add(c.getControlComponent());
       c = getControl(StandardControls.GAIN_CONTROL);
(33)   if ((c != null) &&
          (flags & USE_GAIN_CONTROL) != 0 &&
          c.isOperational())
        add(c.getControlComponent());

       c = getControl(StandardControls.GAINMETER_CONTROL);
(34)   if ((c != null) &&
          (flags & USE_GAINMETER_CONTROL) != 0 &&
          c.isOperational())
        add(c.getControlComponent());}
}
```

addComponents is a long method that does one thing many times. It uses its int argument to determine which control components are added to the control panel. The argument is a bit-wise OR of the values from Table 21.1. With only a slight variation in a few of the cases, each grouping of statements in addComponents tests whether a particular bit is set and, if so, adds the corresponding control component. Let's look at how the start control is handled.

First, the control is retrieved by name using the getControl method [29] introduced in Table 21.2. The name of the control is represented by one of the static final String values defined by StandardControls. The test at [30] is used to determine the control exists and the corresponding bit is set in the input argument. If it is, the start control will be displayed. To affect display of a control component, it is added to the control panel Container [31].

This is more or less the story throughout addComponents. There are, as mentioned, slight variations on this theme. There are three occasions ([32]-[34]) where the AbstractListenerControl method isOperational is tested to determine whether a control component should be added to the control panel. The rationale is that it does not make sense to present a control that does not work. This decision, of course, could be made differently for another subclass of AbstractControlPanel.

The implementations of createControls and addComponents satisfy the second requirement for subclassing AbstractControlPanel. Since we do not require any custom layout or border, optional items (3)-(4) from page 410 are ignored and, instead, we turn our attention to the functionality supplied by StandardControls.

The StandardControls

Since StandardControls extends AbstractControls, it has two methods to implement optional item (5) above. makeControls is responsible for actually creating the control objects that the StandardControls object will manage. setControlComponentState is responsible for setting the display state of control components based on the state of the Controller. As we saw, it is called by controllerUpdate from within AbstractControls.

Implementing makeControls

Listing 21.9 shows the source for makeControls. It is simply a series of pairs of calls to a control-creation method and addControl, repeated for each control to be managed by StandardControls.

Listing 21.9 *StandardControls makeControls Method*

```
private AbstractListenerControl     startControl;
private AbstractListenerControl     stopControl;
private AbstractListenerControl     pauseControl;
private AbstractListenerControl     fastForwardControl;
private AbstractListenerControl     reverseControl;
private AbstractListenerControl     gainControl;
private AbstractListenerControl     gainMeterControl;
private StandardProgressControl     progressControl;

protected void makeControls()
{
    startControl = createStartControl();
    addControl(START_CONTROL, startControl);

    fastForwardControl = createFastForwardControl();
    addControl(FF_CONTROL, fastForwardControl);

    reverseControl = createReverseControl();
    addControl(REVERSE_CONTROL, reverseControl);

    stopControl = createStopControl();
    addControl(STOP_CONTROL, stopControl);

    pauseControl = createPauseControl();
    addControl(PAUSE_CONTROL, pauseControl);
```

(35)
(36)

```
    gainControl = createGainControl();
    addControl(GAIN_CONTROL, gainControl);

    gainMeterControl = createGainMeterControl();
     addControl(GAINMETER_CONTROL, gainMeterControl);

    progressControl = createProgressControl();
    addControl(PROGRESS_CONTROL, progressControl);
}
```

Like `addComponents`, `makeControls` is an example of doing the same thing multiple times. It is responsible for constructing the actual `AbstractListenerControl` objects that will be used in the `Standard-ControlPanel`.

Again limiting our attention to the start control, we see that the `AbstractListenerControl` is first created [35] using a method named in its honor, `createStartControl`. Once created, the `AbstractListener-Control` is added to the list of managed controls [36] using the `addControl` method first seen in EJMF Toolkit Synopsis 21.6 on page 407. The name used to identify each control is defined by a `static final` member data field within `StandardControls`.

Before moving on to `StandardControls`' `controllerUpdate` method, it is worth saying a few words about `createStartControl` and its relatives. If you notice in Listing 21.9, there are calls to methods `createStartControl`, `createStopControl`, etc. Each of these methods returns an `AbstractListenerControl` of the flavor suggested by its name. As an example, `createStartControl` appears in Listing 21.10.

Listing 21.10 *StandardControls createStartControl*

```
protected AbstractListenerControl createStartControl() {
    return new StandardStartControl();
}
```
(37)

As you can see, line [37] finally connects the work in this chapter to the standard `Controls` developed in the previous chapter. All of the create*xxx*`Control` methods appearing in Listing 21.9 do a similar thing. Additionally, all of these methods are `protected`: these are the methods that need to be overridden by subclasses of `StandardControls` to further customize a control panel. We will do exactly that in "The EjmfControlPanel" on page 422.

Implementing setControlComponentState

The enabled state of the control panel components is meant to mirror the state of the associated `Player`. For example, if a `Player` is started, the start button should be disabled so as to not allow the user to invoke the `start` operation.

setControlComponentState should be written to properly manipulate the status of control panel components. In the implementation of setControlComponentState provided by StandardControls, the start, stop, pause and reverse buttons, as well as the progress bar, are all updated by setControlComponent state.

Listing 21.11 *StandardControls setControlComponentState*

```
public void setControlComponentState(int state) {
    boolean on = (state == Controller.Started);

    getStartButton().setEnabled(!on);
    getStopButton().setEnabled(on);
    getPauseButton().setEnabled(on);
    getReverseButton().setEnabled(on);
    if (!on) {
        getProgressControl().setValue(
            getPlayer().getMediaTime().getNanoseconds());
    }
}
```

(38) appears beside the getStartButton block.

(39) appears beside the getProgressControl block.

As a characteristic example, at [38] the start button is enabled if the state argument to setControlComponentState is equal to Controller.Started. Otherwise, the button is disabled. A similar test is repeated for the stop, pause and reverse controls.

At [39] the value of the progress bar control is set based on the current media time if the Controller is stopped. This covers the case when the Controller is stopped and rewound by the stop control.

Recall from Listing 21.5 on page 408 that AbstractControls' controllerUpdate method executes setControlComponentState in the AWT event dispatching thread so we need not worry about that Swing-imposed requirement in the body of the method. However, if you use setControlComponentState directly, it should be called from a Runnable by invokeLater.

The convenience methods, getStartButton, getStopButton, etc., seen in Listing 21.11, are provided by StandardControls.

Overriding controllerUpdate

As we saw in "AbstractControls as a ControllerListener" on page 408, setControlComponentState is called by controllerUpdate within AbstractControls. If additional work is needed from controllerUpdate, it must be overridden. StandardControls overrides controllerUpdate to rewind the media in response to the EndOfMediaEvent. Listing 21.12 shows the source for StandardControls's version of controllerUpdate.

Listing 21.12 *StandardControls controllerUpdate*

```
public void controllerUpdate(ControllerEvent event) {
    if (event instanceof EndOfMediaEvent) {
(40)        player.setMediaTime(new Time(0));
    }
(41)    super.controllerUpdate(event);
}
```

Two points are worth making about this short little method. First, there is a call to `super.controllerUpdate` [41] so that `setControlComponent` is called to affect the default behavior of `controllerUpdate`. Second, `setMediaTime` is called [40] *before* this call. This ensures that the progress bar will be set properly at [39], since the media time is set to zero before the call to `setControlComponentState` in `super.controllerUpdate`.

That concludes the discussion of the work of `StandardControls`. In implementing `makeControls` and `setControlComponent`, `StandardControls` has met the requirement specified by item (5) on page 410. Additionally, item (6) was also addressed by overriding `controllerUpdate` and extending its capabilities. With the `StandardControlPanel` now complete, we can put it to use.

Using the StandardControlPanel

The entire motivation for `StandardControlPanel` is to replace the default control panel. The `CustomCPPlayer` example from the *Essential JMF* examples directory illustrates this. Listing 21.13 excerpts from `CustomCPPlayer` and shows the conventional `begin` method common in *Essential JMF* examples.

Listing 21.13 *CustomCPPlayer Example*

```
private StandardControlPanel        scp;
...
public void begin() {
    playerpanel = getPlayerPanel();
    player = playerpanel.getPlayer();

    player.addControllerListener(this);
    StateWaiter waiter = new StateWaiter(player);
    if (!waiter.blockingRealize()) {
        System.err.println("Can't realized Player");
        return;
    }

(42)    scp = new StandardControlPanel(player);
```

```
        Runnable r = new Runnable() {
            public void run() {
(43)               playerpanel.addControlComponent(scp);
                   playerpanel.addVisualComponent();
            }
        };
        SwingUtilities.invokeAndWait(r);

        if (!waiter.blockingPrefetch()) {
            System.err.println("Can't realized Player");
            return;
        }
        player.start();
}
```

With the exception of [42] and [43], Listing 21.13 is unexceptional. The
`StandardControlPanel` is created at [42] and then added to the `Player-`
`Panel` at [43].

The `CustomCPPlayer` example can be found in `$EJMF_HOME/exam-`
`ples/customcpplayer` directory. This example is run as follows.

• User Input   **Running CustomCPPlayer Example**

% **java ejmf.examples.customcpplayer.CustomCPPlayer **
      $EJMF_HOME/classes/media/safexmas.mov

The `StandardControlPanel` is displayed in all its glory along with the
`Player`'s visual component as previously shown in Figure 21.2. This figure
shows the `StandardControlPanel` used with all of its control components.

Recall from the discussion on page 402 that control components may be
displayed selectively using the two argument constructor for `StandardCon-`
`trolPanel`. Changing [42] on page 417 to

```
scp = new StandardControlPanel(player,
                AbstractControlPanel.USE_START_CONTROL |
                AbstractControlPanel.USE_STOP_CONTROL);
```

would result in a control panel like the one shown in Figure 21.3.

Figure 21.3 *StandardControlPanel Displaying Only Start and Stop Controls*

The above two examples illustrate the flexibility the StandardControl-Panel offers upon construction. Which control components are displayed are determined by the argument to the constructor. There are, however, two additional ways to further customize StandardControlPanel.

First, of course, a subclass can extend StandardControlPanel. We will see that approach in "The EjmfControlPanel" on page 422. Now, though, we are going to take a brief look at customization capabilities provided directly by StandardControlPanel.

Customizing StandardControlPanel

Recall from "Setting the Component and Control Listener" on page 366 that the AbstractListenerControl class provides methods for independently manipulating the control component and the control semantics. In addition, its subclasses makes this functionality public in a type-safe way (see "Type-Safe Setters" on page 370).

The StandardControlPanel brings this functionality directly to its clients. For each standard control available within the StandardControl-Panel there is a pair of methods for setting the control component and control listener. Since these methods are similar across all the control panel controls, we will focus on the StandardStartControl to illustrate their operation.

StandardControlPanel Setters

The two methods for modifying the `StandardStartControl`'s component and listener semantics are described in the *Essential JMF* Toolkit `javadoc` in `$EJMF_HOME/docs`.

EJMF Toolkit Synopsis 21.8 *StandardControlPanel Control Setter Methods*

Class	`ejmf.toolkit.gui.controlpanel.` `    StandardControlPanel`
Method	`setStartButton`
Visibility	`public`
Arguments	`com.sun.java.swing.AbstractButton`
Return	`void`
Description	Sets the GUI Component displayed for the start button within control panel.
Method	`setStartButton`
Visibility	`public`
Arguments	`com.sun.java.swing.AbstractButton` `java.awt.event.ActionListener`
Return	`void`
Description	Sets the GUI Component and the listener semantics for the start button within control panel.

These two methods ensure that any control component assigned to the start button will be an `AbstractButton`. Likewise, they ensure the control listener is an `ActionListener`. For each of the `Controls` within the `StandardControlPanel`, there are analogous methods. For a complete description of these methods consult the *Essential JMF* `javadoc`.

StandardControlPanel Setters In Action

Using the setter that modifies the `AbstractListenerControl` component is the quickest way to a customized control panel. In Listing 21.14, a start and stop button with simple text labels are substituted for the normal `Component` associated with the `StandardStartControl` and the `StandardStopControl`. Listing 21.14 excerpts the `begin` method from a standard *Essential JMF* example, `CustomStdPlayer`.

Listing 21.14 *Use of StandardControlPanel Setter Methods*

```
public void begin() {

    ...

    Runnable r = new Runnable() {
        public void run() {
(44)        scp = new StandardControlPanel(player,
                    AbstractControlPanel.USE_START_CONTROL |
                    AbstractControlPanel.USE_STOP_CONTROL);

(45)        JButton startButton = new JButton("Start");
(46)        scp.setStartButton(startButton);

(47)        JButton stopButton = new JButton("Stop");
(48)        stopButton.setEnabled(false);
(49)        scp.setStopButton(stopButton);

            playerpanel.addControlComponent(scp);
        }
    };
    try {
        SwingUtilities.invokeAndWait(r);
    } (Exception e) {
    ...
    }
    if (!waiter.blockingPrefetch()) {
    ...
    }
}
```

At [44] the `StandardControlPanel` is created, requesting only that the start and stop control components be displayed. A `JButton` is then created [45] and passed as an argument to the `StandardControlPanel`'s `setStartButton` [46] method. Since the control listener was not changed, the new start button will act the same as the default control component. A similar sequence for the stop button is seen at [47]-[49].

The complete listing for this example can be found in `$EJMF_HOME/src/ejmf/examples/customstdplayer/CustomStdPlayer.java`.

To run this example, type the following command.

▶ • User Input   **Running CustomStdPlayer Example**

```
% java ejmf.examples.customstdplayer.CustomStdPlayer \
       $EJMF_HOME/classes/media/noplaceaway.wav
```

Figure 21.4 shows the control panel for `CustomStdPlayer`.

Figure 21.4 *A StandardControlPanel with Custom Buttons*

As you see the start and stop control Components display the Start and Stop strings. In all other respects, they behave as an unadulterated Standard-StartControl and StandardStopControl, respectively.

The EjmfControlPanel

The example custom Players developed in Chapter 18 used the EjmfControlPanel as their default control panel. ejmf.toolkit.gui.controlpanel.EjmfControlPanel extends StandardControlPanel and adds a complete set of custom Components.

Four steps are involved in creating the EjmfControlPanel.

1. EjmfControlPanel extends StandardControlPanel, overriding its constructors, its createControls method and the java.awt.Component method setBackground.

2. ejmf.toolkit.gui.controlpanel.EjmfControls extends StandardControls, overriding all the create*xxx*Control methods and setControlComponentState.

3. New Components are developed.

4. New Controls using the Components developed in (3) are implemented. These Controls extend the corresponding standard Controls developed in Chapter 20, "Creating Control Panel Controls."

Figure 21.5 shows an instance of the EjmfControlPanel displaying its default control components.

Inland Revenue

1 PAYE Reference

Office number	Reference number
764	U7

2 Employee's National Insurance number

| YY | 59 | 10 | 32 | D |

3 Surname

Munro

(Mr Mrs Miss Ms Other)

Dr

First name(s)

ATD

4 Leaving date

Day	Month	Year
25	06	00

5 Continue Student Loan Deductions (Y)

Week 1 or Month 1

6 Tax Code at leaving date. *'X' in the box means Week 1 or Month 1 basis applies*

Code

453 L

7 Last entries on *Deductions Working Sheet* (P11) *If there is an 'X' at item 6, there will be no entries here*

	Week	Month
Week or month number		3
Total pay to date	£	0.00	p
Total tax to date	£	0.00	p

8 This employment pay and tax. ■ *If no entry here, the amounts are those shown at item 7*

Total pay in this employment	£		p
Total tax in this employment	£		p

★ To the employee . . .

Detach this Part 1A and keep it safe
Copies are not available

This form is important to you, so take good care of it.
**You may need the information shown on Part 1A when
completing any Tax Return you are sent at the end of the tax year.**
Please also read the notes on Part 2 attached to this Part 1A. Those notes give some
important information about what you should do next and what to do with Parts 2 and 3.

Employer's name, address and Postcode

UNIVERSITY OF BRISTOL
Finance Office
Senate House
Tyndall Avenue
Bristol. BS8 1TH
03/07/01

To the new employer

If your new employee gives you Parts 1A, 2 and 3 of this form please return this Part 1A
to the employee. Deal with Parts 2 and 3 normally.

P45(Laser-Sheet)

Figure 21.5 *EjmfControlPanel Displaying Default Control Components*

The default set of components mimic the behavior of the default control panel for Sun `Players`. The left-most button toggles between a start button and a pause button depending on whether the `Player` is stopped or started.

The complete set of control components available from the `EjmfControlPanel` is shown in Figure 21.6.

Figure 21.6 *EjmfControlPanel with Full Complement of Control Components*

The full set of control components includes separate start and pause controls as well as fast forward and reverse controls. From left to right in Figure 21.6, there is: start, pause, fast forward, progress bar, reverse, stop, gain control, gain meter.

Let's look now at how these control panels are built.

Extending StandardControlPanel

Extending `StandardControlPanel` first involves overriding its constructors. This is done to provide a default configuration for the `EjmfControl-`

Panel. This is the version used by the custom `Players`. The default configuration is special in that it does not contain a pause button. Instead, like the Sun control panel, the start button acts as a two state start/pause button that displays two vertical bars when the `Player` is started.

The second `EjmfControlPanel` constructor allows for user selection of control components. Listing 21.15 shows both constructors.

Listing 21.15 *EjmfControlPanel Constructors*

```
private static final Color
          myBackground = Color.white;

(50)    public EjmfControlPanel(Player player) {
          this(player,
              AbstractControlPanel.USE_START_CONTROL |
              AbstractControlPanel.USE_STOP_CONTROL |
              AbstractControlPanel.USE_REVERSE_CONTROL |
              AbstractControlPanel.USE_FF_CONTROL |
              AbstractControlPanel.USE_GAIN_METER_CONTROL |
              AbstractControlPanel.USE_GAIN_CONTROL |
              AbstractControlPanel.USE_PROGRESS_CONTROL);

        }

(51)    public EjmfControlPanel(Player player, int buttonFlags) {
            super(player, buttonFlags);
(52)        setBackground(myBackground);

        }
```

The first constructor [50] takes only a `Player` argument and invokes `EjmfControlPanel`'s two-argument constructor selecting all controls but the pause control.

The second constructor [51] is the standard two-argument constructor that allows the user to select which `Controls` will be displayed.

Notice that both constructors call the `setBackground` [52] method. The call is overridden so that it correctly sets the background for all the control `Components` within the panel.

Listing 21.16 *EjmfControlPanel setBackground*

```
public void setBackground(Color bg) {
      super.setBackground(bg);
      if (getControls() != null) {
          AbstractGainButtonPanel gbp = getGainButtonPanel();
(53)      gbp.setBackground(bg);
      }
}
```

Specifically, the background of the `AbstractGainButtonPanel` is set [53]. The important point here is that if you extend `StandardControlPanel` and use composite control components, you will need to override `setBackground` and set the background of the control components as necessary. This is generally true of any of the `java.awt.Component` methods that are overridden within a subclass of `StandardControlPanel`.

The last task of `EjmfControlPanel` when subclassing `StandardControlPanel` is to override the `createControls` method. All this method needs to do is to provide an instance of a subclass of `AbstractControls` that contains the desired `AbstractListenerControls`.

Listing 21.17 *EjmfControlPanel createControls Method*

```
protected AbstractControls createControls(Player player) {
    return new EjmfControls(player);
}
```

Simple enough but, hey, a good segue to the next section where we will look at extending `StandardControls`.

Extending StandardControls

Recall from Figure 21.1 that the `AbstractControlPanel` maintains a reference to an `AbstractControls` object. This reference is provided by a subclass of `AbstractControlPanel` with its implementation of `createControls`. The `AbstractControls` object is a collection of the `Controls` associated with a control panel. Within the constructor of `AbstractControls`, the `makeControls` method, as seen in Listing 21.4 on page 406, creates the necessary controls. Since `EjmfControls` extends `StandardControls`, it relies on `StandardControls`'s implementation of `makeControls` to build the appropriate `Controls`. The `EjmfControls` class must still, however, override the control-creation methods used by `makeControls`. Let's look at what that entails.

Overriding Control Creation Methods

Reviewing Listing 21.9 on page 414 shows that `makeControls` makes a series of calls to `createxxxControl`. Therefore, all `EjmfControls` has to do is provide its own implementation of these methods.

Listing 21.18 *EjmfControls Control Creation Methods*

```
public class EjmfControls extends StandardControls {
    protected AbstractListenerControl
            createFastForwardControl() {
        return new EjmfFastForwardControl();
    }
    protected AbstractListenerControl
            createReverseControl() {
        return new EjmfReverseControl();
    }
    protected AbstractListenerControl
            createStartControl() {
        return new EjmfStartControl();
    }
    protected AbstractListenerControl
            createStopControl() {
        return new EjmfStopControl();
    }
    protected AbstractListenerControl
            createPauseControl() {
        return new EjmfPauseControl();
    }
    protected AbstractListenerControl
            createGainControl() {
        return new EjmfGainControl();
    }
    protected AbstractListenerControl
            createGainMeterControl() {
        return new EjmfGainMeterControl();
    }
    protected StandardProgressControl
            createProgressControl() {
        return new EjmfProgressControl();
    }
    ...
}
```

As you can see, each of the `createxxxControl` methods provides a custom control. All of these new controls extend from their `StandardxxxControl` counterpart and the control component shown in Figure 21.5 on page 423. Only the start control overrides the default semantics of its standard counterpart. Before we look at how that is done, let's look at the final piece of `EjmfControls` that figures in the subclassing of `StandardControls`.

Overriding setControlComponentState

Recall from the initial discussion of `setControlComponentState` (see EJMF Toolkit Synopsis 21.7 on page 409) that its role is to update the display state of the control panel Components in response to Controller state changes.

Since EjmfControlPanel provides a single two state start/pause button, setControlComponentState must accommodate this. Instead of disabling the start button, it changes to display itself as a pause button in response to a StartEvent. Similarly, in response to a StopEvent, it reverts to the start button icon.

Listing 21.19 *EjmfControls setControlComponentState Method*

```
       public void setControlComponentState(int state) {
(54)       EjmfStartButton b =
               (EjmfStartButton) getStartButton();
           if (state == Controller.Started) {
(55)           b.displayAsPause();
           } else {
(56)           b.displayAsStart();
           }
       }
```

In order for setControlComponentState to do the right thing, it relies on additional methods defined by EjmfStartButton. After casting the value returned by the helper method getStartButton to an EjmfStartButton [54], the displayAsPause [55] and displayAsStart [56] methods are available. These methods toggle the look of the start/pause button in response to Start- and StopEvents.

The Essential JMF Control Components

The *Essential JMF* AbstractListenerControl Components differ from the standard control Components in that they are built from Swing Image-Icon objects. The standard components are drawn buttons, that is, they rely directly on the paint method to draw them.

An example will make this clear. We will look at the Component for the EjmfStartControl because it is both characteristic of the *Essential JMF* AbstractListenerControl Components as well as unusual. Listing 21.20 shows the EjmfStartButton code.

Listing 21.20 *EjmfStartButton Implementation*

```
public class EjmfStartButton extends EjmfControlButton {
    private ImageIcon startActive;
    private ImageIcon startPressed;
    private ImageIcon startRollover;
    private ImageIcon startDisabled;
    private ImageIcon pauseActive;
    private ImageIcon pausePressed;
    private ImageIcon pauseRollover;
    private ImageIcon pauseDisabled;

    public EjmfStartButton() {
        startActive =
          Utility.getImageResource("startButton_image");
        startRollover =
          Utility.getImageResource("rolloverStart_image");
        startPressed =
          Utility.getImageResource("pressedStart_image");
        startDisabled =
          Utility.getImageResource("disabledStart_image");

        displayAsStart();
        pauseActive =
          Utility.getImageResource("pauseButton_image");
        pauseRollover =
          Utility.getImageResource("rolloverPause_image");
        pausePressed =
          Utility.getImageResource("pressedPause_image");
        pauseDisabled =
          Utility.getImageResource("disabledPause_image");
    }

    public void displayAsStart() {
        setIcon(startActive);
        setRolloverIcon(startRollover);
        setPressedIcon(startPressed);
        setDisabledIcon(startDisabled);
    }
    public void displayAsPause() {
        setIcon(pauseActive);
        setRolloverIcon(pauseRollover);
        setPressedIcon(pausePressed);
        setDisabledIcon(pauseDisabled);
    }
}
```

(57)
(58)
(59)
(60)
(61)
(62)

The EjmfStartButton is characteristic of the *Essential JMF* control Components because it creates the four icons necessary to reflect the changes to its state ([57]-[58]). It is also unique in that it creates icons for displaying the various states of the pause button ([59]-[60]) and defines the methods ([61] and [62]) `setControlComponentState` relies on.

As an aside, all of the images used by the *Essential JMF* control `Compo-nents` are available using the `static` utility method `getImageResource` from the Toolkit package `ejmf.toolkit.util.Utility`. These images can be found in `$EJMF_HOME/classes/images`.

The Essential JMF Controls

All of the *Essential JMF* `Controls` extend their standard counterparts. Generally, they only override `createControlComponent`. `EjmfStartControl` is an exception in that it provides its own listener. The code for `EjmfStart-Control` appears in Listing 21.21.

Listing 21.21 *EjmfStartControl Implementation*

```
public class EjmfStartControl
               extends StandardStartControl {

      public EjmfStartControl() {
          setControlListener(new ActionListener() {
              public void actionPerformed(ActionEvent event) {
                  Controller c = getController();
                  if (c.getState() == Controller.Started) {
                      c.stop();
                  } else {
                      Time now = c.getTimeBase().getTime();
                      c.syncStart(now);
                  }
              }
          });
      }

      protected Component createControlComponent() {
          return new EjmfStartButton();
      }
}
```

(63)

(64)
(65)

(66)

In the case of `EjmfStartControl`, the constructor is overridden to call `setControlListener` [63]. `setControlListener` installs a new `ActionListener` with the control `Component`. This `ActionListener` differs from the control listener from the `StandardStartControl` class in that it tests for the state of the `Controller` [64] and then stops [65], or starts [66], the `Controller` as appropriate. This behavior allows a single control to support both a start and a pause operation. As we saw in Listing 21.19 on page 427, the implementation of `setControlComponentState` provided by

EjmfControls does the work of displaying the button properly, using displayAsStart [61] and displayAsPause [62].

An important point needs to be made here about the EjmfStartControl. Keep in mind that the single-argument constructor of EjmfControlPanel–the one with no flags for selectively displaying controls–uses this specialized start control. If you want separate start and pause buttons, it is not enough to use EjmfControlPanel's other constructor with flags selecting both the start and pause buttons. You will also have to replace the start button listener with an ActionListener that implements the "normal" start semantics.

Summary

In this chapter we have seen the details of the control panels used by the custom Players from Chapter 18.

Starting with an abstract framework defined by the AbstractControl-Panel and AbstractControls classes, the StandardControls and StandardControlPanel classes were developed to provide a ready-to-use, yet bland, control panel. A StandardControlPanel object provides layout for a collection of Components managed by a StandardControls object. By extending StandardControlPanel and building and using slick-looking icons, we developed a control panel with a little flash, the EjmfControl-Panel.

More importantly, however, with the framework in place, a custom control panel can be easily built by simply providing your own Components.

Chapter 22

CREATING A CUSTOM DATASOURCE

Introduction

In Chapter 18, "Creating a Custom Player," we looked at how to extend the *Java Media Framework* to support new media formats. There we learned how to create a custom Player for an unsupported format, and even how to "register" a new content-type with the JMF. No longer were we confined to the limitations of currently-supported media.

As a Player is defined by the format of the media, a DataSource is defined by the protocol used to transport it. In this chapter we will continue to buck the system and extend the JMF to support new and exciting data transfer protocols. When run-of-the-mill protocols like HTTP just aren't good enough, you need to create a custom DataSource to transfer the media to your Player. Here we will do just that, creating a DataSource to support the NNTP protocol.

The NNTP Protocol

The Network News Transfer Protocol, or NNTP, is the protocol used to transfer news group articles from a network server to a news client. It is the protocol used by news readers to fetch specific articles from a central database that may include thousands of news groups and articles.

In this chapter we will develop a `DataSource` to transfer news group articles to a JMF `Player`. Since news group articles are text-based, the `Player` we will use to display these articles will be the Text `Player` developed in Chapter 18, "Creating a Custom Player." This will culminate nicely our effort to extend both the media format and protocol support of the JMF.

The Text `Player`, as you recall, plays text-based media by slowly scrolling it in a ticker tape `Component`. Though not within the scope of this chapter, an enterprising JMF developer could, were he so inclined, extend the Text `Player` to handle some of the many types of data that are often encoded in news group articles. Imagine, for example, automatically decoding and displaying an AVI video uuencoded in a news group article. The first step in this process would be, of course, to implement a `DataSource` for the NNTP protocol.

Constructing a MediaLocator

As we have seen throughout this book, either a `URL` or a `MediaLocator` can be used to construct a `Player`. The `URL` is more often used because it supports the most common transfer protocols. When an unconventional protocol is utilized, however, a `MediaLocator` must be used in its stead.

A `MediaLocator` takes a form similar to a URL. Both consist of a *protocol* and a *body*, and can be constructed from a `String` of the form

protocol://*body*

The body portion of the `MediaLocator` is not constrained by any particular specification. Its only requirement is that it be understood by the `DataSource` that uses it.

The NNTP MediaLocator

As you may know, every news article is identified by a unique numeric message-id. As a form of classification, these articles are organized into news groups. These news groups in turn reside on a Network News server. This hierarchical series of classification suggests the following `MediaLocator` format:

NNTP://*server*/*newsgroup*/*article*

Thus the NNTP protocol, server, news group, and article will define the `MediaLocator` used by our `DataSource`. Conversely, our `DataSource` will only be able to understand `MediaLocators` of this form.

Retrieving An Article

An NNTP server listens on TCP port 119 for client requests. After connecting to this port, the DataSource will use the following commands to retrieve a specific article.

Table 22.1 *Retrieving a News Article*

Command	Description
GROUP *group*	Specify the news group from which article is to be retrieved
BODY *message-id*	Retrieve the body of the article specified by the unique message-id
QUIT	Close the connection with the NNTP server

After each command that is sent by the client, the server will respond with a three-digit status code indicating whether or not the command was successful. These codes are summarized in Table 22.2.

Table 22.2 *Server Response Codes*

Response	Description
1*xx*	Informative message
2*xx*	Command okay
3*xx*	Command okay so far, send the rest of it
4*xx*	Command was correct, but couldn't be performed for some reason
5*xx*	Command unimplemented, or incorrect, or a serious program error occurred

The success of the command is determined by the first digit of the three-digit response. For our purposes, we will assume that any response beginning with 1, 2, or 3 is successful.

Now that we have nailed down the basics of the NNTP protocol, let's begin looking at how to create our custom DataSource.

Five Steps to a Custom DataSource

As we saw in Chapter 10, "Locating the Player," there are five basic steps that must be taken to create a custom `DataSource`. These steps are outlined below.

1. Create a class called `DataSource` that extends the abstract `javax.media.protocol.DataSource` class.

2. Create a separate class that implements the `javax.media.protocol.SourceStream` interface.

3. Provide a no-argument constructor for the `DataSource` class.

4. Place the `DataSource` class in the *package-prefix*.`media.protocol.`*protocol* package.

5. Register the package prefix with the `PackageManager` class.

The majority of our discussion will be devoted to steps (1) and (2). As we will see, creating a functional `DataSource` does not end with extending the abstract `DataSource` class. Inevitably, a corresponding `SourceStream` must also be implemented for the new protocol being supported.

Like the `Handler` class developed to extend media format support, the `DataSource` class must contain a no-argument constructor that will sufficiently initialize the `DataSource`. This requirement, per step (3), is due to the algorithm followed by the `Manager` class when searching for a `DataSource`. When it has found an appropriate `DataSource` class, it calls the `Class` method `newInstance` to instantiate it. This method, in turn, calls the `DataSource`'s no-argument constructor. If no such constructor exists, a `java.lang.NoSuchMethodError` is thrown and the `DataSource` will not be created.

Steps (4) and (5) were introduced in Chapter 10, "Locating the Player." As you recall, the `Manager` class locates an appropriate `DataSource` based on the protocol specified by the media URL or `MediaLocator`. In order for the `Manager` class to find a `DataSource`, the `DataSource` class must be placed in a package reflective of the protocol it supports, and the package prefix added to the `PackageManager`'s protocol prefix list. This list is referenced by the `Manager` as the first step when looking for a `DataSource`.

DataSource Structure

The abstract `javax.media.protocol.DataSource` class is extended by two classes from the same package. The `PushDataSource` class is used to download push media, while the `PullDataSource` is specific to pull media. Recall that these two types of media transfer are differentiated by which party instigates the transfer.

The abstract `DataSource` class in itself does not define the mechanism by which the media is read. This is done instead by its subclasses, `PushData-Source` and `PullDataSource`. Each of these classes defines the method `getStreams` which returns an array of `SourceStreams`.

Whereas the `DataSource` class manages the support of a protocol, the `javax.media.protocol.SourceStream` interface provides the basis for transferring the media data. In a similar fashion to the `DataSource` class, this interface is extended by the `PushSourceStream` and `PullSourceStream` interfaces to differentiate the type of media transfer. These interfaces define a `read` method to retrieve bytes of data from the media stream.

The `getStreams` method of the `PushDataSource` class returns an array of `PushSourceStreams` that transfer the media data. The corresponding method in the `PullDataSource` class returns an array of `PullSourceStreams`.

Since the NNTP protocol is a pull protocol, the `DataSource` we create will extend from the `PullDataSource` class. Likewise, the `NNTPSourceStream` created to transfer the media will implement the `Pull-SourceStream` interface. This relationship, including the structure of the `DataSource` and `SourceStream` hierarchy, is shown in Figure 22.1.

Figure 22.1 *DataSource Class Structure*

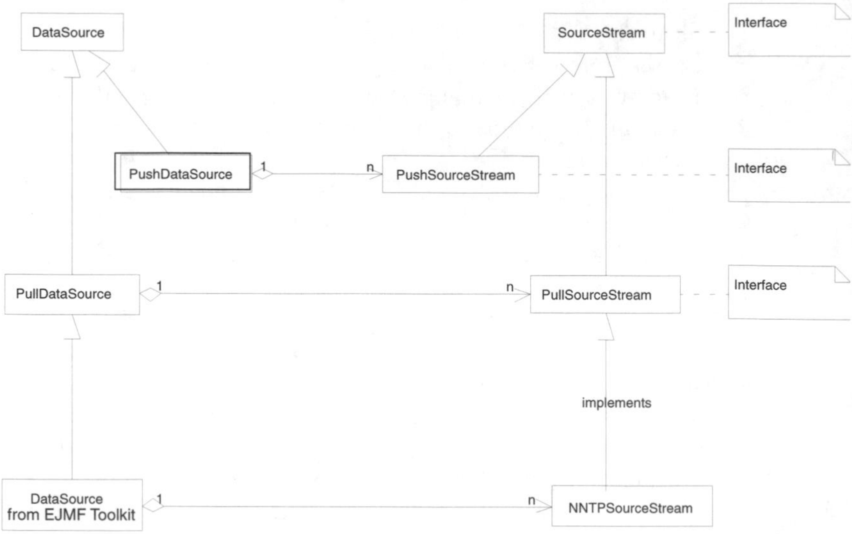

It may seem odd that the DataSource class we create has the same name as one of its ancestors. This naming convention, as mentioned before, is imposed by the Manager class which searches for classes called "Data-Source" when a DataSource is created. Indeed, the rationale for this naming convention may seem questionable, but in reality it poses no extraordinary obstacles to creating a DataSource. Because each DataSource class resides in a different Java package, the Manager can easily distinguish them from each other and their superclass.

Implementing the DataSource Class

The javax.media.protocol.DataSource class contains several abstract methods that need to be implemented. These methods, connect, start, stop, disconnect, and getContentType, specify how the media is transferred to the client. In addition to implementing these abstract methods, the NNTP DataSource will override the setLocator method to enforce additional requirements on the DataSource's MediaLocator.

Following the process outlined in "Five Steps to a Custom DataSource" on page 434, the first step to be taken in this endeavor is to create a class called DataSource. This class will extend the abstract PullDataSource class.

Initializing the DataSource

When the Manager class locates a DataSource that appears to support a particular protocol, it instantiates it using the DataSource's no-argument constructor. Then, to initialize the `DataSource` with a `MediaLocator` object, it calls the `DataSource`'s `setLocator` method.

The NNTP `DataSource` provides no explicit constructor, and thus relies on the no-argument constructor of its superclass. Its `setLocator` method is where the bulk of its initialization takes place. This method is shown in Listing 22.1.

Listing 22.1 *Setting the MediaLocator*

```
private String server;
private String newsgroup;
private String article;

public void setLocator(MediaLocator locator) {
    String remainder = locator.getRemainder();
    StringTokenizer tokenizer =
        new StringTokenizer(remainder, "/", false);

    try {
        server    = tokenizer.nextToken();
        newsgroup = tokenizer.nextToken();
        article   = tokenizer.nextToken();
    }
    catch(NoSuchElementException e) {
        throw new Error(
            "Invalid MediaLocator set on DataSource");
    }
    if( tokenizer.hasMoreTokens() ||
        server    == null || server.length()    == 0 ||
        newsgroup == null || newsgroup.length() == 0 ||
        article   == null || article.length()   == 0 )
    {
        throw new Error(
            "Invalid MediaLocator set on DataSource");
    }

    super.setLocator(locator);
}
```

The `setLocator` method is overridden to ensure that the given `MediaLocator` conforms to the format specified in "The NNTP MediaLocator" on page 432. After retrieving the body of the `MediaLocator` [1], a `StringTokenizer` is then used to parse the individual portions of the news article location. If the server [2], news group [3], or article [4] are not specified, an `Error` is thrown [5] and the `MediaLocator` is not set. A similar `Error` is thrown if any of these fields are `null` or empty [6].

Finally, if the `MediaLocator` conforms to the predetermined NNTP format, then it is set in the `PullDataSource` superclass [7].

Connecting the DataSource

The `DataSource`'s `connect` method establishes a connection between the media client and server. For the NNTP `DataSource`, this takes the form of a socket connection to a Network News server.

Listing 22.2 *Connecting the DataSource*

```
public static final int    NNTP_PORT = 119;
public static final String GROUP_CMD = "GROUP";

private Socket          socket;
private PrintWriter     output;
private InputStream     is;
private DataInputStream input;

public void connect()
    throws IOException
{
    initCheck();

    if(socket != null) {
        disconnect();
    }

    socket = new Socket(server, NNTP_PORT);

    output =
        new PrintWriter(
            socket.getOutputStream(), true);

    is = socket.getInputStream();

    input =
        new DataInputStream(is);

    verifySuccessful();
    command(GROUP_CMD + " " + newsgroup);
}
```

(8) — `throws IOException` line
(9) — `initCheck();`
(10) — `disconnect();`
(11) — `socket = new Socket(server, NNTP_PORT);`
(12) — `output =`
(13) — `is = socket.getInputStream();`
(14) — `input =`
(15) — `verifySuccessful();`
(16) — `command(GROUP_CMD + " " + newsgroup);`

The `connect` method indicates a failure by throwing an `IOException` [8]. Although not explicitly thrown in this method, some of the methods called here do throw an `IOException`. The first of these is the `initCheck` method [9]. Defined in the superclass, this method ensures that a `MediaLocator` has been set on this `DataSource`. If it has not, an `IOException` is thrown and the method is abruptly halted. Most of the `DataSource` methods that we

implement here will call this method as a first step, ensuring that the Data-
Source has been initialized.

After ensuring that a MediaLocator has been set, a java.net.Socket is
then created [11]. This establishes a connection on TCP port 119 to the
Network News server specified in the NNTP MediaLocator. Incidentally, if
a socket connection already exists, it is first disconnected [10] before a new
one is created.

Once the socket is established, a java.io.PrintWriter is created from
the Socket's output stream [12]. This will enable us to easily send commands
to the news server. Note that the PrintWriter is constructed with a true
flag, indicating that the buffer should be flushed after each command.

In a similar fashion, a DataInputStream is constructed [14] using the
Socket's InputStream [13]. This will be used to monitor the server's
responses to the client requests.

The final step in the connect method is to verify that the socket connection was established, and, if so, switch to the news group specified in the
NNTP MediaLocator. The former is done with the verifySuccessful
method [15]. The latter, by sending the GROUP command to the server via the
command method [16]. Both of these are discussed in the next section.

Sending a Command to the Server

Using the PrintWriter constructed in the connect method, the command
method can be called to send an NNTP command to the Network News server.

Listing 22.3 *Sending a Command to the Server*

```
       private void command(String cmd)
              throws IOException
          {
(17)          output.println(cmd);
(18)          verifySuccessful();
          }

       private void verifySuccessful()
              throws IOException
          {
(19)          String response = input.readLine();
(20)          boolean successful =
                  response.startsWith("1") ||
                  response.startsWith("2") ||
                  response.startsWith("3");

              if(! successful) {
(21)              throw new IOException(response);
              }
          }
```

The `command` method contains only two instructions. After printing the given command to the `PrintWriter` [17], the server's response is monitored for errors with the `verifySuccessful` method [18].

The `verifySuccessful` method uses the `DataInputStream` created in the `connect` method. After reading in a line of text from the server [19], the response is then checked for errors. As summarized in Table 22.2, if the text response begins with 1, 2, or 3, then the previous command was successful [20]. Otherwise, the command is assumed to have failed and an `IOException` is thrown [21].

Starting the DataSource

Once the connection to the server is established, the requested data can be sent back to the client. The `DataSource`'s `start` method, called by the media `Player`, requests the specified article from the Network News server.

Listing 22.4 *Starting the DataSource*

```
public static final String BODY_CMD = "BODY";

public void start()
    throws IOException
{
    initCheck();
    command(BODY_CMD + " " + article);
}
```

(22)

For what this method does, you might expect it to be much longer. However, all that is required is that the appropriate command be sent to the server. Using the `BODY` command with the article specified in the NNTP `MediaLocator` as a parameter [22], a request is made for the server to send back the body of the article. As always, this output is preceded by a single-line status indicating whether the command was a success. If it was not, an `IOException` is thrown.

Stopping the DataSource

The `stop` method of the NNTP `DataSource` stops the flow of media to the client.

Listing 22.5 *Stopping the DataSource*

```
public static final String QUIT_CMD = "QUIT";

public void stop()
    throws IOException
{
    initCheck();
    if( socket == null ) {
        return;
    }
    command(QUIT_CMD);
    input.close();
    output.close();
}
```

(23)
(24)
(25)
(26)

If the `DataSource` has not connected to the server, the stop method simply returns [23]. Otherwise, the NNTP `QUIT` command is sent [24], indicating that the data transfer should be stopped. Finally, the input [25] and output [26] streams established in the `connect` method are closed.

Disconnecting the DataSource

In the case of the NNTP `DataSource`, the `disconnect` method simply calls the stop method and returns.

Listing 22.6 *Disconnecting the DataSource*

```
public void disconnect() {
    initCheck();

    try {
        stop();
    } catch(IOException e) {}
}
```

For other `DataSource` implementations, the `stop` and `disconnect` operations may be very different. Some protocols may allow data transfer to be abruptly halted with a `STOP` command. But for the NNTP `DataSource`, since the data is sent in its entirety before a new command can be processed, the `stop` method simply closes the socket connection.

Tying the DataSource to the SourceStream

While the DataSource is the official handler of the protocol specifics, it is the SourceStream which provides the actual media data. In order to retrieve this data, a Player must call the DataSource's getStreams method. The implementation of this method in the NNTP DataSource is shown below.

Listing 22.7 *Getting the SourceStream*

```
public PullSourceStream[] getStreams() {
    MediaLocator locator = getLocator();

    if( locator == null || is == null ) {
        return null;
    }

    if( streams == null ) {
        streams = new PullSourceStream[1];
        streams[0] =
            new NNTPSourceStream(is);
    }
    return streams;
}
```

(27)

(28)

(29)

The getStreams method is defined by the PullDataSource class. This method returns an array of PullSourceStreams that delivers the media data. If the DataSource has not been initialized and connected, then this method returns null [27]. Otherwise, a PullSourceStream[] array is created with an NNTPSourceStream as its only element [28]. Finally, this array is returned in line [29].

Once the Player has acquired a PullSourceStream linking it to the media, the data can be retrieved using the PullSourceStream's read method. This will be discussed in detail shortly.

Additional DataSource Methods

Now that all of the methods involved in the low-level transfer of the media data have been implemented, some of the higher-level DataSource methods can be considered.

Listing 22.8 *Additional DataSource Methods*

```
       public String getContentType() {
           initCheck();
(30)       return "text.plain";
       }

       public Time getDuration() {
(31)       return DURATION_UNKNOWN;
       }
```

The remaining method defined by the DataSource interface is getContentType. Since news media is text-based, this method returns text.plain [30]. It is this content-type on which the Manager class will base its search for a suitable Player. In this case, the Manager will instantiate the Text Player developed in Chapter 18.

The getDuration method is part of the DataSource class by virtue of it implementing the Duration interface. Since the Network News server contains no information relating to the duration of the media, this method returns DURATION_UNKNOWN [31].

Now that we've seen how the specifics of the protocol are addressed, let's look at how the media data itself is transferred. This is handled by our SourceStream implementation, the NNTPSourceStream class.

Having concluded the DataSource implementation, let's look now at the NNTPSourceStream class.

Implementing the SourceStream Interface

As discussed earlier, the NNTPSourceStream class implements the PullSourceStream interface. This interface extends SourceStream to provide methods to explicitly read the media data.

Constructing the NNTPSourceStream

The NNTPSourceStream constructor takes an InputStream argument. It is through this InputStream that the media data will be read.

Listing 22.9 *Constructing the NNTPSourceStream*

```
       private InputStream is;

       public NNTPSourceStream(InputStream is) {
           this.is = is;
       }
```

As we saw in Listing 22.7, the NNTPSourceStream is constructed in the DataSource's getStreams method. As you recall, the InputStream used to construct this class was originally retrieved from `Socket` established in the `connect` method.

The SourceStream Methods

The `SourceStream` interface provides the functionality common to both the `PushSourceStream` and `PullSourceStream` interfaces. These methods are shown below.

Listing 22.10 *The SourceStream Methods*

```
(32)   private boolean endOfStream = false;
(33)   private int readBytes = 0;

       public ContentDescriptor getContentDescriptor() {
           if( content == null ) {
(34)           content = new ContentDescriptor("text.plain");
           }
           return content;
       }

       public long getContentLength() {
           try {
(35)           return readBytes + is.available();
           } catch(IOException e) {
(36)           return readBytes;
           }
       }

       public boolean endOfStream() {
(37)       return endOfStream;
       }
```

The `getContentDescriptor` method plays a role similar to that of the `getContentType` method of the NNTP `DataSource` class. Instead of returning a `String`, however, this method returns a `javax.media.protocol.ContentDescriptor` reflecting the content-type of the media. Since the news articles retrieved with the NNTP protocol are text-based, this content type is `text.plain` [34].

The `getContentLength` method is used to retrieve the number of bytes contained in the media data. Since the Network News server does not provide this information, the best that we can do is return the number of bytes already read or available to be read from the `InputStream`. As we will see in the next section, the `readBytes` variable declared in line [33] is used to track the number of bytes read from the `InputStream`. This value, added to the number of bytes available to be read, is returned in line [35]. If the `InputStream`'s `available` method throws an `IOException`, then only the `readBytes` value is returned [36].

In line [37], the endOfStream variable, declared in line [32], is returned from the endOfStream method. This variable also is updated as media is read from the server. As we will see, when this data is exhausted, the endOf-Stream variable is set to true.

The PullSourceStream Methods

The PullSourceStream interface provides the methods that ultimately retrieve the media data from the server. These methods are shown below.

Listing 22.11 *The PullSourceStream Methods*

```
       public int read(byte[] buffer, int offset, int length)
           throws IOException {
(38)           int result = is.read(buffer, offset, length);
(39)           endOfStream = (result == -1);
               if(! endOfStream) {
(40)               readBytes += result;
               }
(41)           return result;
       }
       public boolean willReadBlock() {
           try {
(42)               return (is.available() == 0);
           } catch(IOException e) {
(43)               return true;
           }
       }
```

The PullSourceStream's read method has the same Java signature as the corresponding method in the InputStream class. It should be no surprise, then, that the read request is simply forwarded [38] to the InputStream passed by the DataSource as an argument to the NNTPSourceStream constructor. If the return value of this method is -1, then the endOfStream variable is set to true [39]. Otherwise, the readBytes variable is incremented by the number of bytes read from the InputStream [40]. In either case, the result of the read method is returned [41].

The willReadBlock method tests whether there are bytes available to be read from the stream. Using the InputStream's available method, will-ReadBlock returns true if there are bytes available, and false otherwise [42]. If that method throws an IOException, willReadBlock returns true [43] since this presumably implies that no bytes are available to be read.

Thus concludes the implementation of the DataSource and NNTPSourceStream classes. Now that steps (1)-(3) from "Five Steps to a Custom DataSource" on page 434 have been satisfied, it is time to move on to steps (4) and (5) and integrate the DataSource into the JMF.

Integrating the NNTP DataSource

The first part of integrating the new `DataSource` involves placing the `DataSource` class just created into a Java package that reflects the protocol that it supports. In this case, the protocol supported is the NNTP protocol. Following step (4), the NNTP `DataSource` class will be placed in the `ejmf.toolkit.media.protocol.nntp` package. This means that the `ejmf.toolkit` package prefix, in accordance with step (5), must be added to the protocol prefix list maintained by the `PackageManager` class.

(44)   `Vector v = PackageManager.getProtocolPrefixList();`
(45)   `v.addElement("ejmf.toolkit");`
(46)   `PackageManager.setProtocolPrefixList(v);`
(47)   `PackageManager.commitProtocolPrefixList();`

This may look remarkably similar to the process discussed in Chapter 18 for adding an entry to the content prefix list. After getting the existing protocol prefix list from the `PackageManager` class [44], the `ejmf.toolkit` prefix is added to the list [45] and set in the `PackageManager` class [46]. Finally, the `commitProtocolPrefixList` method is called [47] to make the addition persistent.

Again as a shortcut, the `ejmf.toolkit.install.PackageUtility` class reduces all of the above to a single method call:

`PackageUtility.addProtocolPrefix("ejmf.toolkit", true);`

Finally, as with the content prefix list, persistent changes to the protocol prefix list can be made manually using Sun's `jmfconfig` utility, which is part of the JMF distribution. This utility simply modifies the JMF's `jmf.properties` file. It is described in Appendix C, "Configuring the Java Media Framework."

Using the DataSource

Now that the `DataSource` has been implemented and registered with the JMF, it can be used as any other `DataSource` would be. Using the `GenericPlayer` class developed earlier, the `DataSource` will be used simply by specifying an NNTP-style `MediaLocator` string on the command line.

▸ **User Input**   **Using the DataSource**

```
% java ejmf.examples.genericplayer.GenericPlayer \
    nntp://news.specialsauce.com/comp.lang.c/238512
```

In this example, the Network News server is `news.specialsauce.com`. The article requested is from the `comp.lang.c` news group and has the unique message-id 238512. With this information, our `DataSource` will connect to the news server and retrieve the article for the Text Player to display.

The resulting `Player` is shown in Figure 22.2.

Figure 22.2 *Using the DataSource*

Summary

In this chapter we learned how to extend the JMF to provide support for a new transfer protocol. Supporting the NNTP protocol, we developed a `Data-Source` that would retrieve news articles from a Network News server and deliver them to a `Player` capable of rendering text data.

The `DataSource` that we developed extended the `PullDataSource` class. This class is provided by the JMF as a base class for supporting pull protocols. Along the way, we also developed the `NNTPSourceStream` class, which provided the specific methods needed to retrieve the media data.

Using the Text Player developed in Chapter 18, we were able to display the news article retrieved with the NNTP `DataSource`. This culminated several chapters devoted to extending the JMF and showed how several of the JMF extensions can operate together.

Part III

BUILDING JMF APPLETS AND APPLICATIONS

Chapter 23   *INTRODUCTION*

Part III of this book provides a couple tools for quickly integrating multiple Players into an application or applet.

What follows is a brief overview of Part III.

A Simple Mixer

In Chapter 24, "A Simple Mixer," an application for combining multiple media files is described. The Simple Mixer application generates HTML for use with a *Java Media Framework* Player within your web pages. Special attention is paid to the MultiPlayer class, a general mechanism for coordinating the playback of multiple media files.

A MultiPlayer Applet

In Chapter 25, "A MultiPlayer Applet," we use the output from a Simple Mixer session together with the MultiPlayer class introduced in Chapter 24 to build an applet that plays multiple media sources.

Chapter 24   *A SIMPLE MIXER*

Introduction

Remember the aspiring rock star from Chapter 9? Well, he has made it huge. He has parlayed his rebel image into a multi record deal with one of the world's largest record labels.[1] The record company has packaged his ersatz rebellion and is selling it to fist-waving, radical poseurs all over the planet who express their revolutionary fervor by buying exactly what their friends are buying.

With all the money that comes our rock star's way, he has decided to build a private recording studio in his thirty-two room mansion. What studio would be complete without a mixing board? And what mixer would be hipper than one written in Java and incorporating the JMF?

In this chapter we will not write *that* mixer, but we will look at a simple mixer that is part of the *Essential JMF* example suite and allows other, still aspiring, rock stars with smaller budgets to easily incorporate music and video into their web pages.

1.We can't mention any names.

This chapter will explore the internals of the SimpleMixer class. The SimpleMixer class is the heart of a useful tool for coordinating the play of multiple media streams, or *tracks*. It does this by using the MultiPlayer class which associates Players with Tracks. By manipulating the start time and playing time of a Track through the SimpleMixer GUI, the user can coordinate the playback of multiple Players, arranging them to start at arbitrary start times, overlapping them as desired.

When a desired configuration is reached, a file can be generated to preserve session information. In Chapter 25 we will see how this output can be used by an applet to drive the coordination of multiple Players.

Let's jump in and see if we can help those Pearl Jam wannabees.

A Simple Mixer

The source for the SimpleMixer class lives in $EJMF_HOME/src/ejmf/ examples/mixer. The related classes we will discuss live in $EJMF_HOME/ src/ejmf/toolkit/multiplayer. It is a rather large amount of code so we will focus only on that code germane to the JMF API. Those readers interested in the details of, say, the use of Swing code in the example can refer to the source code and the javadoc reference pages available from the *Essential JMF* ftp site.

Here we will briefly cover the GUI of the SimpleMixer just to give you a taste for how it works from the outside in. We will also say a few words about its design to give you a taste of how it works from the inside out. We will follow these brief sections with a detailed look at the MultiPlayer and MultiPlayerControl classes, both from the ejmf.toolkit.multiplayer package. These classes are the meat of the SimpleMixer example and useful classes in their own right.

Running SimpleMixer

SimpleMixer actually relies on ejmf.examples.mixer.MixerMain to provide its window, or JFrame, for display. To run the *Essential JMF* Simple Mixer, then, type the following command.

▶ • User Input   **Running the SimpleMixer Example**

% **java ejmf.examples.mixer.MixerMain 4**

The argument to MixerMain determines how many tracks the mixer will display. This number is arbitrary, but practically speaking it must be small.

The SimpleMixer Interface

Figure 24.1 shows a screen shot of the `SimpleMixer` in action.

Figure 24.1 *The SimpleMixer In Action*

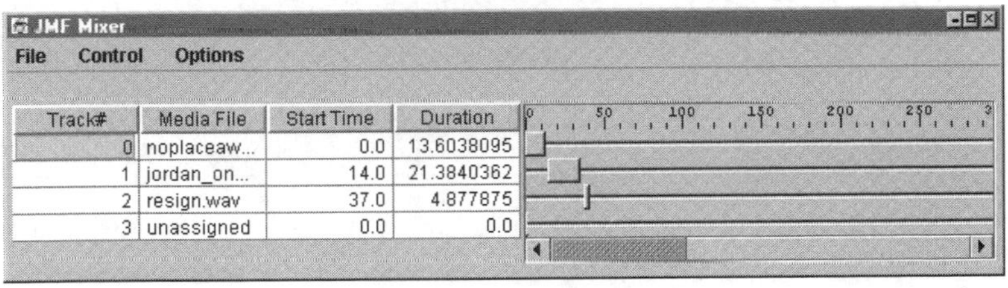

`SimpleMixer` displays any number of tracks. Each track represents a `Player`. The number of tracks is specified on the command line. A track is represented on the left as a row in a table (i.e. a Swing `JTable`) and on the right as a slider. The table displays the `String` representation of the `Media-Locator` from which the `Player` was created, the time at which the media is to start and its playing time. Since the playing time value is editable, it may differ from the value reported by `getDuration`. The start time may be modified from within the table or by using the slider. The slider allows changes in only one second increments. If greater precision is desired, a value can be entered directly into the table cells.

The start time is a real time offset from the point at which the user says "go" by selecting the Play item from the Control menu. This operation is described below. In addition to the control operations provided by the Control menu, the menu bar presents File and Options pull-down menus. The operations available from these menus appear in Table 24.1 and Table 24.2.

Table 24.1 *SimpleMixer File Menu Operations*

Menu	Item	Description
File	Open	Opens a media file, creates a `Player` from it and assigns it to the next available track
	Close	Closes currently selected track
	Load	Loads a MIX file
	Save As...	Saves current track configuration into a MIX file or as HTML
	Exit	Exits the JMF Mixer

Table 24.2 *SimpleMixer Control and Options Menu Operations*

Menu	Item	Description
Control	Play	Plays the current tracks
	Stop	Stops the currently playing tracks
	Query	Reports Track state information for all tracks to System.out
Options	Show Visual	Shows panel for display of Player Components

For the sake of our discussion of the JMF, the above tables sufficiently describe the operation of the SimpleMixer, with two exceptions.

Display of Player Visual Components

First, the Show Visual item under the Options menu displays a JPanel (an instance of ejmf.toolkit.gui.ViewingPanel) in which the Players can display their GUI components. Within this JPanel is a JDesktopPane. Any GUI components displayed by a Player appear within a JInternal-Frame (an instance of ejmf.toolkit.gui.ViewScreen) within the JDesktopPane. Figure 24.2 shows the SimpleMixer with the Show Visual option enabled.

Figure 24.2 *SimpleMixer with Show Visual Enabled*

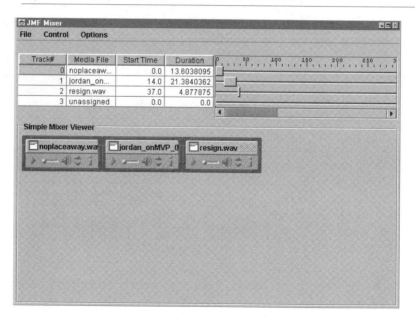

As you can see, the `Player` associated with a track displays its GUI components in the viewing area. If a `Player` has a visual component it will also be shown in the viewing panel.

Saving a SimpleMixer Session

The second item from Table 24.1 that needs elaboration is the Save As operation. A `SimpleMixer` session configuration may be saved in either of two ways. First, HTML can be generated that can be added to your web page and used in conjunction with classes from the *Essential JMF* Toolkit for easy playback within an applet. To save an HTML representation of a mixer session, you can select the HTML filter from the `JFileChooser` as shown in Figure 24.3.

Figure 24.3 *Saving a SimpleMixer Session in HTML*

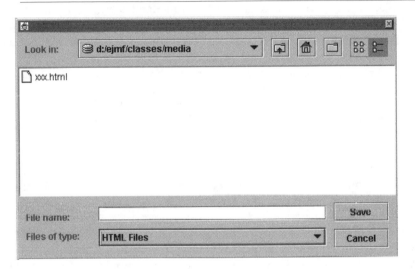

To save your session as HTML, the option menu labelled **Files of type:** must be set to the HTML Files option.

The second way in which a `SimpleMixer` session can be saved is as a MIX file. A MIX file is simply an ASCII file generated by `SimpleMixer` that describes the current track configuration. It is a rudimentary format that captures in a file what is displayed in the `SimpleMixer`. There are plenty of examples of MIX files in the `$EJMF_HOME/classes/media` directory for your perusal.

Both of these formats can be used in conjunction with the `MultiPlayer` class. We will see an example of this in Chapter 25, "A MultiPlayer Applet."

The Design of SimpleMixer

Central to the operation of `SimpleMixer` is the *observer* pattern.[2] The observer pattern defines a relationship between a single *subject* and, possibly many, *observers*. Observers are objects that are interested in changes within the subject. A common implementation of the observer pattern is the model-view-controller architecture where the model acts as the subject and the view and controller pieces act as observers.

The subject piece of the observer pattern is implemented by the `ejmf.toolkit.multiplayer.TrackModel` class. The `TrackModel` class extends the `AbstractTableModel` from the `com.sun.java.swing.table` package. A `TrackModel` object maintains the current status of any number of `Tracks`.

In the `SimpleMixer` example, there are obviously two views observing the `TrackModel`, the table view and the slider view. We will not concern ourselves much with the details here, but the table view is implemented by the `ejmf.toolkit.multiplayer.TrackTable` class, and the slider view is implemented by `ejmf.toolkit.multiplayer.TrackPanel` class. A `TrackPanel`, in turn, has a reference to any number of `ejmf.toolkit.multiplayer.TrackSlider` objects. The controller logic for the respective views also lies within these classes.

In addition to the two views which observe the `TrackModel`, there is a third observer, a `MultiPlayer` object. The `MultiPlayer` acquires from the `TrackModel` a list of the `Tracks` it maintains. It uses this list, a `ejmf.toolkit.multiplayer.TrackList`, to control the operation of its constituent `Players`.

Updates to the status of a `Track` modeled by the `TrackModel` are propagated to all observers. To wit, the table and slider views are changed in response to changes in the `TrackModel` object. The `TrackTable` is notified by virtue of being a `JTable` whose associated model is the `TrackModel`. The `TrackPanel` view is notified of changes by virtue of registering as a `TrackModelListener`. Similarly, the `MultiPlayer` needs to ensure that its internal state is properly updated so it, too, registers as a `TrackModelListener`.

The relationships described above are captured in the class diagram appearing in Figure 24.4.

2. See *Design Patterns*, Erich Gamma, et al., Addison-Wesley, 1995, p. 293-303.

Figure 24.4 *TrackModel Observers*

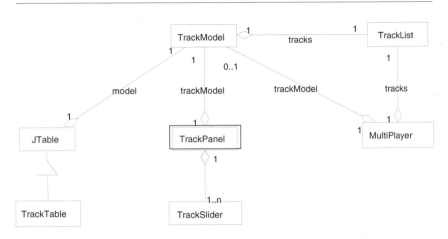

The `TrackTable` object (via `JTable`), the `TrackPanel` object, and the `MultiPlayer` object each has a reference to a `TrackModel`. It is through this reference that they register themselves as a `TrackModelListener` in their role as observers.

This introduction to its design is sufficient background to help you understand the central piece of `SimpleMixer`, the `MultiPlayer` class, most relevant to the JMF. Let's now turn our attention to the `MultiPlayer` class.

The MultiPlayer: An Overview

The `MultiPlayer` class is the heart of the `SimpleMixer` example. It is the class responsible for coordinating the operation of multiple `Players`. First, we will get a top-down perspective by looking at a class diagram. After that overview, we will dive into the code.

MultiPlayer Class Diagram

Figure 24.5 shows a class diagram of the MultiPlayer class. We'll start at the top and work our way down.

Figure 24.5 *Class Diagram for MultiPlayer Class*

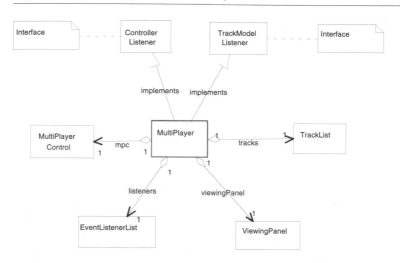

First, the MultiPlayer class implements the ControllerListener interface. This should come as no surprise since, in keeping watch on the Players under its control, a MultiPlayer object will listen for their ControllerEvents.

Moving to the right, we see that MultiPlayer also implements the TrackModelListener interface. Recall from the discussion in "The Design of SimpleMixer" on page 458 that a TrackModel object functions as a subject in the observer pattern. An object that implements the TrackModelListener interface is capable of functioning as an observer, assuming it explicitly registers itself as such. In the implementation of SimpleMixer, we will see an instance of MultiPlayer that does, in fact, register itself as an observer of a TrackModel object. For future examples, it is important to note, though, that a MultiPlayer object need not always have an associated TrackModel on which it registers as a listener.

The MultiPlayerControl

The relationship between MultiPlayer and MultiPlayerControl is an example of the *strategy* pattern.[3] A strategy pattern defines a collection of

---

3. See *Design Patterns*, pp. 315-323.

encapsulated algorithms that are interchangeable. This allows the algorithms to vary independently of their clients.

The `MultiPlayerControl` class defines general operations for control of multiple `Players`. As an `abstract` class, it allows its subclasses to implement the details of those operations. By manipulating a `MultiPlayerControl` reference, the `MultiPlayer` can be used to control multiple `Players` with different algorithms. The particular `MultiPlayerControl` implementation that the `SimpleMixer` relies upon is the `TimerMultiPlayerControl`. `TimerMultiPlayerControl` implements its own internal timer for scheduling the starting and stopping of different `Tracks`. It is in the control strategy class that much of the interesting JMF code resides.

After dispatching with the final pieces of the `MultiPlayer`, we will take a closer look at the `MultiPlayerControl` class.

The TrackList and Track

A `TrackList` is nothing more than a glorified `java.util.Vector`. What is interesting is what lives in that `Vector`. A `TrackList` is a vector of `ejmf.toolkit.multiplayer.Track` objects. A `Track` object encapsulates a `Player` in a way suitable for use within a `MultiPlayer`. Specifically, it allows the setting of various attributes on a `Player` independent of what state the `Player` is in. It maintains these attribute values until such time as they can be retrieved and set in the `Player` directly.

The operation of the `MultiPlayer` is driven by its `TrackList`. It is the `Track` objects on which the `MultiPlayer` operates in response to changes in the model or directives from the `SimpleMixer`. Even in the absence of an association with a `TrackModel`, the `MultiPlayer` references its `Players` through `Track` objects.

The EventListenerList

The `com.sun.java.swing.event.EventListenerList` is the standard list maintenance class provided by Swing for Java event listeners. A client may register with a `MultiPlayer` object as a `MultiPlayerListener`. Upon registration, the client is added to the `MultiPlayer`'s `EventListenerList`. The client is then notified of changes to the `MultiPlayer` object's internal state. `SimpleMixer` is one such client. In order to correctly display various menu items, `SimpleMixer` tracks the state of the `MultiPlayer` and enables and disables menu selections as appropriate.

The ViewingPanel

The `ViewingPanel` was mentioned previously and provides a `JPanel` for display of a `Player`'s GUI components. Whether or not the GUI components of a `Player` are shown in the `ViewingPanel` is controlled by the Show Visual menu option described in Table 24.2.

The Details of the MultiPlayer

For a close-up look at MultiPlayer, we will interleave a discussion of its API with examples of its usage by SimpleMixer. We will start where SimpleMixer does, in its creation of a MultiPlayer object.

Creating a MultiPlayer

A MultiPlayer may be created using one of four different constructors. For now, we will meet only the one used by SimpleMixer. All of the Multi-Player constructors require a MultiPlayerControl strategy object. In addition, the MultiPlayer constructor used by SimpleMixer requires a TrackModel. Recall that the MultiPlayer used by SimpleMixer is an observer of a TrackModel. The TrackModel to which the MultiPlayer listens is passed at construction time.

EJMF Toolkit Synopsis 24.1 *MultiPlayer Constructor*

Class	ejmf.toolkit.multiplayer.MultiPlayer
Constructor	MultiPlayer
Visibility	public
Arguments	ejmf.toolkit.multiplayer.TrackModel ejmf.toolkit.multiplayer.MultiPlayerControl
Description	Creates a MultiPlayer assigns it a TrackModel and a Mul-tiPlayerControl.

Listing 24.1 is an excerpt from SimpleMixer.java that creates the Mul-tiPlayer.

Listing 24.1 *Creating a MultiPlayer from a TrackModel*

```
(1)   private MultiPlayer        multiPlayer;
      private TrackModel         trackModel;

      public SimpleMixer(int numberOfTracks) {
          TrackList trackList = new TrackList(numberOfTracks);
(2)       trackModel = new TrackModel(columnNames, trackList);
(3)       multiPlayer = new MultiPlayer(trackModel,
(4)                   new TimerMultiPlayerControl(trackList));
(5)       multiPlayer.addMultiPlayerListener(this);
      . . .
      }
```

At [2] the TrackModel is created and then passed to the MultiPlayer constructor at [3]. The reference to the MultiPlayer object is stored in the member data field multiPlayer, defined at [1]. At this time, the TimerMultiPlayerControl strategy, a subclass of MultiPlayerControl, is also assigned to the MultiPlayer [4]. As was mentioned above, this is an instance of TimerMultiPlayerControl. The SimpleMixer adds itself as a listener of the MultiPlayer [5]. Recall that the SimpleMixer enables and disables its menu items based on the state of the MultiPlayer so it must listen for changes in the MultiPlayer's state.

The particular version of the MultiPlayer constructor invoked at [3] appears in Listing 24.2.

Listing 24.2 *MultiPlayer Constructor Using a TrackModel*

```
private TrackList              tracks;
private TrackModel             trackModel;
private MultiPlayerControl     mpc;
...
public MultiPlayer(TrackModel tm, MultiPlayerControl mpc)
{
    tracks = tm.getTrackList();
    tm.addTrackModelListener(this);
    trackModel = tm;
    nActiveTracks = addAsListener(tracks);
    setControlStrategy(mpc);
}
```

(6)
(7)

(8)
(9)

This constructor code extracts the TrackList from the TrackModel [6]. The TrackList is used throughout the MultiPlayer code. Since the MultiPlayer needs to track changes to the TrackModel, it registers itself as a TrackModelListener [7]. Additionally, since the MultiPlayer needs to track Player state, it adds itself as a ControllerListener at [8] by calling to one of it helper methods, addAsListener. Since addAsListener iterates over the TrackList installing a ControllerListener on active Tracks, it provides the service of returning how many active Tracks, those with an associated Player, it finds.

Finally, at [9], the MultiPlayer installs its control strategy.

MultiPlayer Control Operations

The `MultiPlayer` provides basic `Player` operations to its clients. These operations are available from the `public` methods described in EJMF Toolkit Synopsis 24.2.

EJMF Toolkit Synopsis 24.2 *MultiPlayer Control Operations*

Class	`ejmf.toolkit.multiplayer.MultiPlayer`
Method	`start`
Visibility	`public`
Arguments	`void`
Return	`void`
Description	Starts the `MultiPlayer`.
Method	`stop`
Visibility	`public`
Arguments	`void`
Return	`void`
Description	Stops the `MultiPlayer`.
Method	`close`
Visibility	`public`
Arguments	`void`
Return	`void`
Description	Closes the `MultiPlayer` and all its `Players`. If the `MultiPlayer` is started, stops it before closing.
Method	`rewind`
Visibility	`public`
Arguments	`void`
Return	`void`
Description	Sets the media time of `MultiPlayer`'s `Players` to 0.0.

The use of the `start` and `stop` methods is shown in Listing 24.3. Specifically, two `ActionListeners` attached to `SimpleMixer`'s Control menu are shown.

Listing 24.3 *Using the MultiPlayer Control Methods*

```
class PlayItemListener implements ActionListener {
    public void actionPerformed(ActionEvent event) {
        multiPlayer.start();
    }
}

class StopItemListener implements ActionListener {
    public void actionPerformed(ActionEvent event) {
        multiPlayer.stop();
    }
}
```

(10)

(11)

The `PlayItemListener` inner class starts the `MultiPlayer` [10] in response to the Play item being selected. Similarly, the `StopItemListener` inner class stops the `MultiPlayer` [11] in response to the Stop item being selected.

Starting the MultiPlayer

The `start` method, like all of `MultiPlayer`'s control operations, delegates to analogous methods provided by the `MultiPlayerControl` object associated with this `MultiPlayer`. The source for `start` illustrates this.

Listing 24.4 *Starting the MultiPlayer*

```
private int startedCount;
private int totalToStart;

public synchronized void start() {
    if (state == STARTED) {
        return;
    }
    startedCount = 0;
    totalToStart = nActiveTracks;
    mpc.start();
    state = STARTED;
    fireMultiPlayerUpdate(STARTED);
}
```

(12)

(13)
(14)
(15)
(16)
(17)

After the necessary state checking code [12], the call out to the `Multi-PlayerControl` is done at [15]. As soon as the call returns, the state value is updated [16] and all listeners notified [17].

The `start` method also performs two other supporting tasks. First, at [13], the `startedCount` data field is set to zero. This variable counts how many `Players` are currently started. It is incremented in response to `StartEvents` and decremented in response to `StopEvents`. The `totalToStart` variable is initialized to the number of active tracks. We will also see this number decremented in the `controllerUpdate` method as `Players` are started. We will see the details of how both of these values are used when we look at `Multi-Player`'s `controllerUpdate` method in just a bit.

The `MultiPlayer` start method assumes all `Players` are prefetched. This assumption gives the greatest freedom to the implementation of the `MultiPlayerControl`. With the `Players` in the `Prefetched` state, the control strategy is free to start them using either the `start` or the `syncStart` method, without requiring any additional work.

The `Players` are initially guaranteed to be in the `Prefetched` state by their being associated with a `Track`. When a `Player` is assigned to a `Track`, the `Track` code prefetches the `Player`. Subsequently, that guarantee must be maintained by the `MultiPlayer` operations.

Stopping the MultiPlayer

The `stop` method provides no surprises.

Listing 24.5 *Stopping the MultiPlayer*

```
public synchronized void stop() {
    totalToStart = 0;
    mpc.stop();
}
```

(18)
(19)

The `stop` method first sets the `totalToStart` variable to zero and then stops the `MultiPlayerControl` [19]. Invoking the `MultiPlayerControl` stop method stops all the `Players`. Setting `totalToStart` to zero indicates that when all currently started `Players` are stopped, the `MultiPlayer` is stopped.

Unlike the `start` method, the `stop` method does nothing to affect the state of the `MultiPlayer`. Bringing the `MultiPlayer` to the `STOPPED` state is the responsibility of the `controllerUpdate` method covered in "MultiPlayer as ControllerListener."

MultiPlayer States

A `MultiPlayer` can be in one of the three states described in Table 24.3. The states are ordered, the "lowest" state being at the top of the table. These values are `static final` variables defined in the `MultiPlayer` class.

Table 24.3 *Ordered MultiPlayer States*

State	Description
INITIALIZED	Initial state. MultiPlayer object has been instantiated and a control strategy has been assigned.
STARTED	The MultiPlayer is started. At least one of its Players is in the Started state.
STOPPED	The MultiPlayer is stopped. All of its Players are in the Prefetched state.

Note that the definition of a started MultiPlayer is that at least one of its Players is started. This is the most liberal definition and allows a MultiPlayer to play several Players in succession and be considered in the STARTED state as soon as its start method is called.

A MultiPlayer can be queried for its current state using the getState method.

EJMF Toolkit Synopsis 24.3 *MultiPlayerListener getState Method*

Class	ejmf.toolkit.multiplayer.MultiPlayer
Method	getState
Visibility	public
Arguments	void
Return	int
Description	Reports the current state of the MultiPlayer.

The range of values returned by getState are listed in Table 24.3. SimpleMixer uses getState to determine the proper enable state of its menu items. For example, when the MultiPlayer is in the STARTED state, the Play item is unavailable.

Below is a call by SimpleMixer to update the enabled state of its Control menu items.

```
setControlMenuState(multiPlayer.getState());
```

Now we will see how a MultiPlayer notifies its listeners of changes to its state.

MultiPlayer State Change Notification

Whenever a MultiPlayer changes state, an update notification is fired. Any object that implements the MultiPlayerListener interface and has registered itself with a MultiPlayer will be notified of any changes to the state of

that MultiPlayer. This notification occurs via an invocation of the Multi-
PlayerListener's multiPlayerUpdate method.

EJMF Toolkit Synopsis 24.4 *Notification of MultiPlayer State Change*

Interface	ejmf.toolkit.multiplayer. MultiPlayerListener
Method	multiPlayerUpdate
Visibility	public
Arguments	int
Return	void
Description	Called on listener object when the MultiPlayer changes state.

SimpleMixer implements the MultiPlayerListener interface so that
it can enable and disable menu selections based on the state of the Multi-
Player.

To register as a listener on a MultiPlayer object, the addMultiPlayer-
Listener method is used.

EJMF Toolkit Synopsis 24.5 *Registering as a MultiPlayerListener*

Class	ejmf.toolkit.multiplayer.MultiPlayer
Method	addMultiPlayerListener
Visibility	public
Arguments	ejmf.toolkit.multiplayer. MultiPlayerListener
Return	void
Description	Registers object passed as argument as a listener on this MultiPlayer.

We saw how the SimpleMixer registered as a MultiPlayerListener in
[5] on page 462. Listing 24.6 shows its multiPlayerUpdate method to set
the enable state of its menu items in response to a state change notification.

Listing 24.6 *SimpleMixer's use of multiPlayerUpdate*

```
(20)    public void multiPlayerUpdate(int state) {
(21)        setControlMenuState(state);
        }

        private void setControlMenuState(int state) {
(22)        int ntracks = trackModel.getNumberOfAvailableTracks();
(23)        boolean canPlay =
                        (state == MultiPlayer.STOPPED ||
                            state == MultiPlayer.INITIALIZED) &&
                        (ntracks < getNumberOfTracks());
(24)        playItem.setEnabled(canPlay);
(25)        stopItem.setEnabled(!canPlay);
        }
```

SimpleMixer's multiPlayerUpdate method [20] simply calls
setControlMenuState [21]. This method queries the TrackModel for the
number of available Tracks at [22]. The canPlay variable is then set based
on the state of the MultiPlayer and whether there are any active Tracks
[23]. The value of canPlay is used to set the enabled state of the menu items
appropriately ([24] and [25]).

MultiPlayer as ControllerListener

The MultiPlayer implements the ControllerListener interface so that
it can track the state of the Players under its control. Specifically, it needs to
know when all the Players are stopped so that it can inform any listeners.
You will notice that the start method in Listing 24.4 calls fireMulti-
PlayerUpdate to inform listeners of the MultiPlayer's transition to the
STARTED state, whereas the stop method in Listing 24.5 does not. The
responsibility for firing notification that the MultiPlayer has stopped falls
to its controllerUpdate method. The controllerUpdate method waits
to hear from all the Players managed by the MultiPlayer before posting a
STOPPED event.

Listing 24.7 excerpts MultiPlayer's controllerUpdate method.

Listing 24.7 *MultiPlayer controllerUpdate Method*

```
      public void controllerUpdate(ControllerEvent event) {
          Player p = (Player)event.getSourceController();
(26)      Track track = tracks.findTrack(p);

(27)      if (event instanceof StartEvent) {
(28)          startedCount++;
(29)          totalToStart--;
(30)          track.setState(STARTED);
          }

(31)      if (event instanceof StopEvent &&
              !(event instanceof RestartingEvent))
          {
(32)          if (track.getState() == STARTED) {
(33)              startedCount--;
(34)              track.setState(STOPPED);
              }
(35)          if (startedCount == 0 && totalToStart) {
(36)              state = STOPPED;
(37)              mpc.rewind();
(38)              fireMultiPlayerUpdate(STOPPED);
              }
          }
          . . .
      }
```

The first thing the controllerUpdate method does is retrieve the Track from the Controller which fired the ControllerEvent [26].

In response to a StartEvent [27], three steps are performed. First, the number of currently started Players is incremented [28]. Second, the number of remaining Tracks to be started is decremented [29]. Finally, the state of the Track whose Player was started is changed to reflect this event [30].

The controllerUpdate also listens for StopEvents [31], explicitly ignoring the RestartingEvent. The MultiPlayer is interested when a Player is stopped for good, not simply reverting to the Prefetching state to access additional media data, perhaps in response to a setMediaTime call.

When it is satisfied it has an honest to goodness StopEvent, controllerUpdate retrieves the state of the Track whose Player fired the event and tests whether it is STARTED [32]. If it is, the startedCount is decremented [33] and the Track's state is set to STOPPED [34]. This additional test of the Track's state prevents multiple StopEvents from the same Controller from mistakenly decrementing startedCount. This scenario can occur if the MultiPlayerControl strategy explicitly stops its constituent Players, causing a StopByRequestEvent. If, due to timing imprecision, the stop request is issued just after the end of media has been reached, two `StopEvents` will reach the `MultiPlayer`, an `EndOfMediaEvent` and a `StopByRequestEvent`.

The `MultiPlayer` knows all of its `Players` are stopped when `started-Count` is zero and `totalToStart` also reaches zero [35]. In other words, the `MultiPlayer` has reached the `STOPPED` state when there are no `Players` started and there are no more to start. At this point, it sets its state to `STOPPED` [36], rewinds the `Players` [37], and fires an update event [38].

MultiPlayer ViewingPanel

A `MultiPlayer` may have an `ejmf.toolkit.gui.ViewingPanel` associated with it for display of the GUI components associated with a `Player`. The `ViewingPanel` provides a default means for displaying these components. The `SimpleMixer` uses the `ViewingPanel` to implement its Show Visual functionality. Specifically, it uses the `setViewingPanel` method provided by the `MultiPlayer` class.

EJMF Toolkit Synopsis 24.6 *Associating a ViewPanel with a MultiPlayer*

Class	`ejmf.toolkit.multiplayer.MultiPlayer`
Method	`setViewingPanel`
Visibility	`public`
Arguments	`ejmf.toolkit.gui.ViewingPanel`
Return	`void`
Description	Provides a default `Container` into which a `MultiPlayer` can display the GUI components of its constituent `Players`.

Once a `ViewingPanel` has been associated with a `MultiPlayer`, the `displayPlayers` method may be used to display the control panel and visual Components of a `MultiPlayer`'s `Players`.

EJMF Toolkit Synopsis 24.7 *Displaying MultiPlayer GUI Components*

Class	`ejmf.toolkit.multiplayer.MultiPlayer`
Method	`displayPlayers`
Visibility	`public`
Arguments	`void`
Return	`void`
Description	If there is a `ViewingPanel` associated with `MultiPlayer`, displays the GUI Component of constituent `Players`.

The `SimpleMixer`'s use of the `ViewingPanel` is shown in Listing 24.8. It appears in the inner class `ShowItemListener`. An instance of `ShowItemListener` is registered as a listener on the Show Visual menu item.

Listing 24.8 *Using the ViewingPanel*

```
       class ShowItemListener implements ActionListener {
           public void actionPerformed(ActionEvent e) {
(39)           if (showItem.isSelected() == true) {
(40)               if (viewingPanel == null) {
(41)                   viewingPanel =
                           new ViewingPanel("EJMF Mixer Viewer");
(42)                   multiPlayer.setViewingPanel(viewingPanel);
(43)                   multiPlayer.displayPlayers();
                   }
(44)               SimpleMixer.this.add(viewingPanel,
                                        BorderLayout.SOUTH);
               }
(45)           if (showItem.isSelected() == false) {
(46)               SimpleMixer.this.remove(viewingPanel);
               }
           }
       }
```

If the Show Visual check box is selected [39] and a `ViewingPanel` has not been created [40], one is created [41] and associated with the `MultiPlayer` [42]. The `Players`' GUI components are then displayed [43] and the `ViewingPanel` is added to the `SimpleMixer`'s main `Container` [44].

If the `ShowItemListener` was invoked as a result of deselecting the Show Visual check box [45], the `ViewingPanel` is removed from the `SimpleMixer`'s `Container` [46]

The `ViewingPanel` is by no means the only way to display the GUI components of the `MultiPlayer`'s `Players`. In fact, it is a rather broad stroke: both GUI components from each of the `Players` are displayed at once. It was designed specifically for the `SimpleMixer`. Most applications using the `MultiPlayer` will want to provide their own `Container` for laying out the GUI components of the `MultiPlayer`'s `Players`. We will see an alternative to the `ViewingPanel` in Chapter 25.

We have now taken a close look at the major pieces of the `MultiPlayer` API. However, before we can appreciate the power of the `MultiPlayer` and understand how it works, either alone or in conjunction with the `SimpleMixer` class, we need to follow its reference to a `MultiPlayerControl`.

The MultiPlayerControl

MultiPlayerControl is an abstract class that describes methods for controlling the operation of multiple Players. As we saw above, it needs to start and stop the Players under its control. It does this with its own start and stop methods (EJMF Toolkit Synopsis 24.2 on page 464). Recall, however, that the primary role of these methods is to delegate the actual control function to a MultiPlayerControl object. The functionality provided by the MultiPlayerControl class to which MultiPlayer delegates is defined by the abstract methods appearing in Table 24.4.

Table 24.4 *MultiPlayerControl Abstract Methods*

Method	Description
init	Initialize the MultiPlayerControl.
restart	Restart the Players controlled by the MultiPlayerControl object
rewind	Rewind the Players controlled by the MultiPlayer, setting their media time to 0.0.
start	Start the Players controlled by the MultiPlayerControl object
stop	Stop the Players controlled by the MultiPlayerControl object
update	Force MultiPlayerControl to evaluate all Tracks in TrackList and update its TrackList.

The assumption behind all of these methods is that an implementation of MultiPlayerControl maintains a TrackList that serves as input to the control algorithm. In the example implementation that we will look at, that TrackList is passed as an argument to the constructor.

The only method that requires a TrackList as an argument is the update method. This provides the client with some flexibility in choosing how to hand off the TrackList to the MultiPlayerControl. If the client provides the control algorithm a copy of the TrackList, the update method provides a means to get an entirely new TrackList to the MultiPlayerControl object if it has changed sufficiently to deem this necessary.

A word about start and restart is in order.[4] The two are provided, again, for flexibility. Depending on your control algorithm, there may be some differences between starting your collection of Players and restarting them. For example, if you were to add a pause feature to the MultiPlayer, restart may be called to start the Players after pausing. This alternative

---

4. Start and restart were in a boat. Start fell out and who was left?

means of starting them would not require any synchronization work. The restart method would simply call any previously started Player's start method.

The TimerMultiPlayerControl

The secret to the flexible playback of Players within the SimpleMixer is the control strategy used by the MultiPlayer. The TimerMultiPlayer-Control maintains a list of events which are triggered by an internal timer. Unlike the synchronization of two Players using addController where the Players are limited to starting at the same time, the TimerMulti-PlayerControl allows playback of multiple Players at arbitrary times.

In the current context, the times at which the various Players are to start, and their playing time, are determined within a SimpleMixer session and recorded within Track objects. The SimpleMixer manipulates the Track-Model which is shared between the GUI code and an instance of Multi-Player. When the user selects the Play menu item, the MultiPlayer is started, using the current TrackList configuration to drive the operation of the Players. The MultiPlayer relies on its MultiPlayerControl strategy, in this case TimerMultiPlayerControl, to start the Players.

Let's look closely at TimerMultiPlayerControl, starting with a class diagram.

TimerMultiPlayerControl Class Diagram

A TimerMultiPlayerControl contains a reference to a Timer, an event list represented as an array of MixerEvents, and a TrackList. These relationships are shown in Figure 24.6.

Figure 24.6 *TimerMultiPlayerControl Class Diagram*

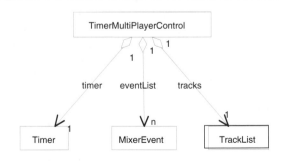

The MixerEvent array is a time-ordered set of events. Each event has a time and a command associated with it. When the Timer reaches the time specified by a particular event, the command is executed. A command is an instance of MixerCommand and encapsulates an operation on a Player.

We have already discussed the TrackList, so we will now direct our attention to the other major pieces of the TimerMultiPlayerControl.

The MixerEvent List

The event list is an array of MixerEvents. All you need to know to understand how a MixerEvent works can be gleaned from its constructor and its execute method. The MixerEvent class is excerpted in Listing 24.9.

Listing 24.9 *Constructing a MixerEvent*

```
public class MixerEvent implements Sortable {
    private MixerCommand        cmd;
    private long                time;

    public MixerEvent(MixerCommand cmd,
                        long time) {
        this.time = time;
        this.cmd = cmd;
    }
    ...
    public void execute() {
        cmd.execute();
    }
    ...
}
```

(47)

(48)

When the time offset represented by the time member field is reached, the execute method [48] is executed, which simply delegates to the MixerCommand execute method. Both the time value and MixerCommand object are passed as arguments to the constructor [47].

Creating the Event List

The TimerMultiPlayerControl builds an array of MixerEvents based on the Track data within its TrackList. The array is then sorted based on the time field values of the MixerEvent entries.

For each active Track in the TrackList, there are two MixerEvents, one for starting the Track, the other for stopping it.

All of this work is accomplished by the convertToEventList method appearing in Listing 24.10.

Listing 24.10 *Creating MixerEvent List*

```
       private void convertToEventList(TrackList tracks) {
(49)       totalEventCount = 0;
(50)       int nt = tracks.getNumberOfTracks();
(51)       eventList = new MixerEvent[nt * 2];

(52)       for (int i = 0; i < nt; i++) {
               long eventTime;
               Track track = tracks.getTrack(i);

(53)           if (track.isAvailable()) {
                   continue;
               }

               Player player = track.getPlayer();
(54)           double eventSecs = track.getStartTime();

(55)           if (player.getStartLatency() !=
                       Controller.LATENCY_UNKNOWN) {
(56)               double latentSecs =
                       player.getStartLatency().getSeconds();

(57)               eventSecs = eventSecs - latentSecs;
               }
(58)           eventTime = (long)(eventSecs * 1000.0);

(59)           eventList[totalEventCount++] =
                   new MixerEvent(new StartCommand(player),
                                   eventTime);

(60)           double playingTime = track.getPlayingTime();
(61)           playingTime = Math.min(playingTime,
                               player.getDuration().getSeconds());

(62)           if (playingTime > 0) {
(63)               long endTime =
                       (long)((track.getStartTime() + playingTime)
                       * 1000.0);
(64)               eventList[totalEventCount++] =
                       new MixerEvent( new StopCommand(player),
                                       endTime);
               }
           }
           if (totalEventCount > 0) {
(65)           QuickSort.sort(eventList, 0, totalEventCount-1);
(66)           normalizeEventTimes(eventList);
           }
       }
```

`convertToEventList` starts by setting the total event count to zero [49]. A new array is then created [51] based on the number of `Tracks` retrieved at [50].

With the array memory in hand, the `TrackList` is iterated over starting at [52]. `Tracks` without a `Player` assigned are skipped [53], otherwise the steps toward creating the appropriate `MixerEvents` are taken for each `Track`.

The first of these steps involves retrieving the assigned starting time from the current `Track` [54].

If the `Player` associated with the current `Track` has a known start latency [55], this value is retrieved [56] and subtracted from the starting time [57]. The accommodation of start latency at this point allows for a uniform starting procedure for all `Tracks`, namely they all can be started "as soon as possible," having built the latency into the requested start time.

In any case, the starting time is converted to milliseconds at [58]. With the start time now adjusted for start latency and in the right units, a `MixerEvent` for the `StartCommand` is created [59], incrementing `totalEventCount` in the process.

With the start event created, `convertToEventList` moves to creating an event for stopping the playback of the `Track`. At [60] the playing time is fetched from the `Track`. At [61] the minimum of the playing time set in the `Track` and the `Player`'s duration is chosen. As a sanity check the `Mixer-Event` is only created [64] if the playing time is greater than zero [62]. Absent a `StopCommand` event, the media will simply run until its end.

The time at which the stop event occurs is calculated by adding the playing time to the start time [63]. Notice that the start time from the `Track` is used, and not the time of the `MixerEvent` created at [59]. The latter has been adjusted for start latency and would result in clipped media if used in this calculation.

After the `MixerEvent` array has been populated, it is sorted [65] and normalized [66]. We now turn to the normalization step.

Normalizing the Event List

Once sorted, the `MixerEvent` array is *normalized* so that the `time` field within each `MixerEvent` represents an offset from the previous entry in the array. Normalization also adjusts for any event time made negative due to start latency. The normalization process is performed by the `normalizeEvent-Times` method appearing in Listing 24.11.

Listing 24.11 *Normalizing the MixerEvent Array*

```
        private void normalizeEventTimes(MixerEvent[] eventList) {
            long timeDelta;
(67)        long prevTime = eventList[0].getTime();

(68)        if (prevTime < 0) {
(69)            eventList[0].setTime(0);
            }
(70)        for (int i = 1; i < totalEventCount; i++) {
(71)            timeDelta =
                    Math.abs(eventList[i].getTime() - prevTime);
(72)            prevTime = eventList[i].getTime();
(73)            eventList[i].setTime(timeDelta);
            }
        }
```

The basic algorithm for `normalizeEventTimes` is to iterate over the `MixerEvent` array subtracting the current time from the time of the previous entry. This work is done in the loop beginning at [70]. The only twist to the algorithm is the accommodation of a possible negative time value in the first element of the array. This condition arises if, within `SimpleMixer`, a `Track` is slated to start at some time less than its associated `Controller`'s start latency.

By the time the `MixerEvent` list reaches `normalizeEventTimes`, the times have been adjusted for start latency. In other words, the value of the start latency has been subtracted from the start time selected within the `Simple-Mixer`. If this computation results in a negative start time, *T*, for some `Track`, then the start time of every `Track` has be shifted ahead by the absolute value of *T* to maintain synchronization. If a negative start time results for multiple `Tracks`, choosing the one with the most negative time will result in the correct shift for all the other `Tracks`. Since the `MixerEvent` array is sorted, the first element will always contain the least value.

It turns out, however, that since the normalized array records an element's time value as an offset from the previous element's time, the shift only need be applied to the first entry. This is done by setting the smallest value to zero and calculating offsets using the original values.

The test for a negative start value is performed at [68]. If the first element's start time is less than zero, it is reset to zero [69].

The main loop of `normalizeEventTimes` then calculates the time offsets of consecutive elements in the event list [71]. At each iteration the time offset is saved in a temporary variable, the previous time is updated [72], and the current element updated with the new offset [73].

After the call to `normalizeEventTimes`, the `MixerEvent` list is ready for processing. This processing is triggered by a `Timer` maintained by the `TimerMultiPlayerControl`.

Timer Ticks and MixerEvents

Once the event list has been normalized, the Timer can do its job. The Timer is created and initialized in the initEventList method shown in Listing 24.12.

Listing 24.12 *Creating the Timer*

```
        private void initEventList(TrackList tracks) {
(74)        nextEvent = 0;
            if (timer == null) {
(75)            timer = new Timer(0, this);
(76)            timer.setRepeats(false);
            }
            convertToEventList(tracks);
        }
```

The creation of the Timer at [75] is what interests us here. This Timer is going to drive the traversal of the event list, executing events, beginning at nextEvent [74], at each "tick." A Timer "tick" manifests itself as an invocation of the actionPerformed method on its listeners. The second argument to Timer's constructor establishes the TimerMultiPlayerControl as an ActionListener on this Timer object. As a good ActionListener, TimerMultiPlayerControl implements the actionPerformed method.

Listing 24.13 *Responding to Timer Ticks*

```
        public void actionPerformed(ActionEvent e) {
            int millis;
(77)        long fireTime = eventList[nextEvent].getTime();

(78)        fireEventsAtOffset(fireTime);

(79)        if (nextEvent < totalEventCount) {
(80)            millis = (int)(eventList[nextEvent].getTime());
(81)            timer.setInitialDelay(millis);
(82)            timer.restart();
            }
        }
```

With the arrival of each timer event, the "firing" time of the next event is extracted from the event list [77]. To affect the execution of the command associated with this event, the fireEventsAtOffset method is called [78]. fireEventsAtOffset steps through event list "firing" events at a given offset, incrementing nextEvent as it goes.

If there are any events remaining [79], the "firing" time of the next event is retrieved [80] and used at the time for the next "tick" [81]. The timer is then restarted.

To fully understand lines [81] and [82], we must return to [76] in Listing 24.12. When the `Timer` is created, the `setRepeats` method is called with a `false` argument. This configures the `Timer` to fire once and then stop. After the `Timer` fires, the `actionPerformed` method restarts it at [82] only after setting the next firing time to the offset found in the next `MixerEvent` [81].

Executing a MixerCommand

The `fireEventsAtOffset` method actually executes the command associated with a `MixerEvent`. As we saw at [78] in Listing 24.13, `fireEventsAtOffset` is called in the `actionPerformed` method with a time value as an argument. This value identifies the offset of the `MixerEvent` whose command is to be executed.

Listing 24.14 *Executing a MixerCommand*

```
      private void fireEventsAtOffset(long offset) {
(83)        if (nextEvent < totalEventCount &&
                  eventList[nextEvent].getTime() == offset) {
(84)          eventList[nextEvent].execute();
(85)          nextEvent++;

(86)          while (nextEvent < totalEventCount &&
(87)                  eventList[nextEvent].getTime() == 0) {
                eventList[nextEvent].execute();
                nextEvent++;
            }
          }
      }
```

The `fireEventsAtOffset` method first executes the `MixerCommand` [84] of the `MixerEvent` whose `getTime` value returns a value equal to the `offset` argument. This will always be the element at the `nextEvent` position in the array since it was just set before the call to `fireEventsAtOffset` call at [77] in Listing 24.13. This renders the test at [83] useless in this context. However, it is meaningful when `fireEventsAtOffset` is called with a zero value when the `TimerMultiPlayerControl` is started.

After the command is executed, the `nextEvent` counter is incremented [85]. If there are still more events to process [86], and as long as they have a zero offset [87], their `MixerCommand` is executed.

The `TimerMultiPlayerControl` currently implements two flavors of `MixerCommand`. Let's look at those now.

The MixerCommand Interface

The `MixerCommand` interface only defines one method of any merit, the `execute` method. Two inner classes of `TimerMultiPlayerControl` support this interface for use with `MixerEvents`.

The StartCommand starts a Player and is excerpted in Listing 24.15.

Listing 24.15 *The StartCommand*

```
class StartCommand implements MixerCommand {
    private Player    player;
(88)    public StartCommand(Player player) {
        this.player = player;
    }
    public void execute() {
        long now = player.getTimeBase().getNanoseconds();
(89)        player.syncStart(new Time(now));
    }
}
```

You can see that when a StartCommand is created, it is passed a Player argument [88] on which it will invoke the syncStart method [89]. The call to syncStart is coded to start "now" since the start latency has already been factored into the time at which the StartCommand is invoked.

The StopCommand is left as an exercise for the user, or if you are on the critical path, you can look at it in the $EJMF_HOME/src/ejmf/toolkit/ multiplayer directory.

At this point we have seen how the MixerEvent list is created and normalized and how the Timer affects the execution of MixerCommands. We have even looked at the implementation of the start and stop commands. We have yet, however, to see the public methods available to the MultiPlayer that controls the TimerMultiPlayerControl. Let's turn to that now.

Starting the TimerMultiPlayerControl

The start method starts the TimerMultiPlayerControl. It must, if necessary, initialize the event list, fire any events scheduled for time zero, and start the timer. The code for these operations is shown in Listing 24.16.

Listing 24.16 *The TimerMultiPlayerControl start Method*

```
public void start() {
    if (eventList == null) {
        initEventList(tracks);
    }
    nextEvent = 0;
    fireEventsAtOffset((long) 0);
    startTimer();
}
```

We have seen all the methods used by start, so the code should be self-explanatory, if it could talk.

The stop method is equally straightforward.

Stopping the TimerMultiPlayerControl

The `stop` method stops the `Timer` and then explicitly calls the `stop` method on each `Player` in its `TrackList`.

Listing 24.17 *Stopping the TimerMultiPlayerControl*

(90)

```
public void stop() {
    timer.stop();
    for (int i = 0; i < tracks.getNumberOfTracks(); i++) {
        Track track = tracks.getTrack(i);
        if (track.isAssigned()) {
            Player player = track.getPlayer();
            if (player.getTargetState()
                    == Controller.Started) {
                player.stop();
            }
        }
    }
}
```

Keep in mind that the `MultiPlayer`'s `stop` method differs from the `StopCommand` in that it stops all the `Players` and is called directly by the `MultiPlayer`. The `StopCommand`, on the other hand, acts on a single `Player` and is the result of a `Timer` event. The normal operation of the `TimerMultiPlayerControl` is that the `Players` run until a `StopCommand` stops them. The `stop` method is more of a preemptive operation provided by a GUI like `SimpleMixer`. As such, it tests only that a `Controller` is destined for the `Started` state.

Summary

We have looked at three major classes in this chapter: `SimpleMixer`, `Multi-Player`, and `TimerMultiPlayerControl`. The `SimpleMixer` class uses a `MultiPlayer` to control multiple `Players` while the `MultiPlayer` relies on the `TimerMultiPlayerControl` to implement the details of that control.

The `TimerMultiPlayerControl` class is one implementation of the `MultiPlayerControl` strategy. A `MultiPlayer` can use any instance of such a strategy but the `TimerMultiPlayerControl` is well-suited to the `SimpleMixer` application. In allowing the playback of multiple `Players` with arbitrary start and stop times, it mirrors how the `SimpleMixer` is used.

Both the `MultiPlayer` and `MultiPlayerControl` classes may be used in your applications and applets. With the help of `SimpleMixer` you can arrange the playback of multiple `Players`, generate a record of that configuration as either a MIX file or HTML and use that data to drive a `Multi-Player` incorporated into your own application or applet. In the next chapter we will look at some examples of how these things can be accomplished.

Chapter 25

A MULTIPLAYER APPLET

Introduction

In this chapter we are going to continue our work with the MultiPlayer class discussed in last chapter. Recall that the MultiPlayer was a general way to control multiple Players using different control algorithms.

We are now going to look at the two output formats generated by Simple-Mixer and learn how they can be used by your application or applet. Specifically, we will look at how to read them and use their data to initialize a MultiPlayer embedded in an application or applet.

The MIX File

The MIX file is a simple ASCII file. The contents of an example MIX file appear below.

```
file:/D:\ejmf\classes\media\noplaceaway.wav 0.0 13.6038095
file:/D:\ejmf\classes\media\jordan_onMVP.wav 14.0 21.38403
file:/D:\ejmf\classes\media\resign.wav 37.0 4.877875
```

This MIX file identifies three sources of media. Each entry in a MIX file consists of three fields:

- A string suitable for constructing a `MediaLocator`.
- The start time in seconds as an offset relative to some arbitrarily chosen time.
- The playing time in seconds.

A MIX file is read using an instance of the `MixFile` object. A `MixFile` object can be constructed in two different ways, both shown in EJMF Toolkit Synopsis 25.1.

EJMF Toolkit Synopsis 25.1 *Constructors for MixFile*

Class	`ejmf.toolkit.util.MixFile`
Constructor	`MixFile`
Visibility	`public`
Arguments	`java.io.File`
Description	Creates a `MixFile` from a `File`.
Constructor	`MixFile`
Visibility	`public`
Arguments	`java.lang.String`
Description	Creates a `MixFile` from a `java.lang.String` representing a file path name.

Once you have a `MixFile` object, you can read the contents using the `read` method.

EJMF Toolkit Synopsis 25.2 *Reading a MIX File*

Class	`ejmf.toolkit.util.MixFile`
Method	`read`
Arguments	`void`
Return	`ejmf.toolkit.util.MixFileData`
Description	Reads a `MixFile`, returning a reference to a `MixFileData`.

The following code snippet illustrates the process of creating and reading a MIX file.

```
String mixFileName = "heavymetal.mix";

MixFile mixFile = new MixFile(mixFileName);
MixFileData v = mixFile.read();
```

The `MixFileData` class represents a collection of `MixTrackData` objects, one for each entry in the MIX file. The number of entries, each corresponding to a track, and a specific track can be accessed with the methods described in EJMF Toolkit Synopsis 25.3.

EJMF Toolkit Synopsis 25.3 *MixFileData Methods*

Class	`ejmf.toolkit.util.MixFileData`
Method	`getNumberOfTracks`
Visibility	`public`
Arguments	`void`
Return	`int`
Description	Returns the number of tracks described by the MIX file.
Method	`getMixTrackData`
Visibility	`public`
Arguments	`int`
Return	`ejmf.toolkit.util.MixTrackData`
Description	Returns the track indexed by the input argument.

The `MixTrackData` class corresponds directly to the data seen in the example MIX file above. It appears in its entirety in Listing 25.1.

Listing 25.1 *The MixTrackData Class*

```
public class MixTrackData {
    public double startTime;
    public double playingTime;
    public String mediaFileName;

    public MixTrackData(String file,
                        double startTime,
                        double playingTime)
        this.startTime = startTime;
        this.playingTime = playingTime;
        this.mediaFileName = file;
    }
}
```

All the member data fields are `public` and can be accessed, without apologies, directly.

With the above collection of methods in hand, it should be clear how you can turn a MIX file into a `TrackList` for use with a `MultiPlayer`. If it is not, then check out the `static` method provided by `TrackList`.

EJMF Toolkit Synopsis 25.4 *Parsing a MixFile*

Class	`ejmf.toolkit.multiplayer.TrackList`
Method	`parseMixFileData`
Visibility	`public`
Arguments	`ejmf.toolkit.util.MixFileData`
Return	`ejmf.toolkit.multiplayer.TrackList`
Description	Returns a `TrackList` representing the data stored in the MIX file passed as an argument.

The source for `parseMixFileData` appears in Listing 25.2

Listing 25.2 *Creating a TrackList from a MixFileData Object*

```
public static TrackList parseMixFileData(MixFileData mfd)
{
    int n = mfd.getNumberOfTracks();
(1) TrackList trackList = new TrackList(n);
    for (int i = 0; i < n; i++) {
(2)     MixTrackData mtd = mfd.getMixTrackData(i);
        try {
            String nm = mtd.mediaFileName;
(3)         Track track = Track.createTrack(i,
                            new MediaLocator(nm),
                            mtd.startTime,
                            mtd.playingTime);
(4)         trackList.addTrack(track);
        } catch (Exception e) {
            e.printStackTrace();
            System.err.println(
                "Can't create Player for" + nm);
            continue;
        }
    }
    trackList.trimToSize();
(5) return trackList;
}
```

After creating an empty `TrackList` [1], `parseMixFileData` relies on the `static` method from the `Track` class, `createTrack`, to generate `Track` entries with which to populate the `TrackList`. The `Track` is created at [3] and added to the `TrackList` at [4]. The `MixTrackData` [2] provides the values for the arguments to `createTrack`. Finally, the `TrackList` is returned at [5].

We can now go from a MIX file to a `TrackList`. We saw in the last chapter how we use a `TrackList` with a `MultiPlayer`. That is a fine approach for applications where reading a file does not require clearance from the National Security Agency. What we really need is a way to get data from a `SimpleMixer` session into an applet. Stay tuned.

HTML Output from SimpleMixer

As we saw in "Saving a SimpleMixer Session" on page 457, generating HTML from a `SimpleMixer` is easy. Like the MIX file, the HTML generated by `SimpleMixer` includes an "entry" for each track. In the case of the HTML output, each entry is introduced by a `PARAM` tag.

Below is example HTML output from a `SimpleMixer` session.

```
<PARAM NAME=TRACKDATA0
    VALUE=file:D:\ejmf\classes\media\xmas.avi;0.0;9.875>
<PARAM NAME=TRACKDATA1
    VALUE=file:D:\ejmf\classes\media\xmas.avi;0.0;9.875>
```

Each `PARAM` tag's `VALUE` attribute contains the values we expect within a `Track`. The `NAME` attribute values differ only by a final number. To convert these contrived names and string `Track` data values to a `TrackList` is just a small matter of software. The *Essential JMF* Toolkit provides two methods that do the trick.

First, we will look at code that collects similarly-named applet parameter values into a `String` array. This method is available as a `static` method from the `Utility` class in the `ejmf.toolkit.util` package.

EJMF Toolkit Synopsis 25.5 *Retrieving Similarly Named Applet Parameters*

Class	`ejmf.toolkit.util.Utility`
Method	`vectorizeParameter`
Visibility	`public`
Arguments	`java.applet.Applet` `java.lang.String`
Return	`java.lang.String[]`
Description	Collects all the applet parameters, the first part of whose `NAME` attribute matches the value of the `String` argument, and returns their `VALUE` attribute values in an array of `String` objects.

To eliminate any mystery surrounding this method, we will lay it bare. Listing 25.3 contains the vectorizeParameter source.

Listing 25.3 *Source Listing for vectorizeParameter*

```
public static String[] vectorizeParameter(
                        Applet app,
                        String name)
{
    String    value;
    Vector    v = new Vector();
    int       i = 0;
    while (
(6)         (value = app.getParameter(name + i)) != null)
        {
(7)         v.addElement(value);
            i++;
        }
        String[] ret = new String[v.size()];
(8)     v.copyInto(ret);
(9)     return ret;
}
```

The secret to vectorizeParameter lies at line [6]. Here the Applet method getParameter tries to retrieve a parameter whose name is constructed by appending a sequentially-generated integer to the end of the name argument. If getParameter returns a non-null value, that value is collected in a Vector [7].

As soon as an attempt to locate a parameter with a generated NAME value fails, the while loop terminates and the Vector of matched values is copied into an array [8]. Finally, the array of Strings is returned [9].

Were this method passed "TRACKDATA" as its second argument and run in an applet whose HTML included the sample generated by SimpleMixer shown above, the array it returned would hold Strings that contained Track data with fields separated by semi-colons.

That means there is still another step to a TrackList object. We can take that step with another *Essential JMF* Toolkit method, this one from the TrackList class.

EJMF Toolkit Synopsis 25.6 *Parsing Strings for TrackData*

Class	`ejmf.toolkit.multiplayer.TrackList`
Method	`parseTrackData`
Visibility	`public`
Arguments	`java.lang.String[]`
Return	`ejmf.toolkit.multiplayer.TrackList`
Description	Returns a `TrackList` representing the data stored in the `String` array passed as an argument.

This method is analogous to the `parseMixFileData` method. Both are convenient methods for creating a `TrackList` from `SimpleMixer` session data.

Now let's take the next step. Given that we have a `TrackList`, let's hand it off to a `MultiPlayer`.

A MultiPlayer Applet

At this point, most of the work is finished. In `SimpleMixer`, we configured a collection of `Players` for playback. We then created some HTML directly from the `SimpleMixer` session. Granted, we had to (manually) add this HTML to an `APPLET` tag in our web page, but we finally ended up with the HTML shown below.

```
<APPLET CODE = ejmf.examples.mixapplet.MPApplet.class
    WIDTH = 180 HEIGHT = 320>
<PARAM NAME=TRACKDATA0
 VALUE=file:/D:\ejmf\classes\media\kickbutt.wav;0.0;15.94>
<PARAM NAME=TRACKDATA1
 VALUE=file:/D:\ejmf\classes\media\resign.wav;16.0;4.8778>
<PARAM NAME=LOOP VALUE=TRUE>
</APPLET>
```

With this input, we can, in a relatively few lines of code, put together an applet that reproduces a previously saved `SimpleMixer` session. Let's look at that applet, the `MPApplet`, starting with its `init` method.

The init Method

Based on the parameters in the applet, `MPApplet`'s `init` method creates a `MultiPlayer` and displays the `Players`' visual components.

Listing 25.4 *The MPApplet init Method*

```
public class MPApplet extends JApplet
        implements MultiPlayerListener, ContainerListener {
    private MultiPlayer mp;

    public void init() {
        boolean loop;
(10)    String[] rawmix =
            Utility.vectorizeParameter(this, "TRACKDATA");
(11)    TrackList trackList =
            TrackList.parseTrackData(rawmix);

        if (trackList.getNumberOfTracks() > 0) {
(12)        mp = new MultiPlayer(trackList,
(13)                new TimerMultiPlayerControl(trackList));

            String ls;
(14)        if (((ls = getParameter("LOOP") != null) &&
                Boolean.valueOf(ls).booleanValue() == true)
                {
(15)            mp.addMultiPlayerListener(this);
                }
(16)        NPlayerPanel npp = new NPlayerPanel(mp);
            getContentPane().add(npp);
        }
    }
    ...
}
```

A quick glance shows that init utilizes much of what we have already seen. At [10], the TRACKDATA parameters are collected together in the rawmix array using vectorizeParameter. This array is then passed to parse-TrackData [11] to create a TrackList. A MultiPlayer is created at [12], passing the newly created TrackList object and an instance of TimerMultiPlayerControl [13] as arguments.

Skipping ahead a few lines, we see that MPApplet also creates an NPlay-erPanel object [16]. An ejmf.toolkit.gui.NPlayerPanel lays out the visual components from the Players within a MultiPlayer using a Grid-Layout. The NPlayerPanel is part of the *Essential JMF* Toolkit and is useful if you need a GridLayout. A complete description of the NPlayerPanel class appears in the javadoc accompanying the *Essential JMF* Toolkit.

There is also a little bonus embedded within the init method. If the LOOP parameter is defined [14] and its boolean value is true, the applet adds itself as a MultiPlayerListener [15]. With the correct code in the applet's multiPlayerUpdate method, we have a looping MultiPlayer. The multiPlayerUpdate method, which listens for changes in the Multi-Player's state, is shown in Listing 25.5.

Listing 25.5 *A Looping MultiPlayer*

```
                public void multiPlayerUpdate(int state) {
                    if (state == MultiPlayer.STOPPED) {
(17)                    mp.start();
                    }
                }
```

Since `MultiPlayer`'s `stop` method is written to rewind all of its `Players`, all the `multiPlayerUpdate` method needs to do is call `start` [17] on the `MultiPlayer` object.

The start Method

The `start` method of `MPApplet` is very simple and reproduced here with no further comment.

Listing 25.6 *The MPApplet start Method*

```
public void start() {
    mp.start();
}
```

The destroy Method

Little needs to be said about the destroy method, except to emphasize again the importance of stopping, and perhaps closing, a `Player` when the web page in which it plays is left. Otherwise, it may continue to play and tie up resources even when the user (i.e. visitor) is finished with it.

Listing 25.7 *The MPApplet destroy Method*

```
public void destroy() {
    mp.stop();
    mp.close();
}
```

Summary

In this chapter we saw how the output from a `SimpleMixer` session can be easily used within an application or applet. The MIX file provides a way for an application to read session configuration information, while HTML is more suited to an applet.

In both cases, the raw data can be transformed into a `TrackList` with methods provided by the unremittingly helpful *Essential JMF* Toolkit. Once you have a `TrackList`, you can use a `MultiPlayer` to play multiple `Players` within your applet faster than Martha Stewart can make pie crust.

Part IV

APPENDICES

Appendix A   *SUPPORTED MEDIA TYPES*

A complete list of all media types supported by release 1.0.1 of Sun's *Java Media Framework* implementation are listed below. For updates to this list consult:

```
http://java.sun.com/products/java-media/jmf/1 0/
   supported.html
```

AIFF (.aiff)

- 8 bits mono/stereo linear
- 16 bits mono/stereo linear 8 kHz
- 16 bits mono/stereo linear 11.05 kHz
- 16 bits mono/stereo linear 22.05 kHz
- 16 bits mono/stereo linear 44.1 kHz
- G.711 mono
- IMA4 ADPCM

AVI (.avi)

Audio:

- 8 bits mono/stereo linear
- 16 bits mono/stereo linear 8 kHz
- 16 bits mono/stereo linear 11.05 kHz
- 16 bits mono/stereo linear 22.05 kHz
- 16 bits mono/stereo linear 44.1 kHz
- DVI ADPCM compressed
- G.711 mono
- GSM mono

Video:

- Cinepak
- Indeo (iv31 and iv32)
- JPEG (411, 422, 111)

GSM (.gsm)

- GSM mono audio

MIDI (.midi)

- Type 1 & 2 MIDI audio files

MPEG-1 (.mpg)

(not available on Solaris x86 platforms)

- Video: MPEG-1
- Audio: MPEG-1, Layer 1 and 2

MPEG audio (.mp2)

(not available on Solaris x86 platforms)

- MPEG layer 1 or 2 audio

Quicktime (.mov)

Audio:

- 8 bits mono/stereo linear
- 16 bits mono/stereo linear 8 kHz
- 16 bits mono/stereo linear 11.05 kHz
- 16 bits mono/stereo linear 22.05 kHz
- 16 bits mono/stereo linear 44.1 kHz
- G.711 mono
- GSM mono
- IMA4 ADPCM
- u-law

Video:

- Cinepak
- H.261
- H.263
- Indeo (iv31 and iv32)
- JPEG (411, 422, 111)
- Raw
- RLE
- SMC

RMF (.rmf)

- Headspace's Rich Media Format audio files

RTP

Audio:

- 4 bits mono DVI 8 kHz
- 4 bits mono DVI 11.05 kHz
- 4 bits mono DVI 22.05 kHz
- 4 bits mono DVI 44.1 kHz
- G.711 mono
- GSM mono

Video:

- JPEG (411, 422, 111)
- H.261
- H.263

Sun Audio (.au)

- 8 bits mono/stereo linear
- 16 bits mono/stereo linear 8 kHz
- 16 bits mono/stereo linear 11.05 kHz
- 16 bits mono/stereo linear 22.05 kHz
- 16 bits mono/stereo linear 44.1 kHz
- G.711 mono

Vivo (.viv)

- Video H.263

Wave (.wav)

- 8 bits mono/stereo linear
- 16 bits mono/stereo linear 8 kHz
- 16 bits mono/stereo linear 11.05 kHz
- 16 bits mono/stereo linear 22.05 kHz
- 16 bits mono/stereo linear 44.1 kHz
- G.711 mono
- GSM mono
- DVI ADPCM (not MSADPCM)

Appendix B *JMF, Browsers and The Java Plug-in*

Introduction

This appendix takes a look at some of the more popular browsers and discusses their compatibility with existing *Java Media Framework* implementations. As we shall see, some browsers don't support some implementations. As an alternative, the Java Plug-in is introduced as a way to provide an up-to-date, fully-compliant and consistent JMF upon which to run *Java Media Framework* applets within a browser.

We will start with a look at the current implementations of the *Java Media Framework*.

Current JMF Implementations

There are multiple implementations of the JMF API. It is important to keep in mind that the published API is just a specification arrived at by a cooperative effort of Sun, Intel and SGI. The implementation of that specification is left to the individual efforts of each vendor.

There are currently four implementations of the JMF `Player` API. These implementations are distinguished by their target platform, which version of the JDK they were written to, and the technique used for writing native code to interface with video and audio devices.

Table 25.1 *Implementations of JMF Player API*

Vendor	Platform	JDK Basis	Native Code Interface
Sun	Solaris	1.1	JNI
Sun	Wintel	1.1	JNI
Intel	Wintel	1.02	1.02 native interface
Intel	Wintel	1.02	RNI

Both of Sun's implementations are based on JDK 1.1 which introduced the *Java Native Interface* (JNI) API. The JNI is the Java-sanctioned way of getting outside of the JMF and into native code. It is also one of the central bones of contention between Sun and Microsoft. Intel avoided this controversy and targeted a larger browser user-base by providing two Wintel implementations of its JMedia Player. Both were written to the JDK 1.02 API but one uses Sun's old-style version of a native code interface while the other uses Microsoft's Raw Native Interface (RNI). As we will see, this has implications for browser compatibility.

Sun has planned a RNI implementation of the JMF for release in Fall 1998.

Browser Compatibility

It would probably not be an exaggeration to say that the biggest stumbling block to getting started with the JMF—at least for the applet writer—is determining which browser supports which implementation. Of course, the question of which browser supports what Java functionality is the bane of applet writers everywhere.

A good rule of thumb: If a JMF implementation uses the JNI, you need a browser whose virtual machine supports JDK 1.1 functionality. There is an immediate corollary to this rule: Microsoft Explorer's VM will not run an applet using Sun's Wintel implementation of the JMF. This is because Microsoft does not support the JNI.

The following table lists various browser configurations along with the JMF implementations that they support.

Table 25.2 *Netscape Navigator/Communicator Support for JMF*

Version	Sun JMF on Solaris	Sun JMF on Wintel	Intel JMF on Wintel
3.x	No	No	Yes
4.03	No	No	Yes
4.03 w/1.1 patch	Yes	Yes	Yes
4.04	No	No	Yes
4.04 w/1.1 patch	Yes	Yes	Yes
4.05	No	No	Yes
4.05 w/1.1 patch	No*	Yes	Yes
4.05 preview	Yes	Yes	Yes

* This is an anomaly due to a bug.

Table 25.3 *Internet Explorer Support for JMF (Wintel Platforms)*

Version	Sun JMF	Intel JMF
3.x	No	Yes
4.x	No	Yes

As you can see from the tables, the Intel JMF provides a fairly complete solution, ignoring *really* old browsers, for the Wintel platform. It does this by limiting its implementation to JDK 1.02 language features. On the other hand, Sun's JMF on either a Solaris or Wintel platform requires a patch to the standard Netscape browser releases. This is because Sun's JMF implementation was written using some features first available in JDK 1.1, namely JNI, as we saw above, and elements from the 1.1 event delegation model.

Downloading Netscape Communicator

The JDK 1.1 patch for Communicator and the preview release of Communicator 4.05 are available from:

```
http://developer.netscape.com/tech/java/index.html
```

The Java Plug-In

The above tables tell only part of the story. By writing your web pages to download the Java Plug-in you can use Sun's JMF with any of the browsers listed above on either Solaris or Wintel platforms. The Java Plug-in enables a browser to run the latest and greatest JMF available from Sun. This allows all applets to take advantage of the latest Java technology, including the JMF.

What is Java Plug-In?

The Java Plug-in is a general solution to the problem of different flavors of browsers either not supporting Java (the official coffee-cup kind) or supporting an "old" version of the JMF. Anyone who has ever been charged with writing an applet that executes within Netscape Navigator 3.x, Netscape Communicator 4.x and Internet Explorer knows the difficulty in writing such an applet. Out of frustration, the temptation has been to fall back on HTML, cgi and perl.

The Java Plug-in will help resist that temptation. The Java Plug-in takes advantage of the extensibility of the leading browsers by allowing an HTML page to request the loading of a specific JMF for execution within that browser. Beyond that, the Java Plug-in is "future-ready," allowing a web page to bring the latest Java features to a browser. This is done by actually identifying within your HTML a specific version of the JMF to be loaded by the browser.

How Does Java Plug-In Work?

The Java Plug-in leverages Netscape's plug-in architecture and Internet Explorer's ActiveX/COM support to load a JMF into the browser's process space. From the page designer's viewpoint, this is done by including the appropriate tags in a web page's HTML. In the case of Netscape, the <EMBED> tag introduces a plug-in. Internet Explorer interprets an <OBJECT> tag as introducing an ActiveX control.

Since this is not intended to be a full-scale treatment of the Java Plug-in, a short example of the use of the <OBJECT> and <EMBED> tags is illustrated below. For complete details, see:

```
http://java.sun.com/products/plugin/1.1/docs/
```

HTML Conversion

To ease the job of converting old HTML documents to use the Java Plug-in, Sun provides a tool, HTMLConverter that takes as input existing HTML pages and inserts additional HTML. The new HTML tags cause the Java Plug-in to run within the browser. HTMLConverter works by recognizing all <APPLET> tags and replacing them with the appropriate <OBJECT> and <EMBED> tags. Both of these tags are inserted into your web page by HTML-

Converter so that the page will work with either of the Netscape browsers and Microsoft's Internet Explorer.

Listing 25.8 contains a simple HTML page containing an <APPLET> tag before conversion.

Listing 25.8 *A Simple HTML Page with an <APPLET> Tag*

```
<applet code=ejmf.examples.browsers.SwingApplet.class
    width=160 height=60>
</applet>
```

After applying the HTMLConverter tool, the resulting HTML appears below.

Listing 25.9 *Converted HTML*

```
<!--"CONVERTED_APPLET"-->
<!-- CONVERTER VERSION 1.0 -->
<OBJECT classid=
    "clsid:8AD9C840-044E-11D1-B3E9-00805F499D93"
    WIDTH = 160 HEIGHT = 60
    codebase-
        "http://java.sun.com/products/plugin/1.1/
        jinstall-win32.cab#Version=1,1,0,0">
<PARAM NAME = CODE
    VALUE = ejmf.examples.browsers.SwingApplet.class >
<PARAM NAME-"type"
    VALUE="application/x-java-applet;version=1.1">
<COMMENT>
<EMBED type="application/x-java-applet,version=1.1"
    java_CODE - ejmf.examples.browsers.SwingApplet.class
    WIDTH = 160 HEIGHT = 60
    pluginspage="http://java.sun.com/products/plugin/1.1/
        plugin-install.html">
<NOEMBED>
</COMMENT>
</NOEMBED></EMBED>
</OBJECT>
<!--
<APPLET CODE = ejmf.examples.broswers.SwingApplet.class
    WIDTH = 160 HEIGHT =60 >
</APPLET>
-->
<!--"END_CONVERTED_APPLET"-->
```

For a complete specification of the use of these tags and how they work within the relevant browser, see http://java.sun.com/products/plugin/1.1/docs/tags.html.

Compatibility Matrix Using Java Plug-In

The Java Plug-in eliminates the need to worry about which browser supports what Java functionality. Like all plug-ins, the Java Plug-in delivers to the browser the resources it needs to render a particular page. Table 25.4 illustrates an updated browser compatibility matrix when using Sun's *JMF* along with the Java Plug-in.

Table 25.4 *Browser Support for Sun JMF Using Java Plug-in*

Browser Version	Sun JMF on Solaris	Sun JMF on Wintel
Navigator 3.x	Yes	Yes
Communicator 3.x*	Yes	Yes
Internet Explorer 3.x	Yes	Yes
Internet Explorer 4.x	Yes	Yes

   * Sun issues a warning on their Java Plug-in web page that Netscape 4.04/4.05 with the 1.1 patch "does not run stably with the Java Plug-in." They recommend moving to a version of Communicator that does not require the patch.

Downloading The Java Plug-In

More information on the Java Plug-in can be found at:

`http://java.sun.com/products/plugin/`

The Java Plug-in can be downloaded from:

`http://java.sun.com/products/plugin/1.1/index.html`

The `HTMLConverter` tool can also be downloaded from this location.

The JMF Run-Time

The foregoing discussion still leaves one question unresolved: How does a visitor to your web page retrieve the run-time libraries necessary to run an applet that incorporates a JMF Player? Current implementations of JMF rely heavily on native libraries to interface with audio and video drivers. Unlike class files that may be associated with an applet and loaded by the applet class loader, the native libraries need to be downloaded and installed by some other mechanism.

Intel provides such a mechanism. Using JavaScript that you can include in your web page, a run-time version of Intel's JMF can be downloaded automatically. If you want to build a web page that launches an applet using a `Player` and without relying on your visitor to have the JMF run-time installed locally, you will need to include the JavaScript available from Intel within your page. This script works only with Microsoft's Internet Explorer 4.x and Netscape's Communicator 4.x. In the former case, the JavaScript code relies on Microsoft's Internet Component Download Service. In the latter case, Netscape's SmartUpdate technology is used. This functionality is much like a plug-in in that a download will only be necessary once. After that, your browser will recognize the presence of Intel's JMF and will not intervene.

Neither Netscape's nor Microsoft's 3.x release browser supports the necessary functionality to download Intel's JMF run-time.

For more information on downloading Intel's JMF run-time including the JavaScript source that affects the download, see

```
http://developer.intel.com/ial/jmedia/Docs/JMFramework/
    Tutorial/Tutorial3H/Tutorial3H.htm.
```

Unfortunately, Sun does not provide the ability to download a JMF run-time from an HTML page. Currently, you can not serve Solaris clients with a run-time version of the JMF. This is a shortcoming of their packaging that needs to be addressed. Barring any additional support from Sun, if you want your applets to use Sun's JMF, you will have to package the appropriate pieces from Sun's distribution and make them available from your site much like Intel does. This is permitted by the licensing agreement governing the use and redistribution of Sun's JMF. The shortcoming of this approach is that you will need to closely track Sun releases or risk being out of date.

appletviewer and HotJava

Two other browsers deserve mention. `appletviewer` and HotJava are both produced by Sun. The `appletviewer` shipped with JDK 1.1 or later will be capable of running an applet incorporating a JMF Player.

When reading HTML files converted to utilize the Java Plug-in, `appletviewer` will complain about finding a <PARAM> tag outside of a <APPLET>...</APPLET> pair. This <PARAM> tag is associated with the <OBJECT> so the message can be ignored. `appletviewer` will proceed to use the <APPLET> tag and properly launch the applet.

HotJava 1.0 is shipped with *Java Runtime Environment* (JRE) from JDK 1.1.1 and, therefore, will also run a JMF-enabled applet.

Early versions of HotJava 1.1.x have some bugs involving the recognition and parsing of the <OBJECT> tag. HotJava 1.1.4 is needed to correctly handle the <OBJECT> tag and properly load the Java Plug-in.

Appendix C

Configuring the Java Media Framework

Configuring JMF

In the `bin` directory of the *Java Media Framework* distribution lies a utility called `jmfconfig`. This application allows you to configure various properties of the JMF. These properties are stored persistently in the `jmf.proper-ties` file located in the `lib` directory of the JMF distribution.

Running jmfconfig

No special environment variables or setup is needed to run the JMF Configuration utility. It can be run as follows.

◀ **•User Input**   **Running jmfconfig**

```
% $JMFHOME/bin/jmfconfig
```

The `jmfconfig` application is shown in Figure C.1.

Figure C.1 *The jmfconfig Utility*

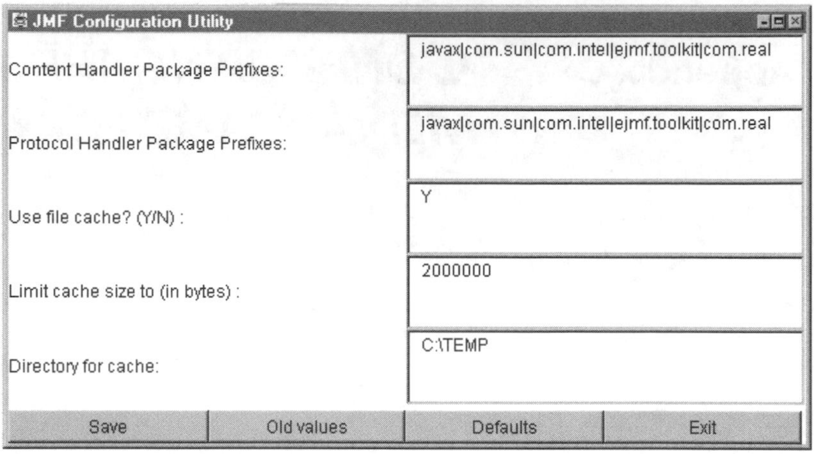

Ignoring the sketchy GUI implementation, the `jmfconfig` utility is quite useful for configuring the JMF.

Configurable Properties

Following is a summary of the properties that can be modified with this utility.

Content Package Prefix List

As discussed in chapter Chapter 18, "Creating a Custom Player," the JMF's content prefix list can be modified to provide support for new media formats. This list is used by the `Manager` class when searching for a suitable `Player` for a given media file. Each entry in this list is a prefix to a package that may contain a `Player` to render the given medium.

This option modifies the `content.prefixes` property of the JMF. Entries within the list are separated by the vertical bar (|) character. The default context package prefix list appears in Table C.1.

Table C.1 *Default Content Package Prefix List*

Platform	Default Value
Solaris	`javax|com.sun`
Windows 95/NT	`javax|com.sun`

If you are running on a Wintel platform that also has Intel's implementation installed, `com.intel` will appear in your content package prefix list. Likewise, if you have installed Real's Player, `com.real` will appear.

Protocol Package Prefix List

As discussed in chapter Chapter 22, "Creating a Custom DataSource," the JMF's *protocol* prefix list can be modified to provide support for different data-transfer protocols. This list is used by the Manager class when searching for a suitable DataSource to handle a given protocol. Each entry in this list is a prefix to a package that may contain a DataSource that understands the given protocol.

This option modifies the protocol.prefixes property of the JMF. Like the content.prefixes property, entries within this list are separated by the vertical bar character. The default protocol package prefix list appears in Table C.2.

Table C.2 *Default Protocol Package Prefix List*

Platform	Default Value
Solaris	javax|com.sun
Windows 95/NT	javax|com.sun

Using File Cache

This entry specifies whether to use caching when downloading media. Caching may improve the quality of the media playback by eliminating delays caused by downloading the media.

This option modifies the cache.use property of the JMF. Valid values for this property are y and n. The default values for use of the disk cache appear in Table C.3.

Table C.3 *Default for Use of File Cache*

Platform	Default Value
Solaris	Enable disk caching (y)
Windows 95/NT	Disable disk caching (n)

File Cache Size

This entry specifies the number of bytes of data to cache when downloading media. With small values, the quality of the media playback may suffer because the JMF may need to stop a Player to repopulate its cache. If media playback is choppy, this value should be increased.

When using the HTTP protocol, this value specifies the number of bytes to download before the playing the media. If the number of bytes remaining in the cache is less than 20% of this number, then the player stops and restarts after the cache has been repopulated.

This option modifies the `cache.limit` property of the JMF. The default cache size values appear in Table C.4.

Table C.4 *Default File Cache Size*

Platform	Default Value
Solaris	5,000,000 bytes
Windows 95/NT	2,000,000 bytes

File Cache Directory

This entry specifies the directory in which to create cache files. This directory should reside on a local file system for faster cache access.

This option modifies the `cache.dir` property of the JMF. The default file cache directory values appear in Table C.5.

Table C.5 *Default File Cache Directory*

Platform	Default Value
Solaris	`/tmp`
Windows 95/NT	`c:/tmp`

jmfconfig Actions

The `jmfconfig` application makes the following actions available to the user.

Save

This action makes the property changes persistent. Properties are stored in the `$JMFHOME/lib/jmf.properties` file.

Old Values

When this action is taken, the values that the JMF properties had at start-up are restored to the text fields. These values will need to be saved to take effect.

Default Values

This action causes the default values of the JMF properties to be restored to the text fields. These default values are defined by the JMF. After taking this action, the properties need to be saved to take effect.

Exit

This action causes the `jmfconfig` application to exit. Any unsaved changes made to the property text fields are discarded.

Appendix D *RESOURCES*

Multimedia Resources

For your browsing pleasure, herein are provided some URLs related to the Java Media effort, related products and just plain old good cyber-places to go to learn more about things you can never know enough about.

Places Where the Sun Does Shine

`http://java.sun.com/` – For Java, Java and more Java.

`http://java.sun.com/products/java-media/jmf` – Home page for the JMF effort at Sun.

`http://java.sun.com/products/java-media/jmf/1.0/supported.html` – For a complete and up-to-date list of supported media and formats.

`http://java.sun.com/products/java-media/` – The jumping-off point for all the Java Media APIs.

513

`http://java.sun.com/products/jfc/tsc/` – The Swing Connection, and we're not talking the latest music craze. Check here daily for the latest on the fastest changing software ever introduced.

`http://java.sun.com/products/jfc/tsc/swingdoc-archive/ threads.html` – For a thorough explanation of the how and why of multi-threading in Swing and official justification on the use of `invokeLater` and `invokeAndWait`.

Places Where Justice Department Lawyers Hang Out

`http://www.microsoft.com/directx/pavilion/dshow/ default.asp` – Microsoft's DirectShow home page.

`http://www.microsoft.com/java/sdk/20/packages/directX/ default.htm` – Information on a collection of Java classes providing access to Microsoft's DirectX functionality.

The Real Thing

`http://www.real.com/` – The "Home of Streaming Media."

`http://www.real.com/realmedia/` – For the RealMedia SDK and its Java Media Player implementation.

`http://www.real.com/g2/overview.html` – For a description of the RealMedia technology.

The First Multimedia Computer Company

`http://www.apple.com/quicktime/developers/qtjava/` – For information on and download of Apple's QuickTime for Java.

Blinded Me by Beatnik Science

`http://www.headspace.com/` – The best sound engine available, lots of music to license, and a slick audio player, all brought to you by an aging rocker.

Get Shocked!

`http://www.macromedia.com/` – Home page of the company that brings you Shockwave.

`http://www.macromedia.com/shockwave/` – Four hundred gazillion web sites can't be wrong.

An Erstwhile Multimedia Company

`http://developer.intel.com/ial/jmedia/` – "Gee, Bill, you are right. We don't need to do multimedia development."

Discussion Lists

For help from fellow JMF programmers there exists at least two relevant discussion groups.

JMF-interest

The jmf-interest list is for people interested in the JMF and can be subscribed to by sending e-mail with:

`subscribe jmf-interest`

in the message body to:

`javamedia-request@sun.com`

JMF-digest

To avoid a flood of e-mail, you may opt for the jmf-digest list. Messages sent to the jmf-interest list are collected and periodically mailed to jmf-digest subscribers.

To subscribe to the jmf-digest list, send e-mail with:

`subscribe jmf-digest`

in the message body to:

`javamedia-request@sun.com`

Javasound-interest

If you are interested in the Java Sound API, the javasound-interest list is where like-minded people exchange questions and suggestions.

To subscribe, send e-mail to `javamedia-request@Sun.COM` with the following text contained in the message body:

`subscribe javasound-interest`

Most of the other Java Media APIs also have a discussion list. See the home page for each effort for more information. Those pages are available from:

`http://java.sun.com/products/java-media/`

Glossary

No need to reinvent the wheel. If you need to look up any unfamiliar terms, see:

`http://www.whatis.com/`

UNIFIED MODELING LANGUAGE NOTATION

Throughout this book appear class diagrams of various pieces of the *Java Media Framework* and the *Essential JMF* Toolkit. All of those diagrams use a notation known as the Unified Modeling Language (UML). This appendix provides a brief introduction to the UML. Described herein are only those elements from the UML that were used in the book. For a complete description of the UML see *Unified Method for Object-Oriented Development* by Grady Booch, et. al. (Rational Software Corporation).

A UML Example

Figure E.1 displays the class diagram used in the discussion of implementing a custom `DataSource`. This particular diagram illustrates all the UML elements seen throughout the book. Some elements have been labelled with numbers to aid in the discussion of their meaning.

Figure E.1 *The DataSource Revisited*

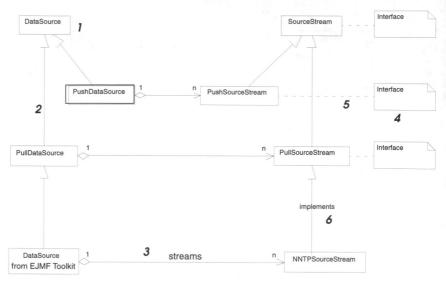

1. A Java class or interface is represented by a rectangular box. The name of the class or interface appears inside the box.

2. A line terminated with a closed arrow is drawn from a subclass to its superclass. This arrow depicts, for example, that `PullDataSource` extends `DataSource`. The precise UML name for this relationship is *generalization*.

3. A line with a diamond at one end and an open arrow at the other depicts a *has-a* relationship. Specifically, the class at which the diamond is located has a reference to an object of the class to which the arrow points. The has-a relationship (3) in Figure E.1 shows that a `DataSource` object has a reference to an `NNTPSourceStream` object.

   A has-a relationship is sometimes labelled with the name of the member data field that maintains the object reference. Here, that member field is named `streams`.

   A has-a relationship also has a *cardinality* associated with it. The cardinality of a has-a relationship defines how many references an object may maintain. In the `streams` has-a relation, the `DataSource` has a single reference, thus the 1 appearing near the diamond, to many, or n, `NNTPSourceStream` objects. A 1-n relationship means that a reference is maintained to a collection of objects, like an array or vector.

4. Since the UML has no good way of depicting a Java `interface`, a UML *note* is used. A note is designed for annotating a UML element. It is used here to mark a rectangle as a Java `interface` instead of a class.

5. A dotted line between a note and a UML element simply associates that note with a particular element.

6. Labelling a generalization relationship with `implements` is a liberty we have taken to emphasize that the arrow does not represent the normal subclassing relationship but, rather, a case of a class implementing a Java interface.

Appendix F

JAVA MEDIA FRAMEWORK API

This page intentionally left blank except for the page number, the title of the appendix, the Official Scribble of the *Essential Java* Series and this message specifying such.

Interface javax.media.CachingControl

public interface CachingControl
extends Control

The CachingControl Interface provides a GUI Component to monitor a Player's media download. A Player may choose not to support the CachingControl interface. If supported, this control it typically retrieved with the Controller.getControls method. A Player that supports a CachingControl will post CachingControlEvents as the media is downloaded.

See Also:

Controller, ControllerListener, CachingControlEvent, Player

Variables

LENGTH_UNKNOWN

public static final long LENGTH_UNKNOWN

Indicates that the CachingControl is unable to determine the length of the media being downloaded.

Methods

isDownloading

public abstract boolean isDownloading()

Indicates whether or not media is being downloaded.

Returns:

Returns true if media is being downloaded; otherwise returns false. .

getContentLength

public abstract long getContentLength()

Gets the total number of bytes in the media being downloaded. Returns LENGTH_UNKNOWN if this information is not available.

Returns:

The media length in bytes, or LENGTH_UNKNOWN.

getContentProgress

public abstract long getContentProgress()

Gets the total number of bytes of media data that have been downloaded so far.

Returns:

The number of bytes downloaded.

getProgressBarComponent

```
public abstract Component getProgressBarComponent()
```

Gets a java.awt.Component for displaying the download progress.

Returns:

Progress bar GUI.

getControlComponent

```
public abstract Component getControlComponent()
```

Gets a java.awt.Component that provides additional download control. Returns null if no such Component is provided.

Returns:

Download control GUI.

Class javax.media.CachingControlEvent

```
java.lang.Object
   |
   +----javax.media.ControllerEvent
            |
            +----javax.media.CachingControlEvent
```

public class CachingControlEvent
extends ControllerEvent

A CachingControlEvent is posted by a Player that supports the CachingControl
interface. It is posted incrementally as the media is downloaded.

See Also:

Controller, ControllerListener, CachingControl

Constructors

CachingControlEvent

public CachingControlEvent(Controller from, CachingControl
  cacheControl, long progress)

Constructs a CachingControlEvent from the given Controller, CachingControl,
and progress length.

Methods

getCachingControl

public CachingControl getCachingControl()

Gets the CachingControl object that generated the event.

Returns:

The CachingControl object.

getContentProgress

public long getContentProgress()

Gets the total number of bytes of media data that have been downloaded so far.

Returns:

The number of bytes of media data downloaded.

Interface javax.media.Clock

public interface Clock

The Clock interface is the most basic part of the Player interface. It provides the timing information needed to support a time-based medium.

See Also:

TimeBase, Player

Variables

RESET

public static final Time RESET

Returned by getStopTime if the stop time is unset.

Methods

setTimeBase

public abstract void setTimeBase(TimeBase master) throws
IncompatibleTimeBaseException

Sets the TimeBase for this Clock. This method can only be called on a Stopped Clock, otherwise a ClockStartedError is thrown. A Clock has a default TimeBase that is determined by the implementation. To reset a Clock to this default, call setTimeBase with a null argument.

Parameters:

master - The new TimeBase or null to reset the Clock to its default TimeBase.

Throws: IncompatibleTimeBaseException

Thrown if the Clock can't use the specified TimeBase.

syncStart

public abstract void syncStart(Time at)

Synchronizes the current media time to the specified time-base time and starts the Clock. The syncStart() method sets the time-base start-time and puts the Clock in the Started state. This method can only be called on a Stopped Clock. If this method is called on a Started Clock a ClockStartedError is thrown.

Parameters:

at - The *time-base time* to equate with the current *media time.*

stop

public abstract void stop()

Stops the Clock, releasing the Clock from synchronization with the TimeBase. After this request is issued, the Clock is in the Stopped state. If stop is called on a Stopped Clock, the request is ignored.

setStopTime

```
public abstract void setStopTime(Time stopTime)
```

Sets the media time at which the Clock is to stop. The Clock will stop when its media time passes its stop time. To clear the stop time, set it to Clock.RESET.

The setStopTime method can always be called on a Stopped Clock. On a Started Clock, however, the stop time can only be set once. A StopTimeSetError is thrown if setStopTime is called and the stop time has already been set.

Parameters:

stopTime - The time at which you want the Clock to stop, in *media time*.

getStopTime

```
public abstract Time getStopTime()
```

Gets the last value successfully set by setStopTime. Returns the default value Clock.RESET if no stop time has been set.

Returns:

The current stop time.

setMediaTime

```
public abstract void setMediaTime(Time now)
```

Sets the Clock's media time. This method can only be called on a Stopped Clock. If it is called on a Started Clock. a ClockStartedError is thrown.

Parameters:

now - The new media time.

getMediaTime

```
public abstract Time getMediaTime()
```

Gets this Clock's current media time. A Started Clock's media time is based on its TimeBase and rate.

Returns:

The current *media time*.

getMediaNanoseconds

```
public abstract long getMediaNanoseconds()
```

Gets this Clock's current media time in nanoseconds.

Returns:

The current *media time* in nanoseconds.

getSyncTime

```
public abstract Time getSyncTime()
```

Gets the current media time or the time until this `Clock` will synchronize to its `TimeBase`. If the `Clock` is Stopped, this method returns the `Clock`'s current media time , which is based on its `TimeBase` and rate. However, when the `Clock` is in the `Started` state but has not yet reached its time-base start time, `getSyncTime` returns the time remaining until the time-base start-time. Once the `TimeBase` reaches the time-base start-time, `getSyncTime` and `getMediaTime` will return the same value.

getTimeBase

```
public abstract TimeBase getTimeBase()
```

Gets the `TimeBase` used by this `Clock`.

mapToTimeBase

```
public abstract Time mapToTimeBase(Time t) throws
    ClockStoppedException
```

Gets the `TimeBase` time that corresponds to the specified media time.

Parameters:

t - The *media time* to map from.

Returns:

The *time-base time* in *media-time* coordinates.

Throws: ClockStoppedException

Thrown if `mapToTimeBase` is called on a *Stopped* `Clock`.

getRate

```
public abstract float getRate()
```

Gets the `Clock`'s rate. The rate defines the relationship between the `Clock`'s media time and its `TimeBase`. A rate of 2.0 indicates that media time will pass twice as fast as the `TimeBase` time once the `Clock` starts. Similarly, a negative rate indicates that the `Clock` runs in the opposite direction of its `TimeBase`.

setRate

```
public abstract float setRate(float factor)
```

Sets the rate for this `Clock`. The given argument is the rate requested of the `Clock`. If the `Clock` cannot support this rate, it will set the rate as close to the requested value as possible. The only rate guaranteed to be supported by all `Clock`s is 1.0.

The `setRate()` method returns the actual rate set in the `Clock`.

Parameters:

factor - The temporal scale factor (rate) to set.

Returns:

The actual rate set.

Class javax.media.ClockStartedError

```
java.lang.Object
   |
   +----java.lang.Throwable
            |
            +----java.lang.Error
                     |
                     +----javax.media.MediaError
                              |
                              +----javax.media.ClockStartedError
```

public class ClockStartedError
extends MediaError

A ClockStartedError is thrown by a started Clock when a method is invoked that is not legal on a Clock in the Started state.

See Also:

Player, Controller, Clock

Constructors

ClockStartedError

public ClockStartedError(String reason)

Constructs a ClockStartedError with the given error message.

ClockStartedError

public ClockStartedError()

Constructs a ClockStartedError with no error message.

Class javax.media.ClockStoppedException

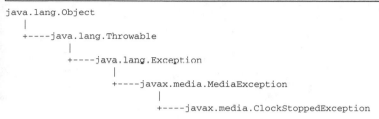

```
java.lang.Object
    |
    +----java.lang.Throwable
            |
            +----java.lang.Exception
                    |
                    +----javax.media.MediaException
                            |
                            +----javax.media.ClockStoppedException
```

public class ClockStoppedException
extends MediaException

A ClockStoppedException is thrown when a method that expects the Clock to be Started is called on a Stopped Clock.

Constructors

ClockStoppedException

public ClockStoppedException()

  Constructs a ClockStoppedException with the given error message.

ClockStoppedException

public ClockStoppedException(String reason)

  Constructs a ClockStoppedException with no error message.

Class javax.media.ConnectionErrorEvent

```
java.lang.Object
   |
   +----javax.media.ControllerEvent
            |
            +----javax.media.ControllerClosedEvent
                     |
                     +----javax.media.ControllerErrorEvent
                              |
                              +----javax.media.ConnectionErrorEvent
```

public class ConnectionErrorEvent
extends ControllerErrorEvent

A ConnectionErrorEvent is posted when an error occurs within a DataSource while obtaining data or communicating with a server.

Constructors

ConnectionErrorEvent

public ConnectionErrorEvent(Controller from)

Constructs a ConnectionErrorEvent for the given source Controller.

ConnectionErrorEvent

public ConnectionErrorEvent(Controller from, String why)

Constructs a ConnectionErrorEvent for the given source Controller and error message.

Interface javax.media.Control

public interface Control

The Control interface provides a way to give the user a finer level of control over some aspect of an Object's operation. Its sole method provides a GUI component that allows the user to interact with the Object in a manner not otherwise provided by the API.

Methods

getControlComponent

public abstract Component getControlComponent()

Gets the java.awt.Component associated with this Control object. This Component should allow a user to control some aspect of the Object that implementats this interface. As an example, this method might return a slider for volume control or a panel containing radio buttons for CODEC control. The getControlComponent() method returns null if there is no GUI Component for this Control.

Interface javax.media.Controller

public interface Controller
extends Clock, Duration

The Controller interface extends the Clock interface to provide resource-allocation state information, event generation, and a mechanism for obtaining objects that provide additional control over a Controller.

Variables

LATENCY_UNKNOWN

public static final Time LATENCY_UNKNOWN

Indicates that the Controller cannot determine its start latency.

Unrealized

public static final int Unrealized

Returned by getState.

Realizing

public static final int Realizing

Returned by getState.

Realized

public static final int Realized

Returned by getState.

Prefetching

public static final int Prefetching

Returned by getState.

Prefetched

public static final int Prefetched

Returned by getState.

Started

public static final int Started

Returned by getState.

Methods

getState

public abstract int getState()

Gets the current state of this Controller. The state is an integer constant as defined above.

Returns:

> The `Controller`'s current state.

getTargetState

```
public abstract int getTargetState()
```

Gets the current target state of this `Controller`. The state is an integer constant as defined above.

Returns:

> The `Controller`'s current target state.

realize

```
public abstract void realize()
```

Asynchronously moves the `Controller` from the `Unrealized` state to the `Realized` state. Acquires non-exclusive resources necessary for the `Controller` to render the media. The media data may be examined in the process. The `realize` method puts the `Controller` into the `Realizing` state and returns immediately. When the realize operation is complete and the `Controller` is in the `Realized` state, the `Controller` posts a `RealizeCompleteEvent`.

prefetch

```
public abstract void prefetch()
```

Asynchronously moves the `Controller` to the `Prefetched` state. Acquires any exclusive resources necessary for the `Controller` to render the media. As much of the media data as necessary may be downloaded to reduce the `Controller`'s start latency to the shortest possible time. The `prefetch()` method puts the `Controller` into the `Prefetching` state and returns immediately. When the realize operation is complete and the `Controller` is in the `Prefetched` state, the `Controller` posts a `PrefetchCompleteEvent`.

deallocate

```
public abstract void deallocate()
```

Abort the current forward transition and cease any activity that consumes system resources. If a `Controller` is not yet `Realized`, it returns to the `Unrealized` state. Otherwise, the `Controller` returns to the `Realized` state. A `ClockStartedError` is thrown if `deallocate` is called on a `Started Controller`.

close

```
public abstract void close()
```

Release all resources and cease all activity. The `close` method indicates that the `Controller` will no longer be used and the `Controller` has shut down. A `ControllerClosedEvent` is posted to indicate the transition. Methods invoked on a closed `Controller` might throw errors.

getStartLatency

```
public abstract Time getStartLatency()
```

Gets the `Controller`'s start latency in nanoseconds. The start latency represents a worst-case estimate of the amount of time it will take to present the first frame of data. This method is useful for determining how far in advance the syncStart() method must be invoked to ensure that media will be rendered at the specified start time. For a Controller that has a variable start latency, the value returned represents the maximum possible start latency. This method returns LATENCY_UNKNOWN if the start latency cannot be determined.

Returns:

The time it will take before the first frame of media can be presented.

getControls

```
public abstract Control[] getControls()
```

Gets a list of the Control objects that this Controller supports. If there are no controls, an array of length zero is returned.

Returns:

A list of Controller Controls.

getControl

```
public abstract Control getControl(String forName)
```

Gets the Control that supports the class or interface specified. The full class or interface name should be specified. null is returned if the Control is not supported.

Returns:

Control for the class or interface name.

addControllerListener

```
public abstract void addControllerListener(ControllerListener
  listener)
```

Specifies a ControllerListener to which this Controller will send events. A Controller can have multiple ControllerListeners.

Parameters:

listener - The listener to which the Controller will post events.

removeControllerListener

```
public abstract void removeControllerListener(ControllerListener
  listener)
```

Removes the specified ControllerListeners from this Controller's listener list.

Parameters:

listener - The listener that has been receiving events from this Controller.

Class javax.media.ControllerClosedEvent

```
java.lang.Object
   |
   +----javax.media.ControllerEvent
          |
          +----javax.media.ControllerClosedEvent
```

public class ControllerClosedEvent
extends ControllerEvent

A ControllerClosedEvent is posted by a Controller when it has closed. It indicates that the Controller is no longer operational.

See Also:

Controller, ControllerListener

Variables

message

protected String message

The error message represented by this ControllerClosedEvent.

Constructors

ControllerClosedEvent

public ControllerClosedEvent(Controller from)

Constructs a ControllerClosedEvent for the given source Controller.

ControllerClosedEvent

public ControllerClosedEvent(Controller from, String why)

Constructs a ControllerClosedEvent for the given source Controller and error message.

Methods

getMessage

public String getMessage()

Obtains the message describing why this event occurred.

Returns:

Message describing event cause.

Class javax.media.ControllerErrorEvent

```
java.lang.Object
    |
    +----javax.media.ControllerEvent
            |
            +----javax.media.ControllerClosedEvent
                    |
                    +----javax.media.ControllerErrorEvent
```

public class ControllerErrorEvent
extends ControllerClosedEvent

A ControllerErrorEvent is posted when an error condition occurs that causes a Controller to cease functioning. Extending from ControllerClosedEvent, a ControllerErrorEvent indicates that the Controller is closed and no longer operational.

See Also:

Controller, ControllerListener

Constructors

ControllerErrorEvent

public ControllerErrorEvent(Controller from)

Constructs a ControllerErrorEvent for the given source Controller.

ControllerErrorEvent

public ControllerErrorEvent(Controller from, String why)

Constructs a ControllerErrorEvent for the given source Controller and error message.

Class javax.media.ControllerEvent

```
java.lang.Object
    |
    +----javax.media.ControllerEvent
```

public class ControllerEvent
extends Object
implements MediaEvent

The ControllerEvent class is the base class for events generated by a Controller. These events are sent to the Controller's ControllerListeners.

See Also:

Controller, ControllerListener, MediaEvent

Constructors

ControllerEvent

public ControllerEvent(Controller from)

Constructs a ControllerEvent for the given source Controller.

Methods

getSourceController

public Controller getSourceController()

Gets the Controller that posted this event. The returned Controller has at least one active listener. (The addListener method has been called on the Controller).

Returns:

The Controller that posted this event.

getSource

public Object getSource()

Gets the Object that posted this event.

Interface javax.media.ControllerListener

public interface ControllerListener

The `ControllerListener` interface is used to handle `ControllerEvents` generated by `Controllers`. Clases that implement this interface should call the `Controller`'s `addController()` method to register with the given `Controller`. Thereafter, `ControllerEvents` are sent to the `ControllerListener` via its `controllerUpdate` method.

See Also:

Controller

Methods

controllerUpdate

public abstract void controllerUpdate(ControllerEvent event)

This method is called when an event is generated by a `Controller` that this listener is registered with.

Parameters:

event - The event generated.

Class javax.media.DataStarvedEvent

```
java.lang.Object
    |
    +----javax.media.ControllerEvent
            |
            +----javax.media.TransitionEvent
                    |
                    +----javax.media.StopEvent
                            |
                            +----javax.media.DataStarvedEvent
```

public class DataStarvedEvent
extends StopEvent

A DataStarvedEvent is posted by a Controller when it has unexpectedly lost or stopped receiving data. If the Controller was started, this event indicates that it has transitioned to a Stopped state.

See Also:

Controller, ControllerListener

Constructors

DataStarvedEvent

public DataStarvedEvent(Controller from, int previous, int current, int target, Time mediaTime)

Constructs a DataStarvedEvent with the given source Controller, previous state, current state, target state, and media time.

Class javax.media.DeallocateEvent

```
java.lang.Object
    |
    +----javax.media.ControllerEvent
            |
            +----javax.media.TransitionEvent
                    |
                    +----javax.media.StopEvent
                            |
                            +----javax.media.DeallocateEvent
```

public class DeallocateEvent
extends StopEvent

A DeallocateEvent is posted by a Controller when it has completed a deallocate transition. It implies that the Controller must be prefetched or realized before it can be started.

See Also:

Controller, ControllerListener

Constructors

DeallocateEvent

public DeallocateEvent(Controller from, int previous, int current, int target, Time mediaTime)

Constructs a DeallocateEvent with the given source Controller, previous state, current state, target state, and media time.

Interface javax.media.Duration

public interface Duration

The Duration interface provides the duration of the media handled by an object. The duration is specified as a Time object. A Controller that supports the Duration interface posts a DurationUpdateEvent whenever its media's duration changes.

See Also:

Controller, DurationUpdateEvent

Variables

DURATION_UNBOUNDED

public static final Time DURATION_UNBOUNDED

Returned by getDuration().

DURATION_UNKNOWN

public static final Time DURATION_UNKNOWN

Returned by getDuration().

Methods

getDuration

public abstract Time getDuration()

Gets the duration of the media represented by this object. The value returned is the media's duration when played at the default rate. If the duration can't be determined (for example, the media object is presenting live video) getDuration() returns DURATION_UNKNOWN.

Returns:

A Time object representing the duration or DURATION_UNKNOWN.

Class javax.media.DurationUpdateEvent

```
java.lang.Object
    |
    +----javax.media.ControllerEvent
            |
            +----javax.media.DurationUpdateEvent
```

public class DurationUpdateEvent
extends ControllerEvent

A DurationUpdateEvent is posted by a Controller when its duration changes or is recalculated.

See Also:

Controller, ControllerListener

Constructors

DurationUpdateEvent

public DurationUpdateEvent(Controller from, Time newDuration)

Constructs a DurationUpdateEvent with the given source Controller, and new duration.

Methods

getDuration

public Time getDuration()

Gets the duration of the media that this Controller is using.

Returns:

The duration of this Controller's media.

Class javax.media.EndOfMediaEvent

```
java.lang.Object
   |
   +----javax.media.ControllerEvent
          |
          +----javax.media.TransitionEvent
                 |
                 +----javax.media.StopEvent
                        |
                        +----javax.media.EndOfMediaEvent
```

public class EndOfMediaEvent
extends StopEvent

An EndOfMediaEvent is posted by a Controller when the end of its media has been reached. As a StopEvent, it indicates that the Controller has moved from the *Started* into the *Stopped* state.

See Also:

Controller, ControllerListener

Constructors

EndOfMediaEvent

public EndOfMediaEvent(Controller from, int previous, int current,
   int target, Time mediaTime)

Constructs a EndOfMediaEvent with the given source Controller, previous state, current state, target state, and media time.

Class javax.media.GainChangeEvent

```
java.lang.Object
    |
    +----javax.media.GainChangeEvent
```

public class GainChangeEvent
extends Object
implements MediaEvent

A GainChangeEvent is posted by a GainControl when its state has changed.

See Also:

GainControl, GainChangeListener

Constructors

GainChangeEvent

public GainChangeEvent(GainControl from, boolean mute, float dB, float level)

Constructs a GainChangeEvent with the given source GainControl.

Methods

getSource

public Object getSource()

Gets the object that posted this event.

Returns:

The object that posted this event.

getSourceGainControl

public GainControl getSourceGainControl()

Gets the GainControl that posted this event.

Returns:

The GainControl that posted this event.

getDB

public float getDB()

Gets the GainControl's new gain value in dB.

Returns:

The GainControl's new gain value, in dB.

getLevel

public float getLevel()

Gets the GainControl's new gain value in the level scale.

Returns:

The GainControl's new gain, in the level scale.

getMute

```
public boolean getMute()
```

Gets the GainControl's new mute value.

Returns:

The GainControl's new mute value.

Interface javax.media.GainChangeListener

public interface GainChangeListener

The GainChangeListener interface is implemented to handle GainChangeEvents generated by GainControls.

See Also:

GainControl, GainChangeEvent

Methods

gainChange

public abstract void gainChange(GainChangeEvent event)

This method is called to deliver a GainChangeEvent when the state of a GainControl changes.

Parameters:

event - The event generated.

Interface javax.media.GainControl

public interface GainControl
extends Control

The GainControl interface is a Control used to manipulate and retrieve audio signal gain. It is retrieved, if applicable, from the Player interface with the Player method getGainControl.

See Also:

GainChangeEvent, GainChangeListener, Control

Methods

setMute

public abstract void setMute(boolean mute)

Mute or unmute the signal associated with this GainControl. Calling setMute with a true argument on an object that is already muted is ignored, as is calling setMute with a false argument on an object that is not currently muted. Going from a muted to an unmuted state doesn't effect the gain.

Parameters:

mute - Specify true to mute the signal, false to unmute the signal.

getMute

public abstract boolean getMute()

Gets the mute state of the signal associated with this GainControl.

Returns:

The mute state.

setDB

public abstract float setDB(float gain)

Sets the gain in decibels. Setting the gain to 0.0 (the default) implies that the audio signal is neither amplified nor attenuated. Positive values amplify the audio signal and negative values attenuate the signal.

Parameters:

gain - The new gain in dB.

Returns:

The gain that was actually set.

getDB

public abstract float getDB()

Gets the current gain set for this object in decibels.

Returns:

The gain in dB.

setLevel

```
public abstract float setLevel(float level)
```

Sets the gain using a floating point scale with values between 0.0 and 1.0. 0.0 is silence; 1.0 is the loudest useful level that this GainControl supports.

Parameters:

level - The new gain value specified in the level scale.

Returns:

The level that was actually set.

getLevel

```
public abstract float getLevel()
```

Gets the current gain set for this object as a value between 0.0 and 1.0

Returns:

The gain in the level scale (0.0-1.0).

addGainChangeListener

```
public abstract void addGainChangeListener(GainChangeListener
    listener)
```

Register for gain change update events. A GainChangeEvent is posted when the state of the GainControl changes.

Parameters:

listener - The object to deliver events to.

removeGainChangeListener

```
public abstract void removeGainChangeListener(GainChangeListener
    listener)
```

Remove interest in gain change update events.

Parameters:

listener - The object that has been receiving events.

Class javax.media.IncompatibleSourceException

```
java.lang.Object
    |
    +----java.lang.Throwable
             |
             +----java.lang.Exception
                      |
                      +----javax.media.MediaException
                               |
                               +----javax.media.IncompatibleSourceException
```

public class IncompatibleSourceException
extends MediaException

An IncompatibleSourceException is thrown by a MediaHandler when the setSource method is invoked with a DataSource that the MediaHandler cannot support.

See Also:

DataSource, MediaHandler, Manager

Constructors

IncompatibleSourceException

public IncompatibleSourceException()

Constructs a IncompatibleSourceException with no error message.

IncompatibleSourceException

public IncompatibleSourceException(String reason)

Constructs a IncompatibleSourceException with the given error message.

Class javax.media.IncompatibleTimeBaseException

```
java.lang.Object
   |
   +----java.lang.Throwable
          |
          +----java.lang.Exception
                 |
                 +----javax.media.MediaException
                        |
                        +----javax.media.IncompatibleTimeBaseException
```

public class IncompatibleTimeBaseException
extends MediaException

An `IncompatibleTimeBaseException` is posted by a `Clock` when its `setTimeBase` method is invoked with a `TimeBase` that the `Clock` cannot support.

See Also:

Clock, Player

Constructors

IncompatibleTimeBaseException

`public IncompatibleTimeBaseException()`

Constructs a `IncompatibleTimeBaseException` with no error message.

IncompatibleTimeBaseException

`public IncompatibleTimeBaseException(String reason)`

Constructs a `IncompatibleTimeBaseException` with the given error message.

Class javax.media.InternalErrorEvent

```
java.lang.Object
   |
   +----javax.media.ControllerEvent
         |
         +----javax.media.ControllerClosedEvent
               |
               +----javax.media.ControllerErrorEvent
                     |
                     +----javax.media.InternalErrorEvent
```

public class InternalErrorEvent
extends ControllerErrorEvent

An InternalErrorEvent indicates that a Controller failed for implementation-specific reasons. This event indicates that there are problems with the implementation of theController.

See Also:

Controller, ControllerListener

Constructors

InternalErrorEvent

public InternalErrorEvent(Controller from)

Constructs a InternalErrorEvent for the given source Controller.

InternalErrorEvent

public InternalErrorEvent(Controller from, String message)

Constructs a InternalErrorEvent for the given source Controller and error message.

Class javax.media.Manager

```
java.lang.Object
   |
   +----javax.media.Manager
```

public final class Manager
extends Object

The Manager class is a utility for obtaining system dependent resources such as Players and DataSources. Using the createPlayer and createDataSource static methods, the Manager class retrieves a Player or DataSource object based on a given media file and protocol.

See Also:

URL, MediaLocator, PackageManager, DataSource, URLDataSource, MediaHandler, Player, MediaProxy, TimeBase

Variables

UNKNOWN_CONTENT_NAME

public static final String UNKNOWN_CONTENT_NAME

Returned if the content-type of the media cannot be determined.

Methods

createPlayer

public static Player createPlayer(URL sourceURL) throws
   IOException, NoPlayerException

Creates a Player for the specified media URL.

Parameters:

sourceURL - The URL that describes the media data.

Returns:

A new Player.

Throws: NoPlayerException

Thrown if no Player can be found.

Throws: IOException

Thrown if there was a problem connecting with the source.

createPlayer

public static Player createPlayer(MediaLocator sourceLocator)
   throws IOException, NoPlayerException

Create a Player for the specified MediaLocator.

Parameters:

    sourceLocator - A `MediaLocator` that describes the media content.

Returns:

    A `Player` for the media described by the source.

Throws: NoPlayerException

    Thrown if no `Player` can be found.

Throws: IOException

    Thrown if there was a problem connecting with the source.

createPlayer

```
public static Player createPlayer(DataSource source) throws
  IOException, NoPlayerException
```

Create a `Player` for the specified `DataSource`.

Parameters:

    DataSource - The `DataSource` that describes the media content.

Returns:

    A new `Player`.

Throws: NoPlayerException

    Thrown if a `Player` can't be created.

Throws: IOException

    Thrown if there was a problem connecting with the source.

createDataSource

```
public static DataSource createDataSource(URL sourceURL) throws
  IOException, NoDataSourceException
```

Create a `DataSource` for the specified media URL.

Parameters:

    sourceURL - The URL that describes the media data.

Returns:

    A new `DataSource` for the media.

Throws: NoDataSourceException

    Thrown if no `DataSource` can be found.

Throws: IOException

    Thrown if there was a problem connecting with the source.

createDataSource

```
public static DataSource createDataSource(MediaLocator
```

sourceLocator) throws IOException, NoDataSourceException

Create a `DataSource` for the specified `MediaLocator`.

Parameters:

sourceLocator - The source protocol for the media data.

Returns:

A connected `DataSource`.

Throws: NoDataSourceException

Thrown if no `DataSource` can be found.

Throws: IOException

Thrown if there was a problem connecting with the source.

getSystemTimeBase

`public static TimeBase getSystemTimeBase()`

Gets the `TimeBase` for the system. Typically this is based on the system's hardware clock.

Returns:

The system time base.

getDataSourceList

`public static Vector getDataSourceList(String protocolName)`

Build a list of `DataSource` class names from the Java Media Framework's *protocol* prefix-list and a protocol name.

Parameters:

protocol - The name of the protocol the source must support.

Returns:

A vector of strings, where each string is a `Player` class-name.

getHandlerClassList

`public static Vector getHandlerClassList(String contentName)`

Build a list of `Handler` class names from the Java Media Framework's *content* prefix-list and a content type.

Parameters:

contentName - The content type to use in the class name.

Returns:

A vector of strings where each one is a `Player` class-name.

Class javax.media.MediaError

```
java.lang.Object
   |
   +----java.lang.Throwable
           |
           +----java.lang.Error
                   |
                   +----javax.media.MediaError
```

public class MediaError
extends Error

A MediaError indicates an error condition that has occurred through incorrect usage of the API.

Constructors

MediaError

public MediaError()

Constructs a ClockStartedError with no error message.

MediaError

public MediaError(String reason)

Constructs a MediaError with the given error message.

Interface javax.media.MediaEvent

public interface MediaEvent

MediaEvent is the base interface for events supported by the *Java Media Framework.*

See Also:

ControllerEvent, GainChangeEvent

Methods

getSource

public abstract Object getSource()

Gets the Object that posted this event.

Class javax.media.MediaException

```
java.lang.Object
    |
    +----java.lang.Throwable
            |
            +----java.lang.Exception
                    |
                    +----javax.media.MediaException
```

public class MediaException
extends Exception

A MediaException indicates an unexpected error encountered in a JMF method.

Constructors

MediaException

public MediaException()

Constructs a MediaException with no error message.

MediaException

public MediaException(String reason)

Constructs a MediaException with the given error message.

Interface javax.media.MediaHandler

public interface MediaHandler

The MediaHandler interface is the base interface for objects that read and manage media content delivered from a DataSource. A MediaHandler is generally a Player or a MediaProxy.

See Also:

Player, MediaProxy

Methods

setSource

```
public abstract void setSource(DataSource source) throws
    IOException, IncompatibleSourceException
```

Sets the media source the MediaHandler should use to obtain content.

Parameters:

source - The DataSource used by this MediaHandler.

Throws: IOException

Thrown if there is an error using the DataSource

Throws: IncompatibleSourceException

Thrown if this MediaHandler cannot make use of the DataSource.

Class javax.media.MediaLocator

```
java.lang.Object
    |
    +----javax.media.MediaLocator
```

public class MediaLocator
extends Object

The MediaLocator class describes the location of media content. It is nearly identical to a URL, but does not require a URLStreamHandler to be installed for the given protocol. A MediaLocator can be constructed from URL, and a URL, if applicable, can be retrieved from a MediaLocator.

See Also:

URL, URLStreamHandler

Constructors

MediaLocator

public MediaLocator(URL url)

Constructs a MediaLocator from the given URL.

Parameters:

url - The URL to construct this media locator from.

McdiaLocator

public MediaLocator(String locatorString)

Constructs a MediaLocator from the given String.

Methods

getURL

public URL getURL() throws MalformedURLException

Gets the URL associated with this MediaLocator.

getProtocol

public String getProtocol()

Gets the beginning of the locator string up to but not including the first colon.

Returns:

The protocol for this MediaLocator.

getRemainder

public String getRemainder()

Gets the MediaLocator string with the protocol removed.

Returns:

The argument string.

toString

```
public String toString()
```

Used for printing MediaLocators.

Returns:

A string for printing MediaLocators.

Overrides:

toString in class Object

toExternalForm

```
public String toExternalForm()
```

Create a string from the URL argument that can be used to construct the MediaLocator.

Returns:

A string for the MediaLocator.

Interface javax.media.MediaProxy

public interface MediaProxy
extends MediaHandler

The MediaProxy interface is a MediaHandler which is able to process content from one DataSource in order to produce another DataSource. This new DataSource is then used to create another MediaHandler. Typically a MediaProxy reads a configuration file that contains information needed to make a connection to a server and obtain media data. From this information, a new DataSource is created which can then be used to create a Player for the actual media.

See Also:

Manager

Methods

getDataSource

public abstract DataSource getDataSource() throws IOException,
  NoDataSourceException

Obtain the new DataSource. The DataSource is already connected.

Returns:

the new DataSource for this content.

Throws: IOException

Thrown when if there are IO problems in reading the the original or new DataSource.

Throws: NoDataSourceException

Thrown if this proxy can't produce a DataSource.

Class javax.media.MediaTimeSetEvent

```
java.lang.Object
    |
    +----javax.media.ControllerEvent
            |
            +----javax.media.MediaTimeSetEvent
```

public class MediaTimeSetEvent
extends ControllerEvent

A MediaTimeSetEvent is posted by a Controller when its *media-time* has been set with the setMediaTime method.

See Also:

Controller, ControllerListener

Constructors

MediaTimeSetEvent

public MediaTimeSetEvent(Controller from, Time newMediaTime)

Constructs a MediaTimeSetEvent with the given source Controller and media time.

Methods

getMediaTime

public Time getMediaTime()

Gets the new media time of the Controller that generated this event.

Returns:

The Controller's new media time.

Class javax.media.NoDataSourceException

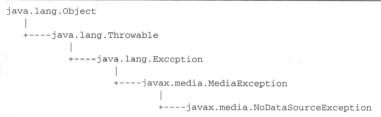

```
java.lang.Object
   |
   +----java.lang.Throwable
          |
          +----java.lang.Exception
                 |
                 +----javax.media.MediaException
                        |
                        +----javax.media.NoDataSourceException
```

public class NoDataSourceException
extends MediaException

A NoDataSourceException is thrown when a DataSource class cannot be found for a particular transfer protocol. This is typically be thrown by the Manager class is response to a failed createDataSource call.

Constructors

NoDataSourceException

public NoDataSourceException()

    Constructs a NoDataSourceException with no error message.

NoDataSourceException

public NoDataSourceException(String reason)

    Constructs a NoDataSourceException with no error message.

Class javax.media.NoPlayerException

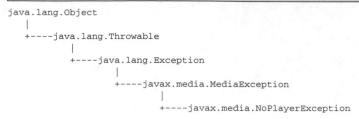

```
java.lang.Object
    |
    +----java.lang.Throwable
            |
            +----java.lang.Exception
                    |
                    +----javax.media.MediaException
                            |
                            +----javax.media.NoPlayerException
```

public class NoPlayerException
extends MediaException

A NoPlayerException is thrown when a Player class cannot be found a particular medium. This is typically be thrown by the Manager class is response to a failed createPlayer call.

Constructors

NoPlayerException

public NoPlayerException()

Constructs a NoPlayerException with no error message.

NoPlayerException

public NoPlayerException(String reason)

Constructs a NoPlayerException with the given error message.

Class javax.media.NotPrefetchedError

```
java.lang.Object
    |
    +----java.lang.Throwable
            |
            +----java.lang.Error
                    |
                    +----javax.media.MediaError
                            |
                            +----javax.media.NotPrefetchedError
```

public class NotPrefetchedError
extends MediaError

A `NotPrefetchedError` is thrown by a `Controller` when a method that requires the `Controller` to be in the `Prefetched` state is called and the `Controller` has not been `Prefetched`.

See Also:

Controller

Constructors

NotPrefetchedError

`public NotPrefetchedError(String reason)`

Constructs a `NotPrefetchedError` with the given error message.

Class javax.media.NotRealizedError

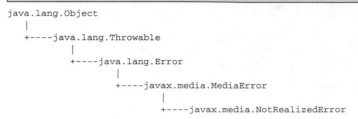

```
java.lang.Object
    |
    +----java.lang.Throwable
            |
            +----java.lang.Error
                    |
                    +----javax.media.MediaError
                            |
                            +----javax.media.NotRealizedError
```

public class NotRealizedError
extends MediaError

A `NotPrefetchedError` is thrown by a `Controller` when a method that requires the `Controller` to be in the `Realized` state is called and the `Controller` has not been `Realized`.

See Also:

Controller, Player

Constructors

NotRealizedError

`public NotRealizedError(String reason)`

Constructs a `NotRealizedError` with the given error message.

Class javax.media.PackageManager

```
java.lang.Object
    |
    +----javax.media.PackageManager
```

public class PackageManager
extends Object

The PackageManager class is used to manipulate and retrieve the *Java Media Framework*'s persistent database of *content* and *protocol* package-prefix lists. The Manager class uses these lists to locate a Player or DataSource for a given medium.

See Also:

Manager

Constructors

PackageManager

public PackageManager()

Methods

getProtocolPrefixList

public static Vector getProtocolPrefixList()

Gets the current value of the *protocol* package-prefix list.

Returns:

The protocol package-prefix list.

setProtocolPrefixList

public static void setProtocolPrefixList(Vector list)

Sets the *protocol* package-prefix list. This is required for changes to take effect.

Parameters:

list - The new package-prefix list to use.

commitProtocolPrefixList

public static void commitProtocolPrefixList()

Make changes to the *protocol* package-prefix list persistent. This method throws a SecurityException if the calling thread does not have access to system properties.

getContentPrefixList

public static Vector getContentPrefixList()

Gets the current value of the *content* package-prefix list.

Returns:

The content package-prefix list.

setContentPrefixList

```
public static void setContentPrefixList(Vector list)
```

Sets the current value of the *content* package-prefix list. This is required for changes to take effect.

Parameters:

list - The content package-prefix list to set.

commitContentPrefixList

```
public static void commitContentPrefixList()
```

Make changes to the *content* prefix-list persistent. This method throws a SecurityException if the calling thread does not have access to system properties.

Interface javax.media.Player

public interface Player
extends MediaHandler, Controller, Duration

The `Player` interface is implemented to provide a mechanism for rendering and controlling time based media data. `Player` extends both the `Controller` and `Clock` interfaces, provides AWT components to controle the media rendering, and has the ability to manage slave `Controllers`.

See Also:

Manager, GainControl, Clock, TransitionEvent, RestartingEvent, DurationUpdateEvent, Component

Methods

getVisualComponent

```
public abstract Component getVisualComponent()
```

Obtain the display `Component` for this `Player`. The display `Component` is where visual media is rendered. If this `Player` has no visual component, `getVisualComponent` returns `null`. The `getVisualComponent` method might return `null` if the `Player` only plays audio.

Returns:

The media display `Component` for this `Player`.

getGainControl

```
public abstract GainControl getGainControl()
```

Obtain the object for controlling this `Player`'s audio gain. If this player does not have a `GainControl`, `getGainControl` returns `null`. The `getGainControl` method might return `null` if the `Player` does not play audio data.

Returns:

The `GainControl` object for this `Player`.

getControlPanelComponent

```
public abstract Component getControlPanelComponent()
```

Obtain the `Component` that provides the default user interface for controlling this `Player`. If this `Player` has no default control panel, `getControlPanelComponent()` returns `null`.

Returns:

The default control panel GUI for this `Player`.

start

```
public abstract void start()
```

Start the `Player` as soon as possible. The `start` method attempts to transition the `Player` to the Started state. If the Player has not been Realized or Prefetched, start automatically performs these actions. The appropriate events are posted as the Player moves through each state.

addController

```
public abstract void addController(Controller newController)
    throws IncompatibleTimeBaseException
```

Assume control of another Controller.

Parameters:

newController - The Controller to be managed.

Throws: IncompatibleTimeBaseException

Thrown if the added Controller cannot take this * Player's TimeBase.

removeController

```
public abstract void removeController(Controller oldController)
```

Stop controlling a Controller.

Parameters:

oldController - The Controller to stop managing.

Class javax.media.PrefetchCompleteEvent

```
java.lang.Object
   |
   +----javax.media.ControllerEvent
           |
           +----javax.media.TransitionEvent
                   |
                   +----javax.media.PrefetchCompleteEvent
```

public class PrefetchCompleteEvent
extends TransitionEvent

A PrefetchCompleteEvent is posted by a Controller when it finishes Prefetching.
This occurs when a Controller moves from the Prefetching state to the Prefetched
state, or as an acknowledgement that the prefetch method was called and the Controller is
already Prefetched.

See Also:

Controller, ControllerListener

Constructors

PrefetchCompleteEvent

public PrefetchCompleteEvent(Controller from, int previous, int
   current, int target)

Constructs a PrefetchCompleteEvent with the given source Controller, previous
state, current state, and target state.

Class javax.media.RateChangeEvent

```
java.lang.Object
    |
    +----javax.media.ControllerEvent
              |
              +----javax.media.RateChangeEvent
```

public class RateChangeEvent
extends ControllerEvent

A RateChangeEvent is a ControllerEvent that is posted when a Controller's rate changes.

See Also:

Controller, ControllerListener

Constructors

RateChangeEvent

public RateChangeEvent(Controller from, float newRate)

Constructs a RateChangeEvent with the given source Controller and rate.

Methods

getRate

public float getRate()

Gets the new rate of the Controller that generated this event.

Returns:

The Controller's new rate.

Class javax.media.RealizeCompleteEvent

```
java.lang.Object
  |
  +----javax.media.ControllerEvent
           |
           +----javax.media.TransitionEvent
                    |
                    +----javax.media.RealizeCompleteEvent
```

public class RealizeCompleteEvent
extends TransitionEvent

A RealizeCompleteEvent is posted when a Controller finishes Realizing. This occurs when a Controller moves from the Realizing state to the Realized state, or as an acknowledgement that the realize method was called and the Controller is already Realized.

See Also:

Controller, ControllerListener

Constructors

RealizeCompleteEvent

public RealizeCompleteEvent(Controller from, int previous, int current, int target)

Constructs a RealizeCompleteEvent with the given source Controller, previous state, current state, and target state.

Class javax.media.ResourceUnavailableEvent

```
java.lang.Object
   |
   +----javax.media.ControllerEvent
           |
           +----javax.media.ControllerClosedEvent
                   |
                   +----javax.media.ControllerErrorEvent
                           |
                           +----javax.media.ResourceUnavailableEvent
```

public class ResourceUnavailableEvent
extends ControllerErrorEvent

A ResourceUnavailableEvent indicates that a Controller is unable to allocate a resource that it requires for operation.

See Also:

Controller, ControllerListener

Constructors

ResourceUnavailableEvent

public ResourceUnavailableEvent(Controller from)

Constructs a ResourceUnavailableEvent for the given source Controller.

ResourceUnavailableEvent

public ResourceUnavailableEvent(Controller from, String message)

Constructs a ResourceUnavailableEvent for the given source Controller and error message.

Class javax.media.RestartingEvent

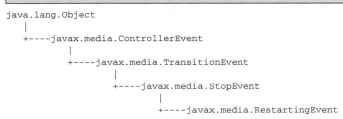

```
java.lang.Object
   |
   +----javax.media.ControllerEvent
           |
           +----javax.media.TransitionEvent
                   |
                   +----javax.media.StopEvent
                           |
                           +----javax.media.RestartingEvent
```

public class RestartingEvent
extends StopEvent

A RestartingEvent indicates that a Controller has temporarily moved from the Started state to the Prefetching state and intends to return to the Started state when Prefetching is complete. This occurs when a Started Player is asked to change its rate or media time and to fulfill the request must prefetch its media again.

See Also:

Controller, ControllerListener

Constructors

RestartingEvent

public RestartingEvent(Controller from, int previous, int current,
   int target, Time mediaTime)

Constructs a RestartingEvent with the given source Controller, previous state, current state, target state, and media time.

Class javax.media.StartEvent

```
java.lang.Object
   |
   +----javax.media.ControllerEvent
           |
           +----javax.media.TransitionEvent
                   |
                   +----javax.media.StartEvent
```

public class StartEvent
extends TransitionEvent

A StartEvent is posted by a Controller to indicate that it has entered the Started state.
A StartEvent provides the time-base time and the media-time at when this transition occurred.

See Also:

Controller, ControllerListener

Constructors

StartEvent

public StartEvent(Controller from, int previous, int current, int
    target, Time mediaTime, Time tbTime)

Constructs a StartEvent with the given source Controller, previous state, current state,
target state, media time, and time-base time.

Parameters:

from - The Controller that has *Started*.

mediaTime - The media time when the Controller *Started*.

tbTime - The time-base time when the Controller *Started*.

Methods

getMediaTime

public Time getMediaTime()

Gets the media time when the Controller was started.

Returns:

The Controller's *media time* when it started.

getTimeBaseTime

public Time getTimeBaseTime()

Gets the time-base time when the Controller was started.

Returns:

The *time-base time* associated with the Controller when it started.

Class javax.media.StopAtTimeEvent

```
java.lang.Object
   |
   +----javax.media.ControllerEvent
          |
          +----javax.media.TransitionEvent
                 |
                 +----javax.media.StopEvent
                        |
                        +----javax.media.StopAtTimeEvent
```

public class StopAtTimeEvent
extends StopEvent

A StopAtTimeEvent is posted by a Controller when it has stopped because it has reached its stop time.

See Also:

Controller, ControllerListener

Constructors

StopAtTimeEvent

public StopAtTimeEvent(Controller from, int previous, int current, int target, Time mediaTime)

Constructs a StopAtTimeEvent with the given source Controller, previous state, current state, target state, and media time.

Class javax.media.StopByRequestEvent

```
java.lang.Object
   |
   +----javax.media.ControllerEvent
           |
           +----javax.media.TransitionEvent
                   |
                   +----javax.media.StopEvent
                           |
                           +----javax.media.StopByRequestEvent
```

public class StopByRequestEvent
extends StopEvent

A StopByRequestEvent is posted by a Controller when it has stopped in response to an explicit stop call. This event is posted as an acknowledgement even if the Controller is already Stopped.

See Also:

Controller, ControllerListener

Constructors

StopByRequestEvent

public StopByRequestEvent(Controller from, int previous, int current, int target, Time mediaTime)

Constructs a StopByRequestEvent with the given source Controller, previous state, current state, target state, and media time.

Class javax.media.StopEvent

```
java.lang.Object
    |
    +----javax.media.ControllerEvent
            |
            +----javax.media.TransitionEvent
                    |
                    +----javax.media.StopEvent
```

public class StopEvent
extends TransitionEvent

A StopEvent is posted by a Controller when it has stopped.

See Also:

Controller, ControllerListener

Constructors

StopEvent

public StopEvent(Controller from, int previous, int current, int
    target, Time mediaTime)

Constructs a StopEvent with the given source Controller, previous state, current state, target state, and media time.

Parameters:

from - The Controller that generated this event.

mediaTime - The *media time* at which the Controller stopped.

Methods

getMediaTime

public Time getMediaTime()

Gets the clock time (media time) that was passed into the constructor.

Returns:

The *mediaTime* at which the Controller stopped.

Class javax.media.StopTimeChangeEvent

```
java.lang.Object
   |
   +----javax.media.ControllerEvent
            |
            +----javax.media.StopTimeChangeEvent
```

public class StopTimeChangeEvent
extends ControllerEvent

A StopTimeChangeEvent is posted by a Controller when its stop time has changed.

See Also:

Controller, ControllerListener

Constructors

StopTimeChangeEvent

public StopTimeChangeEvent(Controller from, Time newStopTime)

Constructs a StopEvent with the given source Controller, and the new media stop time.

Methods

getStopTime

public Time getStopTime()

Gets the new stop time for the Controller that generated this event.

Returns:

The new stop time for the Controller that generated this event.

Class javax.media.StopTimeSetError

```
java.lang.Object
   |
   +----java.lang.Throwable
           |
           +----java.lang.Error
                   |
                   +----javax.media.MediaError
                           |
                           +----javax.media.StopTimeSetError
```

public class StopTimeSetError
extends MediaError

A StopTimeSetError is thrown when the stop time has been set on a Started Clock whose stop time has already been set.

Constructors

StopTimeSetError

public StopTimeSetError(String reason)

Constructs a StopTimeSetError with the given error message.

Class javax.media.Time

```
java.lang.Object
    |
    +----javax.media.Time
```

public class Time
extends Object

The Time class abstracts time in the *Java Media Framework*. It can represent a point in time, as returned by the Clock method getMediaTime, or an amount of time, as returned by the Duration method getDuration().

See Also:

Clock, TimeBase

Variables

ONE_SECOND

public static final long ONE_SECOND

The number of nanoseconds (1000000000) in one second.

nanoseconds

protected long nanoseconds

Time is kept in a granularity of nanoseconds. Converions to and from this value are done to implement construction or query in seconds.

Constructors

Time

public Time(long nano)

Constructs a Time for the given number of nanoseconds.

Parameters:

nano - Number of nanoseconds for this time.

Time

public Time(double seconds)

Constructs a time for the given number of seconds.

Parameters:

seconds - Time specified in seconds.

Methods

secondsToNanoseconds

```
protected long secondsToNanoseconds(double seconds)
```
Convert seconds to nanoseconds.

getNanoseconds

```
public long getNanoseconds()
```
Gets the time value in nanoseconds.

Returns:
The time in nanoseconds.

getSeconds

```
public double getSeconds()
```
Gets the time value in seconds.

Interface javax.media.TimeBase

public interface TimeBase

A TimeBase represents a monotonically-increasing source of time. A TimeBase cannot be manipulated or stopped.

See Also:

Clock

Methods

getTime

public abstract Time getTime()

Gets the current time of this TimeBase.

Returns:

the current TimeBase time.

getNanoseconds

public abstract long getNanoseconds()

Gets the current time of the TimeBase specified in nanoseconds.

Returns:

the current TimeBase time in nanoseocnds.

Class javax.media.TransitionEvent

```
java.lang.Object
    |
    +----javax.media.ControllerEvent
            |
            +----javax.media.TransitionEvent
```

public class TransitionEvent
extends ControllerEvent

A `TransitionEvent` is posted by a `Controller` when it has changed state.

See Also:

Controller, ControllerListener

Constructors

TransitionEvent

public TransitionEvent(Controller from, int previous, int current,
    int target)

Constructs a `TransitionEvent` with the given source `Controller`, previous state, current state, and target state.

Constructs a new `TransitionEvent`.

Parameters:

from - The Controller that is generating this event.

previous - The state that the `Controller` was in before this event.

current - The state that the `Controller` is in as a result of this event.

target - The state that the `Controller` is heading to.

Methods

getPreviousState

public int getPreviousState()

Gets the state that the `Controller` was in before this event occurred.

Returns:

The `Controller`'s previous state.

getCurrentState

public int getCurrentState()

Gets the `Controller`'s state at the time this event was generated.

Returns:

The `Controller`'s current state.

getTargetState

```
public int getTargetState()
```

Gets the `Controller`'s target state at the time this event was generated.

Returns:

The `Controller`'s target state.

Class javax.media.protocol.ContentDescriptor

```
java.lang.Object
   |
   +----javax.media.protocol.ContentDescriptor
```

public class ContentDescriptor
extends Object

The ContentDescriptor class identifies the content-type of a particular medium. Typically this returns the MIME-type of the media data.

See Also:

SourceStream

Variables

CONTENT_UNKNOWN

public static final String CONTENT_UNKNOWN

The default content-type when a content-type cannot be determined.

typeName

protected String typeName

The content-type represented by this object.

Constructor

ContentDescriptor

public ContentDescriptor(String cdName)

Creates a content descriptor with the specified name. To create a ContentDescriptor from a MIME type, use the mimeTypeToPackageName static method.

Parameters:

cdName - The name of the content-type.

Methods

getContentType

public String getContentType()

Obtains a string that represents the content-name for this descriptor.

Returns:

The content-type name.

mimeTypeToPackageName

protected static final String mimeTypeToPackageName(String

`mimeType)`

Maps a MIME content-type to an equivalent string of class-name components. The MIME type is mapped to a string by replacing all slashes with a period, converting all alphabetic characters to lower case, and converting all non-alpha-numeric characters other than periods to underscores (_).

Parameters:

mimeType - The MIME type to map to a string.

Interface javax.media.protocol.Controls

public interface Controls

The Controls interface provides a way to retrieve objects by interface or class name. This is useful when support for a particular interface cannot be determined at runtime, or where a different object is required to implement the behavior. The object returned from the getControl method is assumed to control the object on which getControl was invoked.

Methods

getControls

`public abstract Object[] getControls()`

Obtain the collection of objects that control the object that implements this interface. If no controls are supported, a zero-length array is returned.

Returns:

the collection of object controls

getControl

`public abstract Object getControl(String controlType)`

Obtain the object that implements the specified Class or Interface The full class or interface name must be used. If the control is not supported then null is returned.

Returns:

the object that implements the control, or null.

Class javax.media.protocol.DataSource

```
java.lang.Object
   |
   +----javax.media.protocol.DataSource
```

public abstract class DataSource
extends Object
implements Controls, Duration

A DataSource is used to connect to a medium using a particular transfer protocol. Defined by the protocol that it uses, the DataSource provides the SourceStreams that deliver the media data to a MediaHandler.

See Also:

Manager, DefaultPlayerFactory, Positionable, RateConfigureable

Constructors

DataSource

public DataSource()

A no-argument constructor required by pre 1.1 implementations so that this class can be instantiated by calling Class.newInstance().

DataSource

public DataSource(MediaLocator source)

Constructs a DataSource from a MediaLocator. This method should be overloaded by subclasses; the default implementation just keeps track of the MediaLocator.

Parameters:

source - The MediaLocator that describes the DataSource.

Methods

setLocator

public void setLocator(MediaLocator source)

Sets the connection source for this DataSource. This method should only be called once; an error is thrown if the locator has already been set.

Parameters:

source - The MediaLocator that describes the media source.

getLocator

public MediaLocator getLocator()

Gets the MediaLocator that describes this source. Returns null if the locator hasn't been set.

Returns:

The MediaLocator for this source.

initCheck

```
protected void initCheck()
```

Checks to see if this connection has been initialized with aMediaLocator. If the connection hasn't been initialized, initCheck throws an UninitializedError. Most methods should call initCheck on entry.

getContentType

```
public abstract String getContentType()
```

Gets a string that describes the content-type of the media that the source is providing.

Returns:

The name that describes the media content.

connect

```
public abstract void connect() throws IOException
```

Opens a connection to the source described by the MediaLocator. The connect method initiates communication with the source.

Throws: IOException

Thrown if there are IO problems when connect is called.

disconnect

```
public abstract void disconnect()
```

Closes the connection to the source described by the locator. The disconnect method frees resources used to maintain a connection to the source. If no resources are in use, disconnect is ignored. If stop hasn't already been called, calling disconnect implies a stop.

start

```
public abstract void start() throws IOException
```

Initiates data-transfer. The start method must be called before data is available. connect must be called before start.

Throws: IOException

Thrown if there are IO problems with the source when start is called.

stop

```
public abstract void stop() throws IOException
```

Stops the data-transfer. If the source has not been connected and started, stop does nothing.

Interface javax.media.protocol.Positionable

public interface Positionable

The Positionable interface is implemented by a DataSource to indicate that it can change the media position within the stream.

See Also:
   Datasource

Variables

RoundUp

public static final int RoundUp

RoundDown

public static final int RoundDown

RoundNearest

public static final int RoundNearest

setPosition

public abstract Time setPosition(Time where, int rounding)

   Sets the position to the specified time. Returns the rounded position that was actually set.

   Parameters:

      time - The new position in the stream.

      round - The rounding technique to be used: RoundUp, RoundDown, RoundNearest.

   Returns:

      The actual position set.

isRandomAccess

public abstract boolean isRandomAccess()

   Find out if this source can be repositioned to any point in the stream. If not, the source can only be repositioned to the beginning of the stream.

   Returns:

      Returns true if the source is random access; false if the source can only be reset to the beginning of the stream.

Class javax.media.protocol.PullDataSource

```
java.lang.Object
   |
   +----javax.media.protocol.DataSource
           |
           +----javax.media.protocol.PullDataSource
```

public abstract class PullDataSource
extends DataSource

The `PullDataSource` class is a `DataSource` that is specific to *pull* media data.

See Also:

Manager, Player, DefaultPlayerFactory, DataSource

Constructors

PullDataSource

public PullDataSource()

Methods

getStreams

public abstract PullSourceStream[] getStreams()

Gets the collection of streams that this source manages. The collection of streams is entirely content dependent. The MIME type of this `DataSource` provides the only indication of what streams can be available on this connection.

Returns:

The collection of streams for this source.

Interface javax.media.protocol.PullSourceStream

public interface PullSourceStream
extends SourceStream

The `PullSourceStream` interface is a `SourceStream` that is specific to *pull* media data.

See Also:

PullDataSource

Methods

---

willReadBlock

`public abstract boolean willReadBlock()`

> Find out if data is available now. Returns `true` if a call to read would block for data.

> **Returns:**

>> Returns `true` if read would block; otherwise returns `false`.

read

`public abstract int read(byte buffer[], int offset, int length)`
`throws IOException`

> Block and read data from the stream. Reads up to `length` bytes from the input stream into an array of bytes. If the first argument is `null`, up to `length` bytes are read and discarded. Returns -1 when the end of the media is reached. This method only returns 0 if it was called with a length of 0.

> **Parameters:**

>> buffer - The buffer to read bytes into.

>> offset - The offset into the buffer at which to begin writing data.

>> length - The number of bytes to read.

> **Returns:**

>> The number of bytes read, -1 indicating the end of stream, or 0 indicating `read` was called with `length` 0.

Class javax.media.protocol.PushDataSource

```
java.lang.Object
    |
    +----javax.media.protocol.DataSource
            |
            +----javax.media.protocol.PushDataSource
```

public abstract class PushDataSource
extends DataSource

The `PushDataSource` class is a `DataSource` that is specific to *push* media data.

See Also:

Manager, Player, DefaultPlayerFactory, DataSource

Constructors

PushDataSource

```
public PushDataSource()
```

Methods

getStreams

```
public abstract PushSourceStream[] getStreams()
```

Gets the collection of streams that this source manages. The collection of streams is entirely content dependent. The `ContentDescriptor` of this `DataSource` provides the only indication of what streams can be available on this connection.

Returns:

The collection of streams for this source.

Interface javax.media.protocol.PushSourceStream

public interface PushSourceStream
extends SourceStream

The `PushSourceStream` interface is a `SourceStream` that is specific to *push* media data.

See Also:

PushDataSource

Methods

read

```
public abstract int read(byte buffer[], int offset, int length)
```

Read from the stream without blocking. Returns -1 when the end of the media is reached.

Parameters:

buffer - The buffer to read bytes into.

offset - The offset into the buffer at which to begin writing data.

length - The number of bytes to read.

Returns:

The number of bytes read or -1 when the end of stream is reached.

getMinimumTransferSize

```
public abstract int getMinimumTransferSize()
```

Determine the size of the buffer needed for the data transfer. This method is provided so that a transfer handler can determine how much data, at a minimum, will be available to transfer from the source. Overflow and data loss is likely to occur if this much data isn't read at transfer time.

Returns:

The size of the data transfer.

setTransferHandler

```
public abstract void setTransferHandler(SourceTransferHandler
    transferHandler)
```

Register an object to service data transfers to this stream. If a handler is already registered when `setTransferHandler` is called, the handler is replaced; there can only be one handler at a time.

Parameters:

transferHandler - The handler to transfer data to.

Interface javax.media.protocol.RateConfiguration

public interface RateConfiguration

The RateConfiguration interface represents a configuration of streams for a particular rate.

See Also:

DataSource, RateConfigureable

Methods

getRate

public abstract RateRange getRate()

Gets the RateRange for this configuration.

Returns:

The rate supported by this configuration.

getStreams

public abstract SourceStream[] getStreams()

Gets the streams that will have content at this rate.

Returns:

The streams supported at this rate.

Interface javax.media.protocol.RateConfigureable

public interface RateConfigureable

The RateConfigureable interface is implemented by a DataSource to interface that it can use different RateConfigurations to support multiple speeds of media transfer.

See Also:

DataSource, RateConfiguration, RateRange

Methods

getRateConfigurations

public abstract RateConfiguration[] getRateConfigurations()

Gets the rate configurations that this object supports. There must always be one and only one for a RateConfiguration that covers a rate of 1.0.

Returns:

The collection of RateConfigurations that this source supports.

setRateConfiguration

public abstract RateConfiguration
    setRateConfiguration(RateConfiguration config)

Sets a new RateConfiguration. The new configuration should have been obtained by calling getRateConfigurations. Returns the actual RateConfiguration used.

Parameters:

config - The RateConfiguration to use.

Returns:

The actual RateConfiguration used by the source.

Class javax.media.protocol.RateRange

```
java.lang.Object
    |
    +----javax.media.protocol.RateRange
```

public class RateRange
extends Object

The RateRange class describes the range of rates at which the media data can be transfered.

Constructors

RateRange

public RateRange(RateRange r)

Copy constructor.

RateRange

public RateRange(float init, float min, float max, boolean isExact)

Constructor using required values.

Parameters:

init - The initial value for this rate.

min - The minimum value that this rate can take.

max - The maximum value that this rate can take.

isExact - Set to true if the source rate does not vary when using this rate range.

Methods

setCurrentRate

public float setCurrentRate(float rate)

Sets the current rate. Returns the rate that was actually set. This implementation just returns the specified rate, subclasses should return the rate that was actually set.

Parameters:

rate - The new rate.

getCurrentRate

public float getCurrentRate()

Gets the current rate.

Returns:

The current rate.

getMinimumRate

public float getMinimumRate()

Gets the minimum rate supported by this range.

Returns:

The minimum rate.

getMaximumRate

```
public float getMaximumRate()
```

Gets the maximum rate supported by this range.

Returns:

The maximum rate.

isExact

```
public boolean isExact()
```

Determine whether or not the source will maintain a constant speed when using this rate. If the rate varies, synchronization is usually impractical.

Returns:

Returns `true` if the source will maintain a constant speed at this rate.

Interface javax.media.protocol.Seekable

public interface Seekable

The `Seekable` interface is implemented by a `SourceStream` to indicate that it is capable of seeking to a particular position in the stream.

See Also:

SourceStream

Methods

seek

```
public abstract long seek(long where)
```

Seek to the specified point in the stream.

Parameters:

where - The position to seek to.

Returns:

The new stream position.

tell

```
public abstract long tell()
```

Obtain the current point in the stream.

isRandomAccess

```
public abstract boolean isRandomAccess()
```

Find out if this source can position anywhere in the stream. If the stream is not random access, it can only be repositioned to the beginning.

Returns:

Returns `true` if the stream is random access, `false` if the stream can only be reset to the beginning.

Interface javax.media.protocol.SourceStream

public interface SourceStream
extends Controls

The SourceStream interface represents a stream of media data.

See Also:

DataSource, PushSourceStream, PullSourceStream, Seekable

Variables

LENGTH_UNKNOWN

public static final long LENGTH_UNKNOWN

Returned by getContentLength if the length of the SourceStream cannot be determined.

Methods

getContentDescriptor

public abstract ContentDescriptor getContentDescriptor()

Gets the current content type for this stream.

Returns:

The current ContentDescriptor for this stream.

getContentLength

public abstract long getContentLength()

Gets the size, in bytes, of the content on this stream. LENGTH_UNKNOWN is returned if the length is not known.

Returns:

The content length in bytes.

endOfStream

public abstract boolean endOfStream()

Find out if the end of the stream has been reached.

Returns:

Returns true if there is no more data.

Interface javax.media.protocol.SourceTransferHandler

public interface SourceTransferHandler

The `SourceTransferHandler` interface implements a callback from a `PushSourceStream`.

See Also:

PushSourceStream

Methods

transferData

`public abstract void transferData(PushSourceStream stream)`

Transfer new data from a `PushSourceStream`.

Parameters:

stream - The stream that is providing the data.

Class javax.media.protocol.URLDataSource

```
java.lang.Object
    |
    +----javax.media.protocol.DataSource
            |
            +----javax.media.protocol.PullDataSource
                    |
                    +----javax.media.protocol.URLDataSource
```

public class URLDataSource
extends PullDataSource

The URLDataSource is a DataSource created directly from a URL using a URLConnection. It is the DataSource that handles all protocols supported by a URL.

See Also:

URL, URLConnection, InputSourceStream

Variables

conn

protected URLConnection conn

contentType

protected ContentDescriptor contentType

The content-type of the media.

sources

protected URLSourceStream sources[]

connected

protected boolean connected

Constructors

URLDataSource

protected URLDataSource()

Implemented by subclasses.

URLDataSource

public URLDataSource(URL url) throws IOException

Constructs a URLDataSource directly from a URL.

Methods

getStreams

```
public PullSourceStream[] getStreams()
```
Gets the collection of streams that this source manages.

Overrides:

getStreams in class PullDataSource

connect

```
public void connect() throws IOException
```
Initialize the connection with the source.

Throws: IOException

Thrown if there are problems setting up the connection.

Overrides:

connect in class DataSource

getContentType

```
public String getContentType()
```
Return the content type name.

Returns:

The content type name.

Overrides:

getContentType in class DataSource

disconnect

```
public void disconnect()
```
Disconnect the source.

Overrides:

disconnect in class DataSource

start

```
public void start() throws IOException
```
Initiate data-transfer.

Overrides:

start in class DataSource

stop

```
public void stop() throws IOException
```
Stops the

Overrides:

stop in class DataSource

getDuration

`public Time getDuration()`

Returns `Duration.DURATION_UNKNOWN`. The duration is not available from an `InputStream`.

Returns:

`Duration.DURATION_UNKNOWN`.

Overrides:

getDuration in class DataSource

getControls

`public Object[] getControls()`

Returns an empty array, because this source doesn't provide any controls.

Returns:

empty `Object` array.

Overrides:

getControls in class DataSource

getControl

`public Object getControl(String controlName)`

Returns `null`, because this source doesn't provide any controls.

Overrides:

getControl in class DataSource

INDEX

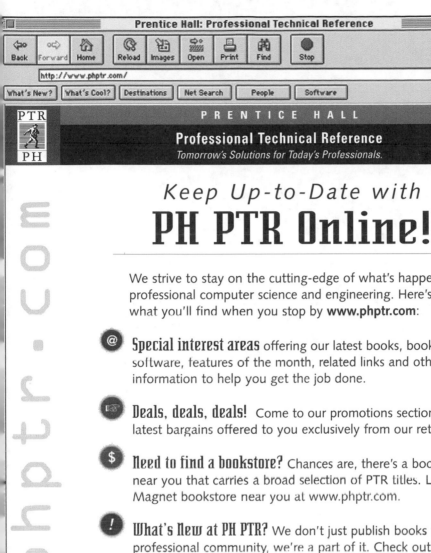